State Power in China, 900–1325

State Power
in China,
900–1325

EDITED BY

PATRICIA BUCKLEY EBREY

and

PAUL JAKOV SMITH

A China Program Book

UNIVERSITY OF WASHINGTON PRESS

Seattle and London

State Power in China was supported by the China Studies Program, a division of the Henry M. Jackson School of International Studies at the University of Washington, and by grants from the Department of History at the University of Washington and the Office of the Provost at Haverford College.

UNIVERSITY OF WASHINGTON PRESS
www.washington.edu/uwpress

Library of Congress Cataloging-in-Publication Data
Names: Ebrey, Patricia Buckley, 1947– | Smith, Paul J., 1947–
Title: State power in China, 900–1325 / edited by Patricia Buckley Ebrey and Paul Jakov Smith.
Description: Seattle : University of Washington Press, 2016. | Includes bibliographical references and index.
Identifiers: LCCN 2016001985 | ISBN 9780295998107 (hardcover : acid-free paper)
Subjects: LCSH: China—History—Liao dynasty, 947–1125. | China—History—Song dynasty, 960–1279. | China—History—Jin dynasty, 1115–1234. | China—History—Yuan dynasty, 1260–1368. | State, The—History—To 1500. | Power (Social sciences)—China—History—To 1500. | Political culture—China—History—To 1500. | Literature and state—China—History—To 1500. | Civil-military relations—China—History—To 1500. | Social change—China—History—To 1500.
Classification: LCC DS750.78 .S73 2016 | DDC 951/.024—dc23
LC record available at http://lccn.loc.gov/2016001985

Contents

Part 3: Statecraft Theory

Part 4: State Power in Practice

Acknowledgments

THE ESSAYS IN THIS VOLUME HAVE THEIR ORIGIN IN THE CONFER-ence on Middle Period China, 800–1400, held at Harvard in June 2014. Organization of the conference began two years earlier when Peter Bol and Patricia Ebrey put out a call for paper proposals for an international, interdisciplinary conference on ninth- through thirteenth-century China. The response to this call went beyond all expectations. In the end, nearly two hundred people came together to discuss 154 precirculated papers. These papers covered the gamut of current academic research, from poetic imagery to the circulation of money, local elites to tomb decoration, interstate interactions to religious practices. This book draws from papers originally presented at the conference, selected for the contribution they make to our understanding of state power. Some of the other papers will appear in other thematic volumes.

The authors and editors wish to express our gratitude to those who funded the conference, including the Chiang Ching-Kuo Foundation and several units at Harvard (the Fairbank Center for China Studies, the Harvard-Yenching Institute, the Weatherhead Center, and the Asia Center), with smaller contributions by the *Journal of Song-Yuan Studies* and the China Studies Program of the University of Washington. We would particularly like to thank those who commented on or moderated discussion of the earlier versions of these papers. They included Sarah Allen, Phillip Bloom, Peter Bol, Stephen Boyanton, Michael Brose, Hui Yu Cheung, Hugh Clark, Xiaonan Deng, Huanli Ge, Robert Hymes, Tomoyasu Iiyama, Takamichi Kobayashi, Martin Kroher, Chang Woei Ong, Sarah Schneewind, Anna Shields, Jimin Sun, and Wai Lun Tam. They all helped us see the significance of our evidence and arguments. At the University of Washington, Peyton Canary also deserves thanks for his assistance with the preparation of the manuscript and the translation of the essay by Li Huarui.

Abbreviations Used in the Notes

CB   *Xu zizhi tongjian changbian* 續資治通鑑長編, by Li Tao 李燾 (1115–1184). Beijing: Zhonghua shuju, 1985.

CBBM   *Huang Song Tongjian changbian jishi benmo* 皇宋通鑑長編紀事本末, by Yang Zhongliang 楊仲良 (fl. ca. 1170–1230). Harbin: Heilongjiang renmin chubanshe, 2006.

FZTJ   *Fozu tongji* 佛祖統紀, edited by Zhi Pan 志磐 (fl. 1269). In Taishō shinshū daizokyō 大正新修大藏經. Tokyo: Taishō Issaikyō Kankōkai, 1929–34. Taibei: Xinwenfeng reprint edition, 1983–87.

LS   *Liao shi* 遼史, edited by Tuo Tuo 脫脫 (1313–1355) et al. Beijing: Zhonghua shuju, 1974.

QSW   *Quan Song wen* 全宋文, edited by Zeng Zaozhuang 曾棗莊 et al. Shanghai: Shanghai cishu chubanshe, 2006.

SCBMHB   *Sanchao beimeng huibian* 三朝北盟會編, by Xu Mengxin 徐夢莘 (1126–1207). See chapter reference list for edition used.

SHY   *Song huiyao jigao* 宋會要輯稿, compiled by Xu Song 徐松 (1781–1848) et al. Beijing: Zhonghua shuju, 1957.

SS   *Song shi* 宋史, edited by Tuo Tuo 脫脫 (1313–1355) et al. Beijing: Zhonghua shuju 1977.

SSJW   *Sushui jiwen* 涑水記聞, by Sima Guang 司馬光 (1019–1086). Vol. 7, part 1, 2003. Reprint, Zhengzhou: Daxiang chuban she, 2008.

WXTK   *Wenxian tongkao* 文獻通考, by Ma Duanlin 馬端臨 (ca. 1254–1323). Beijing: Zhonghua shuju, 2011.

State Power in China, 900–1325

Introduction

PAUL JAKOV SMITH *and*
PATRICIA BUCKLEY EBREY

IN CHINESE HISTORY, THE ERA BETWEEN 900 AND 1350 WAS A multistate one, setting it apart from subsequent periods.[1] The overlapping Liao (907–1123), Song (960–1279), Jin (1115–1234), and Yuan (1215–1368) dynasties occupied larger or smaller chunks of what we can loosely call the China region. All four were monarchies, and all drew on Chinese traditions of statecraft, but the ruling houses were from four different ethnic groups: Kitan, Han Chinese, Jurchen, and Mongol, respectively. The nine chapters in this volume contribute to our understanding of state power in this era, especially that of the Song, by far the best documented of the overlapping states.

Why do we use the term "state" in writing about these entities? It has been the English convention to call Chinese polities "dynasties" or "empires," which tends to obscure the way they were like states elsewhere. "Empire" today is generally reserved for large polities that ruled core territories differently from more distant ones; empires could have states under them.[2] While empire could be used for any of the four states, by using the term "state" we are evoking the ways the Song in particular resembled states in other times and places. The steps dynastic founders took to stabilize their control are much like those used by state-builders in other places; the need to extract revenue to pay for armies is a key feature of states worldwide, past and present, not just in China.

"State" is often taken as a self-evident category, and some books with "state" in the title never define it, using it as interchangeable with government or central government.[3] If a definition is offered, it is often Max Weber's: "a state is a human community that (successfully) claims a monopoly of the legitimate use of physical force within a given territory."[4] The state understood this way has long been a central concern of Chinese historians, who wanted to explain the successes and failures of contenders for power, the institutions they established, the policies they adopted or rejected, and the interpersonal dynamics among those at the political center—rulers, advisors, military men, high officials, their critics, imperial relatives, and so on. These are all topics well documented in the voluminous sources for Chinese history, many generated by the state itself. Many of the pioneers of Western study of the Song, such as Edward A. Kracke and James T. C. Liu, wrote mainly on political and institutional history, explicating the structure of the government, the politics of reform movements, and introducing some of the major actors on the political stage.[5] The generation of scholars who began their studies in the 1960s through the 1980s often wanted to get beyond a state-centered historiography, turning to sources not generated by the government, such as funerary inscriptions, anecdotes, and local histories, in order to see what was going on outside state structures or at odds with them. Many took to focusing on particular places to get closer to the local level. Work on elites is especially notable in this regard (and discussed in some detail later in this chapter).

Beginning in the 1990s, the pendulum seemed to shift back a little toward putting the state at the center of research. This "return of the state" was a general academic trend, not confined to Chinese history, but in the Chinese case was also spurred by the decades-long work on the two volumes of the *Cambridge History of China* on the Five Dynasties (907–960) and Song, which got both junior and senior scholars taking up political, military, and institutional history.[6] Since 2000 a remarkable number of books have been published on the politics, government, war, and statecraft of this period.[7] A particularly important trend has been to investigate more fully the territorial reach of the government, to consider both how the central government could adapt to changing situations far from the capital, and how the prefectural and county governments were elements of local society. Books by Ruth Mostern and Sukhee Lee are notable in this regard.[8]

As we try to advance our understandings of the Song state, the work of modern theorists of the state such as Theda Skocpol and Michael Mann can offer insight.[9] Skocpol defines the state as "a set of administrative, policing, and military organizations headed, and more or less well coordinated by, an executive authority. Any state first and fundamentally extracts resources from society and deploys these to create and support coercive and adminis-trative organizations. Of course, these basic state organizations are built up and must operate within the context of class-divided socioeconomic rela-tions, as well as within the context of national and international economic dynamics."[10] Michael Mann builds on Skocpol, but accentuates two features that are especially pertinent to the chapters in this volume: the state is ter-ritorially delimited and as a consequence states are embedded in geopolitical systems occupied by other states as well. Thus for Mann, geopolitics not only helps shape domestic politics, the two are in fact inextricably entwined.[11] Both Skocpol and Mann elaborate on the connections between states and elites. Skocpol gives the state a conditional autonomy. In her formulation, this autonomy is based on the proclivity of bureaucracies to compete with the dominant classes in appropriating social and economic resources to meet their own needs. Mann attributes this conditional autonomy to the fact that "state elites are diverse and they may be incoherent—especially . . . when monarchies, the military, bureaucrats, and political parties (or in our case bureaucratic factions) cohabit states."[12]

It is around the politics of a state cohabited by diverse and internally fractious elites that our chapters most tightly cohere.

COHABITANTS OF THE SONG STATE

How should we conceptualize the structure of the Song state? Where do the fractious elites fit in? Figure I.1 is our attempt to give the state a visual representation. It depicts a simplified model of the core Song state, its principal cohabitants, and (well out of proportion) the vast population of commoner subjects who were objects of rather than direct agents in shaping its policies and actions. It was through this core set of governmental institutions linking monarch, policy-makers, and administrators and their clerical functionaries in the capital and the provinces that resources from the economy and society were extracted and distributed. They employed a cumulative repertoire of bureaucratic organizations and administrative practices or technologies. All would-be ruling houses and aspiring political elites had to accommodate themselves to customary practices and institutions already in place. Evidence for the limited autonomy of the state can be deduced from the fact that despite significant social, political, and economic changes, the basic structure of the administrative state complex showed remarkable continuity from the Tang through the Ming and even the Qing.[13]

The right side of figure I.1 is occupied by the military. One well-known characteristic of the Song political order was the neutralization of a military class that had enjoyed enormous power and prestige during the Tang and Five Dynasties. Once chief participants in the councils of power, with the ability to enthrone and depose rulers, by Song times the officer corps was defanged and demeaned by a set of laws and cultural prescriptions that relegated military men to the political margins.[14] Neutralizing the military was engineered by the two founding emperors of the Song, Taizu (r. 960–976)

| Emperor | Inner Court consorts, eunuchs, imperial affines, favorites |

Literati elite, composed of ranked civil service officials (2,800 senior and 10,000 executory or probationary posts as of 1086); examination graduates and students; and individuals eligible for office through family connections (the *yin* privilege).	Primary policy-making institutions (Emperors, council of state, academicians, information and rectification organs)	Ranked military officials: 2,500 servitors major and 13,000 servitors minor as of 1086. By 1213 17.2 percent of military officials were drawn from imperial clansmen.
	Central executive authorities, headed by the Two Authorities (Secretariat-Chancellery or Three Departments, and Bureau of Military Affairs)	
	Central administrative agencies (after 1082 the Six Ministries)	
	Civil service territorial administration (circuits, prefectures, counties). / Territorial and logistical administrative functions under the military officials; military chain of command over the imperial, provincial, and local armies.	

Clerical sub-bureaucracy: perhaps 250,000 at a time, but politically demeaned.

Village governance posts requisitioned from among the local wealthy families.

The governed class, including wealthy landowners who staffed village government posts; rich urban merchants; and gradations of the poor and powerless, more or less subject to the coercive powers of the state.

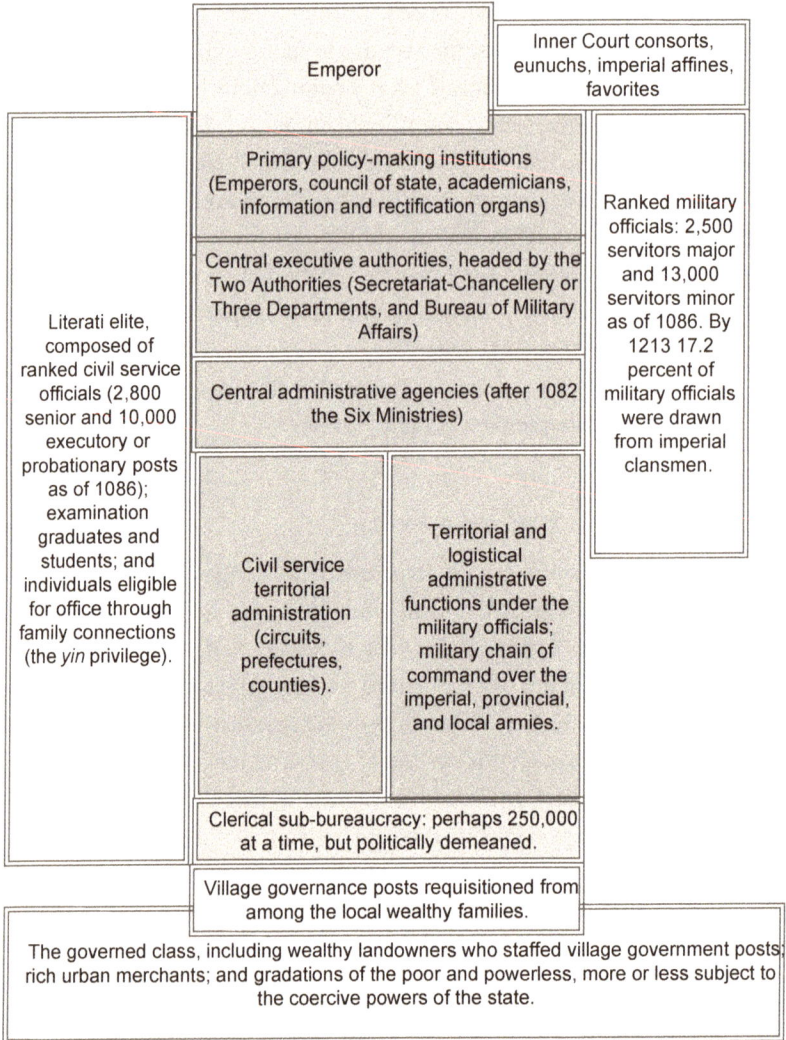

FIGURE I.1. Cohabitants of the Song state. Sources: Chaffee, *Branches of Heaven*; Hartman, "Sung Government and Politics"; Kracke, *Civil Service in Early Sung China*; Liu, "The Sung Views on the Control of Government Clerks"; Lo, *An Introduction to the Civil Service of Sung China*; McKnight, *Village and Bureaucracy in Southern Sung China*.

and Taizong (r. 976–997), who had themselves been at the top of the military ranks. Deposing their generals freed them from worries about a repeat of the military coups that had successively toppled each of the short-lived Five Dynasties, thereby consolidating the power of the monarchy. In a second move of fundamental political importance, Taizong deployed a vastly expanded examination system to recruit a new administrative class—the literati or scholar-officials—dependent on government service and unstintingly loyal to the throne. Even as the Song monarchy successfully reined in such constituents of the inner court as eunuchs, consorts, and scions of the imperial clan, the fast-growing literati class secured its hold on power by banning from the examination halls such potential rivals as merchants, Buddhist and Daoist monks, and clerks.[15] Indeed, it is tempting to cast the history of the Song state in terms of the relationship between these two preeminent cohabitants of the political order.

The chapters in our volume go beyond static depictions of the monarchy and the literati to address the tensions within each group. For despite its veneer of civility, Song political culture pulsated with tensions caused by the ceaseless rivalry between and within the political classes to capture and consolidate control over the institutions of the state. Even the monarchy was susceptible to these concerns.

CONJURING IMPERIAL LEGITIMACY

Denoting emperors as cohabitants of the state may seem to demean the majesty of those who, to anticipate Louis XIV, could claim that "l'Etat, c'est moi." But as the two chapters in part 1 on imperial legitimacy reveal, emperors had to work hard to assert their legitimate place in and impose their will over the political order, especially during transitions or competition for the throne.[16] It is this contest for legitimate status as the rightful ruler of all the territories of the newly unified Song domain that Tracy Miller explores in her chapter. After the Lower Yangzi kingdom of Wuyue capitulated to Song in 978, Taizong appropriated a rare Buddhist relic that had linked the Wuyue rulers to King Asoka, the most famous of the universal Buddhist (or *cákravartin*) kings. In order to house his new treasure, Taizong then commissioned a Wuyue architect to build a soaring tower in Kaifeng with "the power to illuminate the center of the new dynasty" and expand the perceptions of authentic "Chinese" culture to encompass both the old north and the new south.

If all this seems like the confident assertion of despotic monarchical authority, Miller shows that it was also an anxious response to a politically awkward situation. Having immediately claimed the throne on the unexpected death of his brother and political adversary Taizu in 976, Taizong ruled under the cloud of possible fratricide. In addition, his failed attempt to oust the Kitan Liao from the Sixteen Prefectures in 979 compromised his legitimacy with the military men closest to his brother, many of whom had warned against the campaign. Over time Taizong consolidated his rule by nurturing the rise of a new bureaucratic elite recruited through a vastly expanded examination system. But in the short term, his deployment of southern architecture and a powerful Buddhist symbol helped Taizong minimize the embarrassment of his military defeat by a powerful rival state and solidify his claim as ruler of the newly incorporated regions of south China.

The quest for imperial legitimacy is also the subject of Charles Hartman's chapter on the creation of a political myth. Using the hermeneutical tools of "textual archaeology," Hartman demonstrates that the legend of Taizu's oath not to execute officials was an artifact of imperial jockeying for power and reputation in the perilous years surrounding the fall of north China to the Jurchen Jin in 1127. At the onset of the invasions in 1125, Emperor Huizong (r. 1100–1125) abdicated to his son Qinzong (r. 1126–1127) in a desperate effort to save his dynasty and his life.[17] In the course of his short reign, Qinzong purged and even executed many of Huizong's advisors and repudiated his policies, implicitly blaming the military disaster on his father's closest advisors. After the two of them were taken captive and were being transported north, Huizong retaliated by enlisting the inner court favorite and likely imperial affine Cao Xun (1098–1174) to formulate a secret message to Qinzong's brother Prince Kang (later Gaozong), authorizing him to assume the throne and enjoining him to obey the putative Taizu oath, an implicit criticism of elder brother Qinzong.

As Hartman shows, successive versions of the secret message, including those by Cao Xun himself, make it difficult to determine the veracity of either Taizu's oath or Huizong's injunction, as well as the scope of officials to whom it was intended to apply. By dating the variants, however, Hartman is able to link uses of the no-kill legend to the evolving political environment. For Gaozong himself, intent as he was on reaching a peace agreement with the Jurchen that many literati opposed, injunctions against executing officials who criticized his policies was an inconvenience. As a result, he and Cao Xun—now Gaozong's imperial ideologist—downplayed the no-kill edict and created alternative omens to justify Gaozong's rule. More surprising is the absence of references to the no-kill oath in the writings of contemporary literati who would have most benefitted from protections for political speech. Hartman attributes this avoidance to the contempt shared by one group of political stakeholders—the higher officials—for a member of a rival group, the imperial affines and favorites, too closely connected to the monarch to seem like one of them. As Hartman concludes, it is only in the early thirteenth century that the historian Li Xinchuan (1166–1243) elevates the no-kill injunction to an important dynastic principle, making it "a symbol of dynastic constancy and Gaozong's legitimacy." Hartman attributes Li's revitalization of the legend to his own abhorrence of the authoritarian ministerial regimes of Qin Gui (1090–1155) and Han Tuozhou (1152–1207), both of whom had suppressed political remonstrance.

FRACTIOUS ELITES AND THE POLITICAL SYSTEM

Several chapters in this book can be seen as contributions to the long tradition of scholarship on the Chinese elite. In the 1950s and 1960s, the issue was whether to use the term "gentry," which E. A. Kracke pointedly avoided, as he did "class," probably because of its Marxist associations.[18] James Liu tended to use "class," in such phrases as "scholar-official class," "ruling class," and "bureaucratic class."[19] Robert Hartwell, in an influential article, uses the seemingly more objective "elite." Based especially on an analysis of intermarriages, he argues that the early Song had a "founding elite," largely military in origin, that was soon eclipsed by the "professional elite" that often claimed to be descended from Tang official families and who proceeded to dominate the higher echelons of government, placing members in office every generation, almost until the end of the Northern Song, by which time factionalism had reduced the appeal of high office, leading the professional elite to merge into the "gentry" or "local elite," whose power was grounded in their locality and only occasionally held office. He sees the civil service examinations as more important to perpetuating elite status than to gaining it.[20]

A long series of scholars have attempted to test, refine, or build on Hartwell's arguments. John Chaffee disagreed on the number of men who rose through success in the examinations and contended that the impact of the examinations on literati life went well beyond enabling a small number of men to enter government service.[21] Robert Hymes confirmed the Northern Song–Southern Song shift in the prefecture he studied, but argues that there was no sharp line in the Northern Song between the national, professional elite and the local gentry. He takes a stronger stance than Hartwell had on the relationship of the local elite to the state, commenting that "the notion of the elite's real independence of the state is half the message of the book."[22] The volume edited by Hymes and Conrad Schirokauer, *Ordering the World,* shows that a Northern Song–Southern Song shift could be found in intellectual history and especially statecraft thought and not only in marriage connections.[23] Beverly Bossler looks more closely at the evidence for a Northern Song–Southern Song shift and finds that it all depends on what body of evidence one uses. When looking at the families of grand councilors, evidence is strong that they maintained their focus on central government posts after moving south. She also argues that in the Northern Song there were local elites whose members paid attention to local needs; it is just the relative scarcity of sources that keeps us from documenting them in the detail we can for the Southern Song.[24] Sukhee Lee, based on a study of Mingzhou, argues that "the presence of the state, rather than its absence, was essential to the rise of a flourishing local society during this period," and that scholars need to consider "the ways in which the state mattered in actual local society."[25]

"Elite" as Hartwell used it is an objective outsider's category, not what members of the elite called themselves. Others work from the categories the Chinese themselves used, above all *shi* and *shidafu*. There is always some ambiguity in the use of these terms, depending on who is using them and the context. Those high in the central government tended to see themselves and those retired from such posts as the *shidafu* par excellence, while those serving as magistrates far from the capital probably also considered themselves *shidafu*, as did men studying for the examinations in the provinces.[26] Peter Bol, preferring to retain the Chinese terms and talk about the *shi,* has brought the issue of *shi* identity into his analyses of intellectual history.[27] Today, many use "literati" as a translation of *shi* or *shidafu*. In this volume, some of the authors clearly prefer one term or the other—literati or elite. Hartman is fully on the literati side and Chen fully on the elite side, but Zhang and Smith use both seemingly interchangeably. Hartman uses a narrower definition of literati than the other authors, reserving it to refer to occupants of the upper echelons of the government, rather than all men with classical educations.[28] (Li instead uses "class," in such phrases as "ruling class" or "class interest," reflecting mainland Chinese scholars' use of Marxist categories.)

When we turn to the ways the elite and the state developed over time, we can see an evolution of the literati from a creation of the ruling house to a self-conscious social class with claims to political power independent of their relationship to the throne—that is, to independent cohabitants of the state. To briefly review that evolution, following the collapse of Tang rule in the late ninth century fragments of state power were seized by military strongmen in the north and south in ways that made reunification anything but a sure bet.[29] The Song founders Taizu and especially Taizong replaced the military elite from which they had emerged with men of letters, a policy known as "advancing literary learning and suppressing military affairs." Demilitariza-tion was extended further with the peace covenant between the Song and the Kitan Liao signed at Chanyuan in early 1005. With it, the government gave up irredentist claims on the sixteen putatively Chinese prefectures held by the Kitans since 936, acknowledged diplomatic equality between the Song and Liao rulers, and chose the payment of peace tribute as the primary tool for securing the northern borders. The standing army remained large but not battle-ready, while the officer corps was transformed into a bureaucratized appendage of the literati state excluded from decision-making at court.

The expanded civil service examination system played a large role in giving the new literati elite their identity as a politically sophisticated, unstintingly loyal, and highly self-aware social group. From the Song on, civil service examinations and the arts of the literati would command the highest respect in society, surpassing war, money, and religion as paths to social and political eminence. This clustering of social power and influence around the institutions of government cast the exercise of state power in a positive light and made gaining office crucial to maintaining a family's status. But the overall success of the literati soon undermined their group cohesion. Because the size of the bureaucracy was small and relatively fixed—by the mid-eleventh century, the regular bureaucracy numbered some 12,700 posts, ten thousand of which were at the probationary level—there soon was a glut of eligible job candidates at both the junior and senior levels. In order to circumvent the merit-based competitiveness of the examination system, senior officials could help their family retain elite status through use of the so-called *yin* privilege, a form of institutionalized nepotism that granted officials of various ranks the right to nominate sons and other relatives for office. They could also make use of sponsorship, which allowed them to recommend men for better posts and more rapid advancement through the clogged bureaucratic hierarchy than their seniority would have warranted.

The alliance between the throne and the literati focused literati interest, culture, and mobility strategies on the preeminent institutions of the state. The literati were divided, however, by philosophical differences about state policies in particular and the proper scope of state power in general. The fast-developing surplus of examination graduates over the number of available government positions exacerbated the sense of competition. The governing structure often seemed to require factional control over key bureaucratic posts in order to achieve policy objectives. All of these realities quickly undermined any solidarity among members of the literati social class and rendered them internally fractious. Factionalism ineradicably blighted the political culture following the introduction of the New Policies by Shenzong and his minister Wang Anshi in 1069. By the end of the eleventh century, the capacity of government service to satisfy the professional and social aspirations of the literati had been exhausted, and literati were losing faith that an activist state could improve life. Thus from the twelfth century on, Song literati continued to submit themselves to the civil service examinations to certify their place at the top of society, but in many places increasingly turned to local, non-state solutions to pressing social and economic problems.

The three chapters in part 2, by Song Chen, Paul Jakov Smith, and Cong Ellen Zhang, explore the evolving entanglements of the state and the literati from the interconnected perspectives of social demography, reform politics, and funerary commemorations.

Song Chen takes the broadest approach to the new civil service elite in his comparative analysis of prefects in the mid-eleventh and early thirteenth centuries. Employing a quantitative methodology made possible by the increasing availability of digitized prosopographical sources like the *China Biographical Database*, Chen compares the origins, career patterns, and marriage networks of 511 prefects in office in the decade of the 1040s and 534 prefects who served between 1210 and 1219. Chen's findings shed new light on the consequences of the Taizong's and Renzong's expansion of examination and career opportunities as a means of enlisting the support of educated men from the south, a goal of Taizong's that Miller also addresses in her essay.

In terms of regional origins, despite assiduous recruitment efforts, over half of all prefects in the 1040s cohort still came from the North China macroregion, especially the Capital Corridor stretching from Luoyang to the Grand Canal at Yingtian. By the 1210s, with North and Northwest China lost to the Jurchen, the geographic "logic of success" had changed: no single region dominated the supply of prefectural governors as the Capital Corridor had. The capital of Lin'an was itself but a minor producer of prefects, and rather than one overwhelmingly dense core of prefect-producers there were now many, arrayed not by proximity to the capital but rather according to the multiple centers of economic prosperity spanning the eastern seacoast from Fujian to the Lower Yangzi Delta. As wealth and local educational investments were diffused throughout South China, residence in or near the political capital no longer gave officials better chances of rising in the government.

The political maturation of South China's prosperous economic regions is seen as well in patterns of appointment and kinship networks. In both cases Chen finds a dramatic shift towards regionalization. During the 1040s, for example, between 30 and 40 percent of incumbents served in three or more administrative macroregions; by the 1210s this career cosmopolitanism had yielded to the allure of service in one's home region, so that very few men held prefectural governorships in three or more regions. That same pattern characterizes the shift from cosmopolitanism to regional kinship endogamy. By the 1210s, the Northern Song propensity for marriage connections that crossed macroregional boundaries gave way to a pronounced preference for marrying in one's own region. One striking corollary of this regional endogamy was that many fewer thirteenth-century prefects were related to one another the way their eleventh century counterparts had been. The 1040s cohort from North China were connected by marriage to 8.9 other prefects, with four high-ranking individuals like Lü Yijian—for Fan Zhongyan the very embodiment of a network-building oligarch—related to some thirty prefectural colleagues. By contrast, prefects in the 1210s averaged connections to just two or three of their colleagues, while even the three most prominent members were connected to no more than ten.

As Chen concludes, by adding prefects to the finance and policy officials that Hartwell analyses in his pathbreaking article of 1982, it becomes clear that the category of "professional elite"—men who (in Chen's paraphrase) "maintained their main residence in the Song capital region, intermarried with each other regardless of regional origin, and placed most of their sons in the upper echelons of government generation after generation"—was even larger than Hartwell identified. But as the "bureaucratic boom" of the eleventh century succumbed to literati oversupply, factionalism, and the loss of the old North China political heartland to the Jurchen, economic prosperity came to trump politics as the geographic determinant of professional success.

The chapters by Smith and Zhang focus squarely on the reform and funerary politics of that bureaucratic boom era. Smith's comparison of Fan Zhongyan's Qingli-era reforms of the 1040s with Wang Anshi's New Policies of the 1070s shows that the structural changes that Chen finds in the career patterns of prefects were not simply imposed by the sovereign, but were instead contested in hard-fought battles between different coalitions within the literati class itself.

Because the state was the employer of first choice and its examination system the premier arbiter of social prestige, debates and contests over personnel policies, educational institutions, and examination curricula stood near the top of literati concerns. Educated and groomed for careers in the civil service, Northern Song literati tended to see the world from a bureaucratic perspective. Thus despite significant differences in specific policy proposals, the reform programs of both Fan Zhongyan (989–1052) and Wang Anshi (1021–1086) were driven by the shared sense that bureaucratic paralysis was worsening the urgent problems of the day—economic inequality and especially military deterioration in the face of powerful states on their northern borders. That paralysis stemmed in turn from the failure of the selection process to find men able to meet the challenges of the day. Therefore, Fan and Wang agreed that reviving the fortunes of the dynasty entailed recruiting, training, and mobilizing a new cohort of political activists ready and eager to address the challenges the state faced, however differently those challenges were defined.

But it was not enough to mobilize reformers—they had to be put in power. Thus for both Fan and Wang the process of reform entailed purging power-holders they saw as opposing change and getting control of the power to appoint their own men. The openly partisan Fan defined the opposition as an entrenched party of self-serving careerists under the leadership of the oligarchical Lü Yijian; Wang railed against and sought to muzzle anyone who questioned his statist political, ideological, and especially economic measures. In both cases the politics of reform widened the internal rifts among the literati governing class.

From the perspective of the overall flows of power, the reform campaigns of Fan Zhongyan and Wang Anshi underscore the centrality of the throne to the political process: no significant political agenda could be enacted without the support of the emperor—the man who ultimately chose and deposed the chief councilors, embraced or rejected their policy proposals, and welcomed or silenced their critics. Emperors could be cajoled and even manipulated, but they could not be disregarded. Because Wang's policies exactly fit his emperor Shenzong's needs and aspirations, his reform program succeeded where Fan Zhongyan's failed.

Given the close fusion between literati self-identity and the state, the disruptiveness of reform politics extended even to funerary commemoration, as Cong Ellen Zhang shows in her chapter. After the death of Fan Zhongyan, the spirit-path (*shendaobei*) author Ouyang Xiu and epitaph (*muzhiming*) author Fu Bi along with Fan's family sharply disagreed on what should be said about him. The rancor and vitriol that engulfed the political order during the fight over the Qingli reforms were perpetuated and turned inward in the squabbles over how to represent Fan's relationship to his political nemesis Lü Yijian. During the early 1040s Fu Bi and Ouyang Xiu were among Fan Zhongyan's closest lieutenants: Fu Bi was the signatory co-author of the

Qingli reform program, while Ouyang Xiu was the most explicit defender of a self-identified reform faction and prosecutor of reform foes. All three men—Fan, Fu, and Ouyang—were demoted and ousted from the capital in 1045 for their partisanship and promotion of the reforms. With Fan's death in 1052, obituary writers were faced with the problem of whether to highlight Fan's heroically virtuous opposition to a reputedly evil Lü Yijian in the years up to Fan's third rustication in 1036, or to focus on the cooperation between the two men when both were recalled to service to mount a defense against the Tangut Xi Xia invasion of Shaanxi in the early 1040s.

Although Ouyang Xiu had been the most bellicose of the Qingli reformers, it was Fu Bi who continued the Qingli grudges into the next decade by casting his epitaph for Fan as an opportunity to "promote the goodness of [Fan] and expose the evil of the wicked [Lü]." In contrast, Ouyang Xiu used his spirit-path text to describe a rapprochement between Fan and Lü that other sources also confirm, but that Fan's sons refused to concede. In the end Fan's sons deleted the reference to a reconciliation between their father and Lü Yijian when having Ouyang's *shendaobei* inscribed on stone, creating an unbridgeable rift between Ouyang and the Fan family that was later deplored by such Northern Song luminaries as Sima Guang and Su Che, themselves partisans in the factional struggles generated by Wang Anshi's reforms.

As Zhang concludes, epitaph writing in Song China became as politicized as the history writing traced in Hartman's study of Taizu's oath. Although epitaphs never lost their function as an integral component of the burial ritual, they also became public records of an elite man's examination experience, official service, and political and social associations. Not only did epitaph writers have to be attentive to their subject's relationship to the state, they also had to anticipate reactions from the deceased's friends, family, and foes—all stakeholders in the depictions of the life and death of a public figure.

STATECRAFT IN THEORY

Although literati factionalism was often provoked by contests for positions and political power, it also reflected heartfelt differences of opinion over statecraft—that is, the proper scope and uses of state power in society. Li Huarui's and Jaeyoon Song's chapters in part 3 on political theory illustrate the dichotomy between activist and restrictive views of the proper scope of state power. Both perspectives could compete at any one time, as illustrated by Sima Guang's forceful philosophical as well as political opposition to Wang Anshi's New Policies.[30] And as Li shows in his chapter, Mencius could be held up as an inspiration by both the statist Wang Anshi and the state-restrictive Neo-Confucian leader Zhu Xi.[31] Like Zhu Xi, Wang regarded Mencius as the "Second Sage," subordinate in the pantheon of Confucian luminaries only to Confucius himself. Wang was particularly inspired by Mencius's heroic spirit, as embodied in the call to "accomplish great deeds" with which Wang in turn rallied his own rulers. As early as his 1058 "Myriad Word Memorial" to Renzong, Wang emulated Mencius in taking the intent—if not the specific deeds—of Yao, Shun, and the Former Kings as his touchstone for greatness. Mencius's own vision of greatness was bound up in his theory of "humane" or "commiserating" government, which as Wang interpreted it involved the muscular exercise of state power to improve the people's well-being.

Mencius's vision was especially influential in Wang's policies of educational reform and agrarian relief. Li shows that Wang's educational reforms were animated by Mencius's insistence on teaching everyone both the technical skills needed to assure their livelihoods and the interpersonal ethics that were the foundation of human relations. Given his centralizing, state-oriented vision, Wang favored the promotion of government over private schools as the way to "make the customs of the world the same," and to train enough talented agents of the state to "reform the affairs of the world so that they conform to the intentions of the Former Kings."

Mencius's influence on Wang's agrarian policies was less direct. As both Li and Jaeyoon Song explain, a central pillar of Mencius's remedy to overcome economic inequality and stabilize the people's livelihoods was to use the Western Zhou's "well-field system" with its equal allotments of land as a model of inspiration. Although Wang, like many of his contemporaries, initially admired the well-field system, he and Shenzong came to agree that under the commercialized economic system of their day, land could not simply be taken from those who already owned it. Instead, Wang sought to achieve the same result by suppressing those landlords and merchants who "engrossed" more wealth and property than was appropriate, through such policies as Green Sprouts, Hired Service, and State Trade.

In Li's generous reading, Wang Anshi's New Policies adjusted the essence of Mencius's well-field system to the circumstances of Wang's own day in order to successfully "regulate the people's livelihoods." This is not how it turned out in fact. Imperial ambition interacted with Wang's propensity for bureaucratic intervention to undermine the Mencian, social welfare orientation of the New Policies: propelled by Shenzong's insatiable desire to stockpile funds for an irredentist war against the Tangut Xi Xia, Wang's

economic measures were quickly transformed into instruments of massive revenue extraction administered by the incentive-driven agents of an
engorged fiscal bureaucracy.[32]

In the twelfth century, the failures of the New Policies and the military
disaster of the Jurchen invasion led many to doubt the central government's
ability to solve pressing problems. At the same time, the irreversible expansion in the pool of examination graduates competing for the relatively fixed
number of civil service posts, in conjunction with the vitriolic factional
purges that such Malthusian elite growth helped spawn, led literati families
to reconsider their priorities. Jaeyoon Song shows in his chapter that as an
autonomous local elite became increasingly suspicious of a heavy-handed if
not mischievous centralized state, even Mencius's interventionist well-field
and associated land policies lost some of their luster, however laudable their
objectives to the Southern Song survivor Ma Duanlin (1245–1322).

As Song demonstrates, the shared opposition to the state activism of the
Northern Song, especially as represented by Wang Anshi's New Policies, did
not mean that there was a Southern Song consensus about how to deal with
the abundant problems of their day. There were two main camps: the Neo-
Confucians, especially as represented by Zhu Xi, and the Yongjia statecraft
school, as represented by Ye Shi (1150–1223).[33] Both camps expressed their
views about policy and the capacity of the state through their accounts of and
commentaries on the idealized and historical past. Ma Duanlin assembled
those accounts and commentaries in his own encyclopedic *Comprehensive
Survey* (Wenxian tongkao), which offers a systematic historical survey of
views on the political, social, economic, and military institutions of the
realm. Because Ma extensively quotes both Neo-Confucian and Yongjia
perspectives on the historical and institutional issues of the past and present,
his *Survey* constitutes an anthology of Southern Song political thought. In
the end, however, Ma himself adopts the conclusion of the Yongjia thinker
Ye Shi that social problems are best solved not by the state, but rather by the
natural pillars of society—the wealthy. Ma, like Ye, concludes that the "powers of nurturing the people" have shifted from government magistrates to the
beneficiaries of the commercial economy, that is, wealthy landowners and big
merchants. As a result, suppressing the wealthy in order to redress economic
inequality, as Mencius and later Wang Anshi proposed, could not succeed.
Thus Ma shows himself to be an inheritor of the characteristically Southern
Song notion that society and its elites were in many instances superior to the
state. But beyond that he is also the inheritor of a more particularly "statecraft" idea, which is that institutions and policies that may have seemed ideal

in the past—such as the Mencian well-field system—may not be appropriate for and should not be reimposed on the present.

STATE POWER AND THE POWERLESS

Juxtaposing Song's chapter with Li's illustrates two contrasting literati world views, that of the tiny professional bureaucratic class wedded to the central state in the Northern Song and one more in keeping with a local gentry of the Southern Song for whom government service is just one source among many of power and prestige. But the Southern Song local gentry still needs to be see as a cohabitant of the state, stakeholders in a governing class that was relatively small in relation to the entire Song population.[34] Larger by far was the vast governed class, that is, the majority of the Song population of 60 to 100 million individuals who lacked the influence, privileges, and legal protections accorded members of the governing class. The ways these groups were subject to the coercive powers of the state runs through part 4 on the exercise of state power.

Elad Alyagon explores the lowest ranking groups in his study on soldier resistance during the Northern Song. As we have seen, early court efforts to neutralize the military class, demilitarize Song society, and replace war with the practice of buying peace were thwarted by the expansionist ambitions of neighboring states and the irredentist yearnings of Shenzong and his sons. In consequence, Northern Song policy-makers were forced to maintain an army of professional and conscripted soldiers that at its peak numbered 1.4 million men, drawn from the poorest elements of Song society. Alyagon shows that in order to control these products of the underclass, the Song military system relied heavily on coercion, including summary execution in the case of resistance or disobedience and mass tattooing as a form of registration and social control. The most draconian measures were aimed at the lowest-ranking soldiers, in a policy of zero tolerance designed to forestall disobedience with a well-timed flogging or beheading.[35]

Tattooing and the threat of sanctioned violence were exacerbated by harsh conditions, as soldiers were rotated between camps and worked to exhaustion as a method of reform through hard work, or kept in a state of perpetual hunger, misery, and poverty by a provisioning system that could not meet the logistical challenges of supplying the northern frontier. But rather than cowing soldiers into submission, the Song system of mass control based on tattooing, hardship, and harsh punishments drove registered soldiers and potential conscripts to widespread acts of resistance, including evasion, desertion, insubordination, and mutiny. Any one of these forms of defiance could turn soldiers into criminals, creating what Alyagon refers to as "the Northern Song penal-military complex." At the same time, because officials had to be wary of driving soldiers into mass rebellion or desertion, acts of resistance could serve to limit and even reverse the state's policies. Although the social status of soldiers, lower even than that of regular commoners, made them easy targets for victimization by their superiors, when soldiers rose against their superiors, official lives could be put in danger. As a result, "officials had to tread a fine line between ruthlessness and flexibility."

Alyagon's study highlights the wide gap between members of the governing class, who could earn praise for speaking up against other powerful officials, and the soldiers who faced execution for merely talking back to their superiors. Moreover, the Confucian values that governed relations among the elite were rarely extended to the soldiers, whose resistance was met with coercion, violence, and terror. But that does not mean that power only flowed downwards from the state, for there was a dynamic relationship between the governing class and the poorest of the governed. In Alyagon's formulation, even national policies could be affected by the violent interaction between the Song underclass and its state officials. At a still higher level of generalization, Alyagon shows that even as court policy transformed higher society by fostering the emergence of a new literati elite, the imperatives of defense wrought an equally important transformation at the bottom of society by binding a few million soldiers and their families to the Song's military institutions.

But it was not only members of the underclass who were vulnerable to the coercive powers of the state. For war—an inescapable feature of East Asia's multi-state system from the tenth through the fourteenth centuries—could suddenly turn even privileged segments of the population into powerless captives of contending states. In her chapter Ebrey underscores the precipitous and arbitrary nature of war-generated coercion by comparing the practice of forced relocations of civilians across the four principal states of our period: Liao, Song, Jin, and Yuan. Her chapter is the one that goes furthest in examining the larger geopolitical context—one in which each state had rivals and peace among them was always somewhat precarious. To understand this situation, it must also be kept in mind that the economies and political systems of these four states differed in fundamental ways. In the simplest terms, the pastoral components were much more important in the economies of Liao, Jin, and Yuan than the Song, and these three northern states were also organized much more in the form of empires that dominated subordinate units and ruled them differently than their cores.

As Ebrey shows, the three northern states relocated captured subjects in order to weaken the social networks of newly conquered regions, as Liao did with Bohai; or to transfer agricultural workers, skilled craftsmen, and women from conquered, especially formerly Chinese regions to their home territories, as did Liao, Jin, and Yuan; or to decimate a ruling household, as did Jin when it marched Song imperial clansmen north under such harsh conditions that huge numbers of them perished.

The numbers of people moved at any one time could be impressive, with the Kitan relocating households and individuals in multiples of hundreds or thousands, and the Mongols often transporting populations in multiples of ten thousands. But the Song was much less inclined than its northern neighbors and foes to relocate people on a mass scale, which Ebrey attributes to a combination of cultural and institutional factors. Culturally, in those few instances when Song forces did make inroads into non-Han domains (on the Song–Xia border, for example, or in the Tibetan tribal lands of modern Sichuan, Gansu, and Qinghai), Song statesmen were reluctant to relocate non-Han captives deep into Song territory. Nor was there an overwhelming reason to move large populations into Song territory, which was already well populated. Moreover, where there were reasons to relocate individuals or families to new regions, such as in the border regions of Southern Sichuan or along the Song–Xia frontier, Song officials could call on an established repertoire of financial (and career) incentives to recruit volunteers, without having to resort to coercion. In this sense, the relatively weak coercive capacity of the Song state in comparison to its rivals was offset by its much more vibrant and mature commercial economy.

*   *   *

State power is a huge topic, and we have made no effort to treat it comprehensively. Law courts, diplomacy, and succession struggles are among the many important elements of state power that do not appear in these pages. At the same time, there are facets of state power that come out best when these chapters are read against each other. Three examples should suffice.

Key ideas about good government come up in multiple chapters. Cong Zhang and Paul Smith both refer to the notion of the "right kind of men" to be recruited or appointed to office. Both Charles Hartman and Paul Smith discuss the notion of "shared governance" between the monarch and literati officials. In the introduction, we have emphasized the fractious side of the elite, but these common grounds also need to be kept in mind.

The routinized, rule-based practices of the state—its institutional structure—also comes through in several of the chapters, ranging from Hartman's discussion of the political use of omens and Li Huarui's analysis of government charitable ventures to Ebrey's investigation of forced transfers of people. Both Fan Zhongyan and Wang Anshi offered detailed lists of government practices in need of reform, as Paul Smith lays out in his chapter. These ranged from the weight put on seniority in assigning offices, officials' pay, and the flow of information to the emperor. Elad Alyagon's chapter points to government practices that had negative effects on the stability of the state—such as inadequate provisioning of the armies on the northern and northwestern borders. Government practices that were not based on explicit policies often can be detected only statistically. Song Chen, for instance, detects a "practice of rotating prefects all across the empire in the 1040s" along with a preference for assigning them to prefectures in the same administrative macroregion about half the time. He sees this practice as "a compromise between conflicting policy goals and with the constraints of social realities."

The territorial side of the state comes out most clearly in Patricia Ebrey's and Song Chen's chapters. Ebrey's chapter offers examples of state attempts to secure territory. As the Liao, Jin, and Yuan all were aware, an efficient way to "pacify" newly acquired people was to move them to a different part of the country. This cut their ties to their former local identities more effectively than simply announcing to them that they had new rulers. Moving people into an underdeveloped region was a way to possess it, to make it—and the relocated transplants—more firmly a part of the state. As Chen shows in his chapter, the Song state needed to draw resources from its regions, but it also needed to co-opt local elites, so drawing officials from a region was one of the most effective ways to lower the costs of administering it. Chen sees persistent north–south differences during the Song, but also sees major changes in the south. "By the tenth century the 'south' was no longer a single area centered on the Lower Yangzi Delta, but had developed multiple centers of culture and power."

Taken together, the chapters in the volume reveal ways the cohabitants of the core Song state achieved a somewhat surprising equilibrium, given the internal contests for power that often seemed ready to tear them apart. In the end it was the external pressures that brought the Song state down, but descendants of its basic structure and the literati social class that developed in tandem with it endured and even flourished through the nineteenth century.

NOTES

1   On this point, see Chaffee, "Introduction: Reflections on the Sung," 2–3.

2   There is today a large literature on empires in comparative perspective. See, for instance, Scheidel, *Rome and China*, and Burbank and Cooper, *Empires in World History*. Calling the Song or the Liao an empire can also be justified on the grounds that subordinate units were not all treated equally and in more distant regions local powers were often allowed to retain control and follow their own customs and practices. But when compared to empires elsewhere in Eurasia, Chinese empires had very large cores where the attempt was made to apply the same laws consistently and govern through officials dispatched from the center, not local magnates or petty kings.

3   On the common understanding of "state" as government, see Skinner, "A Genealogy of the Modern State," 2. Hymes and Schirokauer, *Ordering the World*, 12–15, sometimes use "political center" or "central politics and institutions," when trying to clarify what they mean by "state," suggesting that their understanding of the term in the phrase "state and society" refers to the central government, not the local magistrate or prefect. Sukhee Lee, *Negotiated Power*, 9, explicitly states that he is using "state" as the equivalent of government, but many others do this without making it explicit.

4   Gerth and Mills, *From Max Weber*, 78.

5   Kracke, *Civil Service in Sung China: 960–1067*; Liu, "An Early Sung Reformer"; *Reform in Sung China*; *Ou-yang Hsiu*.

6   Twitchett and Smith, *Cambridge History of China*, vol. 5, part 1, *The Song Dynasty and its Precursors*; Chaffee and Twitchett, *Cambridge History of China*, vol. 5, part 2, *Sung China*.

7   Some examples include Ji, *Politics and Conservatism in Northern Song China*; Lorge, *War, Politics and Society in Early Modern China, 900–1795*; Wright, *From War to Diplomatic Parity in Eleventh-Century China*; Standen, *Unbounded Loyalty*; Anderson, *The Rebel Den of Nùng Trí Cao*; Smith and von Glahn, *The Song-Yuan-Ming Transition in Chinese History*; Levine, *Divided by a Common Language*; Ebrey, *Emperor Huizong*.

8   Ruth Mostern, *"Dividing the Realm in Order to Govern"*; Sukhee Lee, *Negotiated Power*.

9   Skocpol, *States and Social Revolutions*, chap. 1; Mann, *The Sources of Social Power*, esp. vol. 2, chap. 5.

10   Skocpol, 29. That is, "*Some* offices, especially at higher levels, were functionally specialised; *some* officials or aspects of official duties were subject to explicit rules and hierarchical supervision; and the separation of state offices and duties from private property and pursuits was *partially* institutionalized (though in different particular ways) in each regime. None . . . was fully bureaucratic" (Skocpol, *States and Social Revolutions*, 47–48).

11   Mann, *The Sources of Social Power*, 56.

12   Mann, *The Sources of Social Power*, 92, 51; Skocpol, *States and Social Revolutions*, 30.

13   Charles Hucker's charts of the structure of government for Tang, Song, Yuan, Ming, and Qing offer an illustration if not proof of this assertion: Hucker, *A Dictionary of Official Titles*, 3–96. For an authoritative overview of and bibliography on the Song state and its constituents see Hartman, "Sung Government and Politics."

14   For overviews, see Chen Feng, *Bei Song wujiang*; and Fang, *Power Structures and Cultural Identities in Imperial China*.

15 On monarchical control of the inner court see Chaffee, *Branches of Heaven*, 10–11; Hartman, "Sung Government," 87–92; or, for the view from the emperor's position, Ebrey,
Emperor Huizong. On clerks, Chaffee, *The Thorny Gates*, 53–56, implies that occupa-
tional prohibitions restricting the examinations were rarely enforced. James T. C. Liu,
however, suggests that the number of clerks allowed to take the examinations was
strictly limited: Liu, "The Sung Views on the Control of Government Clerks," 321–22.
Liu, 318–19, cites the estimate by Sudō Yoshiyuki that at least 300 clerks served each prefecture, 150 each county, and over 10,000 the offices of the capital. With 1,207 counties
and 306 prefectures as of the year 1100, this would entail some 282,850 clerks, excluding
those in service at the level of the eighteen circuits and their panoply of agencies.

16 See also Hartman, "Sung Government and Politics," 80–86.

17 For details see Ebrey, *Huizong*, chap. 15.

18 Kracke, *Civil Service*, 69n58. Kracke also went to considerable lengths to avoid the
word "class," writing, for instance, "The social basis of power—the size of the segment
of the population whose views would receive effective expression and consideration—
depended in a considerable degree upon the extent to which different social and geographic groups were represented in the civil service" (65).

19 Liu, "Early Sung Reformer," 15, 16, 18, 20; *Ou-yang Hsiu*, 7, 14–15; *China Turning Inward*,
14, 134.

20 Hartwell, "Demographic, Political, Social Transformations," 405–26.

21 Chaffee, *Thorny Gates*, 10–13, 186–88.

22 Hymes, *Statesmen and Gentlemen*, 4.

23 Hymes and Schirokauer, *Ordering the World*.

24 Bossler, *Powerful Relations*, 204–8.

25 Lee, *Negotiated Power*, 2–8 (quotations from 3 and 8). See also Hymes, "Sung Society
and Social Change," 621–61, for his reconsideration of these issues.

26 For a relatively low official who clearly saw himself as belonging to the *shidafu*, see
Ebrey, *Family and Property in Sung China*, for the views of Yuan Cai.

27 Bol, "The Sung Examination System and the Shih"; *This Culture of Ours*, 32–75; *Neo-
Confucianism in History*, esp. 30–36. Hilde de Weerdt has built on this this work with
Competition over Content.

28 See also Chaffee, "Introduction," 10.

29 In addition to Hymes and Hartman, the following paragraphs draw on, inter alios,
Chaffee, *Thorny Gates*; Ebrey, "The Dynamics of Elite Domination in Sung China"; and
Robert M. Hartwell, "Demographic, Political, and Social Transformations."

30 See Bol, "Government, Society, and State;" Ji, *Politics and Conservatism in Northern
Song China*; and Smith, "Shen-tsung's Reign and the New Policies of Wang An-shih."

31 On Zhu Xi, see the essays by Schirokauer, von Glahn, and Hymes, in Hymes and Schirokauer, *Ordering the World*.

32 Smith, "Shen-tsung's reign," 414–46.

33 For an extended comparison of the two schools see De Weerdt, *Competition over
Content*.

34 As a rough guide to the size of the literati elite, the percentage of adult males possessing
the education to enter the competition for office through the examination system rose
from just under half a percent towards the end of the eleventh century (79,000 candi-

dates out of a total population of 100 million, twenty percent of whom were adult males) to between two and three percent in the thirteenth century (400,000 candidates in an adult male population of 12 million): Ebrey, "Dynamics of Elite Domination," 501, based on data by Chaffee, *Thorny Gates*, 38, fig. 3.

35 For a systematic analysis of control mechanisms that relates coercion and material and symbolic incentives to social and task hierarchies see Etzioni, "Organizational Control Structure."

REFERENCES

Anderson, James A. *The Rebel Den of Nùng Trí Cao: Eleventh-Century Rebellion and Response along the Sino-Vietnamese Frontier*. Seattle: University of Washington Press, 2006.

Bol, Peter K. "Government, Society, and State: On the Political Visions of Ssu-ma Kuang and Wang An-shih." In *Ordering the World: Approaches to State and Society in Sung Dynasty China*, edited by Robert P. Hymes and Conrad Schirokauer, 128–92. Berkeley: University of California Press, 1993.

———. *Neo-Confucianism in History*. Cambridge, Mass.: Harvard University Asia Center, 2008.

———. "The Sung Examination System and the *Shih*." *Asia Major*, 3rd ser., 3, no. 2 (1990): 149–71.

———. *"This Culture of Ours": Intellectual Traditions in T'ang and Sung China*. Stanford: Stanford University Press, 1992.

Bossler, Beverly J. *Powerful Relations: Kinship, Status, and the State in Sung China (960–1279)*. Cambridge, Mass.: Council on East Asian Studies, Harvard University, 1998.

Burbank, Jane, and Frederick Cooper. *Empires in World History*. Princeton: Princeton University Press, 2010.

Chaffee, John W. *Branches of Heaven: A History of the Imperial Clan of Sung China*. Cambridge, Mass.: Harvard University Asia Center, 1999.

———. "Introduction: Reflections on the Sung." In *The Cambridge History of China*. Vol. 5, Part 2: *Sung China, 960–1279*, edited by John W. Chaffee and Denis Twitchett, 1–18. Cambridge, UK: Cambridge University Press, 2015.

———. *The Thorny Gates of Learning in Sung China: A Social History of Examinations*. Cambridge, UK: Cambridge University Press, 1985.

Chaffee, John W., and Denis Twitchett, eds. *The Cambridge History of China*. Vol. 5, Part 2: *Sung China, 960–1279*. Cambridge, UK: Cambridge University Press, 2015.

Chen Feng 陈峰. *Bei Song wujiang qunti yu xiangguan wenti yanjiu* 北宋武将群体与相关问题研究. Beijing: Zhonghua shuju, 2004.

De Weerdt, Hilde. *Competition over Content: Negotiating Standards for the Civil Service Examinations in Imperial China (1127–1279)*. Cambridge, Mass.: Harvard University Asia Center, 2007.

Ebrey, Patricia Buckley. "The Dynamics of Elite Domination in Sung China." *HJAS* 48, no. 2 (1988): 493–519.

———. *Emperor Huizong*. Cambridge, Mass.: Harvard University Press, 2014.

———, trans. *Family and Property in Sung China: Yüan Tsai's Precepts for Social Life*. Princeton: Princeton University Press, 1984.

Etzioni, Amitai. "Organizational Control Structure." In *Handbook of Organizations*, edited by James G. March, 650–77. Chicago: Rand McNally, 1965.

Fang, Cheng-Hua. *Power Structures and Cultural Identities in Imperial China: Civil and Military Power from Late Tang to Early Song Dynasties (A.D. 875–1063)*. Saarbrüken, Germany: VDM Verlag Dr. Müller, 2009.

Gerth, H. H., and C. Wright Mills. *From Max Weber: Essays in Sociology*. New York: Oxford University Press, 1946.

Hartman, Charles. "Sung Government and Politics." In *The Cambridge History of China*. Vol. 5, Part 2: *Sung China, 960–1279*, edited by John Chaffee and Denis Twitchett, 19–138. Cambridge, UK: Cambridge University Press, 2015.

Hartwell, Robert M. "Demographic, Political, and Social Transformations of China, 750–1550." *Harvard Journal of Asiatic Studies* 42, no. 2 (1982): 365–442.

Hucker, Charles O. *A Dictionary of Official Titles in Imperial China*. Stanford: Stanford University Press, 1985.

Hymes, Robert P. 1993. "Moral Duty and Self-Regulating Process in Southern Sung Views on Famine Relief." In *Ordering the World: Approaches to State and Society in Sung Dynasty China*, edited by Robert P. Hymes and Conrad Schirokauer, 280–309. Berkeley: University of California Press.

———. *Statesmen and Gentlemen: The Elite of Fu-chou, Chiang-hsi, in Northern and Southern Sung*. Cambridge, UK: Cambridge University Press, 1986.

———. "Sung Society and Social Change." In *The Cambridge History of China*. Vol. 5, Part 2: *Sung China, 960–1279*, edited by John Chaffee and Denis Twitchett, 526–664. Cambridge, UK: Cambridge University Press, 2015.

Hymes, Robert P., and Conrad Schirokauer, eds. *Ordering the World: Approaches to State and Society in Sung Dynasty China*. Berkeley: University of California Press, 1993.

Ji, Xiao-bin. *Politics and Conservatism in Northern Song China*. Hong Kong: The Chinese University Press, 2005.

Kracke, Edward A. Jr. *Civil Service in Sung China: 960–1067*. Cambridge, Mass.: Harvard University Press, 1953.

Lee, Sukhee. *Negotiated Power: The State, Elites, and Local Governance in Twelfth- to Fourteenth-Century China*. Cambridge, Mass.: Harvard University Asia Center, 2014.

Levine, Ari. *Divided by a Common Language: Factional Conflict in Late Northern Song China*. Honolulu: University of Hawai'i Press, 2008.

Liu, James T. C. *China Turning Inward: Intellectual-Political Changes in the Early Twelfth Century*. Cambridge, Mass.: Harvard University Press, 1988.

———. "An Early Sung Reformer: Fan Chung-yen." In *Chinese Thought and Institutions*, edited by John K. Fairbank, 105–31. Chicago: University of Chicago Press, 1957.

———. *Ou-yang Hsiu: An Eleventh-Century Neo-Confucianist*. Stanford: Stanford University Press, 1967.

———. *Reform in Sung China: Wang An-shih (1021–1086) and His New Policies*. Cambridge, Mass.: Harvard University Press, 1959.

———. "The Sung Views on the Control of Government Clerks." *Journal of the Economic and Social History of the Orient* 10, nos. 2–3 (1967): 317–44.

Lo, Winston W. *An Introduction to the Civil Service of Sung China, with an Emphasis on Its Personnel Administration.* Honolulu: University of Hawaiʻi Press, 1987.

Lorge, Peter. *War, Politics and Society in Early Modern China, 900–1795.* London: Routledge, 2005.

Mann, Michael. *The Sources of Social Power.* Vol. 2: *The Rise of Classes and Nation-states, 1760–1914.* Cambridge, UK: Cambridge University Press, 1993.

McKnight, Brian E. *Law and Order in Sung China.* Cambridge, UK: Cambridge University Press, 1992.

———. 1971. *Village and Bureaucracy in Southern Sung China.* Chicago: University of Chicago Press, 1971.

Mostern, Ruth. *"Dividing the Realm in Order to Govern": The Spatial Organization of the Song State (960–1276 CE).* Cambridge, Mass.: Harvard University Asia Center, 2011.

Scheidel, Walter, ed. *Rome and China: Comparative Perspectives on Ancient World Empires.* Oxford, UK: Oxford University Press, 2009.

Schirokauer, Conrad. 1993. "Chu Hsi's Sense of History." In *Ordering the World: Approaches to State and Society in Sung Dynasty China,* edited by Robert P. Hymes and Conrad Schirokauer, 193–220. Berkeley: University of California Press, 1993.

Skinner, Quentin. "A Genealogy of the Modern State." *Proceedings of the British Academy* 162 (2009): 325–70.

Skocpol, Theda. *States and Social Revolutions: A Comparative Analysis of France, Russia, and China.* Cambridge, UK: Cambridge University Press, 1979.

Smith, Paul Jakov. "Shen-tsung's Reign and the New Policies of Wang An-shih." In *The Cambridge History of China.* Vol. 5, Part 1: *The Sung Dynasty and its Precursors, 907–1279,* edited by Denis Twitchett and Paul Jakov Smith, 347–483. Cambridge, UK: Cambridge University Press, 2009.

Smith, Paul J., and Richard von Glahn, eds. *The Song-Yuan-Ming Transition in Chinese History.* Cambridge, Mass.: Harvard University Asia Center, 2003.

Standen, Naomi. *Unbounded Loyalty: Frontier Crossings in Liao China.* Honolulu: University of Hawaiʻi Press, 2007.

Twitchett, Denis, and Paul Jakov Smith, eds. *Cambridge History of China.* Vol. 5, Part 1: *The Sung Dynasty and its Precursors, 907–1279.* Cambridge, UK: Cambridge University Press, 2009.

Von Glahn, Richard. "Community and Welfare: Chu Hsi's Community Granary in Theory and Practice." In *Ordering the World: Approaches to State and Society in Sung Dynasty China,* edited by Robert P. Hymes and Conrad Schirokauer, 221–54. Berkeley: University of California Press.

Wright, David C. *From War to Diplomatic Parity in Eleventh-Century China: Sung's Foreign Relations with Kitan Liao.* Leiden: Brill, 2005.

PART 1

The Ruling House

1   Invoking Higher Authorities

Song Taizong's Quest for Imperial Legitimacy
and Its Architectural Legacy

TRACY MILLER

IN 989, TAIZONG SAW THE COMPLETION OF THE KAIBAO MONAS-
tery Śarīra Pagoda (Kaibaosi Shelita) in the imperial capital at Kaifeng.[1]
Rather than employing the same craftsmen as Taizu (r. 960–976), the first
emperor of the Song who made over the palaces in the manner of those at
the Western Capital of Luoyang, Taizong (r. 976–997) selected Yu Hao, a
famous builder from the newly acquired Wuyue kingdom, to construct his
towering Buddhist edifice. This act was not a simple expression of conquest.
Instead, it was one element of Taizong's larger program to create a new identity distinct from that of his brother Taizu, who was known for his martial
skills and fondness for Yellow River Valley aesthetics. By visibly demonstrat-
ing the ability to marshal substantial material and human resources toward a
single endeavor, monumental constructions had long been known to bolster
a new ruler's claim to imperial authority. However, not all emperors used
the same types of constructions for this purpose.

The goal of this chapter is to investigate the implications of certain
building projects for the legitimacy and personal power of the first two
Song emperors. Their pattern of building patronage and ritual performance
suggests that much of what characterizes Song visual culture more broadly
emerged from competition between these sibling emperors. By employing Yu
Hao to build the monumental Kaibao Monastery Pagoda in Kaifeng, Taizong
sought to establish himself as the leader of a new realm, one that celebrated
the future as much as it embraced the past. Arguably the most public aspect
of Taizong's cultural patronage, the structure served not only to distinguish
Taizong from his brother, but also to appropriate the new cosmopolitanism
of the Yangzi Delta and its potential as a source of economic, technological,
and spiritual power to enhance his own political capital. The pagoda marked
a turning point away from the aesthetics of cultural legitimacy employed by

rulers of earlier Chinese empires, those centered in the traditional capitals of Chang'an and Luoyang. It was more than a reliquary; it was a "modern" tower employed to herald the coming of a new age.

THE TOWERING PAGODA AT KAIBAO MONASTERY

The Kaibao Monastery Pagoda is perhaps the most often discussed non-extant Buddhist pagoda in Chinese art history.[2] In its prime, the building would have been something to behold. Located outside the northeast gate of the Inner City wall, or Old Fengqiu Gate (Jiu Fengqiu Men), the tower was enclosed in a separate Blessed Success Pagoda Cloister (Fusheng Tayuan), as one part of an expansive imperial Buddhist monastery named after the Kaibao reign period of Song Taizu (fig. 1.1).[3] Prior to its destruction by fire in 1044, the Kaibao Monastery Pagoda was, according to Ouyang Xiu (1007–1072), the tallest in the capital and considered to be an incredible feat of architectural engineering.[4] Although criticized by contemporaries as an example of excess, the same sources tell us the structure was unprecedented, "resplendent in gold and jade green" (*jinbi yinghuang*), and took more than eight years and hundreds of millions in cash (*yiwan*) to complete. According to Yang Yi (974–1020), Li Tao (1115–1184), and Zhi Pan (thirteenth century), the final structure was eleven stories tall, and all sources agree that the octagonal timber pagoda soared to 360 *chi* which, based on excavated Song-period carpenter's squares, would be approximately 111.28 meters high.[5] To give a sense of its height, the structure was roughly 43.97 meters taller than the extant Liao dynasty Fogong Monastery Śakyamuni Pagoda (Fogongsi Shijiata, commonly known as the Yingxian Muta, ca. 1056–95) which stands at 67.31 meters (fig. 1.2).

Perhaps because it was such an architectural wonder, we also know much about Yu Hao, the designer of the tower and the most renowned timber craftsman (*duliaojiang*) of Song China. One of the more detailed accounts of Yu Hao and his famous tower comes from the collected tales of Yang Yi, a favorite of Taizong's who participated in the compilation of the *Veritable Records of Taizong* (Taizong shilu) and later coedited the *Outstanding Models from the Storehouse of Literature* (Cefu yuangui). Yang Yi started his court career as a precocious child who, in 984 at the age of eleven *sui*, was brought to the palace for a personal examination by Taizong and then retained in the Department of the Palace Library as a proofreader.[6] Yang arrived at the capital shortly after the tower's construction had begun. He would likely have had an opportunity to watch the process as both boy and tower grew

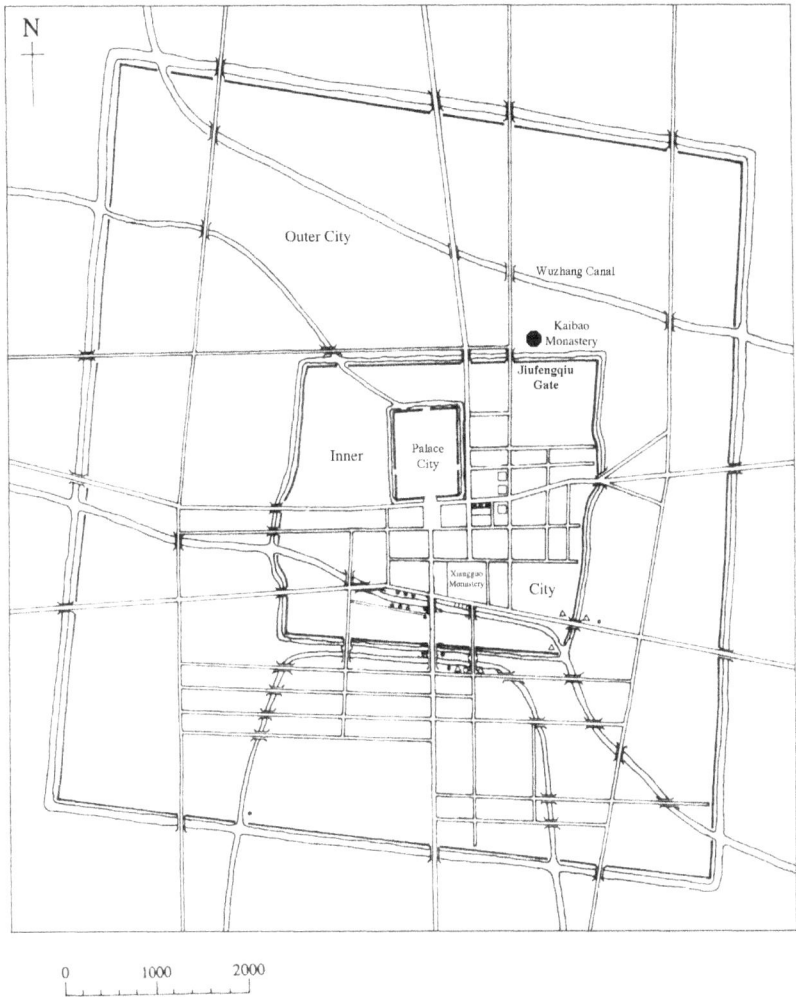

FIGURE 1.1. Kaifeng during the Song dynasty. Scale is in meters. Illustration based on Heng, *Cities of Aristocrats and Bureaucrats*, 153.

to maturity. Yang wrote that Yu Hao was extremely skillful (*jueqiao*) and began his project by presenting a model to the court.[7] Once on the job site, Yu Hao constructed each story secretly behind a curtain, carefully ensuring the stability of each before moving on to the next, so the structure could last 700 years without falling out of alignment (*ci ke qibainian wu qingdong*). Perhaps most famously, when questioned about the slightly higher northern side of the structure, he replied that he had taken environmental conditions into consideration: he claimed the northerly winds and damp ground (because

FIGURE 1.2. Śakyamuni Pagoda, Fogong Monastery, ca. 1056–1095, Yingxian, Shanxi. (Photo courtesy Scott Gilchrist.)

of closeness to the Wuzhang canal) would have an effect on the building and it would, after a hundred years, become level.[8]

Yu Hao was known for more than his skillfulness, however. He was also known because he was from Hangzhou, or Qiantang, the capital of Wuyue. Taizong's choice of Yu Hao may have helped to clarify the Wuyue origin of the relic so important to prove the authentic connection to King Aśoka (ca. 304–232 BCE), the most famous royal patron of Buddhism. The pagoda was constructed to house a smaller reliquary containing one of the nineteen "true" relics of the Buddha originally distributed to China by Aśoka. Taizong ordered this relic moved from the sacred interior (jinzhong) of its pagoda in the Wuyue capital after its ruler Qian Chu (or Qian Hongchu, r. 948–978) capitulated to the Song in 978, an event discussed below.[9] It is important to note here, however, that knowledge of Wuyue architecture may have been deemed critical both to constructing a structurally sound tower of this size and to creating a spiritually effective container for the new relic.

Efficacy, both structural and spiritual, was proven in the ceremony to inter the relic after its completion. Yang Yi tells us that the emperor was carried to the temple in a palanquin to personally place the relic in the *tiangong* within the pagoda. A white light emitted from one corner, causing the emperor to shed tears. The pagoda, now fully charged, caused dozens of palace attendants who witnessed the miracle to decide to become monks.[10] Was the structure worth the great expense of its construction purely as a symbol of political legitimacy? Or could Taizong and members of his court have believed it able to generate true spiritual power? To understand the potential of architecture to project political, cultural, and spiritual affinities it is helpful to review some examples from China's early imperial period before turning to how this Buddhist tower's construction contributed to the Song period shift in focus from center to coast, north to south.

ARCHITECTURE AS A TOOL FOR SPIRITUAL POWER

Large-scale building projects have long played an important role in projecting political power and legitimating claims to authority. At a minimum, monumental structures embody the ability to marshal the financial, material, and human resources necessary for their creation. Often their significance also has a substantial symbolic component, using style or magnitude to suggest alliances with, distinction from, or dominance over neighboring states and/or cultures.[11] And if properly designed, at least some were believed to help actualize that power. Along with military unification and establishment of the imperial bureaucracy in premodern China, the building of highly visible structures was critical to solidifying the authority of a new regime. In the early imperial period, palaces, imperial capitals, and royal temples were the best-known building types used to display state power and acquisition of the Mandate of Heaven—the divine right to demand obedience of a newly conquered population.[12] The "Zhongyong" section of the *Book of Rites* (Liji) describes one understanding of the purpose of rites to spirits only accessible to the emperor: "By the ceremonies of the border sacrifices (to Heaven and Earth), they served God, and by the ceremonies of the ancestral temple they sacrificed to their forefathers. If one understood the ceremonies of the border sacrifices, and the meaning of the sacrifices of the ancestral temple, it would be as easy for him to rule a state as to look into his palms."[13]

Through knowledge and precise performance of the rituals at both open altars and temples, the emperor could manage the needs of the state. These rites show how emperors enlisted spirits commanding natural forces and those of the imperial ancestors to facilitate rulership through the enhanced perspective—one as easy as looking into the palm—afforded by their support.[14]

A very similar motivation lay behind the practice of Buddhism by both common and imperial devotees. Although the celibacy and (at least nominal) rejection of the patriline that accompanied Buddhist monastic life conflicted with indigenous cultural traditions, men and women in early medieval China left their families to join monastic communities in part because Buddhism promised the aspirant the potential to "harness the powers of the spirit world."[15] Using the imperial purse, emperors were able to display their own access to that power by building ever-taller Buddhist towers.[16] For example, according to the *History of the Southern Dynasties* (Nan shi), in 472 Emperor Ming of the Liu-Song dynasty (r. 465–472), another "Song Taizong," set out to build a taller pagoda than the seven-story one constructed by his older half-brother, the former Emperor Xiaowu (r. 454–464).[17] Perhaps because of structural difficulties the planned ten-story pagoda in the new Xianggong Monastery would not stand, so instead he constructed two of five stories.[18] Emperor Ming may also have been competing with the rival Northern Wei. In 467 Northern Wei Xianwendi (r. 465–471) constructed a seven-story pagoda at the Yongning Monastery in his capital of Pingcheng (modern Datong).[19] At 300 *chi*, this pagoda was described as the tallest in the known world at the time.[20]

These building projects seem to have been more than cynical political theater. From the fifth century, we know imperial Buddhist rituals were believed to protect the state and its population from foreign invasion and natural disasters. Two sūtras in particular, the *Sūtra of Golden Radiance* (Jinguangming jing; Skt. Suvarṇa-prabhāsôttama-sūtra) and the indigenous Chinese *Sūtra on Perfect Wisdom for Humane Kings Who Wish to Protect Their States* (Renwang huguo bore buoluomi jing), emphasized that Buddhist ritual practice would grant a ruler's state protection from the Celestial Kings (*tianwang* or *lokapāla*) of the four directions. Both of these works were available in Chinese by the second half of the fifth century and seem to have had immediate influence.[21] The Pingcheng Yongning Monastery Pagoda was also constructed during this period.[22] And, after the move of the capital to Luoyang in 493, a new Yongning Monastery Pagoda was constructed that could be seen "one hundred *li* from the capital."[23] The structure would have provided an expanded view of the ruler's territory, becoming both a sign of the imperial commitment to the Buddha and tool to enhance the ability of soldiers and spirits to protect the empire.[24] Thus, constructing the highly visible Buddhist tower appears to have been an effective way both to proclaim and channel Buddhist support, perhaps even more so during a period of division when new alliances and new empires were being formed.

TAIZU AND KAIBAO MONASTERY BEFORE THE PAGODA

The founding emperors of the Song dynasty inherited this long tradition of using cities, palaces, and ritual structures to express political authority and divine protection for themselves and all under their rule. Neither Taizu nor Taizong rebuilt the imperial capital they inherited from the Later Zhou and both patronized the Kaibao Monastery. Yet, building patronage reveals Taizong's efforts to shift the focus of the empire away from the north, from his brother and the military families who would support him, toward a new source of patronage loyal only to him. As an institution predating the Song, the life of this monastery can offer insights into the changing cultural landscape of the capital.

Kaibao Monastery was an ancient Buddhist site established prior to the imperial capital at Kaifeng. The complex was founded in 559 as Duju Monastery when the Northern Qi ruled the Central Plains. During the Tang Kaiyuan reign period (713–742), Xuanzong (r. 712–756) visited the monastery on his return from performing the Feng and Shan sacrifices and renamed it Feng-Shan Monastery.[25] Thus, by the eighth century the monastery was the recipient of imperial patronage and associated with the most fundamental rituals of imperial legitimacy. Song Taizu was also a major patron. In the third year of the Kaibao reign period (970), he renamed the monastery after his reign, and rebuilt many of the corridors and subsidiary buildings. Its new size totaled approximately 280 areas (*qu*) within which were 24 cloisters (*yuan*).[26]

The depth of Taizu's personal religiosity does not usually dominate discussions of the founding of the "Age of Confucian Rule."[27] Song sources emphasize Taizu's support of Zhou ritual traditions and preference for the cultural heritage of the Yellow River Valley in his choice of imperial capital and the appearance of the palace halls. Kaifeng was the capital of four of the Five Dynasties, including the Later Zhou. The city had been expanded over the course of the tenth century to accommodate a growing population. Its outer wall was constructed under Zhou Shizong (r. 954–959), nominally for the sake of defense.[28] Yet, by constructing an outer wall roughly equidistant from the inner wall on all sides, the imperial palace was located much more centrally than before, thereby conforming to textual descriptions of the

城　　　　　　　　　　　　　　　王

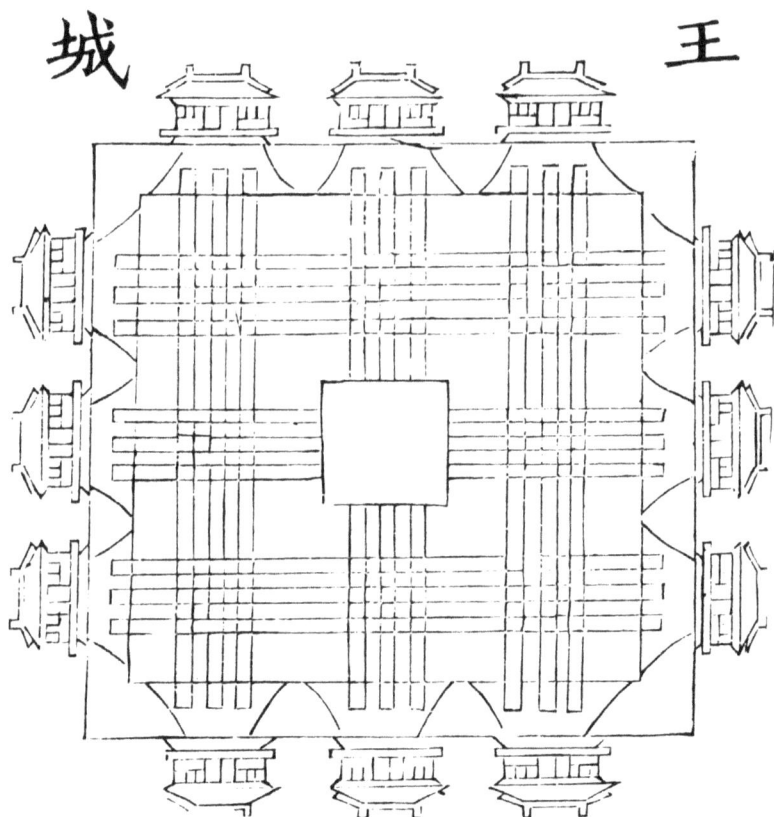

FIGURE 1.3. Royal City (Wangcheng), Nie Chongyi, *Xinding sanlitu*, 962. (Illustration from a reprint of the 1175 edition.)

idealized royal city in the "Kaogongji," a chapter in the classic *Rites of Zhou* (Zhouli). Zhou Shizong also commissioned the Confucian (Ru) scholar Nie Chongyi (tenth century) to undertake a new study of sacrificial implements for the traditional Zhou temple rituals. The resulting *Xinding Sanlitu* was submitted in the fourth month of the third year of Song Taizu's new empire (962) and included an image of the idealized Royal City in the "Kaogongji" (fig. 1.3).[29] The original text does not stipulate the precise placement of an inner city or palace, and the location of these structures in earlier cities was not consistent, nor entirely central.[30] Yet Nie Chongyi's drawing shows the city as a series of concentric squares with a small central square for the palace, in a manner very similar to the Later Zhou and new Song imperial capitals. With the presentation of this text, Taizu acquired a ritually correct fortress. For his accomplishment in explicating the details of the Zhou ritual classics, Taizu awarded Nie Chongyi the purple robe, rhinoceros belt, and silver vessels.[31]

However, Taizu was not fully satisfied with Kaifeng as a capital. Although his official ancestral homeland was Zhuojun (later Zhuozhou) just south of modern Beijing,[32] Taizu was born in Luoyang,[33] and he is said to have liked the customs of the area.[34] In the fifth month of 962, only one month after the submission of the *Xinding Sanlitu*, Taizu decided to refurbish the imperial palaces, sending officers to draw the halls in the palaces in Luoyang. They then followed the drawings in the construction of the new Kaifeng palaces.[35] Taizu's interest in returning to past traditions and locations of empire did not please his ministers or his brother, however. In 976 Taizu expressed his long-held desire move the Song capital to Luoyang, and potentially even to reestablish the capital at Chang'an, a location that had worked to the strategic advantage of the Zhou, Han, and Tang dynasties. This proposition may also have been a veiled threat to Taizong, whose powerbase was in Kaifeng. Taizong responded to Taizu's desire to move west by quoting the Warring States period military strategist Wu Qi (440–381 BCE): "[Defense] is in [the power of] virtue, not in [the use of strategic] passes."[36] Taizu's death, likely an assassination orchestrated by Taizong, took place later that year.[37]

Of course, as we have seen earlier, need for the support of divinities described in the Zhou ritual classics does not obviate the desire to bring the power of other divinities to the imperial cause, including those of Buddhism. In strong contradistinction to Later Zhou Shizong, who suppressed Buddhist practice and image production, Taizu pursued state-supported Buddhism. Taizu's extensive patronage of Buddhist projects may have been motivated by a desire to present himself as a *ćakravartin* (wheel-turning [Buddhist] king; *zhuanlunwang*).[38] Certainly he is cast in this manner in the *Fozu tongji*. The *Song shi* documents that his skin was golden at birth, a hue it retained for three days.[39] Of course, a yellow tint to the skin is a common symptom of infant jaundice, and so not a historical impossibility. Yet, in the *Fozu tongji*, Zhi Pan interprets this detail as an "auspicious sign" of Taizu's destiny to be a great figure in Buddhism (*Fo dashi zhi ruixiang ye*).[40] His actions as an adult support Zhi Pan's case. In 960 the newly enthroned Taizu relaxed restrictions that Zhou Shizong had put on both Buddhism and Daoism in 955.[41] In 966, after completing the conquest of Later Shu the year before, he supported monks to travel to South Asia in search of Sanskrit scriptures, displaying both interest in authentic Buddhist texts and political control of the passes westward.[42] In 969, on his return to Kaifeng after failing to conquer the

Northern Han, Taizu discovered the destruction of a forty-nine-foot bronze sculpture of Avalokiteśvara at Dabei Monastery in Zhenzhou (modern Zhengding). At the request of a local monk, he ordered the casting of the monumental bronze "1,000-arm Avalokiteśvara" in the towering pavilion at the north end of the Longxing Monastery. Work commenced in 971 and four years later the sculpture was completed and housed in the Treasure Pavilion of Great Compassion (Dabei Baoge; also called the Buddha's Fragrance Pavilion or Foxiangge).[43] The body and two arms of the present sculpture are thought to be original to this casting (forty were destroyed in the eighteenth century), which soars to the height of 21.3 meters including the stone Sumeru-style platform (documents record 7 *zhang* 3 *chi*).[44] In 971 Taizu also initiated a full printing of the *Tripiṭaka* (Kaibao zang).[45] Carved in Sichuan, the completed blocks were transported to the capital in 983, shortly after the construction of the Kaibao Monastery tower began.

Taizu's personal efforts at gaining spiritual power also seem to have been based in the Buddhist practice of the Tang capitals Chang'an and Luoyang. Taizu is said to have traveled to Guanghua Monastery, near the Longmen Grottoes outside Luoyang, to pay homage to the preserved body of Śubhākarasiṃha (Shanwuwei 637–735). A South Asian master of esoteric practice, Śubhākarasiṃha famously taught Buddhism in Chang'an after his arrival there in 716.[46] He also translated major works associated with early esoteric Buddhism, including the Mahāvairocanā bhisaṃbodhi-sūtra (A discourse on the enlightenment of Mahāvairocanā), from Sanskrit into Chinese. Huang Ch'i-chang emphasizes that Taizu's worship included removing the preserved body from the funerary tower where it was held and performing a ritual washing, a rite popular among the people of Luoyang.[47] He would likely also have visited the monumental Tang dynasty image of Vairocanā sponsored by Tang Gaozong (628–683) and Wu Zetian (624–705) in the seventh century, an impressive site even in its current damaged state (fig. 1.4).

Vestiges of Tang imperial Buddhism remained in Kaifeng as well. Xiangguo Monastery, the most famous of the Kaifeng monasteries, held numerous objects from the most famous court artists of the Tang dynasty. These included some of the finest examples of Buddhist painting and sculpture available at the time, such as articles from the most famous Buddhist painter of the age, Wu Daozi (b. 680).[48] Perhaps our greatest insight into the perception of artistic style at Xiangguo Monastery in the tenth century is the comment said to have been made by Yu Hao himself. In this well-known story, Yu Hao declared his admiration for the monastery's Tang dynasty gateway. The one flaw (or technical deficiency) was that they did not know how to

FIGURE 1.4. Great Buddha Niche, Longmen Grottoes, late seventh century.
(Photo courtesy Tracy Miller.)

turn up the eaves. Yet, when investigating the structure from underneath, he was unable to understand its principles fully.[49] In his seminal article on the monastery, Alexander Soper interpreted this anecdote as reflecting the "autumnal character" of Northern Song religious art and architecture—it simply could not compare to the Tang. It seems that Taizu would agree with that assessment. Yet, Yu Hao was not only renowned for his incredible abilities as a craftsman, he was decidedly *different*—from a new cultural center with equal claims to legitimacy in the realms of Buddhism and craft technologies.

Although the few timber buildings extant from the Tang period are all from Shanxi, beginning in the tenth century we do have enough examples from different areas across China to identify regional distinctions in architectural style.[50] Most of the extant structures are in remote locations; however, we have some remains from metropolitan regions that can provide insights into urban building styles as well. This evidence suggests that the use of the descending cantilever (*xia'ang*) in the bracket clusters between columns may have been a distinguishing feature of ritual structures along China's east coast, particularly in the areas of modern Zhejiang and Fujian, but also further north in Liaoning.

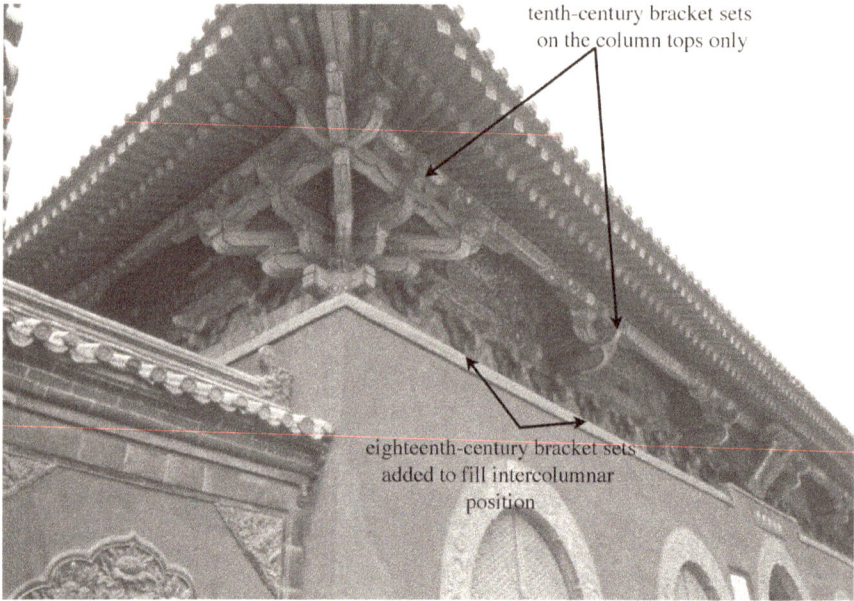

tenth-century bracket sets
on the column tops only

eighteenth-century bracket sets
added to fill intercolumnar
position

FIGURE 1.5. Celestial Kings' Hall (Tianwang Dian), Longxing Monastery, ca. 989, Zhengding, Hebei. (Photo courtesy Tracy Miller.)

The bracket cluster consists of timber arms that reach out from the timber
wall frame to the horizontal eaves purlin supporting the rafters of the roof.
They can be horizontal, vertical, or angled in a cantilever to make use of the
weight of the roof tiles pressing down on the backs of the cantilevers inside
the building in order to lift the eaves. Tenth century buildings in central
and northern Shanxi and Hebei tend to have minimal support for the eaves
purlin between columns—either no bracket arms extend from the wall plane
(fig. 1.5) or smaller bracket arms that do not extend fully outward to the eaves
purlin (fig. 1.6). Examining the roof support of the Jidu Temple Retiring
Palace (Jidumiao Qingong, ca. 973; fig. 1.7), a timber-frame building thought
to have been constructed under Song Taizu's reign, we see a variation from
these more northern buildings in the use of an intercolumnar bracket set that
is the same as the column-top set. But the descending cantilever is not used
at all in this, or a comparable building, the Great Buddha Hall of Dayunyuan
(Dayunyuan Dafo Dian, 940), which is located in the Taihang Mountains east
of modern Pingshun, Shanxi (fig. 1.8).

The descending cantilever supports the upward curvature of eaves along
the facades of buildings rather than just at the corners, and they prolifer-
ated in southern buildings during the tenth century. Evidence suggests that

FIGURE 1.6. 10,000 Buddhas Hall (Wanfo Dian), Zhenguo Monastery, 963, Pingyao, Shanxi, back facade. (Photo courtesy Tracy Miller.)

FIGURE 1.7. Retiring Palace, Jidu Temple (Jidumiao Qingong), ca. 973, Jiyuanxian, Henan. (Photo courtesy Tracy Miller.)

FIGURE 1.8. Great Buddha Hall, Dayun Cloister (Dayunyuan Dafo
Dian), 940, Pingshun, Shanxi. (Photo courtesy Tracy Miller.)

craftsmen regularly used descending cantilevers in bracket clusters between
the columns. Furthermore, in the wider center bays multiple intercolumnar
bracket sets of the same size and configuration as the column-top sets were
employed (figs. 1.9, 1.10). Given the extra support for the eaves provided by
these timbers, these additional descending cantilevers may have been used
to further turn up the eaves, as Yu Hao suggested, distinguishing the new
architecture of the southeast from the old-fashioned buildings of the Yellow
River Valley.

Bracket sets on the tops of columns and between columns are the same configuration and include the descending cantilever (xia'ang)

FIGURE 1.9. Lingyin Monastery Stone Pagoda (Lingyinsi Shita, one of two), 960, Hangzhou, Zhejiang. (Photo courtesy Tracy Miller.)

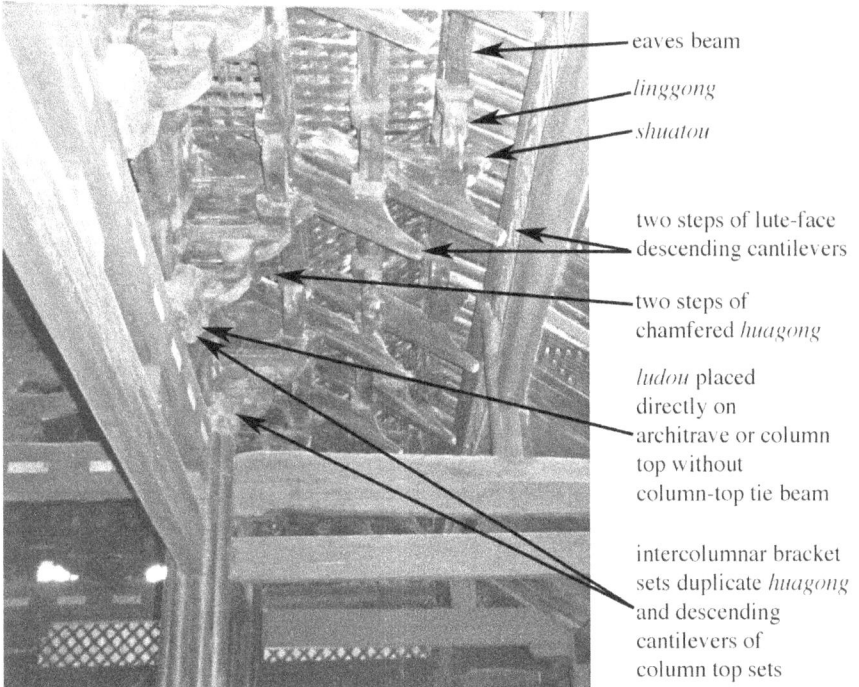

eaves beam

linggong

shuatou

two steps of lute-face descending cantilevers

two steps of chamfered *huagong*

ludou placed directly on architrave or column top without column-top tie beam

intercolumnar bracket sets duplicate *huagong* and descending cantilevers of column top sets

FIGURE 1.10. Mahāvīra Treasure Hall, Baoguo Monastery (Baoguosi Daxiong Baodian), detail of eaves bracketing, 1013, Ningbo, Zhejiang. (Photo courtesy Tracy Miller.)

Perhaps Yu Hao, and his patron Taizong, viewed the Tang dynasty remains in Xiangguo Monastery in a more nostalgic manner, as a modern architect might marvel at the craftsmanship of a Gothic cathedral but not desire to replicate it. Considered from a forward-looking, "modern" perspective, the anecdote might communicate a very different message: an awareness of the differences between the aesthetic of the Yellow River Valley and the Yangzi Delta, differences that came to embody notions of past versus present, old versus new. Not an "ebb-tide" as Soper put it, but a tidal wave of change for a new era.[51]

TAIZONG AND THE TRANSFORMATION OF KAIBAO MONASTERY

Of course, Yu Hao was not transported to the capital at Kaifeng to appraise the buildings of the Tang dynasty; rather, he was part of Taizong's larger campaign to move out from underneath the golden glow of his older brother and remake himself into a different, more spiritually powerful, and more progressive ruler. As described in a recent article by Peter Lorge, Taizong desperately needed legitimacy at the beginning of his reign. Having likely seen to the death of his older brother, Taizong needed to prove his heavenly mandate to solidify the new imperial line and the nascent Song dynasty itself.[52]

During the first decade of his reign, Taizong used numerous military, civil, and spiritual methods to establish legitimate imperial authority.[53] Although he was successful in gaining control over territory sought by Taizu, he was unable to equal his brother on the battlefield. In 978 the last of the independent territories in the south, Zhangquan and the Wuyue kingdom, capitulated, finally solidifying Song rule over the southeast.[54] Taizong succeeded in destroying the Northern Han and demolishing its capital, Taiyuan, in 979. Then, against the advice of his generals, he marched directly against the Liao in an attempt to take the Sixteen Prefectures. This effort ended in a disastrous failure including the loss of at least 10,000 troops at the Gaoliang River in Hebei, which, according to Lorge, compromised his military and imperial legitimacy.[55] In spite of these losses, Taizong persisted in his quest for the Sixteen Prefectures with another futile attack in 986.[56]

Each of these events can be, and has been, interpreted as primarily political—enacted as a means to complete the unification of a sustainable empire based on earlier historical models.[57] This was possibly the more important motive for Taizu as he succeeded in conquering territories in the south and west as well as the north. However, battlefield success also reflects spiritual approval. Taizong's failure to complete his brother's efforts in the north resulted in the disapproval of the generals, who may have interpreted it not only as military incompetence but also as lack of divine support. Taizong's early territorial conquests also show a desire to reunify the "Tang" in spiritual as much as political realms.

By Taizong's accession in 976, the territory under Song control included the Five Marchmounts (Wuyue), but the major Buddhist pilgrimage sites of the day, at Tiantai and Wutai mountains, remained beyond it.[58] The Sixteen Prefectures, including the official Song ancestral home of Zhuozhou, were in Liao territory.[59] Conquest of the southeast, the Northern Han, and the Sixteen Prefectures would have brought all of these locations, and their deities, under the umbrella of the Song. Following the demolition of the Northern Han in 979, Taizong sponsored the rebuilding of Jinci, which included a temple dedicated to the main tutelary deity for the Taiyuan region, Tang Shuyu. This project was completed in 984.[60] In 983 and 984 the court also entertained requests to perform the Feng and Shan sacrifices at Mount Tai, although those were ultimately deemed unfeasible.[61] And of course, Taizong continued to perform the traditional sacrifices to Heaven and Earth at the Circular Mound in the southern suburbs.[62]

Support for Confucian, Daoist, and Buddhist study and practice was also a critical part of Taizong's transformation. Beginning in 977 he dramatically increased the number of *jinshi* awarded in the capital.[63] As Johannes Kurz has described, Taizong also moved the imperial libraries and many officials of the recently conquered Southern Tang to Kaifeng. Constructing a Cloister for the Veneration of Literature (Chongwenyuan), he initiated three major compilation projects: the *Taiping yulan* (977–983), the *Taiping guangji* (977–978), and the *Wenyuan yinghua* (982–987).[64] The *Taiping yulan* contains a large number of Maoshan scriptures, which, as Suzanne Cahill has pointed out, provides evidence that Taizong also sought to bolster religious Daoism.[65] Taizong was willing and able to use the entire range of his imperial "religious repertoire" to prove the spirits supported his rule—a critical aspect of state formation in medieval China.[66]

During the same period, Taizong's Buddhist patronage and performance of Buddhist ritual displayed that he was additionally a contemporary *ćakravartin*. The peaceful acquisition of the Wuyue Kingdom in 978 allowed Taizong to align himself with the most famous *ćakravartin* of them all, King Aśoka. According to Yang Yi, when Aśoka divided the original relics of the Buddha and interred them in 84,000 stūpas to help spread Buddhism, Zhendan (the Land of Breaking Dawn, i.e., China) received nineteen. One such relic was held at the Aśoka Monastery (Ayuwangsi) near Mingzhou (modern Ningbo).[67] Qian Liu (r. 907–932), the first Wuyue king, moved the relic to a timber pagoda in Nanta Monastery south of the capital.[68] Qian Chu continued this association, personally commissioning the construction of 84,000 miniature gilt-bronze pagodas in emulation of Aśoka himself.[69] Qian Chu's efforts also focused on the mass-production of printed Buddhist texts, seemingly as much for power in this life as for merit for the next. The numbers are significant. Zhang Xiumin estimates his patronage efforts resulted in the printing of 682,000 documents including sūtras, *dharaṇis* (spells) and diagrams of multilevel pagodas.[70] Wuyue, possibly because of this effort, also became known for its printing industry.[71] In 958 the Nanta burned, but a monk retrieved the relic from the third floor of the flaming tower. Qian Chu rebuilt the pagoda to house the reliquary in 968.[72] Thus, the authentic relic of Śākyamuni looked over the Wuyue kingdom until they decided to join the Song dynasty peacefully.

Taizong did not plunder his newly annexed kingdom, however, he simply transferred its source of spiritual energy to his own capital.[73] When Qian Chu negotiated his surrender to the Song, he used his advisor Zanning (919–1001), one of the most important Buddhist monks of the time.[74] Officially considered a *vinaya* master, Zanning was ordained at Mount Tiantai. Although Tiantai had suffered under the late Tang suppression of Buddhism, the tradition was revived when Qian Chu sought to retrieve lost Tiantai texts from Korea and Japan.[75] But Zanning's appeal at court seems to have derived, at least partially, from his deep education in Confucian texts and the strong relationship between the literati and Buddhist monks in Wuyue.[76] Although we do not know when Taizong first learned of Zanning's reputation, the *Fozu tongji* describes Zanning's arrival at court with the Śākyamuni relic in 978. Having heard of his fame, and clearly impressed with his erudition, Taizong is said to have summoned him to court seven times in one day.[77] Politically savvy and well-versed in the classics, Zanning was perfectly poised to help Taizong make full use of Buddhism in his efforts to gain spiritual support for his empire.

Indeed one wonders how much influence the arrival of Zanning and the true relic of the Buddha had on Taizong's decisions for the next decade. Did the arrival of the relic from Wuyue bolster Taizong in his quest to conquer the north? Was Zanning able to convince Taizong that the relic helped him to succeed where his brother had failed against the Northern Han, but that more needed to be done to gain control of the Sixteen Prefectures? As Huang Chi-chiang reminds us, in 980, less than a year after the near-death experience fighting the Liao, and at the same time the *Taiping yulan* was being

compiled in the Cloister for the Veneration of Literature, a new Cloister of
Sūtra Translation (Yijing Yuan) was established next to the Taiping Xingguo
Monastery in the capital to house foreign monks returning from South Asia
with Buddhist scriptures.[78] The collation and distribution of textual compilations, be they *Tripiṭaka*, Daoist canon (or Maoshan Daoist texts), or other
encyclopedias, were accompanied by building projects to house the production of these objects and display the nature of Taizong's royal patronage
more generally. The building projects further show a desire to recognize the
spatiality of Buddhist divinities in the creation of his new empire. Also in 980
Taizong sponsored major temple building efforts at Mount Wutai, including
the casting of a gilt-bronze image of the Buddhist deity Mañjuśrī, solidifying
his support for the deity who, by this time, was believed to reside at the newly
reincorporated mountain.[79] The same year he commissioned the casting of
a large bronze sculpture of Samantabhadra on Mount Emei, contributing to
its tenth-century identity as the sacred Buddhist mountain of the west. He
then extended his benevolence to the newly acquired southeast by ordering
the rebuilding of Shouchang Monastery and the production of 516 *luohan*
on Mount Tiantai.[80] Taizong's Buddhist patronage can be seen as initiating
the process of creating a perimeter of Buddhist mountains around the Song
empire parallel to those associated with the imperial cult.[81]

TAIZONG'S MODERN ARCHITECTURE

It was precisely during this period, in the wake of success and then failure on
the battlefield, of massive textual compilation, translation, and transmission,
of patronage of Buddhist and local temples on the western, northern, and
eastern sides of the empire, as well as in the capital, that Taizong commissioned the construction of the Kaibao Monastery Pagoda.[82] By this time the
monastery had already become a location for which Taizong could demonstrate the new direction he was planning to take *his* dynasty. Johannes Kurz's
work has shown how the major imperial compilation projects completed
under Taizong were the result of a transfer of scholars and scholarship from
the southeastern kingdoms, primarily the Southern Tang, to the capital at
Kaifeng.[83] As noted by Eugene Wang, Taizong's first class of imperial exam
graduates, a party of more than 500 including the unprecedented 109
jinshi, were given a feast within the walls of Kaibao Monastery.[84] Evidently,
Taizong believed that a genuine relic of the Buddha from the southeast, one
connected to the renowned imperial Buddhist patron Aśoka, contributed
to the collection. An erudite and politically savvy Buddhist advisor such as

Zanning would have been able to discourse on the historical use of towers to signify the Buddha's support of an empire and its effectiveness in communicating divine support of a new ruler to competing states in the region. After the failure to conquer the Liao in 979, the expense of a Buddhist pagoda to extend the blessings and merit of the relic, and project that power to northern rivals, would have been easily justified.[85] Just in case individuals in Kaifeng failed to appreciate the traditional value of a *cakravartin* to the empire, Taizong commissioned the painter Gao Yi to depict a cycle of the exploits of Aśoka on the corridors of Xiangguo Monastery.[86]

The method of production was also significant. Taizong oversaw the importing of new Wuyue-based technologies for containing and projecting spiritual power, be they mass-produced texts or towering reliquaries. Such a project's success was not guaranteed. As mentioned earlier, Liu-Song Taizong was unable to keep his planned ten-story pagoda standing. Success in constructing an eleven-story pagoda would require the specialized skills of an experienced craftsman. Construction of the pagoda probably began around 982. With such a large scale building project underway, it is perhaps unsurprising that, by 984, the feasting of exam graduates was moved to the Divine-Jade Forest Garden (Qionglinyuan), an imperial pleasure park constructed on the west side of the city outside of Zhengmen (shown in fig. 1.1). One wonders whether this type of displacement fueled the graduates' displeasure with imperial Buddhist patronage.[87] Still, when completed in 989, a tower with the power to illuminate the center of a new dynasty, and one technologically sophisticated enough to soar over the entire capital, would surely have been thought to keep the wheel of the law turning as the printers continued to generate copy after copy of the *Tripiṭaka*.

Moving the nascent Song empire out of the ancient ruins of the past and into a new age was critical for Taizong's political project.[88] But new forms of art must have their own recognizable cultural capital to become models for imitation. The revival of Tiantai in the mid-tenth century was an international event centered on a coastal kingdom that had significantly advanced its technologies of artistic production, the style of which would have been familiar in neighboring polities, including the Liao (916–1125), Goryeo (918–1392), and Heian Japan (794–1185). Architecture may have been its most visible aspect. Thus employing a Wuyue architect to design this pinnacle of southern Buddhist architecture not only enhanced the power of the relic and allowed Taizong to project his identity as *cakravartin*, setting the wheel of cultural change into motion, but also proclaimed a new direction for his dynasty on a greater international stage. No longer was the center of the empire,

FIGURE 1.11. Hermitage of the First Patriarch Main Hall, Shaolin Monastery (Shaolinsi Chuzu'an Zhengdian), 1125, Mount Song, Dengfeng, Henan, view of back and east sides. (Photo courtesy Tracy Miller.)

either politically or spiritually, located in the ancient capitals of Chang'an and Luoyang. By the beginning of the twelfth century even the main hall of the Hermitage of the First (Chan) Patriarch at Shaolin Monastery (Shaolinsi Chuzu'an Zhengdian, 1125), located on China's central marchmount, Mount Song, was constructed in a Wuyue-derived style (figs. 1.11, 1.12). Charged with a true relic from Wuyue, Yu Hao's reliquary tower helped usher in a new age, one that shifted the perceptions of authentic Chinese culture from north to south and from west to east. This shift gained new meaning, and greater importance, as the Song vied with the Liao in their claims to the Mandate of Heaven, and it helped generate a new "international style" of architecture that would express cultural legitimacy for centuries to come.

NOTES

I would like to thank Patricia Ebrey, Paul Smith, Alfred Murck, Lorri Hagman, and two anonymous readers for their very helpful comments on earlier drafts of this chapter. I am also grateful to the National Endowment for the Humanities, the Graham Foundation for Advanced Studies in the Fine Arts, and Vanderbilt University for generously supporting research contributing to this article.

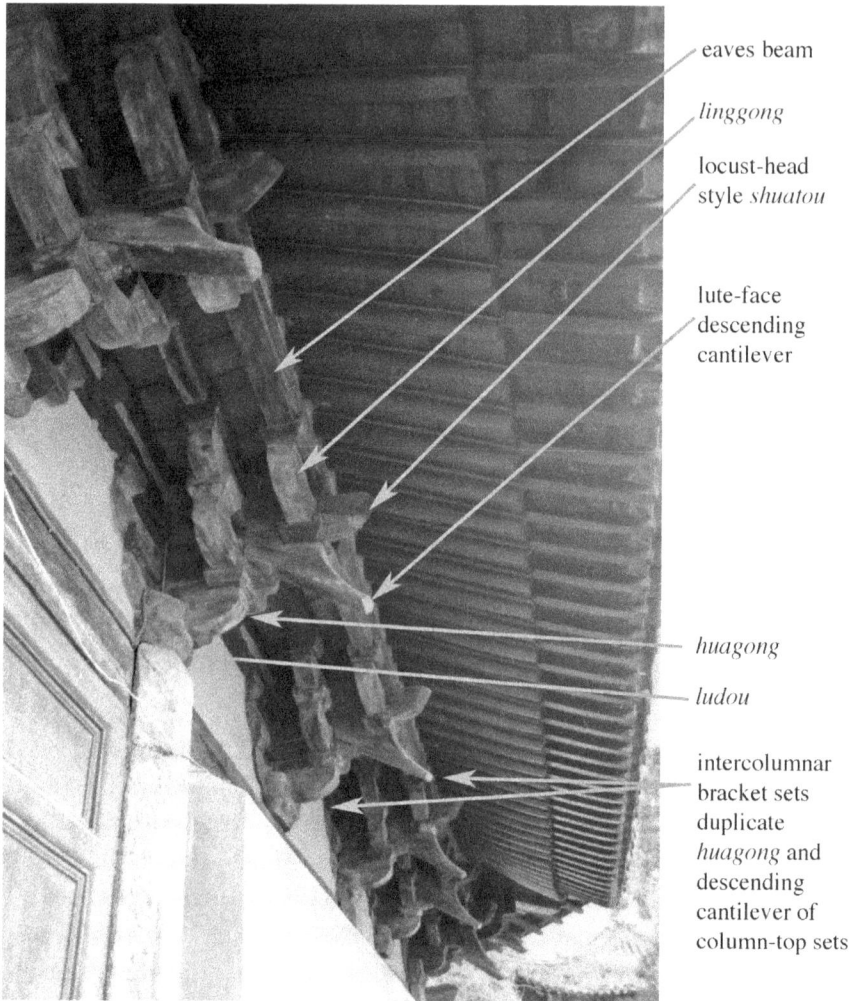

eaves beam

linggong

locust-head
style *shuatou*

lute-face
descending
cantilever

huagong

ludou

intercolumnar
bracket sets
duplicate
huagong and
descending
cantilever of
column-top sets

FIGURE 1.12. Hermitage of the First Patriarch Main Hall, Shaolin Monastery (Shaolinsi Chuzu'an Zhengdian), 1125, Mount Song, Dengfeng, Henan, detail of eaves bracketing. (Photo courtesy Tracy Miller.)

1   In the *CB* both *futu* and *ta* are used to describe the building (e.g., *CB* 30.686, 150.3634), whereas *ta* is used in the *Guitianlu* 1.1. Although perhaps more of a concern for art historians than religious historians, we have no fully acceptable English word to describe the towering structures that are the focus of this chapter. Neither the Portuguese-derived "pagoda" (implying any Asian towering temple from an imperialist-Western perspective) nor the Sanskrit-derived "stūpa" (implying a dome-shaped Buddhist reliquary) are fully appropriate translations the terms *fotu, futu, focha,* and *ta,* the forms of which are still the subject of research. For more on how the East Asian *ta* is related to the towering

Hindu temple see Zhang Gong, *Han-Tang Fosi wenhua shi*, 154–55, and Wu Qingzhou, *Jianzhu zheli, yijiang, yu wenhua*, 127–32. For a discussion of the equation of all of these terms with "stūpa" see Miller, "Perfecting the Mountain." For the sake of clarity, *ta* has been translated in this chapter as "pagoda," because of the latter's towering connotations in English.

2   The Kaibao Monastery Pagoda frequently appears in discussions of Song architecture and technology. See, for example, Soper, "Hsiang-kuo-ssu," 23n15; Liu, "The Water Mill," 566 and 590n6; Hay, "The Mediating Work of Art," 441–42, and Wang, "Picture Idea," 474–75.

3   Wang Shengduo suggests that the tower was probably called by the name of its cloister, Fushengta, prior to being given the name Lingganta in 1013. See Wang Shengduo, *Song-dai zhengjiao guanxi yanjiu*, 560. This is also the name used by Jonathan Hay in "The Mediating Work of Art."

4   *Guitianlu* 1.1. The *CB* 150.3633 records the tower as having burned in the sixth month of 1044.

5   *Yang wengong tanyuan* 107–8, *CB* 30.686–87; *FZTJ* 43.400b and 53.464b. The monk Wenying (d. after 1078) in his *Yuhu qinghua*, 2.21, describes the tower as thirteen stories, but this may be a conflation with the thirteen-story Kaibao Monastery Tieta constructed at the monastery from glazed brick after the conflagration and still standing today. I follow James Hargett and Wenren Jun's calculations where one Song builder's foot (*yingzao chi*) is 30.91 cm. Hargett and Jun, "The Measures Li and Mou," 15–16. If we use the conversion based on the measurement of the Avalokiteśvara in Longxingsi, Zhengding, Hebei, where one *chi* equals 29 cm, then the tower would have been 105 meters tall. It also would have been taller than the locally patronized brick Pota (also known as Xingci Ta and Tianqingsi Ta, 974–90 CE), originally nine stories and 240 *chi* tall, or 74.18 meters using the earlier conversion. See Wang Rui'an and Wei Qianzhi, "Kaifeng Songdai Pota."

6   SS 4.73 and 305.10,079–82. Translations of court titles follow Hucker, *A Dictionary of Official Titles*.

7   In his *Yuhu qinghua* 2.21, Wenying illustrates Guo Zhongshu's skill in architectural rendering by discussing how he was able to identify a structural flaw in Yu Hao's design of the Kaibao Monastery tower. Yu Hao's reputation as a great technician must have still resonated in Wenying's day for the story to have had impact. For more on Guo Zhongshu see Liu, "The Water Mill." I would like to thank Alfreda Murck for reminding me of this comparison.

8   *Yang wengong tanyuan* 107. Also reprinted in *Songchao shishi leiyuan* 43.566.

9   *Yang wengong tanyuan* 108.

10 *Yang wengong tanyuan* 108.

11 For example, the neoclassical architecture of the United States Capitol was selected to recall the order and harmony of the Roman Republic. See Craig et al., *The Federal Presence*.

12 The issue of legitimacy in Chinese and Western contexts has been well treated by Wechsler, *Offerings of Jade and Silk*, and more recently by Eisenberg, *Kingship in Early Medieval China*. Wu Hung has effectively shown how palaces, city walls, and temples were used to assert authority and legitimacy in the Western Han capital of Chang'an, see his *Monumentality*, 150–54.

13 *Liji*, Zhong Yong; Legge, *Li Ki*, 604; Riegel, "Li chi."

14 For more on "religion" in China and how state rituals were part of the religious rites of Han Confucianism described in the *Liji*, see Yu, *State and Religion*, 16–25.

15 Kieschnick, "Buddhist Monasticism," 574.

16 For more on the development of towers within the Warring States and early imperial cityscape, see Lewis, *Construction of Space*, 150–72.

17 *Nan shi* 70.1710. *Jingding Jiankangzhi* 8.1428–2. In this source the tower is called a *futu*. I would like to thank Wang Guixiang for calling this example to my attention.

18 *Nan shi* 70.1710, *Taiping yulan* 658.2939. Also cited in Li Gang, "State Religious Policy," 229 and Li Yuqun, "Classification, Layout, and Iconography," 648.

19 *Weishu* 114.3037. Zhang Gong, *Han-Tang Fosi wenhua shi*, 161, gives a date of 468, the second year of the Huangxing reign period (467–471). In my reading of the *Weishu* passage the construction of the tower appears to be second year of the Tainan period (466–467).

20 *Weishu* 114.3037.

21 Hureau, "Buddhist Rituals," 1232–33. In his essay "Scripture on Perfect Wisdom for Humane Kings," Orzech suggests that although the first documented court use of the scripture was in 559 CE, the sūtra was likely written in the mid-fifth century and would have been in circulation during the second half of the fifth century. Epigraphic evidence of this belief also appears in the Northern Wei grottoes at Longmen outside of Luoyang. See McNair, *Donors of Longmen*, 29–30.

22 Jenner, *Memories of Loyang*, 25–26. Jenner suggests here that much of the increase in patronage of Buddhist temples during this period was driven by the patronage of Han Empress Dowager Feng after the death of Emperor Wencheng (r. 440–465).

23 Yang Xuanzhi describes the height of the Luoyang Yongning Monastery Pagoda as 90 *zhang* (900 *chi*) in his *Luoyang qielan ji*, 1.11. In the *Shuijing zhu* Li Daoyuan described it as being 49 *zhang* (490 *chi*), which would still have been 130 *chi* taller than the tower at Kaibao Monastery. See *Shuijing zhu* 16.398.

24 *Luoyang qielan ji* 1.11.

25 *Bianjing yijizhi* 156. The date given here is Kaiyuan 17, which corresponds to 729 CE. However, it seems Xuanzong performed the sacrifice four years earlier, in 725. See *Jiu Tangshu* 23.898 and Twitchett, "Hsüan-tsung," 388.

26 *CB* 11.241; *Song Dongjing kao*, 254. For more on the imperial commitment made to both Buddhism and Daoism through the use of reign period names, see Wang Shengduo, *Songdai zhengjiao guanxi yanjiu*, 510–25.

27 Following de Bary, Kuhn characterizes Confucianism in the Song dynasty as an intellectual (rather than religious) tradition of "ethical thinking" (*ruxue*) that was transformed into a "philosophical system" (*daoxue*). Taizu, Taizong, and Zhenzong (r. 997–1022) were characterized as model rulers in this system. See Kuhn, *The Age of Confucian Rule*, 29, 99–100, and 291n3. Even Huang Chi-Chiang, whose 1994 article I have depended on heavily here, was reluctant to attribute any actual belief in Buddhism to Taizu in spite of the vast resources he spent producing Buddhist objects. See Huang, "Imperial Rulership and Buddhism," 144–87 (especially 149–51). For more on Song government policy regarding Buddhism and Daoism, see Ebrey, "Song Government Policy."

28 *Huamanlu*, 1.13b. Here Zhang Shunmin relates the tale of Zhou Shizong sending Zhao Kuangyin to ride from the Vermillion Bird Gate (Zhuquemen) until his horse was

exhausted to determine the location of the wall. This would ensure the inner city wall could not be reached in a single ride if the outer wall were breeched.

29 *Xinding sanlitu* 60. Although this figure is from the 1175 printing of the text, the drawing is overall relatively simple, and could have been transmitted according to Nie Chongyi's original version.

30 For more on the connection between the "Kaogongji" and the plans of imperial capitals see Steinhardt, "Why Were Beijing and Chang'an so Different," 339–57.

31 *SS* 431.12794.

32 *SS* 1.1. For the location of Zhuojun/Zhuozhou, see: *Taiping yulan* 162.788. Zhuozhou appears to have been one of the Sixteen Prefectures held by the Liao, giving further reason for the early Song emperors to conquer the area. See Naomi Standen, "The Five Dynasties," 87–88.

33 *SS* 1.2. Taizu named the dynasty Song because he had been *jiedushi* of Songzhou, see *CB* 1.4.

34 *CB* 17.369.

35 *SHY* Fangyu 1.2b.

36 "Zai de bu zai xian" *CB* 17.369. The earliest instance of the quote I have been able to find is in Sima Qian's biography of Wu Qi in the *Shiji* 65.2166–67. For more on the personal entourage of Taizong, see Lau Nap-Yin and Huang K'uan-chung, "Founding and Consolidation of the Sung Dynasty," 245. My thanks to Peter Lorge for emphasizing this point.

37 For more on the assignation of Song Taizu see Lorge, "Sima Guang on Song Taizong," 5–43.

38 Huang Chi-chiang, "Imperial Rulership and Buddhism," 149.

39 *SS* 1.2.

40 *FZTJ* 49, 43.0394a.

41 The dates of the restriction and its reversal can be found in *FZTJ* 43.0394c and Huang, "Imperial Rulership and Buddhism." The restrictions were at least partly intended to procure resources for coin in the form of metal sculpture. In the *Xin Wudai shi* 12.119, Ouyang Xiu records the destruction of Buddhist monasteries and releasing of monks and nuns from their bonds in the fifth month of 955.

42 Huang Chi-chiang, "Imperial Rulership and Buddhism," 171n28. Lau and Huang, "Founding and Consolidation of the Sung Dynasty," 226.

43 Hebeisheng Zhengdingxian Wenwu baoguansuo, *Zhengding Longxingsi*, 1, 10–11. Although the newly cast sculpture was the 1000-arm type, it had forty-two arms. Taizu may have been supportive of this project because of his familiarity with the worship of this esoteric manifestation of Guanyin. The cult of the Dabei Guanyin at Xiangshan Monastery south of Songshan in Henan was focused on an image of the esoteric 1000-armed Guanyin. See Yü, "Pilgrimage and the Creation of the Chinese Potalaka," 192–93.

44 Hebeisheng Zhengdingxian Wenwu baoguansuo, *Zhengding Longxingsi*, 287. One *zhang* equals ten *chi*. Using this comparison, one (or at least one type of) *chi* for North China in the tenth century would be approximately 29 cm.

45 Huang, "Imperial Rulership and Buddhism," 150.

46 Foguang dacidian bianxiu weiyuanhui, *Foguang dacidian*, vol. 5, 4892c–4893c.

47 Huang, "Imperial Rulership and Buddhism," 151 and 173n36.

48 In "Hsiang-kuo-ssu," Soper writes that eleventh-century connoisseur Guo Ruoxu (fl. 1070–1075) described the early paintings of Buddhist and Daoist subjects as superior to those produced in his day. He notes that the comment was, however, a relative one. Other types of painting, such as landscapes, were considered to be superior in the present. Thus, Guo might not have been lamenting the loss of past glories, but celebrating the development of a new aesthetic more appealing to his cohort.

49 *Houshan tan cong* 2.35; and Soper, "Hsiang-kuo-ssu," 27.

50 Fu Xinian, *Zhongguo gudai jianzhu shi*, vol. 2, and Guo Daiheng, *Zhongguo gudai jianzhu shi*, vol. 3. Variety in tenth-century buildings has been discussed in Steinhardt, "Chinese Architecture, 963–66" and in Miller, "Something Old, Something New."

51 Soper, "Hsiang-kuo-ssu," 9.

52 Lorge, "Sima Guang on Song Taizong," 5–43.

53 Here he may have been following the model of Tang Taizong. See Dalia, "The 'Political Career' of Tsan-ning," 165.

54 Hugh Clark notes that they were ready to surrender following the fall of the Southern Tang in 975, but the mourning rituals associated with the sudden death of Song Taizu in 976 caused them to postpone until 978 ("The Southern Kingdoms Between the T'ang and the Sung," 205).

55 Lau and Huang, "Founding and Consolidation of the Sung Dynasty," 248–49; Lorge, "Sima Guang on Song Taizong," 22–23.

56 The Song lost more than 30,000 troops along with talented generals. For more on these battles, see Lau and Huang, "Founding and Consolidation of the Sung Dynasty," 248–51.

57 Comparisons between the Tang's strength and the Song's weakness are common; see, for example, Lau and Huang, "Founding and Consolidation of the Sung Dynasty," 247–48. For more on the conception of what constituted a complete empire in the early Song, see also Lorge, "Fighting Against Empire," 107–39.

58 Documentation of a temple to the Northern Peak in Hunyuan, Shanxi, exists from 435, when the Northern Wei had its capital at Pingcheng. See Guojia wenwu ju, *Zhongguo wenwu dituji, Shanxi fence, zhong*, 127. The temple was relocated to Quyang, in central Hebei, during the reign of Xuanwu (r. 499–515), after the Northern Wei capital was moved to Luoyang. Quyang, within Song territory from the beginning of the dynasty, remained the primary location for worshipping the Northern Peak until it was moved back to Hunyuan in 1660. See Wenhuabu wenwuju, *Zhongguo mingsheng cidian*, 2nd ed., 119. In her "The Temple to the Northern Peak in Quyang," 82, Nancy Steinhardt traces the history of the Quyang temple to the Han dynasty, and the present site of the Yuan period temple's main hall to the Tang dynasty. In *CB* 17.209, we read that worship of the Northern Peak at Dingzhou, where Quyang is located, during Song Taizu's reign was part of the "old" system—already in place prior to the Song founding.

59 *SS* 1.1. A list and map of the Sixteen Prefectures ceded to the Liao in 937 can be found in Naomi Standen, "The Five Dynasties," 87–88.

60 For more on the significance of rebuilding the shrine to Shu Yu of Tang at Jinci, see Miller, *The Divine Nature of Power*, 67–71.

61 *SS* 4.70, 72.

62 *CB* 25.589.

63 In his first examination he awarded more *jinshi* and *zhuke* degrees than the total given

during Taizu's entire reign. For more on Taizong's expansion of examination graduates, see Chaffee, *The Thorny Gates of Learning*, 49–51.

64 For more on the establishment of the Chongwenyuan (here rendered Academy for the Veneration of Literature), see Lamouroux, "Song Renzong's Court Landscape," 50–52, and *SS* 4.57.

65 Cahill, "Taoism at the Sung Court," 38. I am following Wilkinson, *Chinese History: A Manual*, 558, for the compilation dates of the *Taiping yulan*.

66 Campany, "Religious Repertoires and Contestation," 99–141.

67 *Yang wengong tanyuan* 136.107.

68 *Xianchun Lin'an zhi* 76.4044-1-2.

69 *FZTJ* 53.464b.

70 Some of these documents were used to fill the miniature reliquaries mentioned earlier as well as individual bricks for use in building towers like the famous Leifengta in the Wuyue capital. See Shih-shan Susan Huang, "Early Buddhist Illustrated Prints in Hangzhou," 137–39; Zhang Xiumin, "Wudai Wuyueguo de yin shua," 75.

71 Like King Aśoka, Qian Chu sent his textual relics to lands beyond his own empire, publically proclaiming his ability to print the texts, contain them, and disseminate them to surrounding states. Qian Chu's printing efforts were not limited to Buddhist texts as he also printed the Daoist canon in two hundred cases (*han*). Zhang Xiumin "Wudai Wuyueguo de yin shua," 74. Thus, the practice of printing sacred texts went beyond the singular desire to ensure karmic merit. Rather, with the printing industry established, the technology could be marshaled to any cause. Song Taizong seemed to be quite aware of this as well.

72 *Yang wengong tanyuan* 136.107–08. Here we read that Taizong had the sacred interior excavated and the contents transported to Kaibao Monastery to be placed in the new tower. The relic is now in held in the Relic Hall (Shelidian) of Yinxian's Aśoka Monastery outside of Ningbo (Wenhuabu wenwuju, *Zhongguo mingsheng cidian*, 382).

73 *Bianjing yijizhi* 254.

74 My thanks to Daniel Stevenson for highlighting the significance of Zanning in Taizong's court, personal conversation, June 2014.

75 Getz, "T'ien-t'ai Pure Land Societies," 480.

76 Dalia, "The 'Political Career' of Tsan-ning," 157–161.

77 *FZTJ* 43.397b-c; Dalia, "The 'Political Career' of Tsan-ning," 166.

78 Song Taizu initiated the process of acquiring Sanskrit texts directly from India by sponsoring 157 monks to travel to India and Central Asia. This was part of a vast translation project resulting in a centralized printing house for the purpose of transmitting dharma—one explicitly articulated by the renaming of the Cloister of Sūtra Translation as the Cloister of Transmission of the Dharma (Chuanfa Yuan). The newly translated *Tripiṭaka* produced by the imperial printing house in 988 bears a preface written by Taizong himself, and was even given to foreign monks who visited the capital. Huang, "Imperial Rulership and Buddhism," 149–54. For more on the establishment of the Taiping Xingguo Monastery, see Wang Shengduo, *Songdai zhengjiao guanxi yanjiu*, 565–66, 512–14.

79 *FZTJ* 53.464b. This may have been the repair requested by Wei Shaoqin (951–1006) during the Taiping Xingguo reign period (977–984). See *SS* 466.13625. For more on the

development of Mount Wutai as a sacred site and home for Mañjuśrī, see Lin, *Building a Sacred Mountain.*

80 A project that was likely completed before 984; see *FZTJ* 53.464b.

81 The pilgrimage site for Aveloketeśvara (Guanyin) had not yet been established at Putuo-shan, which would become the eastern Buddhist mountain in China. Yü, "Pilgrimage and the Creation of the Chinese Potalaka," 190–245.

82 *Yang wengong tanyuan* 136.107.

83 Kurz, "The Politics of Collecting Knowledge." Here Kurz shows how Taizong, working within a traditional model, effectively shifted the intellectual orientation towards the southeast by employing a majority of southern officials, and materials, for the projects.

84 Wang, "Picture Idea," 476–77. Locating the feast in a Buddhist monastery was a reversal of Later Zhou Xiande-period (954–960) policy, where feasting had been managed by the ministries. In the Tang the feasts had taken place in Qujiang Park, and in other of the Five Dynasties they had been held in famous gardens and Buddhist monasteries; see *CB* 18.393.

85 My thanks to Lennert Gesterkamp for emphasizing the timing of the construction with respect to the campaigns against the Liao in his oral comments at the June 2014 conference.

86 Soper, "Hsiang-kuo-ssu," 33. Although we do not know for certain the date of this cycle, they were commissioned after he was made a Painter-in-attendance of the Hanlin Acad-emy and after Taizong ascended to the throne. They may have been available for viewing during the eight years of the tower's construction. Reduced-scale cartoons of this fresco were kept in the palace storehouse to ensure that the narrative cycle remained legible into the future; see Soper, *Kuo Jo-Hsü's Experiences in Painting*, 47–48; and *Tuhua jian-wen zhi*, 3.10a–b.

87 *SS* 108.3607, *Bianjing yijizhi* 126, and *Song Dongjing kao* 254–56.

88 Proposing the Song dynasty as the beginning of modern China itself has a long history. During the nineteenth century its use was infused with significant political overtones and the introduction of Western-style imperialism into East Asia; see Smith, "Intro-duction: Problematizing the Song-Yuan-Ming Transition," 2–7. My intention here is to emphasize that desire to break from preexisting structures (of all sorts) is not exclusive to the nineteenth century or to Westernization. The introduction of Wuyue-style build-ings to Kaifeng would have been new to the Henan region, allowing Taizong to visibly distinguish himself (and the future dynasty) from his brother while preserving a fragile Song dynastic structure.

REFERENCES

PRIMARY SOURCES

Bianjing yijizhi 汴京遺跡志, by Li Lian 李濂 (Ming). Beijing: Zhonghua shuju, 1999.
Fozu tongji 佛祖統紀, edited by Zhi Pan 志磐 (fl. 1269). In Taishō shinshū daizōkyō 大正新修大藏經. Tokyo: Taishō Issaikyō Kankōkai, 1929–34. Taibei: Xinwenfeng reprint edition, 1983–87.

Guitianlu 歸田錄, by Ouyang Xiu 歐陽修 (1007–1072). Beijing: Zhonghua shuju, 1981, 2006 repr.

Houshan tan cong 後山談叢, by Chen Houshan 陳後山 (Chen Shidao 陳師道) (1053–1101). In *Tang-Song shiliao biji congkan*, vol. 43. Edited by Zhu Lifeng 朱立峰. Beijing: Zhonghua shuju, 2007.

Huamanlu 畫墁錄, by Zhang Shunmin 張舜民 (*jinshi* 1065). In *Baihai*, Ming Wanli edition (明萬曆中會稽半埜堂商濬輯刻本).

Jingding Jiankangzhi 景定建康志 (1261), compiled by Ma Guangzu 馬光祖 (13th cen.), edited by Zhou Yinghe 周應合 (1213–1280). *Song-Yuan fangzhi congkan edition*. Beijing: Zhonghua shuju, 1990.

Jiu Tangshu 舊唐書, by Liu Xu 劉昫 (887–946). Beijing: Zhonghua shuju, 1975, repr. 1991.

Luoyang qielan ji jiaojian 洛陽伽藍記校箋, by Yang Xuanzhi 楊衒之 (d. 555?). Beijing: Zhonghua shuju, 2006.

Nan shi 南史, by Li Yanshou 李延壽 (7th century). Taibei: Dingwen shuju, repr. 1998.

Shi ji 史記, by Sima Qian 司馬遷 (145?–86? BCE). Beijing: Zhonghua shuju, 1962.

Shuijing zhu xiao zheng 水經注校證, by Li Daoyuan 酈道元 (d. 527). Collated by Chen Qiaoyi 陳橋驛. Beijing: Zhonghua shuju, 2007.

Song Dongjing kao 宋東京考, by Zhou Cheng 周城 (Qing). Taibei: Wenshizhe chubanshe, 1990.

Songchao shishi leiyuan 宋朝事實類苑, by Jiang Shaoyu 江少虞 (*jinshi* 1118). Shanghai: Shanghai guji chubanshe, 1981.

Song huiyao jigao 宋會要輯稿 460 *juan*, compiled by Xu Song 徐松 (1781–1848) et al. Beijing: Zhonghua shuju, 1957.

Song shi 宋史, edited by Tuo Tuo 脫脫 (1313–1355) et al. Beijing: Zhonghua shuju, 1985, repr. 1990.

Taiping yulan 太平御覽, edited by Li Fang 李昉 (925–996) et al. Beijing: Zhonghua shuju, 1960, repr. 2006.

Tuhua jianwen zhi 圖畫見聞志, by Guo Ruoxu 郭若虛 (active 1070–1075). Shanghai: Shangwu yinshuguan, 1922.

Weishu 魏書, by Wei Shou 魏收 (506–572). Beijing: Zhonghua shuju, 1974, repr. 1997.

Xianchun Lin'an zhi 咸淳臨安志, by Qian Shuoyou 潛說友 (1216–1277). Song Yuan fangzhi congkan edition. Beijing: Zhonghua shuju, 1990.

Xin Wudai shi 新五代史, by Ouyang Xiu 歐陽修 (1007–1072). Beijing: Zhonghua shuju, 1974, repr. 1995.

Xinding sanlitu 新定三禮圖, by Nie Chongyi 聶崇義 (10th century). In *Zhongguo gudai banhua congkan*, vol. 1, edited by Zheng Chenduo 鄭振鐸. Shanghai: Shanghai guji chubanshe, 1988.

Xu zizhi tongjian changbian 續資治通鑑長編, by Li Tao 李燾 (1115–1184). Beijing: Zhonghua shuju, 1992, repr. 2004.

Yang wengong tanyuan 楊文公談苑, dictated by Yang Yi 楊億 (974–1020). Recorded by Huang Jian 黃鑑 (10th–11th centuries), arranged by Song Xiang 宋庠 (996–1066). In *Song-Yuan biji congshu* 宋元筆記叢書. Shanghai: Shanghai guji chubanshe, 1993.

Yuhu qinghua 玉壺清話, by Wenying 文瑩 (11th century). In *Xiangshan yelu, Xulu, Yuhu qinghua*, by Wenying. Beijing: Zhonghua shuju, 1984, repr. 2007.

SECONDARY SOURCES

Cahill, Suzanne. "Taoism at the Sung Court: The Heavenly Text Affair of 1008." *Bulletin of Sung and Yüan Studies* 16 (1980): 23–44.

Campany, Robert Ford. "Religious Repertoires and Contestation: A Case Study Based on Buddhist Miracle Tales." *History of Religions* 52, no. 2 (2012): 99–141.

Chaffee, John. *The Thorny Gates of Learning in Sung China.* Albany: SUNY Press, 1995.

Clark, Hugh R. "The Southern Kingdoms Between the T'ang and the Sung." In *The Cambridge History of China.* Vol. 5, Part 1: *The Song Dynasty and its Precursors, 907–1279,* edited by Denis Twitchett and Paul Jakov Smith, 133–205. Cambridge, UK: Cambridge University Press, 2009.

Craig, Lois et al. *The Federal Presence: Architecture, Politics, and Symbols in United States Government Building.* Cambridge, Mass.: MIT Press, 1978.

Dalia, Albert A. "The 'Political Career' of the Buddhist Historian Tsan-ning." In *Buddhist and Taoist Practice in Medieval Chinese Society,* edited by David W. Chappell, 146–80. Honolulu: University of Hawai'i Press, 1987.

Ebrey, Patricia. "Song Government Policy." In *Modern Chinese Religion I: Song-Liao-Jin-Yuan (960–1368),* edited by John Lagerwey, 73–137. Leiden: Brill, 2015.

Eisenberg, Andrew. *Kingship in Early Medieval China.* Leiden: Brill, 2008.

Foguang dacidian bianxiu weiyuanhui 佛光大辭典委員會, ed. *Foguang dacidian* 佛光大辭典. Gaoxiong: Foguang chubanshe, 1988.

Fu Xinian 傅熹年, ed. *Zhongguo gudai jianzhu shi, di er juan: Sanguo, Liang Jin, Nan-Bei Chao, Sui-Tang, Wudai jianzhu* 中國古代建築史第二卷：三國，兩晉，南北朝，隋唐，五代建築. 2nd ed. Beijing: Zhongguo jianzhu gongye chubanshe, 2009.

Getz, Daniel A., Jr. "T'ien-t'ai Pure Land Societies and the Creation of the Pure Land Patriarchate." In *Buddhism in the Sung,* edited by Peter N. Gregory and Daniel A. Getz Jr., 477–523. Honolulu: University of Hawai'i Press, 1999.

Guo Daiheng 郭黛姮, ed. *Zhongguo gudai jianzhu shi, di san juan: Song, Liao, Jin, Xixia jianzhu* 中國古代建築史第三卷：宋，遼，金，西夏建築. 2nd ed. Beijing: Zhongguo jianzhu gongye chubanshe, 2009.

Guojia wenwu ju 國家文物局, ed. *Zhongguo wenwu dituji, Shanxi fence, zhong* 中國文物地圖集，山西分冊，中. Beijing: Zhongguo ditu chubanshe, 2006.

Hargett, James M., and Wenren Jun. "The Measures Li and Mou during the Song, Liao, and Jin Dynasties." *Bulletin of Sung and Yüan Studies* 21 (1989): 8–30.

Hay, Jonathan. "The Mediating Work of Art." *The Art Bulletin* 89, no. 3 (Sep. 2007): 435–59.

Hebeisheng Zhengdingxian Wenwu baoguansuo 河北省正定縣文物保管所, ed. *Zhengding Longxingsi* 正定隆興寺. Beijing: Wenwu chubanshe, 2000.

Heng Chye Kiang. *Cities of Aristocrats and Bureaucrats: The Development of Medieval Chinese Cityscapes.* Honolulu: University of Hawai'i Press, 1999.

Huang, Shih-shan Susan. "Early Buddhist Illustrated Prints in Hangzhou." In *Knowledge and Text Production in an Age of Print: China, 900–1400,* edited by Lucille Chia and Hilde De Weerdt, 135–65. Leiden: Brill, 2011.

Huang Chi-Chiang. "Imperial Rulership and Buddhism in the Early Northern Sung." In *Imperial Rulership and Cultural Change in Traditional China,* edited by Frederick P. Brandauer and Chün-Chieh Huang, 144–87. Seattle: University of Washington Press, 1994.

Hucker, Charles O. *A Dictionary of Official Titles in Imperial China.* Stanford: Stanford University Press, 1985.

Hureau, Sylvie. "Buddhist Rituals." In *Early Chinese Religion Part Two: The Period of Division (220–589).* Vol. 2. Edited by John Lagerwey and Lü Pengzhi, 1207–44. Leiden: Brill, 2010.

Jenner, W. J. F. *Memories of Loyang: Yang Hsüan-chih and the Lost Capital (493–534).* Oxford: Oxford University Press, 1981.

Kieschnick, John. "Buddhist Monasticism." In *Early Chinese Religion Part Two: The Period of Division (220–589).* Vol. 1. Edited by John Lagerwey and Lü Pengzhi, 545–74. Leiden: Brill, 2010.

Kuhn, Dieter. *The Age of Confucian Rule.* Cambridge, Mass.: Belknap Press of Harvard University Press, 2009.

Kurz, Johannes L. "The Politics of Collecting Knowledge: Song Taizong's Compilations Project." *T'oung Pao* 87 (2001): 289–316.

Lamouroux, Christian. "Song Renzong's Court Landscape: Historical Writing and the Creation of a New Political Sphere (1022–1042)." *Journal of Song-Yuan Studies* 42 (2012): 45–93.

Lau, Nap-Yin, and Huang K'uan-chung. "Founding and Consolidation of the Sung Dynasty under T'ai-tsu (960–976), T'ai-tsung (976–997), and Chen-tsung (997–1022)." In *The Cambridge History of China.* Vol. 5, Part 1: *The Song Dynasty and its Precursors, 907–1279,* edited by Denis Twitchett and Paul Jakov Smith, 206–78. Cambridge, UK: Cambridge University Press, 2009.

Legge, James (1815–1897), trans. *The Li Ki.* Oxford: Clarendon Press, 1885; Whitefish, Mont.: Kessinger Publishing, repr. 2004.

Lewis, Mark E. *The Construction of Space in Early China.* Albany, NY: State University of New York Press, 2006.

Li Gang. "State Religious Policy." In *Early Chinese Religion Part Two: The Period of Division (220–589).* Vol. 1. Edited by John Lagerwey and Lü Pengzhi, 193–274. Leiden: Brill, 2010.

Li Yuqun. "Classification, Layout, and Iconography of Buddhist Cave Temples and Monasteries." In *Early Chinese Religion Part Two: The Period of Division (220–589).* Vol. 1. Edited by John Lagerwey and Lü Pengzhi, 575–738. Leiden: Brill, 2010.

Lin Wei-cheng. *Building a Sacred Mountain: The Buddhist Architecture of China's Mount Wutai.* Seattle: University of Washington Press, 2014.

Liu Heping. "'The Water Mill' and Northern Song Imperial Patronage of Art, Commerce, and Science." *The Art Bulletin* 84, no. 4 (2002): 566–95.

Lorge, Peter. "Fighting Against Empire: Resistance to the Later Zhou and Song Conquest of China." In *Debating War in Chinese History,* edited by Peter Lorge, 107–39. Leiden: Brill, 2013.

———. "Sima Guang on Song Taizong: Politics, History and Historiography." *Journal of Song-Yuan Studies* 42 (2012): 5–43.

McNair, Amy. *The Donors of Longmen: Faith, Politics, and Patronage in Medieval Chinese Buddhist Sculpture.* Honolulu: University of Hawai'i Press, 2007.

Miller, Tracy. *The Divine Nature of Power: Chinese Ritual Architecture at the Sacred Site of Jinci.* Cambridge, Mass.: Harvard Asia Center, 2007.

———. "Perfecting the Mountain: On the Morphology of Towering Temples in East Asia." *Zhongguo jianzhu shilun huikan* 10 (2014): 419–49.

———. "Something Old, Something New, Something Borrowed: Local Style in the Architecture of Tenth-Century China." In *The Five Dynasties and Ten Kingdoms*, edited by Peter Lorge, 167–222. Hong Kong: Chinese University Press, 2011.

Orzech, Charles. "Scripture on Perfect Wisdom for Humane Kings Who Wish to Protect Their States." In *Religions of China in Practice*, edited by Donald L. Lopez, 372–80. Princeton: Princeton University Press, 1996.

Riegel, Jeffrey K. "Li chi 禮記." In *Early Chinese Texts: A Bibliographical Guide*, edited by Michael Loewe, 293–97. Berkeley: Society for the Study of Early China and the Institute of East Asian Studies, University of California, 1993.

Smith, Paul Jakov. "Introduction: Problematizing the Song-Yuan-Ming Transition." In *The Song-Yuan-Ming Transition in Chinese History*, edited by Paul Jakov Smith and Richard von Glahn, 1–34. Cambridge, Mass.: Harvard University Asia Center, 2003.

Soper, Alexander C. "Hsiang-kuo-ssu: An Imperial Temple of Northern Sung." *Journal of the American Oriental Society* 68 (1948), 19–45.

———, trans. *Kuo Jo-Hsü's Experiences in Painting: An Eleventh Century History of Chinese Painting Together with the Chinese Text in Facsimile*. Washington, D.C.: American Council of Learned Societies, 1951.

Standen, Naomi. "The Five Dynasties." In *The Cambridge History of China*, Vol. 5, Part 1: *The Song Dynasty and its Precursors, 907–1279*, edited by Denis Twitchett and Paul Jakov Smith, 38–132. Cambridge, UK: Cambridge University Press, 2009.

Steinhardt, Nancy S. "Chinese Architecture: 963–966." *Orientations* 26, no. 2 (1995): 46–52.

———. "The Temple to the Northern Peak in Quyang." *Artibus Asiae* 58, no. ½ (1998): 69–90.

———. "Why are Chang'an and Beijing so Different." *Journal of the Society of Architectural Historians* 45, no. 4 (Dec. 1986): 339–57.

Twitchett, Denis. "Hsüan-tsung (Reign 712–56)." In *The Cambridge History of China*, Vol. 3, Part 1: *Sui and T'ang China, 589–906*, edited by Denis Twitchett, 333–463. Cambridge: Cambridge University Press, 1979.

Wang, Eugene. "'Picture Idea' and Its Cultural Dynamics in Northern Song China." *The Art Bulletin* 89, no. 3 (Sep. 2007): 463–81.

Wang Rui'an 王瑞安 and Wei Qianzhi 魏千志. "Kaifeng Songdai Pota" 開封宋代繁塔. *Zhongguo lishi wenwu* (1986): 36–42, 15.

Wang Shengduo 汪聖鐸. *Songdai zhengjiao guanxi yanjiu* 宋代政教關係研究. Beijing: Renmin chubanshe, 2010.

Wechsler, Howard J. *Offerings of Jade and Silk: Ritual and Symbol in the Legitimation of the T'ang Dynasty*. New Haven: Yale University Press, 1985.

Wenhuabu wenwuju 文化部文物局, eds. *Zhongguo mingsheng cidian* 中國名勝詞典. 2nd ed. Shanghai: Shanghai cishu chubanshe, 1986.

Wilkinson, Endymion. *Chinese History: A Manual*. Cambridge, Mass.: Harvard University Asia Center, 1998.

Wu Hung. *Monumentality in Early Chinese Art and Architecture*. Stanford: Stanford University Press, 1996.

Wu Qingzhou 吳慶洲. *Jianzhu zheli, yijiang, yu wenhua* 建築哲理意匠與文化. Beijing: Zhongguo jianzhu gongye chubanshe, 2005.

Yu, Anthony. *State and Religion in China*. Peru, Ill.: Open Court Publishing, 2005.

Yü Chün-fang. "Pilgrimage and the Creation of the Chinese Potalaka." In *Pilgrims and Sacred Sites in China*, edited by Susan Naquin and Chün-fang Yü, 190–245. Berkeley: University of California Press, 1992.

Zhang Gong 張弓. *Han-Tang Fosi wenhua shi* 漢唐佛寺文化史. Beijing: Zhongguo she-hui kexue chubanshe, 1997.

Zhang Xiumin 張秀民. "Wudai Wuyueguo de yin shua" 五代吳越國的印刷. *Wenwu* 12 (1978): 74–76.

2 Cao Xun and the Legend of Emperor Taizu's Oath

CHARLES HARTMAN

IN THE SONG DYNASTY, IT WAS SAID THAT TAIZU, THE FOUNDING emperor, had sworn an oath not to execute officials. Taizu supposedly inscribed his oath on a stone stele, which he erected in a locked chamber of the Ancestral Temple and bound his imperial successors to observe. This legend has remained a central motif in historical constructions of the Song dynasty ever since Wang Fuzhi and Gu Yanwu alluded to the oath in the seventeenth century.[1] The story indeed touches upon major themes in Song history: the personal character of Taizu, the "benevolent" nature of the Song monarchy, the relationship between imperial power and the official bureaucracy in the Song state, and that state's nonmilitary, "literati" character. In the past decade, emphasis on the Song monarchs and the literati as partners in the exercise of a shared governance unique in Chinese history and the related concept of a Song peak in Chinese political, economic, and cultural history has brought renewed attention to Taizu and his oath.[2]

In 1941 the legendary Song historian Zhang Yinlin first questioned the historical foundations of the oath legend. He pointed out that the story derived from only two sources and both presented serious textual problems: Cao Xun's (1098–1174) initial 1127 report to Emperor Gaozong, in which Huizong, then already in captivity, notified the new emperor about the oath, and a detailed description of the oath stele, with a transcription of its text, in a book called *Random Notes Made in Summer* (Bishu manchao) attributed to Lu You (1125–1210). Zhang noted that, although Northern Song sources often cite a generic policy not to execute officials, these sources never mention Taizu's oath or the stele. He maintained that the substance of the oath existed as an unwritten "policy of the ancestors," but that the text of the stele as recorded in the *Random Notes Made in Summer* was a Southern Song fabrication. He nevertheless concluded that the comparative latitude the monarchy accorded to the literati had had both negative and positive impacts on Song political culture. On the one hand, it had fostered interminable policy disputes, political factionalism, and administrative gridlock; on the other hand, the same indulgence had also afforded an intellectual space in which the literati had developed an independent self-awareness that made possible the creativity of Song thought, especially *daoxue*.[3]

Subsequent scholarship has rightly focused on the credibility of these two sources for the oath story, but opinions on the issue have diverged widely. At one end of the spectrum, literal acceptance of both sources supports, unsurprisingly, the historical reality of the legend in all its details.[4] As the spectrum slides, however, toward more critical approaches, differing evaluations of the evidence have generated opinions ranging from total denial to scenarios that attempt to explain the appearance of the legend in these Southern Song sources and the relationship of the sources to each other. For example, Du Wenyu argues that Gaozong and Cao Xun, for their own political purposes, colluded to fabricate Huizong's account of the oath.[5] Li Feng argues that Huizong himself invented the tale and sent it south with Cao Xun in an attempt to ingratiate himself with Gaozong and so improve his chances of returning from captivity.[6] An intermediate position has developed from Zhang Yinlin's original conclusions and acknowledges that, although evidence for the historical existence of the stele is weak, the clear presence of the oath's intent among the "policies of the ancestors" confirms the historical existence of the spirit of the oath in Northern Song policy.[7] Much of this scholarship dwells on the definition of exactly which officials Taizu intended should never be executed, and then compares this definition against the historical records of those that he and succeeding Song emperors actually did execute, including the famous Yue Fei in 1141.[8]

This chapter approaches Taizu's oath from a slightly different perspective and attempts to apply to this problem a group of principles that I have elsewhere termed "textual archaeology." This methodology combines three basic concepts. First, unless there is other supporting evidence, we should not accept an assertion of any fact made in a text as valid evidence for the existence of that fact at a date earlier than the confirmed date for the existence of the text itself. For example, if the *Conversations of Zhu Xi* (Zhuzi yulei) make a claim about the character of Wang Anshi, unless there is other supporting evidence from Northern Song, then Zhu Xi's claim is a Southern Song, not a Northern Song, fact. In essence, this means determining the time interval between a given historical event and that event's first appearance in the surviving record. It also means being cognizant of these intervals when we formulate our understanding of how a group of textual passages—gathered together and deemed pertinent to a given research topic—may relate to each other. This is an exacting standard and a difficult one to apply consistently to our surviving heritage of Song sources. It requires understanding both the compositional history of our sources (and indeed of each distinct passage in the sources) and the history of their transmittal to our time.

Second, whenever a group of texts presents intertextuality, the causes for that intertextuality should be (where possible) determined and used as an aid to establish the chronological affiliation between the texts that participate in the intertextuality. Parallel passages mean that someone has copied (or memorized or remembered) something from an earlier text. After we have arranged these passages in their proper chronological sequence, they will often reveal changes in focus and context—and often in content itself—that a given iteration has imposed upon its predecessors. Third, the political and cultural motivations for these changes should be explored to the fullest. As applied to the texts that make up the story of Taizu's oath and its surrounding contexts, this approach suggests that the problem might profit from a closer look at the career and character of Cao Xun.

Cao Xun's life and career—born 1098, died 1174—spans perfectly the Northern–Southern Song divide. The Jurchen invasions of 1125, the abdication of Emperor Huizong in favor of his son Qinzong, and the political repudiation of the New Policies and their advocates as responsible for the military debacle all combined to force a drastic political realignment and a corresponding reassessment of Northern Song history. This anti–New Policies drive created a view of Song history that elevated Taizu above Taizong as the ultimate source of dynastic values and posited the Qingli and Yuanyou periods, as opposed to the Shenzong and Huizong reigns, as the historical expression of the political values that should undergird the Restoration. Gaozong's decisions in 1131 to return the Song monarchy to the Taizu line was only one among the many concrete manifestations of this Restoration refocus.

But Cao Xun, as well as Gaozong and his closest advisors, were creatures of the Huizong monarchy—the same monarchy whose political and intellectual policies the Restoration, on the one hand, was forced to repudiate, even as, on the other hand, it continued many late Northern Song economic and cultural policies. Huizong had created a monarchy that marshaled the dynasty's Confucian and Daoist elements into a unified synthesis that elevated the emperor into the personification of perfected governance. To buttress this image, the Huizong court fostered a cult of omens and artistic propaganda that glorified his person and his policies. The story of Taizu's oath emerges from this period of contradictions—as Gaozong and his advisors availed themselves of the omens and cultural propaganda of the bygone Huizong era to disseminate a new message of return to the dynasty's supposedly original values.

Whereas most previous scholarship has tended to focus on the few short extracts from Cao Xun's writings that directly mention the oath, in this chapter I attempt to explore his information about the oath in the larger context of the imperial politics of 1127. I also attempt to trace subsequent mentions of Cao Xun and the oath in the Southern Song historical record to demonstrate the connections between his brief references to the issue and the more developed narrative in *Random Notes Made in Summer*. In addition to understanding the origins of Taizu's oath, this chapter seeks to answer the following question: if the meaning of the oath was so central to the struggles of Southern Song literati to limit the power of the monarchy, why are there so few references to the oath in their surviving writings?

THE CAREER AND CHARACTER OF CAO XUN

Cao Xun and his family came directly from cultural center of the Huizong court. Given the career of Cao and his father, Cao Zu, it is probable, although not certain, that the family were imperial affines, descended perhaps from Cao Bin (931–999), one of the founding generals of the Song, through the Empress Dowager Cao (1016–1079), empress of Emperor Renzong. Cao Xun's father had been a member of Liang Shicheng's network, and the powerful eunuch arranged for Cao Zu to receive the *jinshi* by imperial decree in 1121.[9] The elder Cao was an audience attendant in the Postern Gate Office—an "audience usher"—and was posted to the Hall of Profound Thought (Ruisi Dian), Emperor Huizong's inner court scriptorium and cultural center, where he composed propaganda eulogizing the monarchy.[10] Two years later, Cao Xun used his father's patronage protection and another imperial conferral of the *jinshi* to enter military grade rank. By 1125, he had attained mid-level rank in the usher service at the Palace of Dragon Virtue (Longde Gong), Huizong's residence after his abdication.[11] Between 1123 and 1125, Cao Xun had advanced twenty steps on the sixty-step personnel rank system for military officials. On 1127/3/29, he departed with Huizong into northern captivity and arrived with him in Yanshan on 1127/5/17. Sometime before reaching Yanshan, Huizong ordered Cao Xun to attempt an escape and to deliver letters from Consort Wei (Gaozong's mother) and Lady Xing (Gaozong's wife) to Prince Kang. He also instructed Cao Xun to authorize the prince to assume the throne. As evidence of the validity of this mandate, he sent with Cao the famous "collar edict," eight characters personally written and signed on the inside collar of his shirt: 可便即真,來救父母 ("You may at once assume full authority as emperor, then come and rescue your parents"). According to Li Xinchuan, Cao Xun left Yanshan on 1127/5/18 and completed this mission, arriving at Gaozong's court at Yingtian on 1127/7/28.[12] He also delivered a number of other messages and advice, including the information about Taizu's oath. Faithful to Huizong's wishes, Cao proposed a naval mission to rescue the royal party. But Gaozong's advisors, no doubt reluctant to admit a protégé of Liang Shicheng and a close retainer of Huizong into their midst, rejected the plan, and he was not retained at court.

Despite his conferred *jinshi* degree, Cao Xun was not a literatus but an official from the Huizong monarchy's cultural nerve center, a complex of inner court offices staffed by eunuchs, members of the female monarchy, and imperial affines. As such, he was often at odds with the civil literati who staffed top administrative positions. For example, in 1135/3 the chief councilor Zhao Ding blocked a substantive military appointment for Cao on the grounds that he was an unqualified, patronage-seeking dilettante.[13] Literati opposition to Cao continued through his career. When Emperor Xiaozong suggested in 1172 that Cao might be appointed to the important post of recipient of edicts in the Bureau of Military Affairs, the chief councilor Yu Yunwen replied, "He's too low-class a character to be appointed."[14]

However, in 1141 his connections to the former consort, now Empress Wei, placed him center stage in the negotiations to obtain Huizong's coffin and her release from captivity; he was well compensated upon her return and the successful conclusion of the 1142 treaty with the Jin. In 1145, however, he requested a provincial sinecure, presumably to avoid conflict with Qin Gui. His career resumed after Qin Gui's death in 1155, and he served in the Bureau of Military Affairs and in the Palace Security Office, both typical postings for affinal kin.[15] As military tensions with the Jurchen escalated in the late 1150s and early 1160s, the court again utilized his diplomatic experience as negotiator and emissary. Cao Xun eventually attained the highest possible grade of military rank, and Li Xinchuan places him in the category of other imperial "favorites" such as Zhu Mian, Zeng Di, and Jiang Teli, who attained these ranks by imperial dispensation.[16]

Because of his family's record of service to Huizong, he seems to have earned the special trust of both Huizong and Consort Wei, and, through her, of the new Emperor Gaozong. In fact, Cao Xun made the difficult transition from personal servitor of Huizong to personal servitor of Gaozong. When Cao died in 1174, Gaozong composed and personally wrote out a eulogy that summarized his service under four emperors: he had brought back the collar edict that had confirmed the imperial succession; his diplomatic skills had "reunited mother and son" in 1142 and once again restored the status quo after the Jurchen aggression of the early 1160s. Cao's collected works were compiled by his son Cao Si (1137–1197) in forty *juan* in 1190; and this forty-*juan* collection survives via a secure line of transmission to the present.[17] Lou Yue's preface to the collection cites the emperor's personal eulogy as an extraordinary testament to Cao and an honor seldom achieved by literati officials.[18]

Although Cao Si's postface to his father's collected works insists on his family's Confucian and literati credentials, the collection's contents present a clear picture of Cao Xun's station as an affinal retainer of the monarchy, as distinct from a literati official.[19] Over half the collection is social poetry, in regulated verse, *yuefu*, and *ci* genres; many of the latter were composed on imperial order to celebrate the birthdays of Gaozong and Empress Wei, including her seventieth in 1149.[20] Numerous inscriptions for Buddhist sites reveal Cao Xun's close connections to the Buddhist church. Also distinctive in the collection are nine epitaphs—three for affinal kin, three for Buddhist clerics, and three for eunuchs—that represent key segments of Cao's social and political circle.[21]

The collection's many colophons on paintings and calligraphy also reveal Cao's leading role in Gaozong's efforts to rebuild the imperial art collection and continue Huizong's use of art as political propaganda. Zhou Mi quotes a Song work known as the *A Record of Emperor Gaozong's Calligraphy and Paintings* (Siling shuhua ji) that places Cao Xun at the head of a list of connoisseurs who worked to assemble, evaluate, and catalogue Gaozong's collection of paintings and calligraphy. Of the eight names on the list that can be identified, in addition to Cao, two are imperial affines and at least two are eunuchs. Another is Long Dayuan, the great "favorite" of Xiaozong's early years. Another is Song Kuang, a client of Qin Gui and a financial official "from the marketplace" who began his career in the Directorate for Armaments. He was dismissed as acting major of Lin'an in 1151 for permitting the army to make unverified withdrawals from the city treasury, but soon returned as prefect of Qin Gui's home base in Jiankang. Dismissed after Qin Gui's death, he was still active as late as 1169.[22]

CAO XUN ON TAIZU'S OATH

Two locations in Cao Xun's surviving writings describe how he transmitted the story of Taizu's oath from Huizong to Gaozong. The first occurs in a memorial that, although undated, was certainly submitted to Gaozong shortly after Cao arrived at Yingtian in late 1127/7. This text is preserved in his collected works and will be examined later in this chapter.

The second, more extensive mention, occurs in Cao's narrative of his 1127 northern journey, the *Record of Experiences in Northern Captivity* (Bei shou jianwen lu). This one-*juan* work is not included in Cao's collected works and presents a number of difficult bibliographic and textual problems. The date of composition is uncertain. Chen Zhensun lists the book in one *juan* and implies that Cao submitted an initial draft shortly after his arrival at Yingtian.[23] But this initial account was subsequently revised, perhaps several times. The standard edition, as transmitted in Qing period *congshu*, refers to Huizong as Huimiao, a title he obtained only in 1137, two years after his death.[24] This edition also contains a signature line that records Cao's complete official title, presumably at the time he revised or published the work. Liu Pujiang has linked these titles to an 1144 entry in the *Chronological Record* and concluded that the transmitted *Record of Experiences in Northern Captivity* must postdate 1144.[25] However, Cao's titles in the signature line correspond exactly to a minor document concerning his salary in the *Song huiyao*, and this document is clearly dated 1157/10/27.[26] The received version was therefore revised, probably for the last time, in 1157 or 1158, when Cao Xun had just begun to resume his career after Qin Gui's death in 1155. In addition to the received, *congshu* version of the full text, Xu Mengxin's *Compendium of Documents on the Treaties with the North during Three Reigns* (Sanchao beimeng huibian) contains two lengthy quotations from the *Record of Experiences in Northern Captivity*, the second of which, fortunately, records the entire passage concerning the collar edict and Taizu's oath. These quotations refer to Huizong as *taishang* (his retired Majesty) and Gaozong as *dawang* (prince), and derive presumably from an earlier version that predated 1137.[27]

The *Record of Experiences in Northern Captivity* is certainly a subsequently composed memoir and not a contemporary diary. Although the work reflects Cao's role as an intimate of the Huizong court and contains unique details of the northern journey, Cao has crafted his narrative with a keen awareness of the cultural and political circumstances of the Gaozong court. The key passage in question, taken in full into the *Compendium*, articulates in detail the following message: Huizong, with the support of Heaven and other divine authorities as manifested in omens and portents, has authorized the transfer of his authority as emperor to Gaozong. The most likely scenario that accommodates all these facts is that Cao Xun composed an initial version of the work sometime relatively soon after his return, he then revised this version after the return of Empress Wei in 1142, and he then further revised and/or published the work in some form about 1157.

The key passage begins by noting that several days after crossing the Yellow River, Huizong dreamed that he saw four suns appear in the sky. Because he feared this dream might signal that the people of the Central Plains would not support Prince Kang as emperor, he instructs Cao Xun to record it. Cao assures him of the people's loyalty to Song and affirms they will never support Zhang Bangchang. The next day, Huizong instructs Cao, since he is young, quick, and fully knowledgeable of his affairs, to take a message to Prince Kang. That evening, the emperor takes apart the collar of his vest and writes the eight-graph message, followed by his cipher, a total of nine graphs, on the inside lining. He reassembles the garment and gives it to Cao. He also gives him an earring, obtained from Prince Kang's wife that the prince had worn earlier, to serve as verification of the message. He also obtained a letter to the prince from his mother, the Consort Wei.

Cao's narrative then records five additional verbal messages that Huizong instructed him to deliver to Prince Kang. First, the prince should pursue plans to recover the Central Plains without regard for Huizong's safety. Second is the message about Taizu's oath (discussed later). Third, Huizong instructs the prince to follow the model of Han Guangwu and to act quickly to obtain popular support for his restoration and continuation of the Song house. Fourth, to provide further evidence of Cao's bona fides as emissary, Huizong reveals that he had once secretly given the prince a kingfisher-colored pearl and a rhinoceros hide box; and that, fifth, the prince had once suggested in secret that the dikes of the Yellow River might be broken to impede the Jin advance.

Cao's narrative then proceeds to record two messages that Consort Wei deputed him to transmit to her son. First, she reveals that when the prince departed Kaifeng on 1126/11/16 as emissary to Wolibu, there was among the palace women who saw him off a girl named Zhao'er who saw four armed figures, invisible to others, protecting the prince. Consort Wei realizes subsequently that these must have been the Four Sages, to whom she had long been devoted. She explains to Cao that she has continued her devotion to these Daoist divinities on their northern journey, and she urges the prince to observe strict devotion to these divine protectors as manifestations of Heaven's support for the dynasty. Second, she tells Cao that, in an effort to determine if her son will become emperor, she wrote his name on a chess piece and cast it along with other pieces onto the board. The piece labeled "Prince Kang" fell upon the "ninth palace," presaging that her son will become emperor. She is delighted at the outcome of this augury, and Cao informs Huizong of the news. Huizong remarks that his courtiers should congratulate him because these multiple omens pointing towards Prince Kang's ascension give him confidence in his decision to support the prince.[28]

The short segment on Taizu's oath plays but a minor role in this larger narrative, the primary purpose of which is to present the full complexity of Huizong's political message to Prince Kang. In the *Compendium* version, Huizong's second verbal message reads as follows: "And [Huizong] also said: 'Taizu had a covenant that was kept in the ancestral temple, by which he swore not to execute senior officials; and it said that violations [by any later emperor] will be inauspicious. Therefore for successive generations [of emperors from Taizong through Huizong] there was no change [to this covenant]. But I am constantly reminded of the excessive punishments and executions in 1126. Although today's calamity is not solely attributable to this, you should nevertheless consider it as a warning.'"[29]

The crucial phase in this passage reads 不誅大臣言有違者不祥, which I interpret as translated in the preceding paragraph. However, the text of this message in Cao Xun's 1127 memorial to Gaozong, as preserved in his collected works, reads 誓不誅大臣,言官,違者不祥. Most scholars therefore reject the *Compendium*'s reading of 有 as a scribal error for 官.[30] To further complicate matters, the standard edition of the *Record of Experiences in Northern Captivity* reads 不誅大臣用宦官違者不祥—"not to execute senior scholars or employ eunuchs"—which all scholars, save Li Feng, reject as a nonsensical textual corruption.[31]

Therefore, the writings of Cao Xun, as presently transmitted, present three very different textual versions for the second phrase of Taizu's oath. Assuming that Cao Xun did indeed deliver a message about the oath from Huizong to Gaozong, there seems unfortunately no secure way to determine which, if any, of these textual options best represents Huizong's original intention. However, rather than attributing these variations to textual corruption and simply choosing the most convenient reading, we might consider the possibility that each may represent a change that Cao Xun himself introduced into the various iterations of his own memoirs. The different readings may reflect Cao Xun's adaptation of the oath story to the changing political circumstances that he encountered after his return from the north. As Li Feng has suggested, the variability of the phrase concerning "speaking officials" reflects the fact that, for Cao Xun, Taizu's oath was hardly the central focus of Huizong's message.

Within the context of Cao Xun's larger narrative, the purpose of the

Taizu's oath anecdote is to blame Qinzong for the fall of Kaifeng and its aftermath. Cao Xun frames the executions under Qinzong in 1126 as a violation of Taizu's covenant, a policy maintained by all emperors through Huizong himself.[32] Because Qinzong violated this policy, he is responsible for the "inauspicious" fall of Kaifeng. Placed in the context of the written collar edict, Huizong hints that, when Gaozong becomes emperor, he should work to secure his father's return south. He implies that, as "retired emperor," his return—unlike that of the reigning emperor Qinzong—would not threaten Gaozong's status as a new emperor. Those whom Qinzong had executed—Wang Fu, Zhu Mian, Tong Guan, Cai You, Cai Tao, Zhao Liangsi, and Liang Shicheng—had all served as senior officials under Huizong, and he asks Gaozong not to continue retributions against his remaining retainers, of whom Cao Xun himself is one.[33] Later official and private works that cite Cao Xun as a primary source—Wang Mingqing in the late twelfth century, Li Xinchuan in the first decade of the thirteenth century, and the *Huang Song zhongxing liang chao shengzheng*—all truncate this passage after "inauspicious."[34] This editing removes the oath legend from its 1127 provenance—the political maneuvering among the three Song emperors—and foregrounds Taizu's benevolent concern for his officials and their remonstrance.

Given this emphasis, the key phrase is 不誅大臣, which remains constant in all Cao Xun texts. However, the problem of the second clause is further compounded by the possibility that Cao Si may have edited his father's memorials. The reading 言官 is attested not only in the 1127 memorial but also by Wang Mingqing, who had access to the *Record of Experiences in Northern Captivity* later in the century.[35] However, neither the standard edition of *Record of Experiences in Northern Captivity* nor any edition of the *Compendium of Documents on the Treaties with the North during Three Reigns* supports this reading. Therefore, if 言官 was Cao Si's emendation and not Cao Xun's original formulation, then this reading, preferred by virtually all scholars who had addressed this issue, cannot be confirmed earlier than the 1190s. The character 有 indeed appears as an easy scribal mistake for 官, but there is no way to determine which represents the earliest "correct" reading. If, accordingly, we take the collected works text of the 1127 memorial as representing Cao Xun's original text and not a later emendation by Cao Si, then the earliest formulation would indeed be 誓不誅大臣、言官. Less than a month after Cao Xun's arrival at Yingtian, the new administration publically executed Chen Dong (1086–1127) and Ouyang Che (1091–1127), precisely for questioning Gaozong's ascension and for suggesting that Qinzong was still the legitimate emperor. Subsequent suppression of "speakers" during the late 1130s would also have rendered this formulation of the oath unwelcome in the historical record.

Whatever the case may be, the reading 不誅大臣用宦官 is much more difficult to dismiss as textual corruption and probably represents Cao Xun's final 1157 version of his memoirs. But this is also an opaque formulation and difficult to interpret. Presumably, the force of the negative carries through to the second clause, meaning "Taizu swore not to execute senior officials and not to employ eunuchs." Li Feng, has raised the intriguing possibility, however, that the negative may apply only to the first clause, thus making 用宦官 affirmative: "Taizu swore not to execute senior officials and [he swore] to employ eunuchs." Such an understanding seems indeed anomalous on both linguistic and historical grounds.[36] Yet Cao Xun, as Ho Koon-wan has shown, was exceedingly close to the eunuch establishment. And, as Wang Zengyu has shown, Gaozong, although chastened by the eunuchs' role in the Miao-Liu mutiny in 1129, returned in many ways to Huizong's reliance upon them.[37]

At any rate, the obvious reluctance of Cao Xun in his final version of the *Record of Experiences in Northern Captivity* to include "speaking officials" as part of Taizu's oath certainly reflects lingering sensitivity to the many persecutions of those who had opposed the peace treaty under Qin Gui. As Qin Gui's 1155 inscription for the imperial portraits of Confucius and his disciples, which Gaozong himself propagated in 1156/12, makes clear, the state was in no mood to "open the speakers' road" after Qin Gui's death.[38] The updated, and probably emended, version of Cao Xun's memoir fits perfectly with the spirit of this moment in Song history. It also accords well with Cao Xun's desire, after Qin Gui's death, to set the record straight and to remind Gaozong and Empress Wei of his former service to them. Although Cao Xun and Qin Gui differed personally, there is no doubt that Cao supported the treaty that had brought home Empress Wei and the body of his former master, Huizong. As we shall see, another major message of the final version of the *Record of Experiences in Northern Captivity* is that Huizong, despite his initial call to "cleanse the Central Plains" (*qing Zhongyuan*), had supported a negotiated peace with the Jurchen. For all these reasons, we may well understand Cao Xun's own disregard for what would subsequently become the major focus of the oath legend—its concern for "literati officials" (*shidafu*).

AUSPICIOUS RESPONSES TO THE RESTORATION

A painting closely connected to Cao Xun entitled *Auspicious Responses to the Restoration* (Zhongxing ruiying tu) provides important cultural and political context for understanding Cao's role as an intermediately in 1127 between the emperors Huizong and Gaozong, and for understanding the primary message of the *Record of Experiences in Northern Captivity*. Interpreted against Cao's own writings and other surviving sources, the subject matter of the painting reveals how heavenly omens and portents, as well as purported messages to Gaozong from his human predecessors, were used to create propaganda that supported Gaozong's vision of the restoration. As this vision evolved in response to political, military, and diplomatic events after 1127, some early omens became more useful than others, and new omens were created in response to changing political needs. The surviving historical record reflects—but palely—these changes and permits us to understand the first appearance of the story of Taizu's oath as part of the earliest propaganda of the restoration.

Auspicious Responses to the Restoration depicts twelve scenes from Gaozong's life before he became emperor. Each represents an omen or augury of his forthcoming imperial destiny. Cao Xun composed a brief narrative and a versified paean (*zan*) for each of the twelve scenes in the painting and a general preface.[39] A court painter, reputedly Xiao Zhao, a disciple of the great Li Tang, executed the images, but Cao Xun probably participated in the overall creative conception. The original scroll dated from sometime between 1171 and Cao's death in 1174, a period during which he had been called to Lin'an and was under consideration for senior positions. Ming and Qing painting catalogues contain numerous entries on the original twelve-scene version as well as on a reduced series of six scenes. The most important surviving example is a complete twelve-scene scroll that was once in the Qing imperial collection. This scroll disappeared in 1925 but resurfaced "among the people" in 2009 and was sold at auction in Beijing. A full study remains to be undertaken, but preliminary research suggest the scroll is a later copy, not the Song original.[40]

The order of the twelve scenes on the existing hand scroll and in Cao's collected works is identical, and is as follows:

1. At Prince Kang's birth, a golden light and the Four Sages appeared to his mother, then Consort Wei.
2. A deity (one of the Four Sages?) appears to Consort Wei and instructs her not to feed the small prince leftover food from her own table but to prepare food specifically for him.
3. The young prince performs feats of strength that suggest his martial vigor.

4. On 1126/2/5, the Jurchen, fearful of his impressive demeanor, decline to accept Prince Kang as a hostage; he is replaced with Prince Su and thus escapes Jurchen captivity.

5. On 1126/11/16, Prince Kang is appointed emissary to the Jin, with Wang Yun as his deputy. Upon their departure from Kaifeng, a palace girl named Zhao'er sees the Four Sages, who are invisible to the rest of the group, seeing off the prince.

6. On 1126/11/21, at Cizhou, the prefect Zong Ze invites Prince Kang to visit the local temple of the Daoist transcendent Lord Cui. A delegation, bringing a sedan chair and a horse from Lord Cui to assist the prince, receives him. They warn the prince not to proceed northward on his mission. Suspecting that Wang Yun, who urges the prince to continue on his mission, is a spy, the crowd kills him.

7. In 1127/4, on her journey into northern captivity, Consort Wei, in an effort to determine if her son will become emperor, writes his name on a chess piece and casts it along with other pieces onto the board. The Prince Kang piece falls upon the "ninth palace," indicating her son will become emperor. She informs Huizong who is pleased.

8. Prince Kang remains at Cizhou. An old woman diverts Jin solders in the area, and he eludes capture.

9. In 1127/2, at Dongping fu, Prince Kang, attempting to divine his fate, shoots three arrows at the three characters on the placard at the "Flying Immortal Pavilion." All three arrows land in the center of their targeted characters.

10. At Cizhou, Prince Kang shoots a white rabbit. [White is associated with metal and the Jin dynasty].

11. On 1126/12/15, Prince Kang's party crosses the Yellow River over thin ice. Riding a horse, as soon as the prince is safely across, the ice breaks behind him.

12. After his appointment by Qinzong as Grand Field Marshal on 1126/i11/18, Prince Kang, in a dream, sees Qinzong remove his imperial yellow robe and give it to him.[41]

Li Tianming has provided a helpful commentary that scours the surviving record for the historical traces of these omen "stories." He divides his results into five categories based on the relationship of each omen to historical reality as he determines it from the sources. His categories form a sliding scale from stories that accord with "reality" to those that are "myths without factual evidence."[42] But these modern distinctions do little to reveal the evolution of the historical image of the restoration that the scroll presents.

THE OMENS AND THE SOURCES

Although three of the omens are indeed otherwise unattested (numbers 2, 3, and 10), the remaining nine all occur in varying contexts in contemporary sources. These auspicious responses may be overt or subtle, human or superhuman, but they continue a Huizong court tradition that routinely construed natural phenomena as auspicious signs of Heaven's support for the regime, and thus worthy of both a visual record and inclusion in official histories.[43] From the modern perspective, the resulting narrative presents a collage of historical "fact," religious superstition, and political propaganda. Yet this mixture mirrors the precise cultural milieu from which the earliest history of the restoration emerged. An examination of when specific omens entered the historical record can determine their relationship to the collar edict. The resulting chronology can then demonstrate the context in which the Taizu oath legend first became part of, and then disappeared from, restoration history.

When read against the historical sources in this way, Cao Xun's twelve omens can be divided into three broad categories. First are omens whose appearance in the historical record predates the ascension of Gaozong as emperor on 1127/5/1. Second are omens that derive from Consort Wei (numbers 1, 2, 5, and 7). Cao Xun's *Record of Experiences in Northern Captivity* records the two most important of these omens (numbers 5 and 7), which are events that the consort personally witnessed; there is considerable overlap in this group with omens that involve the Four Sages. Third are omens that concern the cult of Lord Cui at Cizhou (numbers 6 and 8). This three-part classification focuses on when, and under what political circumstances, a given omen first entered the historical record. Cao Xun himself in his preface to the omen eulogies distinguishes between three classes: those he learned personally from Empress Wei and transmitted to Gaozong, along with the collar edict, in 1127; those he subsequently learned privately from Gaozong and the empress after her return in 1142; and those that were public knowledge "both here and in Jin."[44]

Deng Xiaonan's study of the legend that Prince Kang crossed the Yellow River on Lord Cui's "mud horse" demonstrates that although the full-blown legend came together only in the thirteenth century, the idea that Lord Cui had divinely assisted the prince at Cizhou first arose in the early 1130s as

Gaozong worked to secure the political support of the cult's many adherents in the north, as well as those who had fled south. The program was part of the restoration government's propaganda initiative to counter the influence of Liu Yu's Qi dynasty regime that the Jurchen had imposed in 1130/9 to administer North China: the program made the political point that because Lord Cui had supported Gaozong, the Lord's followers should do likewise.[45] The cult became a central tenant of Restoration ideology. In 1154 Gaozong established a large temple for Lord Cui on West Lake, and the immortal was entitled "protector of the state" in 1186.[46] Yet evidence suggests that at Cizhou in 1126 Prince Kang did not view Zong Ze nor Lord Cui's intervention as particularly helpful.[47] However, by 1135, as the historical record of the Prince Kang years was being established, Gaozong changed his opinion to accord with the interpretation that the events at Cizhou had been an expression of Heaven's will that he should be emperor.[48]

The omens concerning the Four Sages and Empress Wei probably came into prominence slightly later as diplomatic negotiations for her return intensified.[49] The Four Sages were Daoist guardian deities from the court of the Grand Emperor of Purple Tenuity, whose celestial position corresponded to that of the Song emperor on earth.[50] Early in the dynasty they had helped both Taizu and Taizong, and the founders had built for them an abbey in Kaifeng. Li Xinchuan and other Southern Song sources describe the Empress Wei's devotion to this cult, whose reestablishment in the new capital betokened Gaozong's legitimacy and marked the continuity of his regime with that founded by Taizu. Upon her arrival in Lin'an in 1142, she had constructed on West Lake a temple to continue her adoration and to commemorate the deities' support for the Restoration. In retirement, Gaozong and Empress Wu regularly visited, often accompanied by Emperor Xiaozong.[51]

THE OMENS AND THE COLLAR EDICT

Thus, neither the events at Cizhou—with or without the intervention of Lord Cui—nor the events connected to Empress Wei and the Four Sages were part of the original set of omens that arose prior to Gaozong's ascension on 1127/5/1. When the decision was made on 1127/4/4 that the prince should take the throne, his advisors, including Geng Nanzhong, his son Geng Yanxi, Wang Boyan, and Huang Qianshan, in order to create a public perception of the inevitability of his mandate to rule, prepared a list of omens that, they claimed, had already sanctioned his ascension. They listed seven events. There are no dates in the document; the details in square brackets have been ascertained from other sources:

1. Prior to Prince Kang's departure on a diplomatic mission to Wolibu's camp outside Kaifeng, Emperor Qinzong gave him a jade belt ornament usually worn only by emperors [1126/11/3].
2. Upon notification of his appointment as grand field marshal, Prince Kang dreamed that Qinzong removed his yellow robe and gave it to him [1126/i11/18].
3. A popular interpretation of the two graphs in the Jingkang reign period—to mean "establish him in the twelfth month"—foretells Prince Kang's appointment as field marshal.
4. The prince's three arrows strike the Flying Immortal Pavilion [at Ping-dong fu, 1127/2].
5. A sign (order) from Huizong authorizes the prince to assume command as emperor (*jizhen* 即真).
6. The Yellow River suddenly freezes and permits Prince Kang to cross [1126/12/15].
7. At Jizhou, red auras appear in the sky, an omen of the Song dynasty's "fire virtue" [sometime after arrival at Jizhou on 1127/2/23].[52]

Geng Nanzhong's list adroitly suggests that Heaven, the populace, Qinzong, and Huizong all favor Gaozong's ascension. Three of these omens (numbers 2, 4, and 6) subsequently became scenes in Cao Xun's hand scroll. Yet none of the omens on Geng's list concern Empress Wei, the Four Sages, or Lord Cui. These later omens were all generated by political developments that would occur only after the ascension. Of particular interest is the fifth item, which clearly relates to the collar edict. Geng Nanzhong's document survives only in the *Compendium*, where the 1909 edition reads 太上皇萬里有即真二字之兆. The *Siku quanshu* edition reads 太上皇萬里有即真二字詔. This latter reading, especially, suggests that a two-graph message—即真—had already arrived from Huizong, who had departed Kaifeng on his journey into northern captivity only a week earlier on 1127/3/29.

Five days later, on 1127/4/9, in a court debate about whether Prince Kang should ascend to the throne at his present location in Jizhou or should proceed to the southern capital at Yingtian, Geng Yanxi provided further details about the two-graph message: the two graphs, about two inches square and written in Huizong's own hand, had arrived sealed in wax and hidden in clothing. An escapee had delivered them along with a verbal message from

Huizong that Prince Kang should ascend.[53] The *Compendium* cites these details from the *Diary of the Jianyan Restoration*, a work composed by Wang Boyan, a participant and eyewitness to the events. But the *Compendium* also contains an extract from Geng Yanxi's own primary account of this meeting, the *Record of the Jianyan Restoration*. According to this version, Geng and his allies, arguing on 1127/4/9 for the prince's immanent enthronement at Yingtian, cited a verbal message from Huizong, just received via an unnamed escapee, that "you may inform Prince Kang that he should ascend the throne." However, Geng's own account does not mention any written message from Huizong.[54]

Although Wang did not survive the power struggles around the young Gaozong for long, in 1133/10 the court ordered him to compose a daily calendar to cover the period from Prince Kang's appointment as field marshal through 1127/5/10, ten days after the ascension. Wang submitted five *juan* on 1134/4/22.[55] Gaozong and his councilor Zhao Ding reviewed the work carefully and ordered it sent to the history office on 1135/9/18.[56] It was during their conversation that Gaozong revised his opinion on Zong Ze's actions at Cizhou and accepted them as a manifestation of Heaven's will. Wang's account of this period eventually found its way into the *Qinzong Daily Calendar*, which had been initiated under Qin Gui in 1140, but was not completed by the court history office until 1166. By 1168, the office had condensed the daily calendar into the *Qinzong Veritable Records*, the official history of the reign.[57]

We know that the *Qinzong Veritable Records* conflated these primary accounts by Wang Boyan and Geng Yanxi with the story of Cao Xun's return from Huizong and his transmittal of the eight-graph collar edict. The official, mid-twelfth-century version of what happened on 1127/4/9 reads as follows:

> At that time [the ninth day of the fourth month of 1127] Cao Xun, having escaped and returned from the Hebei battlefield, arrived at the Field Marshal's headquarters. He presented clothing from Emperor Huizong on which His Majesty had written: "You may at once assume full authority as emperor, then come and rescue your parents." As verification, he also instructed [Cao Xun] to tell the prince how previously [Huizong] had secretly given [the prince] a kingfisher-colored pearl and a rhinoceros-hide box and about how the prince had secretly memorialized with a plan to destroy the Yellow River dikes in order to engulf the enemy as they crossed the river. The Xuanhe Empress sent a golden [ear-]ring to the prince and relayed the message that on the day the prince had been dispatched on his

second mission as envoy, the palace girl Zhao'er had seen armed immortals acting as his protectors. The prince, moved to tears, accepted. It was therefore decided that he should proceed to Yingtian.[58]

This passage relies totally upon details from Cao Xun's *Record of Experiences in Northern Captivity*. However, this veritable record's account confuses, or purposely falsifies, the date of Cao's return and thus the date of the transmittal of the collar edict from Huizong to Prince Kang. This version also foregrounds the role of the prince's mother, Empress Wei, as transmitter of the "omen" of the prince's protection from the Four Sages.

In other words, at some point in time, presumably after Empress Wei's return in 1142 and before her death in 1159, the court history office superimposed details from Cao Xun's record onto the chronology and the list of omens that Wang Boyan's *Diary of the Jianyan Restoration* had already established. This manipulation probably occurred between 1140 and 1143 when Qin Gui's son, Qin Xi, reconciled the early history of the restoration with the political propaganda that had been generated to support the peace treaty and the return of Empress Wei in 1142.[59] This rewriting greatly enhanced the significance of the eight-graph edict and the other messages that Cao Xun had brought back from the north. The true chronology—in which Cao had actually arrived almost three months after Gaozong's ascension—rendered the edict little more than another confirmation of a fait accompli. The revised chronology, however, turned Huizong's edict into a powerful affirmation of the former regime's support for Prince Kang's ascension. It also enhanced the role of Empress Wei, the omens that descended from her, and the Four Sages in transfer of the mandate to Gaozong. With this revised chronology, Cao Xun's collar edict assumed its place among the other omens of support for Gaozong's rule, and Geng Nanzhong's truly contemporary but opaque two-graph *jizhen* omen receded from the evolving historical record. Most tellingly, however, this veritable records entry does not mention Cao Xun's transmission of the Taizu oath to Gaozong. Given the punishments meted out to those who opposed the peace treaty, its message no longer suited the monarchy's political needs.

LI XINCHUAN ON TAIZU'S OATH

This revised chronology had become accepted, official history by the late twelfth century. Xiong Ke's *Minor Calendar of the Restoration* and the closely related *Topical Details of our August Court's Restoration*, which date from the late 1180s and early 1190s, both rely upon the *Qinzong Veritable Records* and place Cao's return with the collar edict in 1127/4—before the ascension.[60] This official version of Cao Xun's mission, reinforced by Li Tao's adoption into the *Long Draft*, persisted in Song historical sources well into the Yuan dynasty. Even the *daoxue* historian, Chen Jun (1174–1244) placed Cao Xun's return with the collar edict in 1127/4, where it serves to sanction Gaozong's ascension. There is no mention of Taizu's oath.[61]

Li Xinchuan labored to correct this false chronology in his *Chronological Record*. Relying directly upon Cao Xun's *Record of Experiences in Northern Captivity*, he places the formulation of the plan for Cao to escape, the execution of the collar edict, and the collection of other messages from the prince's wife and mother in late 1127/4. His abridgement follows the original order of Cao's memoir, and he cites in his main text both the eight-graph collar edict and Taizu's oath, thus endorsing the authenticity of both these texts. He deletes, however, all mention of the omens related to Empress Wei.[62] Likewise, his entry for 1127/4/4, when the decision was made that Prince Kang should ascend the throne, omits all mention of Geng Nanzhong's omen list.[63] His entry for 1127/4/9, where omens again figure centrally in the decision that the prince should proceed to Yingtian, also edits out the references to omens in the primary sources. He does, however, citing Geng Yanxi's memoir, quote receipt of a verbal message from the "two emperors" confirming Gaozong's ascension. His note here firmly rejects Wang Boyan's account of the two-graph edict as well as the *Qinzong Veritable Records'* placement of Cao's return on this day. He notes that Cao's own account of his arrival in late 1127/7 with the eight-graph collar edict accords with a similar mention of the same event in Li Gang's memoir of this period.[64]

Having made all these corrections to the existing record, Li Xinchuan then extracted Cao Xun's *Record of Experiences in Northern Captivity* to construct an entry for the *Chronological Record* that foregrounds the collar edict and Taizu's oath:

> About two weeks after crossing the Yellow River, Huizong said to the Administrator of the Dragon Virtue Palace and Audience Attendant Cao Xun: "I dreamt that four suns appeared together in the sky; this is a sign that there will be a struggle for ultimate authority in the Central Plains. I am not certain if the people of the Central Plains are willing to support Prince Kang or not." The next day he took lining from his imperial clothing and personally wrote inside the collar: "You may at once assume full authority as emperor, then come and rescue your parents." . . . He

also told Cao Xun: "If you see Prince Kang, tell him to proceed with all plans to retake the Central Plains without consideration for me." And he also said: "Taizu had a covenant that was kept in the ancestral temple, by which he swore not to kill senior officials or policy critics. Violations [by any later emperor] will be inauspicious." He also told him, for verification, how he had once secretly given the prince a kingfisher-colored pearl and a rhinoceros-hide box and about how the prince had secretly memorialized with a plan to destroy the Yellow River dikes in order to engulf the enemy as they crossed the river.[65]

Li Xinchuan's efforts thus not only restored the proper chronology of Cao Xun's mission but also brought the legend of Taizu's oath—actually for the first time—into the mainstream of Song history. However, given the sources at his disposal, his version is a compromise. On the one hand, his truncations and excerpts of the primary sources remove the collar edict and the oath from their initial context among the omens, the political propaganda, and the machinations that surrounded the three Song emperors and the tenuous future of Song rule in 1127. On the other hand, his version foregrounds the notion of "no-kill" (不殺) and its application to "speakers" as a policy that descended from Taizu himself and that Huizong transmitted as an important dynastic principle to his new successor. In Cao Xun's original narrative and in the *Qinzong Veritable Records* (Qinzong shilu), the Four Sages had represented this dynastic continuity, which the devotion of Empress Wei had enabled Huizong to transmit to Gaozong. In Li Xinchuan's history, however, Taizu's oath replaced the Daoist sages as a symbol of dynastic constancy and Gaozong's legitimacy.

There is good evidence that Li's revisions reflect not only his own passion for historical accuracy but also contemporary notions of what the oath was coming to mean. In Li's text of the oath, 不殺 replaces the earlier reading 不誅. This change is already present in the only other twelfth-century source to discuss the oath, Wang Mingqing's conversation with Zhu Dunru (1081–1159), as recorded in Wang's *Records of One Who Wields the Chowry* (Huizhu lu). Wang explains that he heard about the oath from Cao Xun and that Cao had relayed its contents verbally from Huizong to Gaozong. Wang frames the oath in the context of the dynasty's system of laws that spells out gradations of punishment for official transgressions and does not sanction arbitrary impositions of the death penalty. Wang cites four examples. For their crimes, the early Song councilors Lu Duoxun and Ding Wei would have suffered death in previous dynasties, but both returned alive from southern exiles. However, Wang writes that factional politics after 1086—in-fighting and mismanagement among the literati them-selves—undermined the older imperial policy of forbearance. Therefore Cai Que and Zhang Dun, both chief councilors (大臣), had died in exile. But their deaths were not the fault of the monarchy. Zhang's own exces-sively partisan politics had instigated his own exile. As for Cai, who had written poetry that slandered the reigning Empress Dowager Gao, Wang observes that his death in exile resulted from a few overzealous Yuanyou officials. He concludes that high officials in previous dynasties would have used similar circumstances as a pretext to slaughter large numbers of their political opponents, but the monarchy's policy of restraint had curtailed similar bloodletting in Song.[66]

Since Zhu Dunru died in 1159, and the *Later Records of One Who Wields the Chowry* (Huizhu houlu) was not completed until 1194, precise dating of this entry is difficult. Even though Wang acknowledges Cao Xun as the source of the oath story, his entry already divorces the oath text from its original 1127 context and places it in the larger context of Song law. Although he does not use the term 祖宗之法, Wang links the magnanim-ity and transparency of Song law to a policy that emanated from Taizu and that he believes demarcated the Song from earlier dynasties. Although all of Wang's examples concern chief councilors, his examples suggest that, for Wang and Zhu Dunru, the effect of the oath functioned like a pact between the monarchy and its chief councilors not to allow factional politics to result in death sentences for political actors. Wang's entry reflects an understand-ing that the policy, as reflected in Song legal practice, applied to all officials (臣下所犯) and thus suggests that he perceived the oath as extending to a larger class of officials than simply the 大臣 and perhaps 言官 of Cao Xun's original message.

The *Records of One Who Wields the Chowry* was among Li Xinchuan's sources for the *Chronological Record*. Although he does not directly cite this passage, Li's presentation of the oath issue develops the late twelfth-century view of the oath's meaning that Wang's entry reflects. Li Xinchuan's annota-tion addressing the chronology of the Cao Xun's mission is one of thirty-six interlinear notes that he inserted into an earlier draft of the *Chronological Record* in preparation for the work's submission to court following the assassination of Han Tuozhou in 1207 and the beginning of the new admin-istration under Shi Miyuan. Many of these annotations introduced changes into the official daily calendar (*rili*) that strengthened the negative image of Qin Gui and attempted to correct the distortions that his son Qin Xi had introduced into the historical record.[67] Li's corrections to the history of Cao Xun's mission fall into this category of changes.

But, although Li properly corrected the chronology of the Cao mission, his version also introduced new elements into the story. For example, his text for the oath—不殺大臣及言事官—is new, and does not derive from any surviving Cao Xun formulation. He adopts Wang Mingqing's reading of 殺 for 誅, thus strengthening the oath's injunction. He also introduces the reading 言事官, and inserts the graph 及, thus removing all possible ambiguities from Cao's earlier, shifting formulations of the oath's content. This rephrasing of the oath reinforced its relevance to contemporary politics. In Li Xinchuan's view, authoritarian administrations under Qin Gui and Han Tuozhou had both suppressed remonstrance. The portrait of Qin Gui that emerges from the *Chronological Record* can in fact be read as a type for Han Tuozhou and was probably intended as a warning to the new administration not to follow along the path of its two predecessors. Li Xinchuan's enhancement of Huizong's message about Taizu's oath expresses his opinion that the Southern Song political establishment had fallen short of the oath's lofty commitment to political restraint. Of course, neither Li nor his contemporary audience could have missed the irony of 不殺大臣, since Han Tuozhou was indeed the only "great minister" openly assassinated in Song. Although Li Xinchuan detested Han Tuozhou's politics, he certainly understood the oath, as Wang Mingqing before him, as a pact between the monarchy and its top officials to restrain from the degree of political violence that had removed Han from office.

THE LU YOU ACCOUNT

As we have seen, Huizong sent a complex, contemporary political message to Gaozong via Cao Xun. Despite conflicts in the primary sources, there seems no doubt that Cao indeed served as a courier between the two parties and that he arrived at Yingtian in late 1127/7. Of course, there is no way to prove that Huizong invented the oath story as part of his move to discredit Qinzong. Likewise, there is no way to prove that Cao Xun and Gaozong themselves concocted the story. Given the history of his family's service to Huizong, the former scenario seems much more likely. But, whatever the case may be, Gaozong doubtless found the message politically useful at the moment he received it. Although he probably did not relish the prospect of his father's return, the insinuation of Qinzong's failure as emperor strengthened the case for his own assumption of the office. Likewise, at a time when

Gaozong sought literati-official support for his restoration and its return to the policy of the ancestors, Huizong's vivid reminder of one of the most fundamental of those policies reinforced Gaozong's contemporary agenda. Several months before Cao Xun's return, Gaozong had issued a broad-based amnesty that included even those who had supported the Zhang Bangchang regime.[68] Acceptance of the "warning" from Huizong would affirm that the executions that had marred the Qinzong administration would not continue during the restoration. Acceptance of the oath also played into the scenario that Gaozong's restoration was a return to the ideals of Taizu, the dynastic founder.

However, presuming that Huizong's initial message, as relayed by Cao Xun, did indeed include an injunction not to kill "speakers," Gaozong had no incentive to promote such a message after the late 1130s when he and Qin Gui did indeed suppress those who opposed a negotiated peace with the Jin. Even after Qin Gui's death, Gaozong again expressed the need for political conformity to support the peace policy.[69] Later, in a well-known incident from 1179, Emperor Xiaozong even hinted he might revisit his ancestors' reluctance to execute top officials.[70] Under these imperial sentiments, the monarchy had little interest in recording or promoting the contents of Taizu's oath; the earlier examination of the historical record in the mid-twelfth century reflects this fact. What little evidence does survive from Wang Mingqing and Li Xinchuan suggests that the literati themselves promoted the legend and broadened it to cover a wide spectrum of officials.

The pseudo–Lu You account preserved in *Random Notes Made in Summer* is best read in this light. According to this fully developed version of the legend, in 962 Taizu carved the oath upon a stone stele that he then placed in a secret, locked chamber within the ancestral temple. Following the ascension of each successive emperor, an illiterate eunuch would prepare the chamber and lead the new emperor, alone, into the room, where he memorized the oath. Each Northern Song emperor kept the contents of the oath and the nature of this ritual secret even from his most trusted advisors. During the fall of Kaifeng, the Jurchen ransacked the temple, and the hidden chamber and its stele were revealed. There were reportedly three lines of text. The first mandated that members of the former Zhou dynasty's ruling lineage were to be spared punishment for minor crimes; any who plotted rebellion were to be executed in prison, not in public, and their relatives were not to be harmed. The second was, "do not kill officials or those who send up memorials critical of policy." The third line threatened Heaven's retribution against future monarchs who violated the oath. After the fall of Kaifeng, since the new emperor was unable to visit the chamber, Emperor Huizong, from his northern captivity, deputed Cao Xun to travel south and notify Gaozong about the oath.[71]

The surviving *Random Notes Made in Summer* is a collection of twenty-eight extracts copied from eighteen Tang, Song, and Yuan anecdote books. The story of Taizu's stele is quoted from a work called the *Secret History* (Bishi), but no such Song work has been identified. Furthermore, neither the existence of the book nor its attribution to Lu You can be shown to predate the mid-Ming.[72] Thus, there is no way to fix in time either the account of Taizu's stele from the *Secret History* or the compilation of *Random Notes Made in Summer*. Although the collection is quite diverse, its compiler seems sensitive to the issue of extrajudicial imperial executions. Immediately following the legend of Taizu's oath he cites another anecdote that reinforces the same theme. According to Cai Tiao's *Conversations from Iron Enclosure Mountain* (Tiewei shan congtan), Taizu had inherited from the previous dynasty a warehouse in the palace that stored various poisons used to assassinate disloyal officials. Since the poisons were never use in the Song, Huizong eventually ordered the warehouse dismantled and its contents destroyed, thus reflecting the "benevolent" character of Song rule.[73] Of course, the pairing of these two anecdotes could have occurred at any time, but the resonance from their juxtaposition perhaps suggests sensitivity to the executions of literati officials under the early Ming.

Despite these bibliographic problems, most scholars treat the *Random Notes Made in Summer* account of Taizu's oath-stele as a Southern Song text. Yet no other genuine Southern Song source cites its many details or its stele text. This fact suggests its account is mid- to late thirteenth century or later. At least one other version of the oath legend survives from this period in the collected works of Yu Delin, but the details are very different. Taizu vows not to kill "senior officials, meritorious officials, or remonstrance officials" as token of which he places three broken arrows in the ancestral temple. Huizong writes the oath, not the collar edict, on his shirt and has Cao Xun, here a eunuch, deliver it to Gaozong.[74] Liu Pujiang understands Yu's version as an elaboration of the Cao Xun and pseudo–Lu You material.[75] But Yu Delin's drastically differing details might also indicate that, even by the late thirteenth century and the end of Song, the Lu You version may still not have existed, or, if it did, that a definitive, authoritative version of the legend had still not coalesced.

Scholars also differ on whether the *Random Notes Made in Summer* is, as Zhang Yinlin maintained, a fictional "elaboration" based on Cao Xun, or constitutes a second, independent primary source on the oath/stele.[76] Related to this issue is the proper assessment of the crucial second "line" of the oath. As we have seen, Cao Xun's "best" version reads "he swore not to execute senior officials or policy critics" (誓不誅大臣、言官); the *Random Notes Made in Summer* reads "do not kill officials or those who send up memorials critical of policy" (不得殺士大夫及上書言事人). Some scholars consider these two versions "close enough" in meaning and use this supposed convergence to conclude that these two independent sources thus confirm the authenticity of the stele text.[77]

But the meanings of the two versions are quite different. On the one hand, Cao Xun's *dachen* and *yanguan* refer to officials who hold specific posts, essentially members of the Council of State, censors, and remonstrators—perhaps a dozen to twenty officials at any given time.[78] On the other hand, the *Random Notes Made in Summer* phrasing is much broader. *Shidafu* can refer to any ranked civil or military official—over 40,000 in the late twelfth century—or to literati-officials in general. Similarly, *shangshu yanshi ren* is a general phrase referring to anyone who submits criticism, including, for example, Chen Dong and the other "student protesters" of 1126. Therefore, Cao Xun's text designates a small number of senior administrators; the later text refers to a broadly conceived social class of literati.[79] One may perhaps conceive the former as a strict construction of the oath concept and the latter as a looser construction that, as Zhang Yinlin first suggested, evolved from the former.

CONCLUSION

All scholars agree there existed in Northern Song a general understanding between the monarchy and its senior administrators that the dynasty should not execute its top officials. However, as Li Feng and Deng Xiaonan have argued, the monarchy's small concession of absolute authority did not result from any initial commitment from the dynastic founder but emerged slowly from literati struggles with the sovereign over an independent space for political dissent. Fan Zhongyan in 1043 was the first to proclaim that "since the times of the ancestors, officials have never been rashly executed." The Yuanyou councilor Lü Dafang reaffirmed this principle again in 1093, and both political factions during the post-Yuanyou period generally upheld the concept.[80] However, none of these Northern Song passages ever name Taizu or his oath as the origin of this policy; they name only, as does Fan Zhongyan, generic "ancestors."

The direct link to Taizu and his oath first appears in connection with Cao Xun's mission as political emissary from Huizong to Gaozong in 1127. In that context, although this first formulation of the oath draws vaguely upon Northern Song sentiment, its function is not generally to affirm such a sentiment as policy but, much more narrowly, to accuse Qinzong of violating its spirit. Soon after Qinzong began his reign as emperor, as corollary to his purge of Cai Jing and others who were now labeled as advocates of the New Policies, he embraced in 1126/2 a Yuanyou-inspired program of political reform whose rhetoric advocated a return to the policies of the ancestors.[81] The clear implication was that Huizong had deviated from these policies. Little over a year later, Huizong and Cao Xun formulated the link between Taizu and the Northern Song "no-kill" policy. Most probably rhetorical hyperbole, their language served three purposes. It defended Huizong's legacy; it weakened the link between Qinzong and his professed adherence to the policies of the ancestors; and it accused Qinzong of directly violating a policy that descended from the ultimate ancestor, Taizu, thus freeing Gaozong to assume that mantle. Nothing in the Cao Xun material suggests that Huizong intended to pass on the contents of a "secret covenant" to Gaozong. This motif emerges only in the later thirteenth-century elaborations of the legend.

The Huizong/Cao Xun message thus encouraged and authorized Gaozong to cloak the Restoration in the mantle of Taizu, a process that was already well underway when Cao arrived at Yingtian in 1127/7. But, although the Taizu/Gaozong analogy would become a centerpiece of the Restoration, the policy of "no-kill" proved more difficult to implement as practice than as propaganda. The oath legend had come wrapped together with a package of omens and prognostications that proved much more useful as historical justification for Gaozong's rule and for use in the propaganda war against Liu Yu's Qi dynasty. After the peace of 1142 and the return of Empress Wei, these elements in Cao Xun's original message assumed prominence in the historical record. The message of Taizu's oath became merely a distasteful reminder of how fierce the opposition to the peace had been. Indeed, if our texts are accurate, Cao Xun in fact removed the oath's reference to "speakers" in the 1157 revision of his memoirs. Although later in life, he often recalled his mission and the collar edict, he never again mentioned the oath.[82] Rather, his "Auspicious Responses to the Restoration" are the major remembrance of his former service to the dynasty.

A major question remains why, save for Wang Mingqing's single entry, references to Cao Xun's account of the oath appear virtually unknown among twelfth-century sources. Certainly, as Emperor Xiaozong's 1179 testy exchange with Shi Hao makes clear, the political rise of *daoxue* had brought once again to the fore the efforts of literati officials to constrain the sovereign's unilateral exercise of authority. Likewise, the integrity of the remonstrance function remained a principle literati concern until the end of the dynasty. And both issues are central to Cao Xun's formulation of the oath. Yet there is not a single mention of Taizu's oath in the *Conversations of Zhu Xi*—that most omnivorous compendium of late twelfth-century opinion—or indeed in any other Southern Song *daoxue* work.

The answer lies most probably in the nonliterati character of Cao Xun and his circle. He was first and foremost a servitor of the monarchy—first of Huizong, then of Gaozong. Unlike many *daoxue* inspired literati officials, Cao Xun did not conceive of his service to the dynasty as separate from or opposed to the monarchy. And Gaozong's fulsome eulogy shows that the monarchy appreciated his loyalty. His career trajectory and collected works, as well as Li Xinchuan's informed opinion, mark him as a member of "the close" (*jinxi*), and a member that an influential literatus such as Yu Yunwen could dismiss as "too low-class a character to be considered." Even if Cao Xun personally believed in the reality of the oath—a big if—he did nothing, in the face of the monarchy's reluctance, to spread word of its existence to the very literati audience that might make the most of its potential meaning—but also an audience that had shown him such personal distain.

Much research remains to be done before we can judge how well Li Xinchuan balanced his perception of historical accuracy and his desire that the *Chronological Record* should present a "comprehensive mirror" for contemporary policy post–Han Tuozhou. The fact remains, however, that the *Chronological Record* is the earliest surviving effort to place Cao Xun's account of Taizu's oath in a larger historical perspective. Although Li Xinchuan's reworking of the legend follows Wang Mingqing's lead, his expansive interpretation of the oath as a link to Northern Song policy resonates well with the general hopes among literati in 1208 for a return to the "policies of the ancestors" under the new administration of Shi Miyuan, in which Li Xinchuan's brother, Li Daochuan, played a direct role.[83] Despite the dissolution of the *Chronological Record*, Li Xinchuan's version of the oath found its way into the *Song History*, and thus into the historical mainstream. Cao Xun's biography in the *Song History* is composed entirely of extracts from the *Chronological Record*, including Li Xinchuan's account of Cao Xun's 1127 mission.[84] This biography descended from the *Xiaozong Veritable Records* (Xiaozong shilu) and the *State History of the Four Restoration Courts*

TABLE 2.1. Chronological evolution of the text of Taizu's oath

Date	Text	Source
1127	誓不誅大臣、言官	曹勳:《進前十事札子》
1157?	誓不誅大臣、用宦官	曹勳:《北狩見聞錄》
1194	誓不殺大臣、言官	王明清:《揮塵後錄》
1208	誓不殺大臣及言事官	李心傳:《建炎以來繫年要錄》
Late Song/Early Yuan	誓不殺大臣、不殺功臣、不殺諫臣	俞德鄰:《佩韋齋集》
Late Song to Early Ming?	不得殺士大夫及上書言事人	《避暑漫抄》

(Zhongxing sichao guoshi); Li Xinchuan worked on both of these during his service at the court history office in the 1220s and 1230s.[85]

Nevertheless, despite the theoretical attraction of the Taizu oath legend to the growing ranks of *daoxue* adherents in the thirteenth century, the compilers of histories for this audience did not use Li Xinchuan's version but continued to reprocess, via Li Tao's *Long Draft*, the mid-twelfth-century version of Cao Xun's mission that emphasized the omens and omitted the oath. Thus, it was not until the seventeenth century that the wider implications of the oath legend began to impact scholarly conceptions of Song history. Wang Fuzhi cites the pseudo–Lu You version; Gu Yanwu cites Li Xinchuan's version, probably via Cao Xun's biography in the *Song History*.

In conclusion, there is little evidence that either the oath or the stele ever existed as a historical reality. The story arose from the political entanglements among the three Song emperors and from the complex and shifting politics of the Northern–Southern transition. Although the message was favorably received at Gaozong's court, subsequent developments disinclined the monarchy or its messenger, Cao Xun, from disseminating or further developing the potential of the legend to speak to larger issues of Song governance. Although those issues were actively discussed in Southern Song—often with direct reference to Northern Song prototypes—Taizu's oath did not become part of that conversation. Most twelfth-century literati were likely unaware of what Cao Xun had reported. If they were aware, they probably saw little to be gained from attempting to separate the messenger from his message. Outside of his own memoir, Cao Xun's account of Taizu's oath probably did not become part of the official twelfth-century historical record. Li Xinchuan's efforts to correct that record and reframe the meaning of the oath in the immediate wake of Han Tuozhou's assassination had little subsequent impact. It was only after the emergence of the pseudo–Lu You narrative that scholars of Song history focused again on Cao Xun's mission—and reapplied the message of his report to the larger issues of Song history. In essence, what began as a metaphor to undermine the memory of the unfortunate Emperor Qinzong took life again as a metaphor to describe the benevolence of the dynastic house from which he had come.

NOTES

1   *Song lun* 1.4–5; *Rizhi lu* 15.48a–b.

2   Zhang Qifan, "'Huangdi yu shidafu gongzhi tianxia' shixi," 116; Yu Yingshi, *Zhu Xi de lishi shijie*, 259–60, 271–85; cf. Hartman, "Zhu Xi and His World," 128–31. For a critique of overstated notions of "Song peak," see Zhang Bangwei, "Bubi meihua Zhao Song wangchao."

3   Zhang Yinlin, "Song Taizu shibei ji zhengshi tang keshi kao," 14–16.

4   Yang Haiwen, "'Song Taizu shibei' de wenxian ditu."

5   Du Wenyu, "Song Taizu shibei zhiyi."

6   Li Feng, "Lun Bei Song 'bu sha shidafu'"; Li Feng, "Song Taizu shiyue 'bu zhu dachen, yanguan' xinlun."

7   Xu Gui, "Song Taizu shiyue bianxi"; Zhang Xiqing, "Song Taizu 'bu zhu dachen, yanguan' shiyue kaolun"; Liu Pujiang, "Zuzong zhi fa."

8   Gu Hongyi, "Yue Fei zhi si yu Song Taizu 'bu sha dachen' shiyue kao," for example, argues that Taizu's injunction applied only to civil officials; therefore Gaozong's execution of Yue Fei, a military official, did not violate the oath.

9   *SHY* Zhiguan 61.18b–19a; Fu Xuancong, *Song dengkeji kao*, 621.

10 *Jianyan yilai xinian yaolu* 4.114 (hereafter cited as *Yaolu*). Lou Yue's epitaph for Cao Si, Cao Xun's son, contains details of the family's history; see *QSW* 266:5997.66–69. For Cao Zu's prose-poem on Huizong's "Magic Marchmount," the *Genyue*, see *Huizhu lu Houlu* 2.80–84.

11 *SS* 23.422, 379.11700; Fu Xuancong, *Song dengkiji kao*, 631.

12 *Yaolu* 5.135, 7.191. For a detailed account of Huizong's journey into captivity see Ebrey, *Huizong*, 475–90.

13 *Yaolu* 87.1442–43.

14 *SS* 383.11798.

15 *Yaolu* 153.2462, 169.2774, 170.2779.

16 *Jianyan yilai chaoye zaji* Jia 12.240 (hereafter cited as *Chaoye zaji*). Cf. *Yaolu* 178.2940 where an edict, using the imperial affine Zheng Zao as precedent, grants Cao Xun permission to receive his full salary in cash.

17 Zhu Shangshu, *Songren bieji xulu*, 18.872–74.

18 *Gongkui ji* 52.9b–10a; *QSW* 264:5949.110.

19 For the postface see Zhu Shangshu, *Songji xuba huibian*, 27.1286–87.

20 *Songyin wen ji* 38.4a–9b.

21 These are the only surviving epitaphs for Song eunuchs; for a detailed study see Ho Koon-wan, "Xiancun de san pian Songdai neichen muzhiming," 33–63, esp. 57–59.

22 *Qi dong ye yu* 6.93. On Song Kuang, see *Yaolu* 162.2635; *SHY* Zhiguan 70.42a, 76.57a

23 *Zhizhai shulu jieti* 5.156. Chen writes, in error, that Cao arrived at Yingtian in 1128/7. The *Siku* editors, following this error, suggest that the book was first submitted to the court in 1128; *Qinding Siku quanshu zongmu* 51.717.

24 *SS* 22.417.

25 Liu Pujiang, "Zuzong zhi fa," 148, citing *Yaolu* 151.2434. Zhang Xiqing, "Song Taizu 'bu zhu dachen, yanguan' shiyue kaolun," 47, 49, places the composition of the *Record of Experiences in Northern Captivity* in 1144. Jing Xinqiang, "Cao Xun *Bei shou jianwen lu* zhiyi" argues that the standard edition is much later than 1127 and suggests that the work was perhaps composed as late as 1144. However, he does not consider the relationship of the citations in the *Compendium of Documents on the Treaties with the North during Three Reigns* to the standard edition.

26 *Song huiyao jigao bubian*, Gemen yizhi 90.2. This document is the source for Li Xinchuan's entry at *Yaolu* 178.2940.

27 *SCBMHB* 89.1a–7a, 98.6a–9a.

28 *SCBMHB* 98.6a–9a; for the corresponding passage in the standard edition see *Bei shou jianwen lu*, 186–87.

29 *SCBMHB* 98.7a; *Sanchao beimeng huibian* (Siku quanshu ed.), 98.8a.

30 *Songyin wen ji* 26.2a; *QSW* 191:4201.24.

31 See Li Feng, "Lun Bei Song 'bu sha shidafu,'" 34. Yang Haiwen, "'Song Taizu shibei' de wenxian ditu," 141, conveniently assembles all the textual variants.

32 The 1127 memorial text and the standard *Bei shou jianwen lu* text reinforce this meaning by writing 故七聖相襲，未嘗輒易.

33 For the tense relations between Huizong and the Qinzong court after Huizong's abdication, see Ebrey, *Huizong*, 434–48.

34 *Huizhu lu* Houlu 1.69; *Yaolu* 4.114. The passage at *Huang Song zhongxing liang chao shengzheng* 1.3b also occurs verbatim in *Songshi quanwen* 16A.873. The relationship of this passage to Li Xinchuan's treatment at *Yaolu* 4.114 is a complex problem and will be discussed later.

35 *Huizhu lu* Houlu 1.69.

36 Li Feng, "Lun Bei Song 'bu sha shidafu,'" 34.

37 Wang Zengyu, "Cheng hu she shu" 571–95.

38 Li and Hartman, "A Newly Discovered Inscription," 387–448.

39 For the texts in Cao Xun's collected works, see *Songyin wen ji* 29.1a–4b; *QSW* 191:4206.102–6.

40 Wang Yu, "'Zhongxing ruiying tu' yanjiu," 2–17. For an exhaustive study of the scroll, its versions, and its sources see Murray, "Ts'ao Hsün," which first established the date of the painting. For a recent study see Deng Xiaonan, "Tuhua zuopin yu Songdai zhengzhishi yanjiu," 624–27. Deng notes differences in the text of Cao Xun's preface, as recorded on the painting and in his collected works, and suggests that Cao Si may have softened his father's original language. Another painting, *Welcoming the Imperial Carriage* (Yingluan tu), depicts the return of Empress Wei, Gaozong's mother, in 1142. The emperor commissioned the painting and presented it to Cao Xun after the peace treaty to commemorate his efforts toward her release. Later in life, Cao composed a preface and ten prose-poems that narrated his recollection of those historical events. He inscribed seven

of these poems on the scroll after the painting and passed the scroll to his descendants as a private, family heirloom. For the texts see *Songyin wen ji* 1.1a–5a. Cao Xun's inscription and the subsequent colophons on *Welcoming the Imperial Carriage* became detached from the painting sometime in the past. Xu Bangda, "'Songren hua Renwu gushi' ying ji 'Yingluan tu' kao," 61–63, identified the unknown subject of a painting in the Shanghai Museum as *Welcoming the Imperial Carriage*. Murray, "A Southern Sung Painting Regains Its Memory," 109–24, linked the painting with its inscriptions, which are now in a private collection in Japan. For Murray's recent views on both paintings see Murray, *Mirror of Morality*, 82–84.

41 For more detailed synopses see Murray, "Ts'ao Hsün," 1–3.

42 Li Tianming, "Ruiying tu de gushi," 18–29.

43 Bickford, "Huizong's Paintings."

44 *Songyin wen ji* 29.1a–b; *QSW* 191:4206.102–3.

45 Deng Xiaonan, "Guanyu 'nima du Kangwang,'" 101–8; for Gaozong's diplomatic offensive against Liu Yu see Cho-ying Li and Charles Hartman, "Primary Sources for Song History," 318–33.

46 *Xianchun Lin'an zhi* 13.16a–18b; *Zhuzi yulei* 127.3056–57; *Chaoye zaji* Jia 2.81; Deng Xiaonan, "Guanyu 'nima du Kang wang,'" 107–8.

47 Deng Xiaonan, "Guanyu 'nima du Kangwang,'" 105, citing *Yaolu* 6.155.

48 *Yaolu* 93.1548–49.

49 Jing Xinqiang, "Cao Xun *Bei shou jianwen lu* zhiyi," argues that Cao Xun's account of his transmission of the collar edict is accurate history, but that Cao fabricated the additional "messages" from Huizong and the empresses, especially Empress Wei's account of the omens, at a much later date to ingratiate himself with Gaozong.

50 Among the Four Sages were the Black Killer (Heisha) and the Perfected Warrior (Zhenwu). In addition to their role as dynastic protectors, both deities were the objects of Daoist exorcistic cults that were popular, especially in military circles, in South China during the twelfth century. See Davis, *Society and the Supernatural*, 67–86.

51 *SS* 33.631. Li Xinchuan (*Chaoye zaji* Jia 2.81) notes that the empress financed the shrine. Zhang Duanyi (*Gui'er ji* 1.4) records that the empress brought back pictures of the deities from the north and ordered the eunuch Zhang Quwei to build the shrine within the inner palace. But Qin Gui objected that lavish religious installations had caused the fall of Northern Song and insisted on a simple, public structure on West Lake.

52 *SCBMHB* 90.5a–b; *QSW* 122:2636.202.

53 *SCBMHB* 92.8a; for a discussion of the two passages, especially the latter as an explication of the former, see Deng, "Guanyu 'nima du Kangwang,'" 104–5.

54 *SCBMHB* 92.8b–9a.

55 Both the submission memorial and the preface survive at *SCBMHB* 165.6b–9a; *QSW* 138:2969.18–19, 2970.24–25; see also Chen Lesu, "*Sanchao beimeng huibian* kao," 294–95.

56 *Yaolu* 93.1548–49.

57 Cai Chongbang, *Songdai xiushi zhidu yanjiu*, 44–45, 104–5; Hartman, "The Reluctant Historian," 101–12.

58 *Xu Zizhi tongjian changbian jishi benmo* 150.3b; *Xu Zizhi tongjian changbian shibu* 60.1909. Li Xinchuan's commentary at *Yaolu* 4.103, which contains the date 1127/4/9,

confirms that this passage derived ultimately from the *Qinzong shilu*, and that Li Tao took it from that source into the *Changbian*.

59 On the court history office under Qin Gui see Hartman, "The Making of a Villain," 69–72.

60 *Zhongxing xiaoli*, printed as *Zhongxing xiao ji* 1.5; *Huangchao zhongxing jishi benmo* 1a.6b. Neither mentions the two-graph edict or Taizu's oath.

61 *Zhongxing liang chao biannian gangmu* 1.4a, a popular abridgment of the *Long Draft*, continues the same wording and chronological placement.

62 *Yaolu* 4.113–14.

63 *Yaolu* 4.95. Li Xinchuan does, however, record the arrival of Zheng An, a messenger bearing a note from Qinzong written in blood.

64 *Yaolu* 4.103. For the Li Gang text, see his *Jianyan jintui zhi* 3.81. Li Gang's memoir seems the textual origin of the entry at *SCBMHB* 111.1a–b where Gaozong reveals the collar to his court officials. The *Huibian*, however, dates this event to 1127/7/7, before Li Gang's arrival in Yingtian on 1127/7/11.

65 *Yaolu* 4.113–14. Li Xinchuan begins his entry with the phrase 過河十餘日, which differs slightly from the surviving *Record of Experiences in Northern Captivity* versions. This identical phrase, however, also occurs in *Huang Song zhongxiang liang chao shengzheng* 1.3b and in the subsequent *Songshi quanwen* 16A.873, which both contain a shortened version of Li Xinchuan's account. As Liang Taiji has pointed out, the present text of the *Huang Song zhongxiang liang chao shengzheng* is a reworking by a commercial bookseller of the official *shengzheng* for the Gaozong and Xiaozong reigns. During this process, the anonymous editor inserted many entries from the *Chronological Record* into the official *shengzheng*. Therefore, although the *Gaozong shengzheng* was completed in 1166, I am inclined to believe that this passage was not part of the original *shengzheng*, but originated with Li Xinchuan in 1208. See Liang Taiji, "*Shengzheng* jinben fei yuanben zhi jiu xiangbian," 314–20.

66 *Huizhu lu* Houlu 1.69. Wang Mingqing seems to have known Cao Xun personally and probably obtained a copy of the *Record of Experiences in Northern Captivity* from him. Another passage at *Huizhu lu* Houlu 2.71 cites Cao Xun as the source for the omen stories about Empress Wei and the Four Sages and her augury at the chess board; Wang's language closely tracts the text of the *Record of Experiences in Northern Captivity*.

67 Kong Xue, "*Jianyan yilai xinian yaolu* zhushu shijian kao," 53–56.

68 *Yaolu* 4.112–13; Du Wenyu, "Song Taizu shibei zhiyi," 22.

69 Li and Hartman, "A Newly Discovered Inscription," 417–26.

70 *Chaoye zaji* Yi 3.545–46; cf. Liu Pujiang, "Zuzong zhi fa," 156; Deng Xiaonan, *Zuzong zhi fa*, 474–76. In his detailed rebuttal to the emperor's threat, the chief councilor Shi Hao, referencing Taizu, emphasizes that "no-kill" is fundamental to the Song "policies of the founders" (*zuzong zhi jiafa*). However, he views the policy not as a Song innovation, but, quoting *Mencius*, as an embrace of ideal administrative principles that originated in antiquity. Since these were abandoned in Qin and Han, their reemergence in Song thus constitutes a return to antiquity. Despite its direct relevance to his theme, Shi Hao does not mention Taizu's oath; see *Maofeng zhenyin manlu* 10.9a–12a.

71 *Bishu manchao* 6; *Shuofu* 39.9a–10a; Djang and Djang, *A Compilation of Anecdotes of Song Personalities*, 10–11.

72 Liu Pujiang, "Zuzong zhi fa," 150–51 presents full details.

73 *Bishu manchao*, 6–7; *Tiewei shan congtan* 1.18–19.

74 *Peiwei zhai ji* 17.10b.

75 Liu Pujiang, "Zuzong zhi fa," 152.

76 Li Feng, "Song Taizu shiyue 'bu zhu dachen, yanguan' xinlun," 61–62.

77 Liu Pujiang, "Zuzong zhi fa," 151; Zhang Xiqing, "Song Taizu 'bu zhu dachen, yanguan' shiyue kaolun," 50.

78 For a helpful list, see Zhang Xiqing, "Song Taizu 'bu zhu dachen, yanguan' shiyue kaolun," 53.

79 Cao Xun's account would seem to argue against the existence of an oath stele in Kaifeng. Cao does not mention a stele, only a "covenant" whose format he does not specify. In addition, as Du Wenyu, "Song Taizu shibei zhiyi," 20, points out, after the Jurchen departure from Kaifeng, Song armies still controlled the city. Gaozong sent envoys there in 1127/7 to retrieve items from the ancestral temple, and they returned two months later with no report of the stele, which supposedly had been open for public inspection for over six months.

80 CB 145.3499, 480.11416–17. Li Feng, "Lun Bei Song 'bu sha shidafu,'" 31–32; cf. Deng Xiaonan, *Zuzong zhi fa*, 527–28. Zhang Xiqing, "Song Taizu 'bu zhu dachen, yanguan' shiyue kaolun," 51–53 collects fifteen similar passages from Song sources, seven from Northern Song; see also Yang Haiwen, "'Song Taizu shibei' de wenxian ditu," 142–45.

81 See for example *Jingkang yaolu jianzhu* 2.251, 322.

82 See for example 挂冠說, dated 1165, at *Songyin wen ji* 37.3b–4a; *QSW* 264:4204.72–73.

83 Kobayashi Akira, "Nansō Neisōchō ni okeru Shi Bien seiken no seiritsu to so no igi," 35–64. For a detailed study of the submission of the *Chronological Record* see Liang Taiji, "*Xinian yaolu, Chaoye zaji* de qiyi jishu ji qi chengyin," 200–205.

84 SS 379.1700–01; *Yaolu* 4.113–14, 87.1443, 141.2276. 142.2291, 144.2313, 145.2332, 182.3023, and 183.3053.

85 Cai Chongbang, *Songdai xiushi zhidu yanjiu*, 107–8, 138–39.

REFERENCES

PRIMARY SOURCES

Bei shou jianwen lu 北狩見聞錄 [Record of experiences in northern captivity], by Cao Xun 曹勳 (1098–1174). Quan Song biji ed. Zhengzhou: Daxiang chubanshe, 2008.

Bishu manchao 避暑漫抄 [Random notes made in summer], by Lu You 陸游 (1125–1210). Congshu jicheng ed.

Gongkui ji 攻媿集, by Lou Yue 樓鑰 (1137–1213). Siku quanshu ed.

Gui'er ji 貴耳集, by Zhang Duanyi 張端義 (1179–1235?). Beijing: Zhonghua shuju, 1958.

Huang Song zhongxing liang chao shengzheng 皇宋中興兩朝聖政. Taibei: Wenhai chubanshe, 1967.

Huangchao zhongxing jishi benmo 皇朝中興紀事本末, by Xiong Ke 熊克 (1111?–1189?). Beijing: Beijing tushuguan chubanshe, 2005.

Huizhu lu 揮麈錄 [Records of one who wields the chowry], by Wang Mingqing 王明清 (1127–1215?). Beijing: Zhonghua shuju, 1961.

Jingkang yaolu jianzhu 靖康要錄箋注, by Wang Zao 汪藻 (1079–1154). Chengdu: Sichuan daxue chubanshe, 2008.

Jianyan jintui zhi 建炎進退志, by Li Gang 李綱 (1083–1140). Quan Song biji ed. Zhengzhou: Daxiang chubanshe, 2008.

Jianyan yilai chaoye zaji 建炎以來朝野雜記, by Li Xinchuan 李心傳 (1166–1243). Beijing: Zhonghua shuju, 2000.

Jianyan yilai xinian yaolu 建炎以來繫年要錄 [Chronological record of events since 1127], by Li Xinchuan 李心傳 (1166–1243). Beijing: Zhonghua shuju, 1988.

Maofeng zhenyin manlu 鄮峯真隱漫錄, by Shi Hao 史浩 (1106–1194). Siku quanshu ed.

Peiwei zhai ji 佩韋齋集, by Yu Delin 俞德鄰 (1232–1293). Siku quanshu ed.

Qi dong ye yu 齊東野語, by Zhou Mi 周密 (1232–1308). Beijing: Zhonghua shuju, 1983.

Qinding Siku quanshu zongmu 欽定四庫全書總目, by Ji Yun 紀昀 (1724–1805). Beijing: Zhonghua shuju, 1997.

Quan Song wen 全宋文, ed. Zeng Zaozhuang 曾棗莊 et al. Shanghai: Shanghai Cishu chubanshe, 2006.

Rizhi lu 日知錄, by Gu Yanwu 顧炎武 (1613–1682). Siku quanshu ed.

Sanchao beimeng huibian 三朝北盟會編, by Xu Mengxin 徐夢莘 (1126–1207). Shanghai: Shanghai guji chubanshe reprint of 1908 edition, 2008; also Siku quanshu ed.

Shuofu 說郛, by Tao Zongyi 陶宗儀 (14th century). Shuofu sanzhong 說郛三種 ed. Shanghai: Shanghai guji chubanshe, 1988.

Song huiyao jigao 宋會要輯稿, edited by Xu Song 徐松 (1781–1848) et al. Beijing: Zhonghua shuju, 1957.

Song huiyao jigao bubian 宋會要輯稿補編, compiled by Xu Song 徐松 (1781–1848) et al. Beijing: Xinhua shudian, 1988.

Song lun 宋論, by Wang Fuzhi 王夫之 (1619–1692). Beijing: Zhonghua shuju, 1964.

Song shi 宋史, edited by Tuo Tuo 脫脫 (1313–1355) et al. Beijing: Zhonghua shuju, 1977.

Songshi quanwen 宋史全文. Harbin: Heilongjiang renmin chubanshe, 2004.

Songyin wen ji 松隱文集, by Cao Xun 曹勳 (1098–1174). Songji zhenben congkan ed.

Tiewei shan congtan 鐵圍山從談 [Conversations from iron enclosure mountain], by Cai Tiao 蔡絛 (12th century). Beijing: Zhonghua shuju, 1983.

Xianchun Lin'an zhi 咸淳臨安志, edited by Qian Yueyou 潛說友. Song Yuan difang zhi congshu 宋元地方志叢書 ed. Taipei: Dahua shuju, 1987.

Xu Zizhi tongjian changbian jishi benmo 續資治通鑑長編紀事本末, by Yang Zhongliang 楊仲良 (13th century). Taibei: Wenhai chubanshe, 1967.

Xu Zizhi tongjian changbian shibu 續資治通鑑長編拾補, by Huang Yizhou 黃以周 (1828–1899) et al. Beijing: Zhonghua shuju, 2004.

Zhizhai shulu jieti 直齋書錄解題, by Chen Zhensun 陳振孫 (fl. 1211–1249). Shanghai: Shanghai guji chubanshe, 1987.

Zhongxing liang chao biannian gangmu 中興兩朝編年綱目. Zhonghua zaizao shanben ed. Beijing: Beijing tushuguan chubanshe, 2006.

Zhongxing xiaoli 中興小曆, printed as Zhongxing xiao ji 中興小紀, by Xiong Ke 熊克 (1111?–1189?). Fuzhou: Fujian renmin chubanshe, 1984.

Zhuzi yulei 朱子語類 [Conversations of Zhu Xi], by Zhu Xi 朱熹 (1130–1200). Beijing: Zhonghua shuju, 1994.

SECONDARY SOURCES

Bickford, Maggie. "Huizong's Paintings: Art and the Art of Emperorship." In *Emperor Huizong and Late Northern Song Culture: The Politics of Culture and the Culture of Politics*, edited by Patricia Buckley Ebrey and Maggie Bickford, 453–513. Cambridge, Mass.: Harvard University Asia Center, 2006.

Cai Chongbang 蔡崇榜. *Songdai xiushi zhidu yanjiu* 宋代修史制度研究. Taibei: Wenjin chubanshe, 1993.

Chen Lesu 陳樂素. "*Sanchao beimeng huibian kao*" 《三朝北盟会编》考. *Lishi yuyan yanjiusuo jikan* 6, no. 2 (1936): 193–341.

Davis, Edward L. *Society and the Supernatural in Song China*. Honolulu: University of Hawai'i Press, 2001.

Deng Xiaonan 鄧小南. "Guanyu 'nima du Kangwang'" 關于'泥馬渡康王'. *Beijing daxue xuebao* (1995.6): 101–8.

———. "Tuhua zuopin yu Songdai zhengzhishi yanjiu" 圖畫作品與宋代政治史研究. In *Yudi, kaogu yu shixue xinshuo: Li Xiaocong jiaoshou rongxiu jinian lunwenji* 輿地、考古與史學新說: 李孝聰 教授榮休紀念論文集, edited by Beijing daxue Zhongguo gudaishi yanjiu zhongxin, 615–27. Beijing: Zhonghua shuju, 2012.

———. *Zuzong zhi fa* 祖宗之法. Beijing: Sanlian shudian, 2006.

Djang, Chu, and Jane C. Djang. *A Compilation of Anecdotes of Song Personalities*. New York: St. John's University Press, 1989.

Du Wenyu 杜文玉. "Song Taizu shibei zhiyi" 宋太祖誓碑質疑. *Henan daxue xuebao* (1986.1): 19–22.

Ebrey, Patricia. *Emperor Huizong*. Cambridge, Mass.: Harvard University Press, 2014.

Fu Xuancong 傅璇琮. *Song dengkeji kao* 宋登科記考, edited by Gong Yanming and Hui Zu. Nanjing: Jiangsu jiaoyu chubanshe, 2009.

Gu Hongyi 顧宏義. "Yue Fei zhi si yu Song Taizu 'bu sha dachen' shiyue kao" 岳飛之死與宋太祖'不殺大臣'誓約考. *Huadong shifan daxue xuebao* 33, no. 1 (Jan. 2001): 114–16.

Hartman, Charles. "The Making of a Villain: Ch'in Kuei and *Tao-hsüeh*." *Harvard Journal of Asiatic Studies* 58, no. 1 (1998): 59–146.

———. "The Reluctant Historian: Sun Ti, Chu Hsi, and the Fall of Northern Sung." *T'oung pao* 89 (2003): 100–48.

———. "Zhu Xi and His World." *Journal of Song-Yuan Studies* 36 (2006): 107–31.

Ho Koon-wan 何冠環. "Xiancun de san pian Songdai neichen muzhiming" 現存的三篇宋代內臣墓誌銘. *Zhongguo wenhua yanjiusuo xuebao* 52 (Jan. 2012): 33–63.

Jing Xinqiang 景新強. "Cao Xun *Bei shou jianwen lu* zhiyi: Jian bian *Siku tiyao* zhi wu" 曹勳《北狩見聞錄》質疑: 兼辨《四庫提要》之誤. *Xibei daxue xuebao* 40, no. 3 (May 2010): 47–50.

Kobayashi Akira 小林晃. "Nansō Neisōchō ni okeru Shi Bien seiken no seiritsu to so no igi" 南宋寧宗朝における史彌遠政権の成立とその意義. *Tōyō gakuhō* 91, no. 1 (2009): 35–64.

Kong Xue 孔學. "*Jianyan yilai xinian yaolu* zhushu shijian kao" 《建炎以來繫年要錄》著述時間考. *Henan daxue xuebao* 36, no. 1 (Jan. 1996): 53–56.

Li, Cho-ying, and Charles Hartman. "A Newly Discovered Inscription by Qin Gui: Its

Implications for the History of Song *Daoxue*." *Harvard Journal of Asiatic Studies* 70, no. 2 (2010): 387–448.

———. "Primary Sources for Song History in the Collected Works of Wu Ne." *Journal of Song-Yuan Studies* 41 (2011): 295–341.

Li Feng 李峰. "Lun Bei Song 'bu sha shidafu'" 論北宋'不殺士大夫'. *Shixue yuekan* (2005.12): 31–35.

———. "Song Taizu shiyue 'bu zhu dachen, yanguan' xinlun: Jian yu Zhang Xiqing, Liu Pujiang deng xiansheng shangque" 宋太祖誓約'不誅大臣、言官'新論: 兼與張希清、劉浦江等先生商榷. *Shilin* 137 (2012): 53–63.

Li Tianming 李天鳴. "Ruiying tu de gushi 瑞應圖的故事. In *Wenyi Shaoxing: Nan Song yishu yu wenhua. Tushu juan* 文藝紹興: 南宋藝術與文化. 圖書卷, edited by Li Tianming, 18–29. Taibei: Guoli gugong bowuyuan, 2010.

Liang Taiji 梁太濟. "*Shengzheng* jinben fei yuanben zhi jiu xiangbian" 《聖政》今本非原本之舊詳辨. In *Tang Song lishi wenxian yanjiu conggao* 唐宋歷史文獻研究叢稿 by Liang Taiji, 311–41. Shanghai: Shanghai guji chubanshe, 2004.

———. "*Xinian yaolu, Chaoye zaji* de qiyi jishu ji qi chengyin" 《繫年要錄》、《朝野雜記》的岐異記述及其成因. In *Tang Song lishi wenxian yanjiu conggao* 唐宋歷史文獻研究叢稿 by Liang Taiji, 171–205. Shanghai: Shanghai guji chubanshe, 2004.

Liu Pujiang 劉浦江. "Zuzong zhi fa: Zai lun Song Taizu shiyue ji shibei" 祖宗之法: 再論宋太祖誓約及誓碑. *Wenshi* 92 (2010.3): 145–58.

Murray, Julia K. *Mirror of Morality: Chinese Narrative Illustration and Confucian Ideology.* Honolulu: University of Hawai'i Press, 2007.

———. "A Southern Sung Painting Regains Its Memory." *Journal of Sung-Yuan Studies* 22 (1990–92): 109–24.

———. "Ts'ao Hsün and Two Southern Sung History Scrolls." *Ars Orientalis* 15 (1985): 1–29.

Wang Yu 王瑀. "'Zhongxing ruiying tu' yanjiu" '中興瑞應圖'研究. Master's thesis, Zhongyang meishu xueyuan, 2012.

Wang Zengyu 王曾瑜. "'Cheng hu she shu': Song Gaozong shi de huanguan yu yiguan Wang Jixian" '城狐社鼠': 宋高宗時的宦官與醫官王繼先. In *Yue Fei he Nan Song qianqi zhengzhi yu junshi yanjiu* 岳飛和南宋前期政治與軍事研究, edited by Wang Zengyu, 571–95. Kaifeng: Henan daxue chubanshe, 2002.

Xu Bangda 徐邦達. "'Songren hua Renwu gushi' ying ji 'Yingluan tu' kao" '宋人畫人物故事' 應即'迎鑾圖'考. *Wenwu* (Aug. 1972): 61–67.

Xu Gui 徐規. "Song Taizu shiyue bianxi" 宋太祖誓約辨析. In *Yangsu ji* 仰素集, edited by Xu Gui, 589–92. Hangzhou: Hangzhou daxue chubanshe, 1999.

Yang Haiwen 楊海文. "'Song Taizu shibei' de wenxian ditu" '宋太祖誓碑'的文獻地圖. *Xueshu yuekan* 42, no .10 (Oct. 2010): 138–47.

Yu Yingshi 余英時. *Zhu Xi de lishi shijie* 朱熹的歷史世界. Taibei: Yunchen wenhua gongsi, 2003.

Zhang Bangwei 張邦煒. "Bubi meihua Zhao Song wangchao—Songdai dingfenglun xianyi" 不必美化趙宋王朝: 宋代頂峰論獻疑. *Sichuan shifan daxue xuebao* 38, no. 6 (Nov. 2011): 130–43.

Zhang Qifan 張其凡. "'Huangdi yu shidafu gongzhi tianxia' shixi—Bei Song zhengzhi jiagou tanwei" "皇帝與士大夫共治天下"試析: 北宋政治架構探微. *Jinan xuebao* 23, no. 6 (Nov. 2001): 114–23.

Zhang Xiqing 張希清. "Song Taizu 'bu zhu dachen, yanguan' shiyue kaolun" 宋太祖 '不誅大臣、言官'誓約考論. *Wen shi zhe* 329 (2012.2): 46–56.

Zhang Yinlin 張蔭麟. "Song Taizu shibei ji zhengshi tang keshi kao" 宋太祖誓碑及政事堂刻石考. *Wenshi zazhi* 1, no. 7 (Jan. 1941): 14–18.

Zhu Shangshu 祝尚書. *Songji xuba huibian*宋集序跋彙編. Beijing: Zhonghua shu, 2010.

———. *Songren bieji xulu* 宋人別集敘錄. Beijing: Zhonghua shuju, 1999.

PART 2

The Literati and the Political System

3 Governing a Multicentered Empire

Prefects and Their Networks in the 1040s and 1210s

SONG CHEN

AFTER A SERIES OF SUCCESSFUL UNIFICATION CAMPAIGNS between 963 and 979, the Song territory more than doubled while the population under its control tripled. To effectively govern this newly expanded territory presented a challenge. In the earliest years, Song rulers met this challenge in two ways. They sent trusted men from their entourage across the new empire to govern metropolitan prefectures of the conquered states, while at the same time, forced former officials and even local militia leaders of those states to relocate to the Song capital where many of them were recruited into the Song bureaucracy. Lü Yuqing (927–976), for example, had been on the personal staff of Zhao Kuangyin (Taizu, r. 960–976) while Zhao was still a military governor in the Zhou state (951–959). For many years, Lü had followed Zhao when he was transferred from one province to another. When Zhao Kuangyin proclaimed his new dynasty, Lü became the first governor of its capital, Kaifeng. In subsequent years, he was made the first governor of Tan prefecture and then Chengdu and also the second governor of Jiangling, following the Song conquest of the regimes in Middle Yangzi and Sichuan.[1] Likewise, Pan Mei (921–987), a long-time confidant of Taizu, was made the first governor of Guang prefecture and Taiyuan after the annexation of the Southern (917–971) and Northern Han (951–979) states.[2] At the same time, royal families, bureaucrats, and even local militia leaders of southern states were escorted to Kaifeng on the orders of Song rulers.[3] Many of them established their new residence there and entered the service of the new dynasty.[4] Qian Chu (929–988), the last ruler of Wuyue (907–978), was sent to Kaifeng with his clansmen and officials after his surrender and appointed governor of Deng in 987.[5] Similarly, Meng Xuanzhe (938–992), heir of the last Shu (934–965) ruler, moved to Kaifeng and held a number of governorships in North China and Huainan.[6] In the early decades of the Song, therefore, mandatory relocations combined with career opportunities in the new dynasty remolded the political families of the northern and southern states into a political elite based in North China, especially the Song capital region.

When the civil service examinations expanded under Taizong (r. 976–997), they seemed primarily a tool for this elite to perpetuate itself by participating in a shared culture. Descendants of these North China families, including those of former officials in the southern states who now lived in the Song capital region, entered the civil service in large numbers through these examinations.[7] By the time of Meng Xuanzhe's death in 992, for example, four of his eleven adult sons had passed the *jinshi* examination, and six others had become palace attendants and servitors presumably through the *yin* privilege.[8] North China men made up about 84% of the *jinshi* graduates between 960 and 997. They dominated finance and policy offices as well as the prefectural governorship of Hang in the first two reigns of the Song.[9]

In contrast, the examinations in these decades offered little opportunity for men from less prominent backgrounds still residing in South China. South China men made up only about 16% of the *jinshi* conferred in the first two reigns of the Song. Opportunities only began to increase after the ascension of Zhenzong (r. 997–1022). In his reign, South China's share of *jinshi* nearly doubled.[10] The fact that Kou Zhun (961–1023) was said to have stubbornly favored northerners, probably in part due to his animosity with the southern man Ding Wei (966–1037), nevertheless attests to the growing influence of southerners at Zhenzong's court.[11]

The increasing number of southern men in Song government seems to have built the momentum for more significant changes in Renzong's reign (1022–1063), which saw repeated efforts to make educational resources and political opportunities more available outside the capital and especially in the south. Quotas for prefectural examinations were expanded for Sichuan in 1029 and for various regions across south China in 1060.[12] At the same time, many local officials set up government schools in the 1020s and 1030s.[13] During the Qingli reform (1043–1045), the court required that government schools be established in all prefectures and also in counties with a sizable population of students.[14] As a result, 41% of prefectural schools and 20% of county schools known from the Song period were established or restored in Renzong's reign.[15] They coincided with an unprecedented southern success in the examinations and a steep decline in the proportion of North China men holding policy, finance, and prefect offices.[16] Those who passed examinations in this period were not necessarily beneficiaries of government-financed education, but the decisions to expand examination quotas and finance education outside the capital clearly signaled a general interest in the leadership in expanding political participation beyond those already residing in the capital region. New agricultural technologies, rivalry between states, expansion of maritime trade, and the arrival of new immigrants, including the educated elites who fled the chaos in North China, spurred southern development in the late Tang and the Five Dynasties period. By the tenth century the "south" was no longer a single area centered on the Lower Yangzi Delta, but had developed multiple centers of culture and power.[17] With the scope of political participation broadened in the eleventh century, the political implications of these developments began to surface.

The rising number of southern men in Song civil service brought far more than a change in the composition of the Song political elite. It also led to new career patterns and marriage practices that made the political elite after the mid-eleventh century significantly different from that of Tang and early Song.[18] These changes are evident in the two cohorts of prefects examined here: those who were in office between 1040 and 1049 and those between 1210 and 1219. These two decades were chosen for both practical and methodological reasons. On the practical side, admittedly, to expand the universe of the study to the entire Song period demands significantly more time and energy for collecting new datasets and cleaning existing ones. Methodologically, comparing two discrete periods highlights the most salient aspects of historical change, which may then be built on in future studies.

The cohorts of the 1040s and the 1210s are particularly suited for a comparative study. The 1040s cohort of prefects, who on average received their appointments to prefect governorship at the age of fifty-two, entered government service largely around 1020. They were therefore the generation who served at a time when southerners had become a notable presence in Song officialdom while northerners remained predominant. Those in the 1210s, in contrast, represent the Song political elite at the close of the dynasty but before the impacts of Mongol invasions were felt. Moreover, the *Song Biographical Index* (Songren zhuanji ziliao suoyin) also reports a more impressive corpus of surviving biographical material for prefects of these decades than most of the other periods.[19]

This chapter draws from several major sources of data. It begins with the dated rosters of prefects compiled by Li Zhiliang and recently digitized by the editorial group of the China Biographical Database (CBDB) project.[20] The CBDB is also a major data source on kinship and migration. The list of prefects who served under the Song in the 1040s and the 1210s, first compiled from the rosters of Li Zhiliang, was then checked against the CBDB for data on kinship relations and places of affiliation.[21] This is supplemented further by kinship and migration data from a third source, my own database built from a nearly exhaustive collection of funerary biographies on Sichuan men and women in the Song period.[22] The combined dataset from the three sources was checked for internal consistency and identified problems were corrected before the following analysis.[23]

REGIONAL ORIGINS OF THE PREFECTS

Any effort to decide where a prefect hailed from is difficult, because Song officials were a highly mobile group. Since the goal of this chapter is to understand the political opportunities afforded to men living in different parts of the Song, an official's place of origin is defined here as the place he most likely considered "home" in his formative years prior to his entry to government service, rather than the family's remote ancestral seat or addresses the official moved to later on in his career. The place of origin under this definition was where his parents maintained a primary residence, which is determined on the basis of several factors, in particular, careers and burial sites of his recent ancestors.

I start with places of affiliation registered in the CBDB and update them with data on the family history of office holding and migration gleaned from surviving funerary biographies for the prefects or their close relatives and biographies in the dynastic history. Unless explicitly mentioned in the biographical materials, it is assumed that a family relocated in the generation that started a new gravesite away from its former address. This new address is regarded as the "home" of subsequent generations.

A study of the regional origins of these two cohorts of prefects reveals a considerable proportion of men from various southern regions in Song prefectural administration, though it also confirms the continuing dominance of northerners well into the mid-eleventh century.[24] As table 3.1a shows, the northerners monopolized prefectural governorships in the 1040s as much as, if not more strongly than, they did high policymaking and financial positions in the central government. The regional origin can be identified for 328 of the 511 prefects serving between 1040 and 1049. Of these 328 officials, 60% were from two physiographic macroregions of North and Northwest China.[25] Men from Kaifeng alone accounted for over 16% of the national total. Together with those from Henan, Zheng, Xu (Yingchang), and Yingtian prefectures,

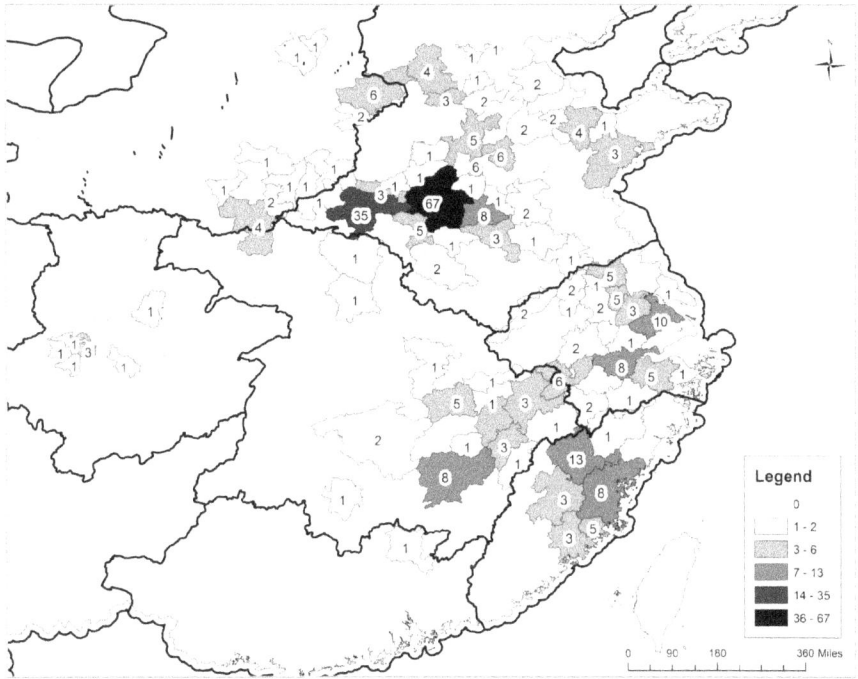

MAP 3.1A. Prefects in the 1040s cohort by home prefecture. Prefectural boundaries in this map are based on Robert Hartwell's "China Historical Studies" GIS datasets, published by the China Historical GIS project (www.fas.harvard.edu/~chgis/data/hartwell/). They are an approximation of Northern Song prefectural boundaries ca. 1080. Thus, for example, the numbers of prefects in our 1040s cohort from Kaifeng (54) and Zheng (13) are aggregated in this map, because Zheng prefecture was abolished into Kaifeng between 1072 and 1085. Thick lines indicate boundaries of G. William Skinner's physiographic macroregions.

men living in the five prefectures along this narrow corridor comprising the principal Song capital with its two auxiliary ones (henceforth, the Capital Corridor) constituted more than one-third (35%) of all prefects in the 1040s, or 59% of the northern-born prefects (table 3.1a). The domination of the Capital Corridor is equally pronounced when the length of term is considered. Men from these prefectures claimed 36% of the total office-years of the prefectural governorship in the 1040s (table 3.1b). Outside this Capital Corridor, by contrast, no prefecture in the north contributed more than six prefects to the cohort.[26]

The ancestral origin of the North China men and their migratory paths will be the subject of a further study. But a cursory inspection of the list reveals a large number of descendants of early Song political elite which

TABLE 3.1A. Regional origin of prefects in the 1040s and 1210s

Physiographic Macroregion	Prefects, 1040–1049		Prefects, 1210–1219	
	No.	%	No.	%
North China	177	54	—	—
Capital Corridor†	*115*	*35*	*—*	*—*
Northwest China	21	6	—	—
Lower Yangzi	58	18	117	42
Grand Canal Band‡	*36*	*11*	*48*	*17*
Coastal Stretch§	*42*	*13*	*169*	*61*
Southeast Coast	33	10	97	35
Middle Yangzi	30	9	41	15
Gan Basin‖	*21*	*6*	*31*	*11*
Upper Yangzi	8	2	22	8
Lingnan	1	0	2	1
Total	328 (183)*	100	279 (255)*	100

Notes: * The number of prefects whose regional origin cannot be identified is in parentheses.

† The Capital Corridor comprises five prefectures in the Song capital region: Henan, Zheng, Xu, Kaifeng, and Yingtian.

‡ The Grand Canal Band comprises a total of seven prefectures, including six along the southern segment of the Grand Canal (Yang, Run, Chang, Su, Xiu, and Hang) and one (Yue) on the Grand Canal's extension.

§ The Coastal Stretch includes ten coastal prefectures (Su, Xiu, Hang, Yue, Ming, Tai, Wen, Fu, Xinghua, and Quan) and two of their inland neighbors (Wu and Hu). Note that although the Coastal Stretch is listed here under the Lower Yangzi macroregion for convenience, it spans two physiographic macroregions, including seven prefectures from the Lower Yangzi and five from the Southeast Coast. Note also that there is an overlap of four prefectures (Su, Xiu, Hang, and Yue) between the Grand Canal Band and the Coastal Stretch.

‖ The Gan Basin includes six prefectures: Ji, Fu, Linjiang, Hong, Rao, and Nankang.

Taizu and Taizong helped mold shortly after the conquest. As far as we can tell from the surviving sources, close to half of the prefects (58 of 115) from the Capital Corridor had a family tradition of officeholding predating the Song conquest. Thirty-seven of them had fathers, grandfathers, or great-grandfathers who served in one or more of the Five Dynasties, while

TABLE 3.1B. Regional origin of prefects in the 1040s and 1210s (percentage of office-years)

Physiographic Macroregion	Prefects (% of office-years) (1040–1049)	Prefects (% of office-years) (1210–1219)	Policy† (% of offices) (1023–1063)	Finance† (% of office-years) (1014–1040)	Finance† (% of office-years) (1041–1067)
North China	57	—	51	48	46
Capital Corridor	36	—	—	—	—
Northwest China	6	—	9	12	7
Lower Yangzi	18	41	15	17	22
Grand Canal Band	12	16	—	—	—
Coastal Stretch	12	59	—	—	—
Southeast Coast	8	32	9	11	8
Middle Yangzi	9	17	10	8	11
Gan Basin	6	13	—	—	—
Upper Yangzi	2	10	6	4	7
Lingnan	0	1	1	1	0
Total Number of Offices or Office-Years	1793 (618)*	1116 (723)*	492	609	777

Notes: * Number of office-years for prefects whose regional origin cannot be identified is in parentheses.

† Data on policy-making and finance appointments are included from Hartwell, "Demographic, Political, and Social Transformations of China, 750–1550," 414–15, for comparison with office-holding patterns in prefectural administrations.

sixteen were descendants of rulers and officials in the southern states. Five others were from families which had served under the Kitans and the warlords of Hebei. Jia Changling (d. 1040), for example, descended from a prominent family that claimed to be natives of Hebei but resided in Kaifeng for many generations. His grandfather Yan was on the personal staff of Taizong and his great-grandfather Wei was a secretariat drafter in the Later Jin (936–947). By early Song the Jia had become a big descent group and produced many officials, including another prefect in our 1040s cohort.[27] Chen Yaozuo (963–1044), in contrast, was the son of Xinghua (939–1006), a Sichuan man and official of Later Shu who moved to Zheng and enlisted himself in the Song officialdom. All of Xinghua's three sons passed the civil service examinations under Taizong and Zhenzong, and two ranked first. Yaozuo and one of his brothers would eventually become grand councilors.[28] Likewise, Qian Yanyuan (994–1050) and his brother Mingyi (1015–1071) were members of the Wuyue royal family discussed earlier in this chapter. Their father Yi (*jinshi* of 999) and uncle Kun (*jinshi* of 992) placed high in the examinations.[29]

In sharp contrast with the north, no place in the south dominated the way the Capital Corridor did. Measured by the number of native sons each had in the 1040s cohort, the five most successful places in the south did not cluster at all, but were scattered across three different macroregions: Jian and Fu in the Southeast Coast claimed home to thirteen and eight of the 1040s prefects respectively, Su and Hang in Lower Yangzi claimed ten and eight respectively, and Ji in the Gan Basin of Middle Yangzi claimed another eight (map 3.1a). In the south, what comes closest to the Capital Corridor is a band of prefectures extending along the Grand Canal south of the Huai River: Yang, Run, Chang, Su, Hang, and Yue.[30] Together this Grand Canal Band of prefectures were home to the vast majority (62%) of prefects of Lower Yangzi origin, but they counted only for 28% of all southern-born prefects of the 1040s, or 11% of all prefects in the 1040s cohort whose geographical origin is identified. Although centuries of economic and cultural development in the Lower Yangzi Delta certainly contributed to this success, this distinctive geographical distribution suggests strongly the extended political influence of the Song capitals, to which the Grand Canal provided convenient access. In fact, the canal was a major waterway that also ran through most of the prefectures in the Capital Corridor.

Southern success in the 1040s, however, was largely limited to the east of the mountain ranges that formed the western and southern borders of Middle Yangzi, separating it from the Sichuan basin (Upper Yangzi) and

TABLE 3.2. Regional origin of southern-born prefects

Physiographic Macroregion	Prefects, 1040–1049		Prefects, 1210–1219	
	No.	%	No.	%
Lower Yangzi	58	48	117	42
Grand Canal Band	*36*	*28*	*48*	*17*
Coastal Stretch	*42*	*32*	*169*	*61*
Southeast Coast	33	25	97	35
Middle Yangzi	30	23	41	15
Gan Basin	*21*	*16*	*31*	*11*
Upper Yangzi	8	6	22	8
Lingnan	1	1	2	1
Total	130	100	279	100

Lingnan. Only a negligible fraction of the 1040s prefects claimed the latter two as home.

At first sight, this pattern of multicentered political success in South China seems to have continued into the early thirteenth century. The Lower Yangzi continued to contribute about 42% of the men who headed prefectural administration in the 1210s, roughly comparable to its share (48%) of southern-born prefects in the 1040s (table 3.2). The Southeast Coast gained considerably, much at the expense of the Middle Yangzi. This was largely the result of the extraordinary success gained by the two coastal prefectures of Tai and Wen (Rui'an) by the early thirteenth century. While they did not contribute any prefect in the 1040s, in the 1210s they together contributed thirty-three. The rest of the Southeast Coast, by comparison, in the 1210s contributed almost exactly the same share of southern-born prefects (23%) as it did in the 1040s (25%).

The remarkable achievements of Tai and Wen men in the 1210s signaled a new pattern of political success in the early thirteenth century, which favored coastal prefectures. This pattern was concealed by the apparent continuity in macroregional-level statistics, because the rise and fall of fortunes between the 1040s and 1210s often occurred *within* macroregional borders and tended to cancel out in the aggregates. Besides Tai and Wen, several other prefectures also reaped great success in the 1210s. These include Ming

(Qingyuan) and Xiu (Jiaxing), located on the coast of the Lower Yangzi region, and two of their neighbors, Hu (Anji) and Wu. In the 1040s these four prefectures produced only three prefects (i.e., 5% of those of Lower Yangzi origin), while in the 1210s fifty-seven of their sons made it to prefectural governorship (i.e., close to 49% of the prefects from the Lower Yangzi).[31] Their success was at the expense of the Grand Canal Band, whose share of southern-born prefects dropped from 28% to 17%. Prefectures located along this Grand Canal near the Song–Jin border and away from the coast (i.e., Yang, Run, and Chang) experienced the most remarkable reversal of fortune. The number of men from this cluster of prefectures holding prefectural governorships declined in absolute terms even though the Lower Yangzi region as a whole contributed twice as many prefects in the 1210s than it did in the 1040s. In the Southeast Coast, there was a similar trend in favor of coastal prefectures. Fu prefecture, south of Wen on the coast, gained at the expense of its northern inland neighbor of Jian. The number of Fu prefecture natives increased from eight in the 1040s to twenty-five in the 1210s, while that of Jian (Jianning) plummeted from thirteen to five. Further down the coast, Xinghua and Quan prefectures also had a significantly larger number of native sons holding prefectural governorship in the 1210s than in the 1040s. In Xinghua the number doubled, and in Quan it tripled.

These extraordinarily successful prefectures, along with Su (Pingjiang), Hang (Lin'an), and Yue (Shaoxing), formed a continuous stretch along the coast of East China Sea, extending from Quan prefecture in the south, meandering along the coast and through the Lower Yangzi Delta all the way to Su prefecture in the north. Sprawling across the macroregions of Lower Yangzi and the Southeast Coast, this stretch consisted of ten coastal prefectures and two of their inland neighbors (Wu and Hu), including the top eleven prefectures which contributed the largest number of prefects to the 1210s cohort. Together, this Coastal Stretch of twelve prefectures supplied 169 prefects in the 1210s, or 61% of the entire cohort. Its success in the 1210s even overshadowed that of the Capital Corridor of the 1040s.

This pattern suggests a logic of success completely different from the 1040s. First, no single prefecture in the 1210s dominated the supply of prefectural governors in the way Kaifeng did during the 1040s. Men from even the most successful prefecture of the 1210s accounted for only less than 9% of the entire cohort. Second, this most successful prefecture was Fu, not the new capital Lin'an. Lin'an fell far short of what Kaifeng had achieved and contributed a mere 4% of the 1210s cohort, and its success was surpassed by that of several other prefectures besides Fu, most of which did not border the new capital. The prefectures bordering the capital, in contrast, were a mix of successful and unsuccessful ones. In other words, political success in the 1210s seems to derive from the prosperity of the coast rather than the influence of the political center.

That no single prefecture in the 1210s could overshadow their neighbors in the supply of prefects was a general trend in the south. In the Upper Yangzi, a total of six prefectures in the 1040s produced eight prefects, of whom Chengdu alone claimed home to three. In the 1210s, by contrast, the twenty-two prefects of Upper Yangzi origin hailed from a total of twelve prefectures. Despite the continuing importance of Chengdu, which claimed home to three of the twenty prefects, its success was overtaken by that of Mei and Long, each producing three and five prefects in the 1210s respectively. Even outside the Chengdu plain, prefectures like Guang'an and Lu also had natives holding prefectural governorship in the 1210s.

In the Middle Yangzi, too, although the traditional centers of success along the Gan River, Ji and Hong (Longxing) in particular, continued to thrive in the 1210s, their neighbors located on other tributaries of the Poyang Lake such as Nankang, Rao, and Fu were quickly catching up. Through the prefectures of Hui (known in the 1040s as She), Qu, Chu, Jianning, and Shaowu lying in between, which were almost equally successful, the runner-up band of prefectures in the Gan–Poyang area was spatially connected to the superstars of the Coastal Stretch, forming a largely contiguous expanse of territory that supplied the vast majority of prefects in the 1210s (map 3.1b).

This finding, however, needs to be qualified, because of data lacuna on governors of Sichuan prefectures in the Li Zhiliang lists. While Li has surveyed all prefectures in Fujian, Liangzhe, and Jiangnan East and West, he has included only eleven of the sixty-three prefectures in Sichuan in his study. Since Sichuan men entered civil service in large numbers only after the 1040s and after the late eleventh century they tended to hold local offices only inside Sichuan, the combined effect of these trends implies that the prefectures ignored in Li Zhiliang's lists are likely to report a higher proportion of Sichuan-born prefects in the 1210s than the prefectures Li surveys.[32] Correction of this bias therefore means a somewhat higher proportion of Sichuan-born prefects in the 1210s cohort and a lower proportion of those from other regions. This is unlikely to shake the dominance of men from coastal prefectures in the 1210s, but it will certainly reduce the magnitude of that dominance.[33]

The foregoing discussions suggest two conclusions. First, prefectural governorship in the 1040s was vested, first and foremost, in the hands of a

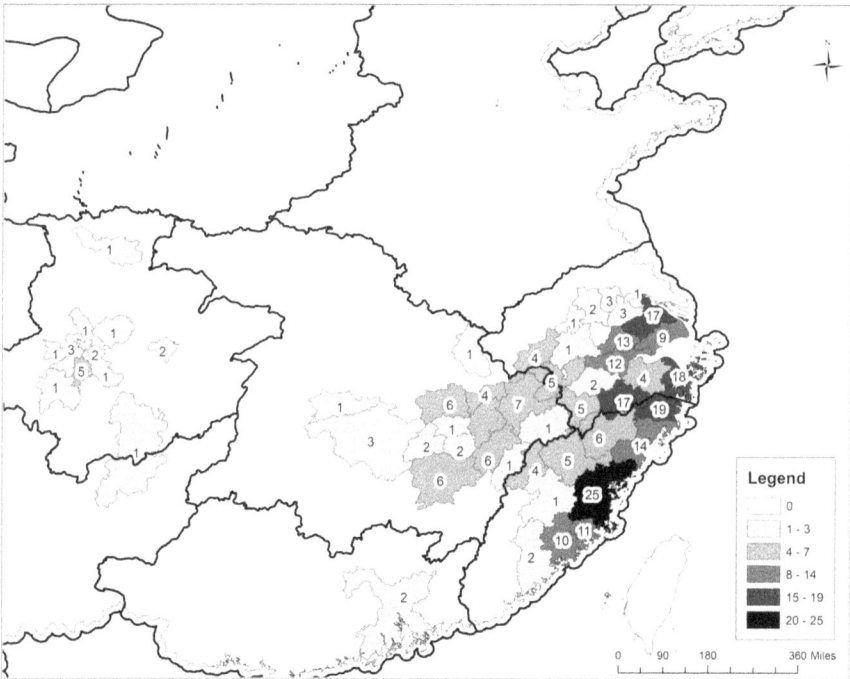

MAP 3.1B. Prefects in the 1210s cohort by home prefecture. Prefectural boundaries in this map are based on Robert Hartwell's "China Historical Studies" GIS datasets, published by the China Historical GIS project (www.fas.harvard.edu/~chgis/data/hartwell/). They are an approximation of Southern Song prefectural boundaries ca. 1200. Thick lines indicate boundaries of G. William Skinner's physiographic macroregions.

capital-oriented, though not necessarily capital-dwelling, political elite. The capital region of the Northern Song (Henan–Yingtian corridor) and, in part due to its extended influence, the band of prefectures along the southern segment of the Grand Canal, supplied about half of the men who headed prefectural administration between 1040 and 1049. By the 1210s, however, the influence of the capital had waned, while economic prosperity and by implication educational investment had become the main determinants of political success. As a result, the new center of success which produced at least half of the prefects in the 1210s was now a stretch of prefectures, extending along the eastern seacoast from Fujian to the Lower Yangzi Delta.

Second, by the time the Song finished its unification campaigns in the late tenth century, the spatial pattern of development in South China had become significantly different from that in the north. Instead of having one center, it had many. This multicenteredness seems to have continued into the

1040s, when the Lower Yangzi Delta, Northern Fujian, and the Gan Basin each claimed one or two of the top four most successful southern prefectures. One might say that this multicenteredness of South China also continued into the 1210s. But by then access to political power had spread to such an extent that what had been relatively isolated pockets of success in Fujian, Liangzhe, and Jiangnan West had now been connected into a contiguous expanse, facilitating social interactions between officials of varied prefectural origins and rendering previous demarcations of different southern regions unrecognizable and arguably irrelevant. Only Sichuan existed as a center of political success in the west, separated from those in the east by the political backwaters of Jinghu and Guangnan.

PATTERNS OF APPOINTMENT IN THE 1040S

A recent study of the late Tang political elite notes a clear distinction between capital and provincial elites that persisted into the ninth century. While capital elites, based nearly exclusively in the twin capitals of the Tang (Chang'an and Luoyang), had strong family traditions of officeholding and served in offices of national prominence all across the empire, their provincial counterparts were usually born to families with very weak or no links to Tang officialdom and tended to serve occasionally and in only local offices near their homes.[34] In other words, political power as late as in the ninth century was largely monopolized by capital-based elites and beyond the reach of those living in the provinces.

Consistent with earlier scholarship on Song examinations and bureaucracy, the preceding discussions on regional origin of Song prefects suggest a far more open political system in the mid-eleventh century. Although officials in the Song Capital Corridor continued to claim a disproportionate share of prefectural governorships in the 1040s, an equally impressive number of prefects in the 1040s were nevertheless recruited from men outside the capital region. Whether these men at some point in their life relocated to Kaifeng or Luoyang, thus joining the ranks of the Song capital elite, is a different issue. The point here is that they formed a group different from both the capital elite and the provincial elite of late Tang: they were of provincial origins but nevertheless carved out a career of national prominence.

An investigation of the entire set of Li Zhiliang's lists shows that prefects of the 1040s typically had assignments in more than one region over the course of their life, regardless of their place of origin. Since administrative boundaries are likely more relevant than the physiographic macroregions in the Song think-

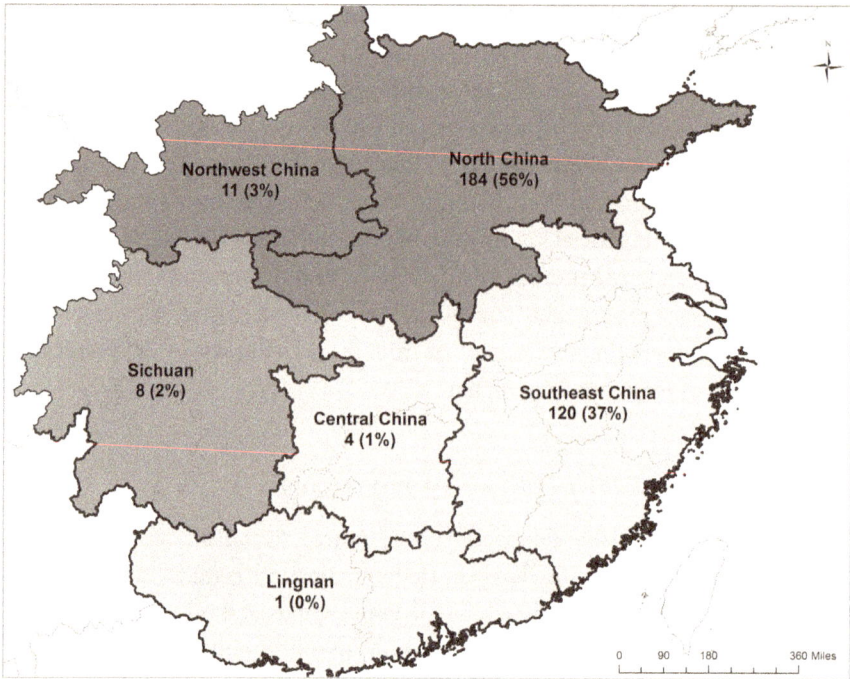

MAP 3.2A. Prefects in the 1040s cohort by home administrative macroregion (AMR). AMR boundaries in this map are based on Northern Song circuit boundaries ca. 1080 in Robert Hartwell's "China Historical Studies" GIS datasets, published by the China Historical GIS project (www.fas.harvard.edu/~chgis/data/hartwell/).

ing on bureaucratic appointments, here I redraw the borders of macroregions along circuit boundaries. Thus, the Song dynasty is divided into six administrative macroregions (AMRs), which are employed as the geographical units of analysis in the following analysis (maps 3.2a and 3.2b). These AMRs are North China, Northwest China, Southeast China, Sichuan, Central China, and Lingnan, each consisting of several circuits specified in the notes of table 3.3.[35]

Excluding those who have only one prefect appointment documented in Li's lists, which by definition limits the geographical scope of their service to one AMR, the vast majority (78%) of the men from the 1040s cohort served as prefects in two or more AMRs and 40% served in three or more AMRs (table 3.3). This is true for both North China and Southeast China, the two AMRs which supplied the largest number of prefects in the 1040s. A comparison between prefects hailing from the Capital Corridor and those from other places in North China, too, does not yield any significant difference in their pattern of geographical rotation.

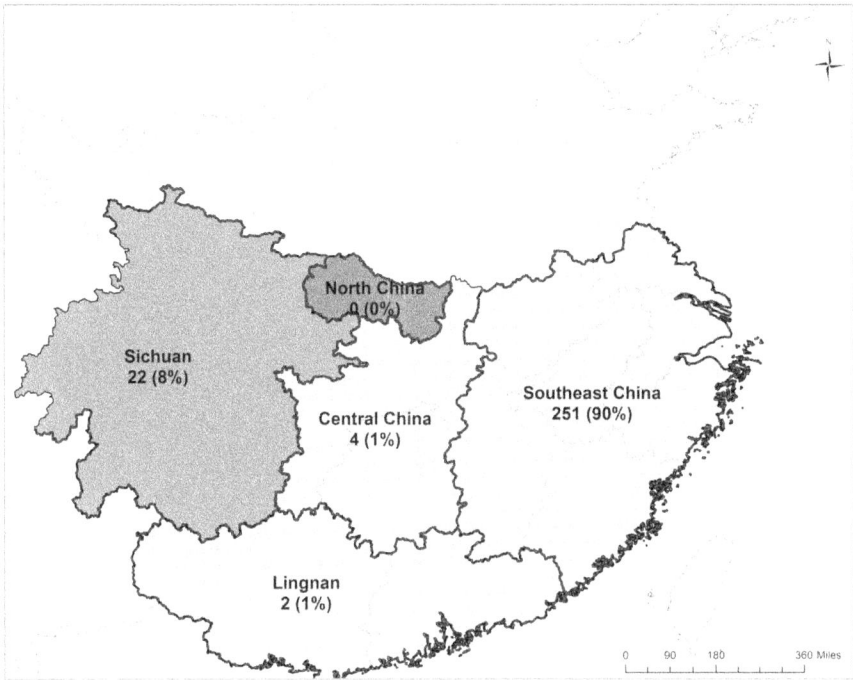

MAP 3.2B. Prefects in the 1210s cohort by home administrative macroregion (AMR). AMR boundaries in this map are based on Southern Song circuit boundaries ca. 1200 in Robert Hartwell's "China Historical Studies" GIS datasets, published by the China Historical GIS project (www.fas.harvard.edu/~chgis/data/hartwell/). Thus, for example, some prefectures along the western end of Song–Jin border (e.g., Jie, Xihe, and Jin), which became part of Lizhou circuit in Southern Song, are included in the Sichuan AMR.

The practice of rotating prefects all across the empire in the 1040s, however, was counterbalanced by a willingness to give officials prefect appointments near their homes. Table 3.4a reports the appointments to prefectship received by officials from a given AMR as a percentage of all known appointments to prefectship they received through their life. As before, those who have only one appointment to prefectship documented in Li Zhiliang's rosters are excluded from these calculations. The statistics in this table show that men from North, Northwest, and Southeast China, which comprised the vast majority of the 1040s cohort of prefects (315 of 328), received about half of their prefect appointments in their home AMR. These numbers remain robust after excluding those who, to the best of our knowledge, served only in a single AMR (table 3.4b). This means that even those who had the experience of being transferred across different

TABLE 3.3. Careers of prefects from 1040–1049 and 1210–1219

	No. of AMRs Posted to as Prefect							
	Number and Percentage of Officials in the 1040s Cohort Posted as Prefect to One or More AMRs					Number and Percentage of Officials in the 1210s Cohort Posted as Prefect to One or More AMRs		
Home AMR	One	Two	Three	Four	Five	One	Two	Three
North China	34 (22%)	60 (38%)	42 (27%)	19 (12%)	2 (1%)	—	—	—
Capital Corridor	26 (27%)	38 (39%)	23 (23%)	10 (10%)	1 (1%)	—	—	—
Northwest China	0	3 (43%)	4 (57%)	0	0	—	—	—
Southeast China	23 (25%)	36 (39%)	20 (22%)	12 (13%)	1 (1%)	92 (55%)	66 (39%)	10 (6%)
Grand Canal Band	11 (38%)	5 (17%)	7 (24%)	6 (21%)	0	21 (62%)	13 (38%)	0
Coastal Stretch	9 (31%)	10 (34%)	6 (21%)	4 (14%)	0	72 (61%)	44 (37%)	3 (3%)
Central China	0	2 (67%)	0	1 (33%)	0	0	1 (50%)	1 (50%)
Sichuan	0	1 (25%)	3 (75%)	0	0	5 (45%)	2 (18%)	4 (36%)
Lingnan	0	0	0	1 (100%)	0	0	0	1 (100%)
Total	57 (22%)	102 (39%)	69 (26%)	33 (13%)	3 (1%)	97 (53%)	69 (38%)	16 (9%)

Notes: Only officials with appointment to more than one prefecture recorded in Li Zhiliang's lists are included in this analysis. When an official received multiple governor appointments to the same prefecture, only one is counted. In this analysis, the Song dynasty is divided into six administrative macroregions (AMRs). North China includes Kaifeng and the circuits of Jingdong East and West, Jingxi North and South, Hebei East and West, and Hedong; Northwest China includes the two Shaanxi circuits of Yongxingjun and Qinfeng; Southeast China includes Huainan East and West, Liangzhe, Jiangnan East and West, and Fujian; Sichuan includes Chengdufu, Tongchuanfu, Lizhou and Zizhou circuits; Central China includes Jinghu North and South; and Lingnan includes Guangnan East and West.

TABLE 3.4A. Proportion of prefect appointments inside home AMR

| | No. and Percentage of Prefect Appointments Inside Home AMR | | | |
| | The 1040s Cohort | | The 1210s Cohort | |
Home AMR of the Prefect	No. (%)	N=	No. (%)	N=
North China	468 (53%)	888	—	—
Northwest China	18 (46%)	39	—	—
Southeast China	297 (57%)	518	401 (78%)	512
Central China	2 (13%)	16	4 (44%)	9
Sichuan	0	18	24 (53%)	45
Lingnan	3 (43%)	7	2 (50%)	4
Total	788 (53%)	1486	429 (75%)	570

Note: Only officials with appointment to more than one prefecture recorded in Li Zhiliang's ros-ters are included in this analysis. When an official received multiple governor appointments to the same prefecture, only one is counted. Sample size (N) is the total number of prefect appointments recorded in Li Zhiliang's lists for men of each region whose place of origin can be identified.

TABLE 3.4B. Proportion of prefect appointments inside home AMR

| | No. and Percentage of Prefect Appointments Inside Home AMR | | | |
| | The 1040s Cohort | | The 1210s Cohort | |
Home AMR of the prefect	No. (%)	N=	No. (%)	N=
North China	395 (51%)	779	—	—
Northwest China	18 (46%)	39	—	—
Southeast China	227 (51%)	442	146 (59%)	248
Central China	2 (13%)	16	4 (44%)	9
Sichuan	0	18	19 (58%)	33
Lingnan	3 (43%)	7	2 (50%)	4
Total	645 (50%)	1301	171 (58%)	294

Note: Only officials who served as prefects in more than one AMR are included in this analysis. When an official received multiple governor appointments to the same prefecture, only one is counted. Sample size (N) is the total number of prefect appointments recorded in Li Zhiliang's lists for men of each region whose place of origin can be identified and who is known to have served as prefects in more than one AMR during his entire career.

administrative regions nevertheless held half of their prefectural governor-ships in their home region. This is consistent with the findings of Brian E. McKnight in his study on governors of Hang and Fu prefectures during Northern Song. He shows that since Renzong's reign (1022–1063) governors of both prefectures had come predominantly from nearby regions. He also shows that prefects of Hang were also most likely to be serving in nearby circuits immediately before and after their assignment to Hang.[36] A notable exception is Sichuan. Prefects of Sichuan origin in the 1040s cohort were not appointed as governor of any prefecture in Sichuan over the course of their life. This resulted from a policy prohibiting native incumbency of local offices that lasted longer in Sichuan than elsewhere.[37] Men from Central China also seem to have received a lower percentage of appointments as prefects in their home AMR on average, though the sample size (a total of eighteen appoint-ments made to three prefects) for this region is extremely small.

The case of Liu Hang (995–1060) helps illustrate the way in which a ten-dency toward native incumbency existed alongside empire-wide rotations. Liu was a native of Ji prefecture, Jiangnan West circuit, who obtained his *jinshi* degree in 1030. Li Zhiliang's series report a total of thirteen prefectures he governed during his lifetime. Nine of them were in the south, five of which were in Southeast China (including three in the Jiangnan circuits, one in Huainan West, and another in Fujian) and four in Central China. But he also received three appointments in North China and one in the Northwest. Thus, even though he had a career that spanned four different macroregions, seven of his prefect appointments were within an approximately three-hundred-mile radius of his home prefecture. His most distant appointment to prefec-tural governorship was in Yongxing, about seven hundred miles northwest of home.[38]

This combination reflects a compromise between conflicting policy goals and with the constraints of social realities. First, the Song administrative geography differs from its geography of political success. In the 1040s, as shown earlier, the political elite came predominantly from a small number of prefectures in North China and along the Grand Canal. They were more from economic and political centers than elsewhere. By comparison, the administrative geography followed a different logic. Prefectures, more often a tool of the state for establishing military control than extracting revenues, were more likely than counties to be found away from major population and economic centers.[39] This created problems of not just financing, but also staffing. From the early years of the Song, officials had frowned upon appointments to places that were located in less developed areas and far away from home. Recruiting local men without necessary educational and administrative credentials was a possibility, but it raised the question of loyalty and was in obvious conflict with the professed ideals of those who ran the Song bureaucracy. The tension between effectiveness and loyalty is the second issue the Song confronted. An effective government favors appointments of men who came from a place close to their jurisdiction. It minimizes expenses of travel and lowers linguistic and cultural barriers. But loyalty to dynastic interests demands frequent rotations and appointments away from the official's home region in order to avoid conflicts of interests. Obviously, the challenge of staffing local administrations was most serious on the frontiers, where the supply of native officials was short, the positions least attractive, and concerns about loyalty paramount.

In the first decades of Song rule, concerns over loyalty prevailed over all the others. In 982 the court issued an edict that banned natives of the south from serving as prefects, vice prefects, or fiscal intendants in their home circuits.[40] It also forbade officials posted to the south from bringing their family along with them, which made appointments to these places even more undesirable.[41] In order to staff these local offices, the court offered incentives to those serving there, such as higher salaries, quicker promotions, and a shorter waiting period between appointments.[42] But it also did not hesitate to force through its will. Around 976, for instance, when a junior official complained of his recent assignment as prefectural registrar in Guangnan, the court exiled him to an even more distant island, making an example of him to all those who tried to evade assignments in distant places.[43] It also used a disproportionately high number of aged, incapable, and corrupt officials as governors of distant prefectures, but their malfeasance raised concerns at court and also provoked local protests.[44]

In the early years of his reign, Renzong undertook a series of measures to reform and regularize the personnel system. By this time, and perhaps much earlier, prohibitions against southern men serving in their home circuit had also been lifted, except in Sichuan, where a series of rebellions following the Song conquest persuaded the court to keep it under watchful eyes for a few more years.[45] The court also gave candidates more liberty in choosing the places they wanted to serve.[46] The most important change came with a ruling in 1027. By then the Song had legislated a system known as "qualification sequence" (*zixu*), in which an official had to acquire adequate experience in a series of local offices at lower levels before he could be promoted to higher level positions. What the ruling of 1027 did was it regularized the geography of appointment by incorporating postings to distant and near places into this sequence of qualifications and requiring the fulfillment of a certain number of terms in distant circuits.[47]

PATTERNS OF APPOINTMENT IN THE 1210S

The spatial logic of employing men more or less close to their homes becomes more pronounced at a higher level of aggregation. Defining North and South China roughly along the Huai and the Han rivers, which approximates the dividing line between the Five Dynasties and the southern states in the preceding period of disunity, it becomes clear that northerners in the 1040s cohort served predominantly in the north, whereas southerners in the south. Sichuan natives, barred from serving in Sichuan, were posted predominantly to prefectures in the south (table 3.5). Thus, in the 1040s, with the exception of the Sichuanese, the average distance from a perfect's home locale to where he was posted was roughly in the range of 300 to 400 miles, though on the other side the standard deviation for the distance was also very high (table 3.6).

The tendency to employ officials as governors of prefectures in their home region persisted into the early thirteenth century and became stronger. The court became more tolerant of officials who refused appointments too far from their homes. In the Southern Song, with its smaller territory, the Ministry of Personnel offered a new definition of "distant" and "near" appointments in 1133. Whereas the distant circuits (Fujian, Guangnan, and Sichuan) in the Northern Song were usually over 800 miles away from the capital, the new definition regarded any assignment 1000 *li* (384 miles) away from the court as "distant."[48] Consistent with this stipulation, tables 3.4a and

TABLE 3.5. The North–South contradistinction in office-holding among the 1040s cohort

| From | Posted To | | | |
	The North	Sichuan	The South	Sample Size
The North	677 (71%)	24 (3%)	257 (27%)	958
Sichuan	8 (36%)	0	14 (64%)	22
The South	174 (31%)	5 (1%)	391 (69%)	570

Note: The North and the South are defined roughly along the course of the Huai and the Han rivers. As will be discussed later, Sichuan represents a special case and is treated separately. Thus, the two AMRs of North China and Northwest China constitute the North in this table; the Sichuan AMR is coextensive with Sichuan here; all other AMRs are considered part of the South.

3.4b show that compared to their 1040s counterparts, the 1210s cohort generally received a higher proportion of appointments to prefectures in their home region. By the 1210s, even Sichuan men were no longer an exception. Like those from other parts of the Song, Sichuan-born prefects in the 1210s typically had half of their appointments in Sichuan. The average distance from a Sichuan man's home to the prefecture where he was posted, therefore, dropped dramatically from over 840 to about 470 miles (table 3.6). There is reason to believe that even these figures are conservative estimates. As noted earlier, only eleven out of sixty-three prefectures in Sichuan are included in Li Zhiliang's surveys while his lists are far more comprehensive on most of the other southern regions. To include more Sichuan prefectures in the dataset will almost certainly increase the number of appointments given to Sichuan natives and shrink further the geographical scope of bureaucratic rotations among Sichuan-born prefects. In fact, my earlier study of Sichuan men's careers based on funerary epitaphs shows that between 1128 and 1241 about 94% of Sichuan-born officials received 80% or more of their local government assignments within Sichuan itself.[49]

This finding remains robust in a more detailed analysis, which looks at subdivisions of the AMRs, each consisting of no more than two circuits (tables 3.7a and 3.7b). That the diagonal values are the greatest in nearly every row of table 3.7b means that the 1210s cohort of prefects, regardless of their geographical origins, consistently received the largest proportion of their prefect appointments in or very close to their home circuit. This

TABLE 3.6. The geographical scope of prefect appointments

	Distance from Home to the Prefecture Posted To (miles)					
	The 1040s Cohort			The 1210s Cohort		
Home AMR of the Prefect	mean	s.d.	N	mean	s.d.	N
North China	318.6	223.8	915	—	—	—
Northwest China	294.2	231.6	43	—	—	—
Southeast China	367.5	249.0	546	319.2	204.2	595
Central China	445.6	186.5	17	280.5	161.0	11
Sichuan	843.3	217.3	22	456.7	361.3	56
Lingnan	291.1	322.2	7	449.1	404.3	5
Empire-wide	343.9	241.9	1550	331.1	225.7	667

TABLE 3.7A. Patterns of prefect appointments by subregion of AMRs: Geographical distribution of prefect appointments made to the 1040s cohort

Home AMR and Subregions	Percentage of Prefect Assignments Received in AMR and Its Subregions														N=
	I	II	III	IV	V	VI	VII	VIII	IX	X	XI	XII	XIII	XIV	
North China															
I. Kaifeng	2	10	19	20	4	16	13	3	6	1	3	1	0	2	259
II. Jingdong	3	19	13	10	5	16	10	8	7	2	3	2	0	2	222
III. Jingxi	4	6	20	17	5	20	8	7	3	1	4	2	0	4	275
IV. Hebei	1	7	5	28	8	20	4	8	4	2	5	3	2	5	106
V. Hedong	2	13	13	23	11	25	4	2	2	0	4	2	0	0	53
VI. Northwest China	0	2	9	9	7	47	7	9	0	0	2	2	2	2	43
Southeast China															
VII. Huainan	3	9	10	9	0	10	23	16	12	3	2	1	0	2	105
VIII. Liangzhe	3	6	3	2	2	10	12	31	13	9	4	1	1	5	173
IX. Jiangnan	2	5	14	4	2	7	14	6	22	5	12	1	0	6	161
X. Fujian	4	2	8	3	1	3	14	17	17	14	7	1	0	10	107
XI. Central China	0	0	24	6	0	24	6	12	12	0	12	0	0	6	17
Sichuan															

XII. Chengdufu and Tongchuanfu	5	5	10	0	0	0	19	0	19	19	14	0	5	0	0	0	5	21
XIII. Lizhou and Kuizhou	0	0	0	0	0	0	0	0	0	0	<u>100</u>	0	0	0	0	0	0	1
XIV. Lingnan	0	14	0	0	0	0	0	0	0	0	29	0	14	0	14	0	**43**	7

Note: Sample size (N) is the number of all prefect appointments received by prefects from each AMR or its subdivision *during his entire career*. Only prefect appointments documented in Li Zhiliang's lists are included. When an official received multiple governor appointments to the same prefecture, only one is counted. Prefect appointments made to men whose regional origin cannot be identified are also excluded from this table. The columns give the AMRs (or its subregions) where a prefect was posted. The largest number in each row is bold face if it is also on the diagonal line, indicating that the home AMR (or subregion) of the prefects were also where they received the largest percentage of prefect appointments; it is underlined if it is not on the diagonal line, indicating that the largest percentage of appointments to prefectship were outside the prefects' home AMR (or subregion).

TABLE 3.7B. Patterns of prefect appointments by subregion of AMRs: Geographical distribution of prefect appointments made to the 1210s cohort

Home AMR and Subregions	Percentage of Prefect Assignments Received in AMR and Its Subregions									
	III	VII	VIII	IX	X	XI	XII	XIII	XIV	N=
North China										
III. Jingxi	0	0	0	0	0	0	0	0	0	0
Southeast China										
VII. Huainan	0	0	0	<u>100</u>	0	0	0	0	0	1
VIII. Liangzhe	2	15	**32**	27	9	11	1	1	3	340
IX. Jiangnan	1	15	19	**25**	12	13	5	5	6	128
X. Fujian	1	10	13	18	**24**	10	0	3	21	126
XI. Central China	9	0	9	27	0	**45**	0	0	9	11
Sichuan										
XII. Chengdufu and Tongchuanfu	2	6	7	11	2	20	**39**	13	0	54
XIII. Lizhou and Kuizhou	0	0	0	0	0	0	0	**100**	0	2
XIV. Lingnan	0	20	0	0	0	0	20	0	**60**	5

Note: See table 3.7a.

proportion was consistently between 20% and 30% where the sample size is large.[50] I think we should see this as further development of a practice the Song had already adopted in the 1040s. An analysis of the careers of the 1040s cohort in table 3.7a shows that it was already common in the mid-eleventh century for men from many different parts of the Song, north and south alike, to receive 20% or more of their prefect appointments in or very close to their home circuit.

As we have seen in the careers of the 1040s cohort, serving most often in one's home region does not necessarily preclude one from also having some experience of serving in a few other regions. But there is clearly a parallel shift toward less geographical diversity in the careers of the 1210s cohort of prefects. As discussed earlier, although the 1040s prefects often received 40% to 50% of appointments inside their home AMR, most of them nonetheless had fairly rich experience governing prefectures in multiple other regions. About 40% of them received appointments to prefectship in three or more

AMRs. This was true for both North and Southeast China, which supplied the vast majority of prefects in the 1040s. In sharp contrast, a mere 6% of the prefects from Southeast China in the 1210s had such experience. Li Zhi-liang's data do show a higher percentage of prefects born in Central China, Lingnan, and Sichuan serving in more than two AMRs, but again Li's data for these regions are limited and that for Sichuan skewed.

Compare Liu Hang with Zhao Shanxiang (*jinshi* of 1196), the person from the 1210s cohort with the greatest number of prefect appointments recorded in Li's lists. An imperial clansman, his father fled the Jurchen invasions and settled in the Ming prefecture in the early Southern Song. He was made prefect in nine different locations over the course of his career, with five in Liangzhe (including one to his home prefecture), three in Huainan, and one in Jiangnan East. All appointments were in the Southeast China macroregion, all but one within 300 miles of his home. He was offered an opportunity to serve in Chengdu, but he declined.[51]

The practice of employing men to govern prefectures close to their homes created in Liangzhe and the heartland of Sichuan (i.e., Chengdufu and Tong-chuanfu circuits) a situation during the 1210s where prefectural administrations were predominantly headed by natives of these regions (table 3.8b). But less successful regions had fewer natives to fill up all the vacancies of prefectural governorship, so much so that they relied on their successful neighbors for additional manpower. Again, the rule of geographical proximity was at work, leading to a clear division of labor between the successful regions. As table 3.8b shows, prefects in the peripheral circuits of Sichuan (Lizhou and Kuizhou circuits) hailed predominantly from the heartland of Sichuan, while Liangzhe in the 1210s supplied most of the men needed to run prefectural administrations in Central China, Jiangnan, and Fujian. The reason why Fujian, itself a very successful region in the 1210s, had many of its prefectures governed by Liangzhe men seems to be that the Fujianese were employed in large numbers to staff prefectural positions in Lingnan (table 3.8b).

Again, here one can see notable parallels and contrasts with the 1040s (table 3.8a). Back then the division of labor was between men from North China, in particular Kaifeng, and those from Southeast China. Much like in the 1210s, natives of Liangzhe and Jiangnan, where all but one of the Grand Canal Band prefectures were located, claimed the largest share of prefectural governorships in these circuits in the 1040s. More than any of the other regions, they also provided the human resources needed for governing prefectures in Central China and Fujian, whereas Fujian overshadowed all other circuits as the chief source of talents for staffing the office of prefect in

TABLE 3.8A. Regional origin of prefects by subregion of AMRs: Prefects in office between 1040 and 1049

| | Regional Origin (%) of Prefects Posted to AMR and Its Subregions | | | | | | | | | | | | | |
Home AMR and Subregions	I	II	III	IV	V	VI	VII	VIII	IX	X	XI	XII	XIII	XIV
North China														
I. Kaifeng	**26**	23	19	**35**	**23**	18	**20**	4	10	7	20	9	25	7
II. Jingdong	21	**26**	13	9	19	13	16	12	9	10	9	18	25	4
III. Jingxi	21	15	**30**	23	19	**22**	11	12	7	7	9	**27**	0	11
IV. Hebei	5	9	2	13	10	9	3	7	4	3	6	18	25	11
V. Hedong	0	6	3	7	13	4	1	0	1	0	3	9	0	0
VI. Northwest China	0	0	2	3	10	8	3	3	0	0	3	0	0	4
Southeast China														
VII. Huainan	5	8	7	3	0	5	15	6	3	3	3	0	0	4
VIII. Liangzhe	16	8	3	2	3	11	11	**34**	18	**24**	9	9	25	14
IX. Jiangnan	0	2	10	4	3	4	10	3	**24**	**24**	**26**	0	0	14
X. Fujian	5	4	7	0	0	2	6	13	13	21	11	9	0	**25**
XI. Central China	0	0	3	0	0	2	0	1	3	0	0	0	0	0

Sichuan

	1	2	3	4	5	6	7	8	9	10	11	12	13	14
XII. Chengdufu and Tongchuanfu	0	0	0	0	0	2	3	4	3	0	3	0	0	4
XIII. Lizhou and Kuizhou	0	0	0	0	0	0	0	0	1	0	0	0	0	0
XIV. Lingnan	0	0	0	0	0	0	0	0	1	0	0	0	0	4
N =	19 (0)	53 (7)	88 (6)	98 (11)	31 (4)	131 (18)	79 (14)	68 (29)	67 (31)	29 (14)	35 (24)	11 (5)	4 (3)	28 (36)

Note: Sample size (N) is the total number of prefect appointments documented by Li Zhiliang in each AMR or its subdivision between 1040 and 1049. The number of prefect appointments made to men whose regional origin cannot be identified are given in parentheses but excluded from the calculations. The columns give the AMRs (or its subregions) where a prefect was posted. The largest number in each column is bold face, highlighting the major source of prefects in each AMR (or subregion) between 1040 and 1049.

TABLE 3.8B. Regional origin of prefects by subregion of AMRs:
Prefects in office between 1210 and 1219

| Home AMR and Subregions | Regional Origin (%) of Prefects Posted to AMR and Its Subregions | | | | | | | | |
	III	VII	VIII	IX	X	XI	XII	XIII	XIV
North China									
III. Jingxi	0	0	0	0	0	0	0	0	0
Southeast China									
VII. Huainan	0	0	0	1	0	0	0	0	0
VIII. Liangzhe	**56**	**60**	**73**	**58**	**45**	**39**	5	19	26
IX. Jiangnan	11	25	13	19	19	25	21	19	12
X. Fujian	11	12	10	15	36	16	0	19	**56**
XI. Central China	11	0	1	1	0	7	0	0	3
Sichuan									
XII. Chengdufu and Tongchuanfu	11	1	2	6	0	13	**74**	**31**	0
XIII. Lizhou and Kuizhou	0	0	0	0	0	0	0	13	0
XIV. Lingnan	0	1	0	0	0	0	0	0	3
N =	9 (4)	68 (36)	82 (41)	104 (67)	42 (20)	56 (48)	19 (10)	16 (13)	34 (52)

Note: Sample size (N) is the total number of prefect appointments documented by Li Zhiliang in each AMR or its subdivision between 1210 and 1219. The number of prefect appointments made to men whose regional origin cannot be identified are given in parentheses but excluded from the calculations. The columns give the AMRs (or its subdivisions) where a prefect was posted. The largest number in each column is bolded, highlighting the major source of prefects in each AMR (or subregion) between 1210 and 1219.

Lingnan. In contrast, officials of Kaifeng, Jingdong, and Jingxi origins were the largest group among the prefects of Hebei, Hedong, Huainan, Northwest China, and the distant Sichuan.

With North China men out of the picture in the 1210s, their role was largely taken over by Liangzhe men, and the new division of labor was between them and those from Sichuan and Fujian. Without the rivalry of northerners, the percentage of prefect appointments made to Liangzhe men throughout Southeast China increased from about 20% to 30% to around 50% to 60% or greater. They also outnumbered Jiangnan men among the

TABLE 3.9A. The east–west contradistinction in officeholding among the 1210s cohort: Sichuan versus the South

From	The North	Sichuan	The South	Sample Size
		Posted To		
Sichuan	1 (2%)	30 (54%)	25 (45%)	56
The South	9 (1%)	23 (4%)	579 (95%)	611

Note: For definitions of the North, the South, and Sichuan, see table 3.5.

TABLE 3.9B. The east–west contradistinction in officeholding among the 1210s cohort: by administrative macroregions (AMRs)

From	North China	Southeast China	Central China	Sichuan	Lingnan	Sample Size
			Posted To			
Southeast China	8 (1%)	454 (76%)	66 (11%)	22 (4%)	45 (8%)	595
Central China	1 (9%)	4 (36%)	5 (45%)	0	1 (9%)	11
Sichuan	1 (2%)	14 (25%)	11 (20%)	30 (54%)	0	56
Lingnan	0	1 (20%)	0	1 (20%)	3 (60%)	5

Note: For definitions of the North, the South, and Sichuan, see table 3.5.

prefects of Central China. In contrast, Fujian men's traditional role in governing Lingnan prefectures continued, whereas prefectural administrations in Sichuan, which had earlier been dominated by northerners, were now handed over mainly to the Sichuan natives.

Therefore, the contradistinction between northerners and southerners (mostly southeasterners) as observed for the 1040s (table 3.5) had, by the 1210s, transformed into one between the southeasterners and the Sichuanese. As table 3.9a shows, in the 1210s, almost all appointments to prefectship received by men from the south were in the south. With the exception of a few, these officials were predominantly from Southeast China. Table 3.9b shows further that the vast majority of prefect appointments the southeasterners received were also in Southeast China itself. When they did serve elsewhere, they usually ended up in Central China and Lingnan, not Sichuan. Though the tables show Sichuan-born prefects receiving a considerable proportion of their assignments outside Sichuan, this is the result of the data bias in Li's rosters in which Sichuan men with only local appointments in Sichuan were significantly underrepresented. Thus, for the 1210s cohort of prefects, the overlap between areas where Sichuan men served as prefects and those where the southeasterners did had shrunk considerably.

KINSHIP NETWORKS

The fact that Sichuan men were employed mostly in Sichuan and the south-easterners in the southeast around the early thirteenth century was associated with a significant change in the social behavior of the Song political elite. This stands out most clearly in the way in which prefects of the 1040s and the 1210s were related by blood and marriage. For this purpose, kinship data—here broadly defined to encompass all data on agnatic or affinal relations—from the CBDB and my previous work on Sichuan are combined and then symmetrized (that is, say, for a record indicating X as the son of Y, a symmetrical record is created indicating Y as the parent of X). The two lists of prefects, from the 1040s and the 1210s respectively, are used as the starting point for querying this dataset for kinship records. All kin found for these prefects are then used to query the database again in search of those who were the kin of the kin of the prefects. This query is repeated for four rounds in the belief that this is sufficient to exhaust all close relatives of the prefects registered in the database. The relationship is then calculated between each prefect and the kin found in the four rounds of query.[52] From this master list of kinship data, only records indicating a kinship relation *between* two prefects are preserved for analysis, and others discarded. The query results are then checked for internal consistency.[53] When multiple types of kinship relations exist between two prefects, the one directly registered in the databases and/or involving fewer marriages is used.

As social network theorists have argued convincingly that any two persons have a connection when a sufficient number of intermediaries are allowed, it only makes sense to look at whether two prefects were *reasonably closely* related. But how close is "reasonably close"? This chapter defines a kinship relation as a reasonably close one if it involves no more than two marriages[54] and no more than two units of collateral distance.[55] It also defines "marriage" broadly as any kinship relation across patrilineal descent groups.[56] Since this chapter looks only at kinship relations within each cohort of prefects, most of kinship relations used in the analysis are by nature between persons who were either of the same generation or removed by only one generation. Only a small number of relations are between men who were two generations removed. Kinship relations that meet the above criteria are found for 211 prefects (out of a total of 511) in the 1040s cohort and 118 prefects (out of a total of 534) in the 1210s cohort.

The results reported in figures 3.1a and 3.1b and table 3.10 reveal sharp contrasts between the two periods in regard to the structure of kinship networks of the prefects. For the 1040s cohort, all but twelve of the 211 prefects ended up in one big component. That is, as far as we can tell with available data, more than 40% of the 511 prefects in the 1040s cohort were part of a single interconnected group. By contrast, the kinship network of prefects from the 1210s was structurally more fragmented. First, only 118 prefects, that is less than a quarter of all known prefects from the 1210s, had agnatic or affinal ties with one another from the same decade. Second, these 118 prefects did not form one connected group. Instead, they broke down into a total of twenty disconnected groups (or "components," to use the technical term of network analysis), and even the largest component could claim only less than half of the 118 prefects as its members (table 3.10).

An analysis of the regional origin of prefects in these network components (table 3.11) reveals a notable tendency toward regional clustering in the 1210s compared to the 1040s. While it was fairly common in the 1040s for prefects from different macroregions to be related to each other through marriage, it was far less so in the 1210s. In the 1040s, the giant component (component A) involves participants from all macroregions of the eleventh century. Although four of the other five components involved prefects from only the same region, three of them were held together only by agnatic ties that by nature limited its geographical scope. In the 1210s, however, even after those components held together exclusively through agnatic ties are excluded, only two of the remaining ten components crossed macroregional borders, and these are the top two components by size (components G and H).

Furthermore, inside these top two big cross-regional components, there was a clear structural division between the Sichuan-born prefects and the Southeasterners. Component G was essentially a cluster of prefects hailing from the broad area of Southeast China, while component H was almost exclusively a Sichuan cluster, involving half of the twenty-one prefects of Sichuan origin in the 1210s. In both clusters the connection between Sichuan-born prefects and the southeasterners was established through only one marriage tie.[57] In component G, this one affinal tie was mediated through a high-ranking Sichuanese official (i.e., Zhang Jun [1097–1164]) who relocated to Central China, which was one of the very few cases of elite

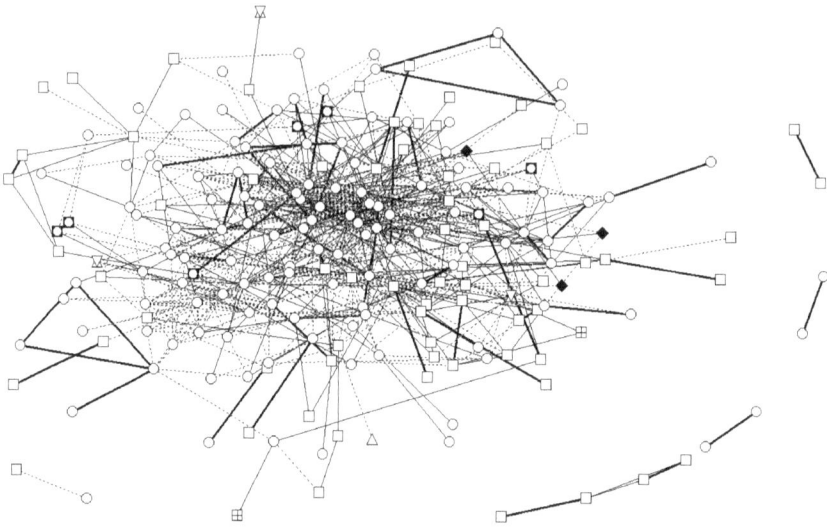

FIGURE 3.1A. Kinship networks among prefects of the 1040s. Each node in the network graph represents a prefect from the period. Nodes are shaped differently according to the home AMR of the prefect. Three styles of lines denote different kinds of connections between each pair of prefects: thick solid lines represent agnatic ties, thin solid lines direct affinal relations, and dotted lines affinal ties via a third party.

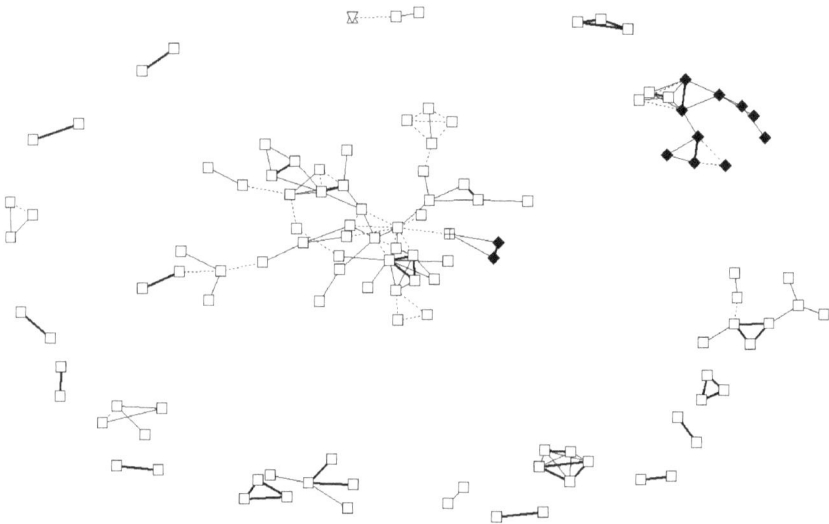

FIGURE 3.1B. Kinship networks among prefects of the 1210s. For symbology legend, see fig. 3.1a.

emigration from Sichuan in the Southern Song prior to the Mongol invasions, making the marriage tie in question all the more special.

This, however, is not evidence that officials of the 1040s did not prefer
marriages with families from their home region, while their counterparts
in the 1210s did. Looking more closely into the networks of the 1040s
prefects, one finds that the tendency to contract marriages within a family's
home region, be it due to preference or convenience, was already notable in
the mid-eleventh century. The calculations here employ "patrilines," each
consisting of any number of prefects related through exclusively father-son
ties, as the unit of analysis and consider only those marriages that linked two
patrilines of prefects together (thus excluding indirect affinal relationships
where two patrilines were related through a third party with which both
contracted marriages). The focus here is on connections between patrilines
established through marriage, not each individual instance of marriage.
Therefore, even when marriages are contracted repeatedly between two
patrilines, they establish only one affinal connection in the following calculations. Due to technical difficulties, the following calculations also exclude
patrilines whose regional origin cannot be identified and those which had
more than one AMR registered as its place of origin, either a result of its
recent migrations or having different descent lines living in different places.
Of the 115 patrilines in the 1040s that meet the above criteria, sixty-seven
of them were from North China and thirty-eight from Southeast China. The
data reports that 64% (86 of 134) of the affinal connections involving North
China patrilines were with each other while 61% (40 of 66) of those involving
Southeast China patrilines were with families outside their home region. In
other words, Southeast China patrilines' affinal connections crossed regional
borders 54% more often, while the North China ones crossed borders 44%
less often. But one should not jump to the conclusion that prefects from
Southeast China preferred establishing affinal ties with those outside their
home region, because the smaller number of Southeast China patrilines
in the data relative to those from North China significantly decreased the
likelihood of their becoming in-laws. Given the relative size of patrilines
from North and Southeast China in the dataset, even in a hypothetical,
purely random situation where marriage ties are evenly distributed between
patrilines regardless of their regional origins (i.e., where the regional origin
of potential marriage partners is not a consideration when making marriage decisions), one expects that patrilines from Southeast China are 3.2
times more likely to have affinal connections across regional borders than
within them, whereas those from North China are 45% *more* likely to do

TABLE 3.10. Structure of kinship networks among prefects, the 1040s versus the 1210s

Cohort of Prefects	Size of Component	No. of Components
I. Networks via Kinship Ties Involving Two or Fewer Marriages		
1040s (N=211)	199	1
	4	1
	2	4
Total		**6**
1210s (N=118)	49	1
	13	1
	9	1
	5	2
	4	1
	3	5
	2	9
Total		**20**

(continued)

so.[58] Compared with expected probabilities in this scenario, what the data shows here, in fact, is a strong tendency of *both* groups to establish affinal ties within regional borders.

What truly makes the marriage practice of prefects in the 1040s different from those in the 1210s, I think, is a notable degree of cosmopolitanism among the 1040s prefects. Just as their tendency to serve near their homes did not prevent them from also having administrative experience in multiple regions, their tendency to look for an in-law from their home region did not turn them away from getting one from elsewhere. In fact, 61% (23 of 38) of the Southeast China patrilines and 43% (29 of 67) of the North China ones were linked by marriage to those outside their home region, both very close to the expected percentages of such patrilines in a random situation (67% and 42% respectively).

The situation in the 1210s was drastically different. The tendency of regional endogamy grew more intense. There are a total of fifty-two patrilines in the 1210s set that meet the criteria for this analysis, including forty-three from Southeast China, eight from Sichuan, and one from Central China.

TABLE 3.10. *(continued)*

Cohort of Prefects	Size of Component	No. of Components
II. Networks via Kinship Ties Involving One or No Marriages		
1040s (N=189)	171	1
	4	2
	2	5
Total		8
1210s (N=110)	31	1
	12	1
	7	1
	5	2
	4	1
	3	6
	2	14
Total		26

Note: The kinship network of each cohort of prefects is partitioned into several components of varying size. A component is a maximal connected subgroup of prefects (i.e., a subgroup of prefects each of whom was connected through kinship ties to at least another in the component but not to any other prefect outside the component). This table reports the number of components each kinship network contains and the size of each component (i.e., the number of prefects in each component). For example, when kinship ties are defined as agnatic or affinal connections involving no more than two marriages, the resulting kinship network of the 1040s cohort consists of six components, one of which contains 199 prefects, another four prefects, and four others two prefects each. As a robustness test, part 2 of this table redefines kinship ties more narrowly as agnatic or affinal connections involving only one marriage and recalculates how the kinship network is partitioned under this narrower definition. Sample size (N) is the total number of prefects with documented kinship relationships that meet the criteria specified here and in the chapter.

Given the overwhelming number of prefects of southeastern origin, affinal connections of Southeast China patrilines are expected to be more than twice as likely within the group than otherwise, while the small percentage of Sichuan men in the 1210s cohort means that affinal connections of Sichuan men would be 11.6 times more likely to occur across regional borders. The data shows, however, that affinal connections of Sichuan men were nearly as exclusively confined to their home region as that of the southeasterners. More importantly, the data reveals low percentages in both regions of patrilines with affinal ties across regional borders (1 of 43 in Southeast China and

TABLE 3.11. Number of prefects in each component of kinship networks, by regional origin

Home AMR	Prefects, 1040–1049						Prefects, 1210–1219																			
	A	B	C	D	E	F	G	H	I	J	K	L	M	N	O	P	Q	R	S	T	U	V	W	X	Y	Z
North China	121		2	1		2																				
Northwest China	7																									
Southeast China	62	4		1	2		46	3	9	5	5	4	2	3	3	3	3	2	2	2	2	2	2	2	2	2
Central China	2						1																			
Sichuan	3						2	10																		
Lingnan	1																									
Origin Unknown	3												1													
Total	199	4	2	2	2	2	49	13	9	5	5	4	3	3	3	3	3	2	2	2	2	2	2	2	2	2

Note: Underlined components consist only of prefects who were agnatic kin, which by nature limits the scope of the component to a single AMR.

2 of 8 in Sichuan), both significantly lower than the expected percentages of such patrilines in a random situation (17% and 85% respectively). As a result, the kinship networks of prefects in the 1210s included two major components (G and H), comprised of southeasterners and Sichuan men respectively, disconnected from each other.

Another significant difference between networks of the two periods is that those in the 1040s had a core–periphery structure in favor of the North China prefects, making them not only numerically superior but also structurally dominant. The network of prefects is partitioned into core and periphery here by identifying the subgroups of maximal size in the network, whose members are directly connected—that is, through agnatic relations, marriage, or marriage to the same third party—to a specified number (k) of other members of the group (i.e., the "k-core" approach).[59] By varying the number k, one is able to define the core group in more or less inclusive ways. The largest value for k obtained in the network of the 1040s cohort is seven. At this level the core group contains forty-six prefects (table 3.12a, fig. 3.2a), who were predominantly from North China (38 of 46, or 83%), especially the Capital Corridor (29 of 46). As table 3.12a shows, even if the size of the core group is expanded by lowering the value of k to six and then five, the proportion of North China men in the core group remains at high levels (>75%), way beyond the percentage of North China men in the entire network (126 of 211, or 60%). Conversely, although prefects of Southeast China origin counted toward 33% (69 of 211) in the whole network, they were disproportionately located in the periphery: 78% (54 of 69) of them would not be considered members of the core group until the value of k is lowered to four or less. Accordingly, prefects of North China origin in the 1040s, as a whole, were far better connected than those from elsewhere. On average, each of them had connections to 8.8 others. The four best connected members, Lü Yijian (979–1044), Zhang Mian (983–1060), Han Yi (972–1044), and Lü Gongbi (1007–1073) were each related to thirty or more prefects in the 1040s network. In comparison, prefects from Southeast and Northwest China on average had ties to only four or five prefects in the network, and those from Central China, Sichuan, and Lingnan even fewer (table 3.13).

The core–periphery structure was much weaker in the network of the 1210s cohort (table 3.12b). The largest k value obtained for this network is four. No matter how inclusively the core group is defined, the proportion of southeasterners fluctuates between 80% and 92%, consistently in close range of the percentage of southeasterners in the entire network (88%, or 104 of

TABLE 3.12A. Core–Periphery structures in kinship networks: Networks of prefects in the 1040s cohort

Coreness Value (k)	North China	Northwest China	Southeast China	Central China	Sichuan	Lingnan	Unknown	Size of k-core
1	15	0	17	1	0	1	1	35
2	17	0	13	1	1	0	0	32
3	7	3	15	0	2	0	0	27
4	12	2	9	0	0	0	2	25
5	27	1	5	0	0	0	0	33
6	10	0	3	0	0	0	0	13
7	38	1	7	0	0	0	0	46
Total	126	7	69	2	3	1	3	211

Heading: **Regional Origin** (spanning North China through Unknown)

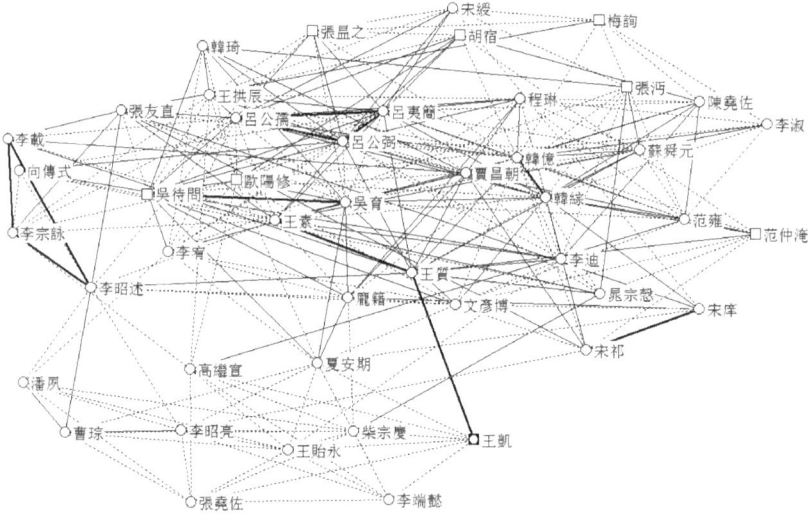

FIGURE 3.2A. Core group in kinship networks of the 1040s prefects (7-core). For symbology legend, see fig. 3.1a.

TABLE 3.12B. Core–Periphery structures in kinship networks: Networks of prefects in the 1210s cohort

	Regional Origin of Members in the k-core				
Coreness Value (k)	Southeast China	Central China	Sichuan	Unknown	Size of k-core
1	47	0	3	1	51
2	32	1	7	0	40
3	17	0	0	0	17
4	8	0	2	0	10
Total	104	1	12	1	118

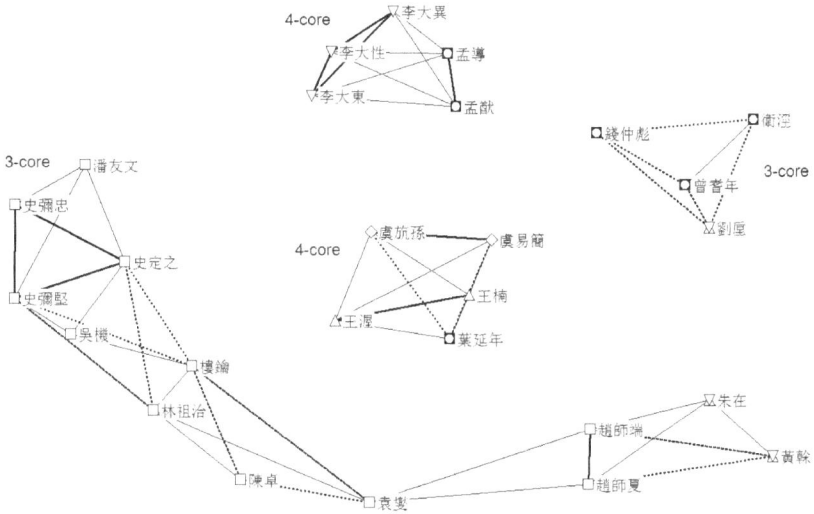

FIGURE 3.2B. Core groups in kinship networks of the 1210s prefects (4- and 3-core). Each node in the network graph represents a prefect from the period. Nodes are shaped differently according to the home circuit of the prefect. Three styles of lines denote different kinds of connections between each pair of prefects: thick solid lines represent agnatic ties, thin solid lines direct affinal relations, and dotted lines affinal ties via a third party.

TABLE 3.13. Number of connections possessed by prefects, average by home AMR

Home AMR	Average Number of Connections	
	1040s	1210s
North China	8.8	—
Northwest China	4.9	—
Southeast China	5.0	2.4
Central China	1.5	3.0
Sichuan	3.0	2.8
Lingnan	1.0	—
Unknown	4.0	1.0
Empire-wide average	7.2	2.5

118). The core itself became more fragmented in the 1210s. While a sizable number (44%, or 92 of 211, under a k value of five) of prefects in the 1040s were well connected to each other and formed one fairly densely connected group, there were only a few small pockets of well-connected groups in the network of the 1210s (four separate clusters comprising 26%, or 27 of 104, of the prefects under a k value of three, see fig. 3.2b). Regardless of regional origin, prefects of the 1210s each had connections to only two to three others in the cohort. Even the top three best connected prefects of the 1210s, Lou Yue (1137–1213), Shi Mijian (d. 1232), and Shi Dingzhi, had connections to only seven to ten others in the cohort.

CONCLUSION

In his seminal article on social and political changes in middle period China, Robert Hartwell defined a semihereditary professional elite that occupied a disproportionate number of incumbents to finance and policy offices between 983 and 1086. It claimed descent from the great Tang clans and imitated the behavior of the Tang elite: they maintained their main residence in the Song capital region, intermarried with each other regardless of regional origin, and placed most of their sons in the upper echelons of government generation after generation. He contrasted it with the founding elite and the gentry, the two other groups in Northern Song bureaucracy. He argued that

GOVERNING A MULTICENTERED EMPIRE 141

the gentry based their power in local society, engaged in a wide range of occupations, and preferred marriage with those from the same native county. It is important to note that in Hartwell's view, the professional elite comprised a fairly limited number of families and that even at the peak of its power, it claimed less than 30% of policy offices and finance office-years. By contrast, the majority of these offices at almost all times during the Northern Song were staffed by the gentry. In the late eleventh century, with the expansion of examinations and factional struggles at court, the professional elite eventually disappeared as a separate status-group and became indistinguishable from the gentry families.[60]

Subsequent studies show, however, that maintaining a capital residence and contracting marriage alliances with those of different regional origins were strategies widely pursued by Northern Song officials.[61] This raises the question of whether the gentry existed at all in Northern Song bureaucracy as a separate group with distinctive social practices. These studies suggest that the professional elite, defined by its residential and marriage practices, was much larger and more inclusive than Hartwell suggested. Until the late eleventh century, local elites who succeeded in the examinations often relocated to the capital (or places with convenient access to it) and married with those from outside their native region, thus transforming themselves into new members of the professional elite.

The formation of this professional elite in the early Song, I think, is in large measure the product of a conscious Song effort to unite the political elites in northern and southern states into a new one based in the Song capital. And it continued to be shaped by the vicissitudes of Song ruling strategies. By expanding the examination system and making resources for political success more available outside the capital, the Song not only allowed more to join the capital elite by succeeding in the examinations and relocating to the capital, but it also made it increasingly practical for elite families to stay in their home region and still achieve political prominence. This, I think, was what distinguishes the Song from the Tang: as Tackett demonstrates, even in late Tang elites based in the provinces had little hope of gaining political prominence. This changed the rules of the game.

This chapter looks at these changes and their consequences by focusing on a small sample of Song administrators. It studies the prefects when the power of these changes was just unleashed and compares them to those who were in office 170 years later right before the Mongols attacked. Through the window of these samples, it argues that economic and cultural developments in South China and the Song attempt to tap into these developments profoundly transformed both the composition and social behavior of the Song political elite.

First, North China, especially those from the Capital Corridor, continued to claim a share of prefect offices in the 1040s significantly greater than its share of the total population and occupied dominant positions in empire-wide elite networks. But consistent with Hartwell's data on financial and policy-making officeholders, they now filled only half of the vacancies and left the rest mainly in hands of men from different regions of the south, who counted toward nearly 40% of all prefects in the 1040s with identifiable geographical origins. The geographical pattern of success in the south during the mid-eleventh century exhibited the multicentered character it had acquired in earlier centuries. Although the Lower Yangzi was the flagship of southern accomplishments, there were also separate pockets of success in modern Jiangxi and Fujian.

Second, the geographical pattern of southern success changed dramatically between the 1040s and the 1210s, indicative of significant differences in the logic of political prominence between the two periods. In the 1040s, despite the broadened geographical scope of political participation, the influence of the capital continued to be felt in the south, where the leading area of success were a band of prefectures situated along the southern segment of the Grand Canal, a major waterway providing convenient access to the principal and auxiliary Song capitals. In sharp contrast, the driving force of success in the 1210s was economic. Being the seat of the new capital gave Lin'an no competitive edge. Instead, men holding prefectural governorship in the 1210s came predominantly from a cluster of prefectures stretching along the coast of the East China Sea.

Third, the large number of southern-born officials offered the Song the opportunity to try out a new way of staffing its field administration. Scholars have noted that local offices in Sichuan were often staffed by Sichuan natives after the late eleventh century. As the data here illustrates, this reflects what seems to have already been a national trend in the 1040s, which continued in a more intensified form into the 1210s. With the notable exception of Sichuan where special policies applied, in both periods, men, regardless of their regional origins, were more likely to serve as prefects in their home region than any of the other regions. On average, the geographical scope of a prefect's place of assignment in both periods was limited to a radius of three hundred to four hundred miles. In the 1040s this led to a pattern of southerners serving mostly in the south and northerners in the north. This north–south contradistinction transformed into an east–west one in the 1210s as Sichuan-born officials grew in numbers and northerners completely dropped out of sight after the Jurchen invasions.

A notable degree of cosmopolitanism, nevertheless, distinguished prefects of the 1040s from their counterparts in the 1210s. This is the fourth finding in this chapter. Despite the inclination to serve relatively close to home, around 40% of the prefects in the 1040s, whatever their regional origin, had experience serving in three or more broadly defined administrative regions in their career. By the 1210s, however, the inclination of serving close to home went to such great lengths that men serving as prefects in three or more regions became extremely rare.

The cosmopolitan character in kinship networks of the 1040s likewise made them structurally different from those of the 1210s. Despite a notable tendency toward regional endogamy in both periods, the substantial number of prefects in the 1040s from North and Southeast China alike who contracted marriage across regional borders joined prefects of different regional origins in a huge interwoven web of connections. By the 1210s, however, the tendency of marrying within regional borders had so intensified that kinship networks of prefects broke down into regional clusters.

This discussion suggests a more general model of understanding the profound social and political implications of a new, multicentered south and the transition from Northern to Southern Song. Development in South China provided essential resources for regional independence as it did in the tenth century, but it also offered the human, economic, and cultural resources that could be mobilized for running the new empire. The Song consciously tapped into these resources by recruiting southern men into civil service and employing them as local administrators, often close to home but also in other regions. This not only changed the composition of the Song political elite, but the policies implemented to achieve this end (such as the spread of schools and expanded quotas in prefectural examinations) significantly undermined the capital's monopoly of political and cultural resources and redistributed them in favor of wealthy areas, fundamentally changing the driving forces behind political success. As the political elite was no longer clustered only around the capital, the tendencies of serving and marrying close to home emerged. As these tendencies ran their full course in the Southern Song, the capital elite disappeared, and along with it capital-oriented elite networks.

TABLE 3.14. Appendix: Data distribution in Li Zhiliang's rosters of prefects, 1040–1049 and 1210–1219

Circuit	Prefectures Surveyed by Li Zhiliang		Prefects Listed in Li Zhiliang's Rosters				Percentage of Listed Prefects with Identifiable Regional Origin	
	Total by Circuit	% of All Prefectures*	Total by Circuit (1040s)	Average Per Prefecture (1040s)	Total by Circuit (1210s)	Average Per Prefecture (1210s)	The 1040s Cohort	The 1210s Cohort
North China								
Kaifeng	1	100	19	19	—	—	100	—
Jingdong East	4	44	22	6	—	—	77	—
Jingdong West	7	70	38	5	—	—	95	—
Jingxi North	9	90	80	9	—	—	96	—
Jingxi South	5	56	14	3	16	4†	79	69
Hebei East	7	37	56	8	—	—	95	—
Hebei West	8	42	53	7	—	—	87	—
Hedong	8	32	35	4	—	—	89	—
Northwest China								
Yongxingjun	12	50	109	9	—	—	89	—
Qinfeng	9	36	40	4	—	—	85	—
Southeast China								
Huainan East	12	80	58	5	56	5	81	68
Huainan West	10	83	35	4	48	5	91	65

Liangzhe East	7	100	47	7	58	8	68	64
Liangzhe West	8	100	50	6	65	8	72	69
Jiangnan East	9	100	41	5	78	9	76	69
Jiangnan West	11	100	57	5	93	8	63	54
Fujian	8	100	43	5	62	8	70	68
Central China								
Jinghu North	9	60	28	3	42	5	75	67
Jinghu South	7	70	31	4	62	9	45	45
Sichuan								
Chengdufu	2	13	8	4	15	8	100	47
Tongchuanfu	3	20	8	3	14	5	38	86
Lizhou	3	18	5	2	17	6	80	47
Kuizhou	1	7	2	2	9	9	0	67
Lingnan								
Guangnan East	10	67	51	5	64	6	51	39
Guangnan West	5	18	13	3	22	4	15	41
Total	175	50	943	5	721	7	79	60

Notes: * Since the number of prefectures in each circuit changes from time to time during the Song period, the total number of prefectures used here to calculate the percentage in each circuit is inevitably a rough estimate based on the Geography Treatise (*dili zhi*) of the dynastic history of Song.
† In the Southern Song, seven of the nine prefectures previously in Jingxi South remained under Song control and four of them are surveyed by Li Zhiliang; Jun, Jin, Ying, and Xiangyang. In the Southern Song, Jin prefecture was moved under the jurisdiction of Lizhou circuit.

NOTES

1 *SS* 263.9098ff.

2 *SS* 258.8990.

3 On mandatory relocations, see also Ebrey's chapter in this volume.

4 Lin, "Song chu zhengquan," 1–19; Chen, "Managing the Territories from Afar," 102–7, 110, 239–45.

5 Qian's appointment to Deng does not seem honorific, since he died in the prefectural office of Deng (*fushu*) the following year. *QSW* 3:65; *SS* 480. 13897ff.

6 *QSW* 6:418.

7 Lin, "Song chu zhengquan," 17–19.

8 *QSW* 6:418.

9 Hartwell, "Demographic, Political, and Social Transformations," 414–15; McKnight, "Administrators of Hangchow," 192. Percentage of North China men in the examinations is calculated from table 21 in Chaffee, *The Thorny Gates of Learning*, 132. Taizong's attempt to mold northern and southern elite families into a capital-based political elite is consistent with his attempt to legitimate the new dynasty and his own reign by integrating northern and southern architectural traditions; see Tracy Miller's findings in this volume.

10 Percentage of South China men in the examinations is calculated from table 21 in Chaffee, *The Thorny Gates of Learning*, 132.

11 *QSW* 222:198.

12 *SHY* Xuanju 15.15.

13 Zhou Yuwen, *Songdai de zhou xian xue*, 6. *QSW* 10:329. Terada Gō, *Sōdai kyōikushi gaisetsu*, 25–31.

14 *SHY* Chongru 2.4, Xuanju 3.23; *CB* 147.3563–65, 153.3714–15.

15 Zhou Yuwen, *Songdai de zhou xian xue*, 72.

16 Chaffee, *The Thorny Gates of Learning*, 134; Hartwell, "Demographic, Political, and Social Transformations," 414–15; McKnight, "Administrators of Hangchow," 192.

17 For a summary of these developments, see Clark, "The Southern Kingdoms," 171–97; Bol, *Neo-Confucianism in History*, 15–16.

18 For a prosopographical study of the late Tang political elite, see Tackett, *The Destruction of the Medieval Chinese Aristocracy*.

19 Wang, *Songren zhuanji ziliao suoyin (dianzi ban)*. Included in the full-text database of Scripta Sinica.

20 It should be noted that only prefects of Kaifeng and four of the Song circuits (Liangzhe, Jiangnan East and West, and Fujian) are thoroughly surveyed in these volumes; for the other circuits only governors of selected prefectures are included in the lists. As a result, the number of prefectures included varies significantly from one region to another. As shown in table 3.14, Sichuan and Guangnan West were among the least surveyed circuits. For example, the volume on Guangnan includes ten of the fifteen prefectures in Guangnan East but only five of at least twenty-five prefectures in Guangnan West. Similarly, only eleven out of about sixty-three prefectures in the four circuits of Sichuan are included in Li's lists. This creates a problem for interpretation, which will be discussed later along with the findings. Li, *Bei Song jingshi ji dong xi lu dajun shouchen kao*; Li, *Song Chuan Shan dajun shouchen yiti kao*; Li, *Song Fujian lu junshou nianbiao*; Li, *Song Hebei Hedong dajun shouchen yiti kao*; Li, *Song Liangguang dajun shouchen yiti*

kao; Li, *Song Lianghu dajun shouchen yiti kao*; Li, *Song Lianghuai dajun shouchen yiti kao*; Li, *Song Liangjiang junshou yiti kao*; Li, *Song Liangzhe lu junshou nianbiao*. The CBDB is a prosopographical database project that began with the late Robert Hartwell and has grown considerably over time through the collaboration of many development teams led by Peter Bol, Michael Fuller, Stuart Shieber, Deng Xiaonan, Luo Xin, Lau Nap-yin, Liu Cheng-yun, and Hilde De Weerdt, among others, as well as data contributions from an even larger group of scholars. For a description of the project and its core institutions and contributors, visit the CBDB website: http://isites.harvard.edu/icb/icb.do?keyword=k16229.

21 Some of the data in the CBDB are legacies from the research of Robert Hartwell, but more has been harvested by the project team from various sources, including, above all, Wang Deyi's revised electronic edition of the *Song Biographical Index*.

22 For a full list of biographical materials used to build this Sichuan database, see Chen, "Managing the Territories from Afar," 357–86, appendix 1. What I refer to as "funerary biographies" include a variety of genres, such as descriptions of conduct (*xingzhuang*), tomb epitaphs (*muzhiming*), and spirit-path steles (*shendaobei*).

23 One of the major tools used for checking data integrity here is the index year assigned by the CBDB team, which are best estimates of a person's sixtieth year of life. For example, a prefect from the 1040s with an index year earlier than 1020 or greater than 1100 raises a red flag. These checks suggest that data problems are few for the size of this dataset. The most common ones relate to the disambiguation of persons, that is, the failure to identify a prefect with the right person in CBDB. This happens most often when two or more persons in CBDB have the same name and when a person is known by an alternative name or has characters in his name written in a variant form. Occasionally there are also issues with misidentification of places and editorial errors of kinship relations.

24 For the rationales behind using burial sites as the clue to a family's address of primary residence, see Bossler, *Powerful Relations*, 42.

25 On physiographic macroregions, see G. William Skinner, *The City in Late Imperial China*, 211–20.

26 Here I borrow the term "Capital Corridor" from Nicolas Tackett, but use it to refer to a different region. In his study of the late Tang elite, Tackett uses the Capital Corridor to refer to the zone between the twin Tang capital cities (Chang'an and Luoyang). See Tackett, *The Destruction of Medieval Chinese Aristocracy*. The Capital Corridor in this chapter refers to a region comprising five prefectures extending from Henan (Luoyang) in the west to Kaifeng and Yingtian in the east.

27 *SS* 285.9622. For the epitaph of Jia Changling, see *QSW* 19:51.

28 Hu and Cai, "Songdai Langzhou Chen shi yanjiu," 51–62.

29 *SS* 317.10344–45. *QSW* 62:34.

30 One exception is Xiu prefecture. Despite its location between Su and Hang along the Grand Canal, no prefect in the 1040s is known to be from Xiu. I also include Yue in this band of prefectures, though strictly speaking, Yue is not on the Grand Canal but is linked to the southern terminus of it via the Zhedong Canal.

31 This is consistent with John Chaffee's findings about the sudden and exceptional success of the Zhe Coast in the civil service examinations in the Southern Song. Chaffee, *The Thorny Gates of Learning*, 148–56.

32 Chen, "Bunken tōchika ni okeru zaichi shakai to kōiki chihō," 157; Smith, *Taxing Heaven's Storehouse*, 98–108.

33 Unlikely, because the proportion of prefects Liangzhe, Fujian, and Jiangnan East and West each contributed to the 1210s cohort (51%, 21%, and 18% respectively) was roughly in line with their share of *jinshi* in the period between 1163 and 1224 (35%, 29%, and 19% respectively). Sichuan on average produced only about 14% of all *jinshi* in Southern Song, which fell far short of Liangzhe, Fujian, and Jiangnan East and West combined. The calculation of each region's share of *jinshi* is based on the numbers provided in Chaffee, *The Thorny Gates of Learning*, 132–33.

34 Tackett, *The Destruction of the Medieval Chinese Aristocracy*, 10, 72, 84–87.

35 Admittedly, a degree of arbitrariness always enters into such decisions. The boundaries of these AMRs are decided based on several factors. First, AMRs should be relatively similar in size for meaningful comparisons. Thus, Fujian, roughly Southeast Coast physiographic region, would be too small to be considered an AMR on its own. Second, the AMRs are modeled as much as possible on Song administrative vocabulary. For example, since Song official documents often use phrases such as "Chuan Xia" 川峽 and "Lingbiao" 嶺表, all circuits of Sichuan are placed inside one AMR and, likewise, all those of Lingnan in another. Similarly, Jiangnan West and East are not assigned to different AMRs since the Song texts very often referred to both with the term "Jiang" 江 or "Jiangnan" 江南. I also, for example, assign Huainan to the same AMR as Jiangnan circuits instead of Jinghu because Song documents pair Huai 淮 more often with Jiang than with Jinghu. Finally, an effort is also made to match the boundaries of the AMRs to those of G. William Skinner's physiographic regions as closely as possible for making rough comparisons.

36 McKnight, "Administrators of Hangchow," 192, 200.

37 Though cases of Sichuan men assigned to Sichuan began to appear by the 1040s, the most important prefectures in Sichuan, which are the only ones surveyed by Li Zhiliang, remained off-limits. On changes in personnel policy on Sichuan, see Lo, *An Introduction to the Civil Service of Sung China*, 204–6; Smith, *Taxing Heaven's Storehouse*, 98–108; Chen, "Managing the Territories from Afar," 138–43.

38 *SS* 285.9605–9. Li, *Song Lianghu dajun shouchen yiti kao*, 12, 47, 239, 281–82; Li, *Song Lianghuai dajun shouchen yiti kao*, 401; Li, *Song Liangjiang junshou yiti kao*, 10, 300, 342; Li, *Song Chuan Shan dajun shouchen yiti kao*, 252; Li, *Bei Song jingshi ji dong xi lu dajun shouchen kao*, 16–17, 176, 327; Li, *Song Fujian lu junshou nianbiao*, 47. Li, by mistake, records Liu's appointment to Jiang prefecture as Ling Jingyang's (Li, *Song Liangjiang junshou yiti kao*, 342; Li, *Song Lianghuai dajun shouchen yiti kao*, 401). This mistake is corrected in the dataset here.

39 Mostern, *"Dividing the Realm in Order to Govern,"* 41–51.

40 *SHY* Zhiguan 59.3. *CB* 23.531. Note that in 982 the jurisdiction of a circuit (*dao*) was larger than later in the Song.

41 *CB* 22.506, 6.149. Chen, "Managing the Territories from Afar," 112–13, 112n173.

42 *CB* 7.178, 11.248, 18.403, 47.1015, 48.1058, and 108.2526

43 *SS* 159.3721. For punishments of officials refusing to accept distant appointments, see *CB* 7.178.

44 For an example of court officials expressing their concerns, see *CB* 32.721. For an example of such protests, see *Jiayou ji jianzhu*, 99–104.

45 Chen, "Managing the Territories from Afar," 138–43.

46 *CB* 107.2504; *SHY* Zhiguan 11.2–3.

47 *SHY* Zhiguan 47.6; *SS* 159.3721. See also *CB* 178.4318, 468.11177–80. On "qualification sequence," see Deng Xiaonan, *Songdai wenguan xuanren zhidu zhu cengmian*, 105–7.

48 *SHY* Zhiguan 8.18–19. This new definition was quoted later in *SHY* Xuanju 24.25. On Northern Song definition of distant and near places, see *SHY* Xuanju 24.25.

49 Chen, "Bunken tōchika ni okeru zaichi shakai to kōiki chihō," 156–57.

50 A further study which employs the circuit as the unit of analysis fails to reveal a similar pattern. In other words, even the 1210s cohort of prefects did not always receive the largest proportion of prefect appointments inside their home circuit, but instead they very often served in a neighboring circuit. Of the 1210s prefects, only those from the following four circuits received the largest proportion of prefect appointments inside their home circuit: Fujian (24%), Guangnan East (40%), Jiangnan West (17%), and Lizhou (100%). But for Lizhou and Guangnan East circuits, the sample size is too small to make these numbers meaningful. By contrast, men from other parts of the Southern Song were more likely to serve in an adjacent than their home circuit. For instance, men from Chengdufu circuit served most often as prefects in the nearby Tongchuanfu circuit, and vice versa. The same is true for men from Liangzhe East and West. Men from Huainan West served most often as prefects in Jiangnan West, from Jiangnan East in Jiangnan West, and from Jinghu South in Jinghu North. Whether one held prefectural governorship most often in his home circuit or an adjacent one, such appointments usually count toward about one-fifth of all prefect appointments documented for men from Fujian, Jiangnan, and Liangzhe where the sample size is large.

51 *SS* 413.12400.

52 Both CBDB and my own database on Song dynasty Sichuan code kinship data following a defined set of symbols described in Fuller, *The China Biographical Database User's Guide*, 13–14. For example, if it is known from sources that person X is person Y's nephew on the paternal side and that person Z is X's father, X is then coded in the database as the BS (i.e., brother's son) of Y, and Z the F (father) of X. This allows the querying algorithm of the database to uncover the agnatic relationship between Y and Z through X and represent it as BSF (by concatenating BS and F), which can then be converted into a more direct relationship of B (brother). Sometimes when the conversion involves ambiguity that cannot be resolved (say, it is impossible to tell if X's father's grandson is X's own son or his brother's), the conservative path is taken to maximize the kinship distance between the two (in the case above, this means interpreting the kinship as X's brother's son).

53 The most important criterion used here is generational depth. For example, a prefect serving in the 1040s could not be more than three generations removed from another prefect serving also in the 1040s, and a prefect from the 1210s could not be the son of someone serving in the 1040s.

54 I have tested the results of defining a close kinship relation more strictly as one that involves no more than one marriage (table 3.10, part 2). Although the network graph, not unexpectedly, becomes more fragmented, all the conclusions I draw remain robust.

55 Following the CBDB conventions, this chapter computes collateral distance by counting the total number of B (brothers) and Z (sisters) present in the string, after the neces-

sary concatenations and conversions, indicating the relationship between two persons. See Fuller, *The China Biographical Database User's Guide*, 41. In fact, after meeting the criterion of involving only two or fewer marriages, only a tiny fraction of the kinship data used here has more than two units of collateral distance. By definition, this also excludes vaguely expressed agnatic ties, such as lineal ancestor or descendant (denoted by the letter G in the CBDB) and lineage kin (denoted by K).

56 As such, for example, the relationship between a person and his mother's brother or his daughter's son is considered involving one instance of marriage.

57 In component H, the connection was established through Yu Fangjian (b. 1164), who was a grandson of Yunwen (1110–1174) and married the granddaughter of Wang Zi (*jinshi* of 1138) from Chi prefecture. In component G, it was established through a marriage between a daughter from the Yuwen family and Zhang Jun, whose grandson Zhongshu (1174–1230) married a daughter of Wang Zhengji (1119–1196) from Ming prefecture.

58 Calculation of the probabilities of intraregional and cross-regional affinal connections is informed by sociological discussions of E-I Index. See Krackhardt and Stern, "Informal Networks and Organizational Crises," 123–40. The probability of a particular regional group having affinal connections inside (or across) regional borders is obtained by dividing the maximum possible of such connections by the maximum possible of all the affinal connections (both within and across regional borders) that patrilines in that particular regional group could establish. The maximum possible is determined by the size (i.e., the number of patrilines) of the regional group and the entire network. The probability of North China patrilines to have cross-regional affinal connections, for example, is $R^*(N\text{-}R)/[R!/2!^*(R\text{-}2)!+ R^*(N\text{-}R)]$, wherein N is the total number of patrilines in the entire network (in this example, N is 115) and R is the number of patrilines in the particular regional group being considered (in this example, R is 67 for North China).

59 On the analytical applications and technical details, see Seidman, "Network Structure and Minimum Degree," 269–87.

60 Hartwell, "Demographic, Political, and Social Transformations," 405–6, 408–10, 423–24.

61 Examples include Hymes, *Statesmen and Gentlemen*; Bossler, *Powerful Relations*; Lee, *Negotiated Power*; Chen, "Managing the Territories from Afar."

REFERENCES

PRIMARY SOURCES

Jiayou ji jian zhu 嘉祐集箋注, by Su Xun 蘇洵 (1009–1066). Edited by Zeng Zaozhuang 曾棗莊 and Jin Chengli 金成禮. Shanghai: Shanghai guji chubanshe, 1993.

Quan Song wen 全宋文, by Zeng Zaozhuang 曾棗莊 et al. Shanghai: Shanghai cishu chubanshe, 2006.

Song huiyao jigao 宋會要輯稿, compiled by Xu Song 徐松 (1781–1848). Beijing: Zhonghua shuju, 1957.

Song shi 宋史, edited by Tuo Tuo 脫脫 (1313–1355). Beijing: Zhonghua shuju, 1977.

Xu zizhi tongjian changbian 續資治通鑑長編, by Li Tao 李燾 (1115–1184). Beijing: Zhonghua shuju, 1985.

SECONDARY SOURCES

Bol, Peter K. *Neo-Confucianism in History.* Cambridge, Mass.: Harvard University Asia Center, 2008.

Bossler, Beverly J. *Powerful Relations: Kinship, Status, & the State in Sung China (960–1279).* Cambridge, Mass.: Harvard University Press, 1998.

Chaffee, John W. *The Thorny Gates of Learning in Sung China: A Social History of Examinations.* Albany: State University of New York Press, 1995.

Chen, Song 陳松. "Bunken tōchika ni okeru zaichi shakai to kōiki chihō: Sōdai Shisen o chūshin toshite" 分権統治下における在地社会と広域地方―宋代四川を中心として―. In *Chūgoku Sōdai no chiiki zō: hikakushi kara mita sensei kokka to chiiki* 中国宋代の地域像―比較史からみた専制国家と地域, edited by Ihara Hiroshi 伊原弘, Ichiki Tsuyuhiko 市來津由彦 and Sue Takashi須江隆, 143–77. Tokyo: Iwata-shoin, 2013.

———. "Managing the Territories from Afar: The Imperial State and Elites in Sichuan, 755–1279." PhD diss., Harvard University, 2011.

Clark, Hugh R. "The Southern Kingdoms between the T'ang and the Sung, 907–979." In *The Cambridge History of China*, Vol. 5: *Part One: The Sung Dynasty and Its Precursors, 907–1279*, edited by Denis Twitchett and Paul J. Smith, 133–205. Cambridge, UK: Cambridge University Press, 2009.

Deng Xiaonan 鄧小南. *Songdai wenguan xuanren zhidu zhu cengmian* 宋代文官選任制度諸層面. Shijiazhuang: Hebei jiaoyu chubanshe, 1993.

Hartwell, Robert M. "Demographic, Political, and Social Transformations of China, 750–1550." *Harvard Journal of Asiatic Studies* 42, no. 2 (1982): 365–442.

Hu Zhaoxi 胡昭曦 and Cai Dongzhou 蔡東洲. "Songdai Langzhou Chen shi yanjiu" 宋代閬州陳氏研究. In *Songdai Sichuan jiazu yu xueshu lunji* 宋代四川家族與學術論集, edited by Zou Chonghua 鄒重華 and Su Pinxiao 粟品孝, 51–78. Chengdu: Sichuan daxue chubanshe, 2005.

Hymes, Robert P. *Statesmen and Gentlemen: the Elite of Fu-chou, Chiang-hsi, in Northern and Southern Sung.* Cambridge, UK: Cambridge University Press, 1986.

Fuller, Michael. *The China Biographical Database User's Guide.* Accessed March 24, 2014. http://isites.harvard.edu/icb/icb.do?keyword=k16229.

Krackhardt, David, and Robert N. Stern. "Informal Networks and Organizational Crises: An Experimental Simulation." *Social Psychology Quarterly* 51, no. 2 (1988): 123–40.

Lee, Sukhee. *Negotiated Power: The State, Elites, and Local Governance in Twelfth- to Fourteenth-Century China.* Cambridge, Mass.: Harvard University Asia Center, 2014.

Li Zhiliang 李之亮. *Bei Song jingshi ji dong xi lu dajun shouchen kao* 北宋京師及東西路大郡守臣考. Chengdu: Ba Shu shushe, 2001.

———. *Song Chuan Shan dajun shouchen yiti kao* 宋川陝大郡守臣易替考. Chengdu: Ba Shu shushe, 2001.

———. *Song Fujian lu junshou nianbiao* 宋福建路郡守年表. Chengdu: Ba Shu shushe, 2001.

———. *Song Hebei Hedong dajun shouchen yiti kao* 宋河北河東大郡守臣易替考. Chengdu: Ba Shu shushe, 2001.

———. *Song Liangguang dajun shouchen yiti kao* 宋兩廣大郡守臣易替考. Chengdu: Ba Shu shushe, 2001.

———. *Song Lianghu dajun shouchen yiti kao* 宋兩湖大郡守臣易替考. Chengdu: Ba Shu shushe, 2001.

———. *Song Lianghuai da jun shouchen yiti kao* 宋兩淮大郡守臣易替考. Chengdu: Ba Shu shushe, 2001.

———. *Song Liangjiang junshou yiti kao* 宋兩江郡守易替考. Chengdu: Ba Shu shushe, 2001.

———. *Song Liangzhe lu junshou nianbiao* 宋兩浙路郡守年表. Chengdu: Ba Shu shushe, 2001.

Lin Huangda 林煌達. "Songchu zhengquan yu nanfang zhu xiangguo zhu chenzi de hudong guanxi" 宋初政權與南方諸降國臣子的互動關係. Accessed April 8, 2011. www.scu.edu.tw/history/song/thesis/th15.pdf.

Lo, Winston Wan. *An Introduction to the Civil Service of Sung China: With Emphasis on its Personnel Administration*. Honolulu: University of Hawai'i Press, 1987.

McKnight, Brian. "Administrators of Hangchow under the Northern Sung: A Case Study." *Harvard Journal of Asiatic Studies* 30 (1970): 185–211.

Mostern, Ruth. *"Dividing the Realm in Order to Govern": The Spatial Organization of the Song State (960–1279 CE)*. Cambridge, Mass.: Harvard University Asia Center, 2011.

Seidman, Stephen B. "Network Structure and Minimum Degree." *Social Networks* 5 (1983): 269–87.

Skinner, G. William, ed. *The City in Late Imperial China*. Stanford: Stanford University Press, 1977.

Smith, Paul J. *Taxing Heaven's Storehouse: Horses, Bureaucrats, and the Destruction of the Sichuan Tea Industry, 1074–1224*. Cambridge, Mass.: Harvard University Press, 1991.

Tackett, Nicolas. *The Destruction of Medieval Chinese Aristocracy*. Cambridge, Mass.: Harvard University Asia Center, 2013.

Terada Gō 寺田剛. *Sōdai kyōikushi gaisetsu* 宋代教育史概説. Tōkyō: Hakubunsha, 1965.

Wang Deyi 王德毅. *Songren zhuanji ziliao suoyin (dianzi ban)* 宋人傳記資料索引(電子版). Taibei: Institute of History and Philology at Academia Sinica, 2005.

Zhou Yuwen 周愚文. *Songdai de zhou xian xue* 宋代的州縣學. Taibei: Guoli bianyiguan, 1996.

4 Anatomies of Reform

The Qingli-Era Reforms of Fan Zhongyan and the
New Policies of Wang Anshi Compared

PAUL JAKOV SMITH

"Hang your reforms!" said Mr. Chichely. "There's no greater humbug
in the world. You never hear of a reform, but it means some trick to
put in new men."

—GEORGE ELIOT, *Middlemarch*

ALTHOUGH THE TERMS "MINOR" AND "MAJOR" HAVE BEEN USED
to differentiate between Fan Zhongyan's (989–1052) Qingli-era reforms of
1043–44 and Wang Anshi's (1021–1086) New Policies (Xin Fa) of the 1070s
and 1080s, had Fan's reform policies succeeded there would have been nothing minor about their impact.[1] They failed, however, so if a descriptive label
is needed we might call them the "abortive reforms" of 1043. But why were
they aborted, when the far more intrusive and controversial reforms of Wang
Anshi prevailed? My aim here is to suggest some answers to that question, by
comparing the two initiatives from the perspective of bureaucratic politics.
I argue that the triumph of the New Policies *as a political campaign*—which
implies nothing about the success or failure of the policies themselves—can
be attributed to Wang's success in five key domains: capturing key institutions of government, creating powerful new reformist organizations,
neutralizing political foes, mobilizing bureaucratic followers, and above all
retaining the unwavering support of his emperor for the reforms.

Institutional reform involves efforts by a segment of the political elite
to significantly alter the functional scope and institutional structure of the
government, in ways that transform the internal operations of the state and
its relationship to the economy and society as a whole. Such reform is different from the kinds of changes associated with dynastic transitions. The

warfare and violence that propels dynastic transitions allows new ruling houses—be they native or foreign—to impose the massive political changes they deem necessary to consolidate their power. These changes are the fruits of military victory, decreed from the top down and enforced where needed by coercion, rather than the outcome of a political process. Following the turmoil of dynastic change politically potent classes adjust to the new ruling house, and the political system as a whole enters a phase of stability and the entrenchment of interests that make further structural alterations difficult. Eventually, burgeoning domestic and external problems may prompt calls for change, especially to the personnel, fiscal, and military institutions of the state. But the constellation of interests and institutions that made up the traditional Chinese polity were crafted with an eye toward durable equilibrium.[2] As a result, significant internally generated reform efforts throughout the last millennium on the scale of Zhang Juzheng's reforms in the late sixteenth century, the Self-Strengthening and post-Boxer reforms of the late Qing—and even Deng Xiaoping's modernizing program of the 1980s—were relatively rare, and often provoked only by a pointed sense of crisis. It is in this category that the abortive reform campaign of Fan Zhongyan and the triumphant New Policies of Wang Anshi fall.

THE REFORMERS' VISIONS

The Qingli and Xining reform movements—so-called because of the era-names within which they were promulgated—are not just linked by categorical affinity, for Song observers thought that Wang's reforms were instigated by the failure of Fan Zhongyan's. The most extensive elaboration of that view is by the thirteenth-century literatus Lü Zhong (*jinshi* 1247). In a provocative set of essays on Northern Song politics Lü observes, "Had the Qingli reforms been completely enacted then the turmoil of both the [New Policies and the subsequent antireform Restoration] could have been avoided. Had Fan Zhongyan's advice been taken, then Anshi's mouth would have stayed shut."[3] Wang may well have agreed, for he referred to Fan as "the teacher for our entire generation," and in his own reform manifesto of 1058 blamed the failure of the Qingli reforms on Emperor Renzong's too-ready capitulation to Fan's opportunistic opponents.[4] The very fact that in the decade following Fan Zhongyan's movement Wang Anshi—among many others—was again calling for reform underscores how two generations of political activists perceived an ongoing crisis in the middle decades of the Northern Song.

By the 1030s, Fan Zhongyan spearheaded the view that government had been captured by the long-time grand councilor Lü Yijian (979–1044) and his oligarchy of factional leaders—many of them descendants of early bureaucratic entrants from the north with claims to illustrious Tang lineages—who manipulated the personnel system in their own favor. In response, he launched a series of political battles on behalf of a younger generation of aspiring activists that in the late 1030s almost brought governing to a halt.[5]

Factional paralysis was serendipitously averted by the sudden onset of war. As outlined in this volume's introduction, both the monarchy and the literati consolidated their hold on the early Song state by neutralizing the once-powerful military class and, with the signing of the Chanyuan peace treaty with the Kitan in 1005, replacing warfare with the payment of peace tribute as the primary strategy of national defense. At the same time that bureaucrats used three decades of peace to solidify their multigenerational hold on office, the Ordos-based Tangut Xi Xia took advantage of the Chanyuan demobilization to expand their territory and raise their diplomatic stature.[6] When in 1038 the Song court refused to grant "the upstart Tangut chieftain" Li Yuanhao equal status as a third Son of Heaven, Yuanhao launched a massive series of attacks that exposed the hollowed-out state of Song defenses. In the absence of competent military commanders, the court turned for help to a coterie of brilliant civilians headed by Fan Zhongyan and Han Qi. During their three years on the Shaanxi–Xi Xia front, the two men and their lieutenants neutralized the battlefield prowess of the Tanguts with the organizational powers of the Song bureaucracy.[7] It was Fan's success in the field that prompted Renzong to summon him to the capital to enact a reform program the emperor hoped would end the war. A treaty was concluded in 1044—undermining the rationale for Fan's reform—but animosities were reignited in the 1060s by Tangut encroachment on the failing Tibetan polity of Gansu and Qinghai that had buffered the Song's northwestern flank and provided the bulk of its warhorses. At the same time, the postwar maintenance of huge but ineffective standing armies all along the northern front consumed over 80 percent of the state's cash income by 1065, pushing the government into its first officially registered deficit.[8]

It was the inconclusive outcome of the war and reforms of the 1040s that animated the challenges faced by Renzong's grandnephew Shenzong when he assumed the throne in 1067 at the age of nineteen. At the time of his accession, the bloated civil service was as demoralized as it had been before the Sino-Tangut war, the government was in debt, and senior advisors were torn between accommodating the Tanguts or launching a preemptive war of choice. Shenzong, who came to the throne determined to repudiate the Chanyuan model and redefine the political map through irredentist conquest and expansion, resolutely favored war. Although Wang Anshi was far less bellicose than the new emperor, on their first meeting, in 1068, Wang's insistence that "the time for great deeds is right now" persuaded Shenzong that Wang was the right man to help him achieve his objectives. The following year Shenzong appointed Wang to the Council of State, over the objections of senior ministers who feared Wang would "change things and disrupt the empire."[9] Thus whereas Renzong tolerated Fan's reforms in the hope that they would end an unwanted war of necessity, Shenzong actively promoted Wang's New Policies in order to ready his realm for irredentist wars of choice.

Because the thrust of the two reform movements was so different, it is important to appreciate just how similar were their animating concerns. Fan articulated his reform vision in a series of razor-sharp critiques submitted between 1025 and 1036 that denounced the political culture of complacency, nepotism, sycophancy, and censorship personified by Lü Yijian.[10] Three times Fan's audacious broadsides earned him expulsion from the capital. But each demotion just served to energize and enlarge a tight-knit fraternity of young supporters who shared Fan's idealistic "ancient style" (*guwen*) vision of morally charged government, and who clamored for Renzong to promote Fan and his 1043 reform agenda. It was the failure of Fan's reforms that in 1058 prompted Wang Anshi to submit his "Myriad Word Memorial," in an attempt to revive Renzong's commitment to change that though fruitless at the time was to become Wang's own reform manifesto.[11]

Underscoring the urgency of their messages, both Fan and Wang predicted disaster for the dynasty if major changes were not enacted. In his 1027 memorial to the councilors of state, Fan boldly warned that "if the councilors do not alter their approach to governance and just maintain the status quo, then in one morning chaos will strike, at the cost of centuries of blood and flesh."[12] Although the dynasty did just barely survive the disaster of the Tangut invasions, Wang perpetuated Fan's jeremiad by insisting that without fundamental change the good luck through which the realm had averted catastrophe could not long be relied on.[13]

Both men thought one of the first places luck might fail was on the frontier, where defensive preparations were in dire need of reform. In 1025 Fan, who would excel as a civilian commander in the Sino-Tangut war, lamented the willful ignorance of warfare that had resulted from two decades of peace; he warned that if the Kitan were to "again knock at the gates of Chanyuan, how could it possibly end well?"[14] Fan's fears were borne out in the Song's hapless response to the Tangut invasions, and Wang Anshi saw little improvement in the postwar military preparedness. But for Wang the culprit was no longer the lulling effect of peace, but rather the foolhardy arrogance of a literati class that despite the lessons of the Qingli war still spurned all thought of military matters: "Today's students regard civil and military matters as completely separate, declaring that 'I am familiar with civil governance and that's enough!' As a result when it comes to service on the frontiers, that is all foisted on the rank and file, comprised solely of violence-loving riff-raff."[15]

Dangers on the frontier were just a symptom of the larger problem identified by Fan and Wang: a fundamental failure of the institutions established by the Song founding emperors to train and mobilize a professional class of officials ready and able to meet the challenges of the day. As Wang Anshi put it, even if the emperor were of a mind to reform the regulations and institutions of the realm to conform with the intent of the ancient kings—his imagined ideal—he would find no one to put his commands into action, "because in the world today there are too few men of talent."[16] In his 1058 memorial Wang located the source of this shortage in the departure from the sagely models of instruction (*jiaozhi zhi dao*), nurturance or support (*yangzhi zhi dao*), selection (*quzhi zhi dao*), and appointment (*renzhi zhi dao*). Wang's typology of the ideal personnel system provides a useful way to identify where his views and Fan's differ and converge.

INSTRUCTION

The social esteem of the literati class vis-à-vis other claimants to power (the military, merchants, the clergy) was based on their mastery of literary learning. But for both Fan and Wang, the bookish pedantry and literary embellishments that characterized high culture and the examination curriculum contributed nothing to the ancient goal of learning: to prepare men for the tasks of governing.[17] For Fan Zhongyan, a leading advocate of the ancient style movement to which most of the Qingli reformers subscribed, the way to reinstate sagely learning and save "this culture of ours" was to replace the frivolous writing style of a morally corrupt age with the pristine, unembellished style of the sage kings.[18] During his short time in power Fan tried to bring his educational views to fruition by emphasizing the Six Classics over poetry and literary prose in the examination system, and by ordering every prefecture and county to establish a school overseen by a teacher who had mastered the Classics.[19]

Wang was even more dismissive of the examination curriculum, which cultivated strong memories at the expense of practical knowledge. Rejecting completely the model of the ideal official as a generalist, Wang insisted that "a man's abilities are brought to fruition through specialization and undermined by dilettantism." The sages enforced this insight by assigning men to the tasks for which they were best suited, and by prohibiting scholars from studying anything but "the Way of the ancient kings. As for the heterodox writings of the Hundred Schools, since they were all rejected no one dared study them." In the present day, however, it was exactly those fields favored by the sages as crucial for governance—the rites, music, punishments, and administration—that students scorned as "the concerns of mere bureaucratic functionaries, and hence not something with which they need be familiar." When given responsibility for public affairs such students prove incompetent.[20]

SELECTION AND PROMOTION

Both Fan and Wang objected to the way candidates were selected for office, not only because they were not judged on merit but also because a disproportionate number of offices went to the kin of high officials through the protection privilege. In Fan's view, the all-important county magistrates and prefectural administrators were chosen on the basis of seniority and their ability to avoid taking actions that would subject them to grudges and slander, rather than on their moral probity and dedication to the welfare of the people.[21] The weakened sense of public duty spawned by a mechanical application of formal selection criteria was seriously exacerbated, in Fan's view, by open misuse of the protection privilege to transform bureaucratic office into the hereditary preserve of the well-connected. Local officials, rather than take their public responsibilities seriously, scrambled to accumulate wealth and advance the career prospects of their relatives.[22] Further up the rank hierarchy, capital officials and senior ministers used their disproportionate protection privileges to leapfrog their kin to the top of the employment lists, while ordinary "civil and military officials wait years for a vacancy."[23] And where merit did propel men of humble families to office, their posts were likely to be in distant and unpleasant locales, "while the sons of the powerful" rarely leave the capital."[24]

The Sino-Tangut war obliged the court to recruit men based on merit rather than pedigree, catapulting the careers of brilliant newcomers like Ouyang Xiu (1007–1072), Yin Zhu (1001–1047), Cai Xiang (1012–1067), Fu Bi (1004–1083), and others, and shaking the hold on power of the prewar bureaucratic oligarchy.[25] Although Wang Anshi is less obsessed with the powers of entrenched oligarchs than Fan, he shares Fan's scorn for a system that put well-connected young men in office with no training or assessment of their abilities.[26] Both men evoked the model of the former kings: have the ruler select the right kind of men for his senior positions, and then charge those senior ministers with appointing like-minded men to fill the posts below them.[27] In essence, Fan and Wang were simply proposing that the ministers who currently controlled the appointments process—the entrenched oligarchs for Fan and the unnamed multitudes of incompetent ministers for Wang—be replaced as arbiters of selection by men of their own kind. Fan put his plan into practice when in 1043 he charged the newly designated surveillance investigators (*anchashi*) with vetting and, if needed, replacing every circuit, prefectural, and county official in the realm. Wang's ecumenical approach to personnel selection crystallized around the mobilization of "bureaucratic entrepreneurs" from among the ranks of officials and commoners alike, and by the delegation of extensive appointment rights to reform-oriented agency chiefs.[28]

APPOINTMENT

Although Fan and Wang agreed that the Song personnel system failed to educate or select the right men to govern the realm, they diverged over how to define the right kind of men and how those men should be employed, motivated, and controlled. Whereas Fan sought to train and promote a cohort of idealists dedicated to the common good, Wang looked to mobilize an army of talented experts whose own wills were bound to the goals of their emperor. In Fan's view, the ideal official should excel in the four traits Confucius used to distinguish among his own disciples: ethical behavior, sound administrative skills, frank and honest speech, and cultural learning. Similarly the ideal career for such a man was characterized by *extensive* experience throughout the bureaucracy rather than *intensive* specialization in a functionally defined field. It was precisely this broad experience that the oligarchs precluded when they monopolized good court offices for their kin: "The sons of men of power and status rarely leave the capital to rotate through the duties of the hundred offices, and so they are completely ignorant about affairs throughout the empire."[29]

By contrast, Wang thoroughly rejected the virtues of the generalist, instead privileging the kind of functional specialization that Max Weber would later identify as a hallmark of the modern bureaucracy.[30] Wang deplored the usual practice of assigning a man who advanced to office on the basis of literary learning to a post in finance, say, only to then transfer him to law, or ritual, with no concerns about his lack of training. "Thus any given individual must be ready to fill *every* office, so that it is difficult to match their abilities to *any* office." The mismatch between skills and responsibilities aggravated administrative inefficiency, for "when men are charged with tasks for which they are ill-prepared, there is little they are able to accomplish individually . . . [so that] little is achieved overall."[31] Instead, Wang invoked the mythical bureaucrat-heroes of the past, who were all kept in one office for their entire lives, to argue that the combination of functional specialization (*zhuan*) and long tenures in office (*jiuren*) were the key to personal and collective achievement. Ultimately, the appointment of technical specialists to long terms in reform-oriented agencies was to be a hallmark of the New Policies under Wang Anshi.[32]

SUPPORT

Once in office, incumbents needed to be adequately paid, motivated, socialized, and controlled, personnel functions Wang bundled under the category of "nurture" or "support" (*yang*). Both Wang and Fan agreed that officials required adequate salaries, official recognition, and the fear of punitive sanctions if they were to remain honest, fulfill their responsibilities, and enact their sovereign's will. Fan just touched on the issues of motivation and enforcement in his 1030s memorials, with some expansion in the 1043 reform agenda.[33] But Wang explicitly sought to bind the interests of the men molded by a revamped personnel system to the objectives of the state. In a formulation that anticipates modern theories of organizational control, Wang subdivided "support" into three constituent elements: the provision of an adequate salary (*raozhi yi cai*), the socialization to appropriate behavior through ritual restraint (*yuezhi yi li*), and the enforcement of behavioral norms and compliance with the ruler's wishes through the threat and application of harsh punishments (*caizhi yi fa*).[34] Behavioral codes and punitive sanctions operated for Wang as external constraints that keep men in check despite their inner desires. The key, for Wang, was to fuse the inner desires of the functionaries to the goals of the ruler. Ideally men should want to act on behalf of the public good, regardless of their material circumstances. But Wang recognized that most men—including 99 percent of the literati!—occupied a shifting moral ground: "If poor, they will behave like scoundrels, while if prosperous they will act like superior men." When establishing systems to regulate behavior the ancient kings took this morally average man as the standard and "sought to use men's desires to lead them along, in the hope that by giving average men something they could hold onto they could be motivated to further the king's intentions for the world and the coming generations." In a detailed analysis of official salaries, however, Wang showed that current-day officials were paid far less than needed to sustain themselves and their families, forcing them to engage in trade, to beg, to take bribes and squeeze the commoners, and to become so lax in their official duties that all hope for good governance was lost.[35] The solution Wang offered in 1058 was to provide sufficient income to keep officials both honest and devoted to the interests of the state. When Wang had a chance to put his theory to the test, he used carefully calibrated financial incentives and normative rewards to motivate line officials into fulfilling New Policies objectives.[36]

THE POLITICAL ENVIRONMENT OF REFORM

To summarize the discussion so far, Fan Zhongyan and Wang Anshi concurred that the post-Chanyuan deterioration of military institutions and the professional culture of the literati had put the long-term survival of the dynasty in jeopardy. But because of the very different pre- and postwar political environments, Fan and Wang translated their shared diagnoses into quite different policy prescriptions.

Fan Zhongyan's sense of crisis was forged in an era of restricted political space. Fan obtained his *jinshi* degree in 1015 and assumed a minor post directly thereafter. For the first two and a half decades of his professional career, the court was dominated by the Empress (and then from 1022 Dowager Empress) Liu (969–1033) and the senior ministers who struggled to consolidate their influence over the regent and her young charge while expanding their own political networks.[37] Beyond monopolizing choice posts for their followers, the ministerial oligarchs enforced tight restrictions on the "paths of speech" (*yanlu*)—that is, who could submit memorials and on what kinds of topics—and declined to fill positions in the Censorate (Yushitai) and Bureau of Policy Criticism (Jianyuan), the two oversight agencies intended in part to curb the power of the grand councilors.[38] In response, Fan repeatedly called on the young emperor to recapture sovereign authority from his usurpatious ministers by reinvigorating the remonstrance bureaus, opening and expanding the scope of political memorializing, and—above all—by choosing the right men for the top positions of responsibility.[39] For in Fan's uncompromising view, the fate of the realm depended on the outcome of a contest between an insurgent "party" (*dang*) of public-minded reformers versus the opposing party of self-serving careerists: "In the realm of all under Heaven these two parties are constantly at war. Whether the world be ordered or in chaos hinges on which of these two parties wins."[40]

Wang Anshi was no less militant in the charge he urged on Renzong, now far more seasoned than before the war and some ten years Wang's senior. Wang was politic enough to blame the failure of the Qingli reforms on the "court" (*chaoting*) and not the emperor himself, observing that "as soon as convention-bound opportunists expressed their discontent [the court] aborted [the reforms] and refused to proceed." Once again, Wang encouraged Renzong to emulate the rulers of old, for "Whenever the ancients aspired to great deeds, they never failed to exterminate [their opponents] as a prelude to attaining their goals"; he continued, "If His Majesty sincerely hopes to bring the world's talents to the fore, then this minister urges that you decide once and for all, and let that be that!"[41]

Ironically, for a man whose measures were to inspire the most paralyzing era of factionalism in the history of the dynasty, Wang himself did not view the obstacles to change as a partisan battle between virtuous and evil parties in the governing class. Unlike Fan, Wang even praised Renzong's chief ministers and the impartial way they were selected.[42] For the postwar political environment that shaped Wang's reform vision was far less constricted than Fan had faced. The war itself had broken whatever monopoly the oligarchs really had on power, by forcing the recruitment of talented administrators like the proreformers Fu Bi and Ouyang Xiu and the antireformers Zhang Fangping (1007–1091) and Bao Zheng (999–1062) regardless of political views. As a result, from the 1050s through the onset of the New Policies in 1069 factional struggles receded as a defining characteristic of the political environment, with the Council of State mixing Qingli-era reformers and opponents both.[43] Similarly, in response to the natural disasters of the late 1030s and the Tangut war itself, Renzong had felt obliged to open avenues of policy discourse and to expand and strengthen the Censorate and the Bureau of Policy Criticism.[44] In fact, Wang thought too much airing of divergent opinions was an obstacle to good governance, arguing in 1070 that "if the Court's officials are not united in mind and virtue so that they collaborate as one then none of the affairs under Heaven can be achieved."[45]

From Wang's postwar perspective, then, the chief problems facing the realm were no longer political but rather financial. By the time of Wang's 1058 memorial the economy had become an overriding political issue of the day. The Sino-Tangut war had doubled the number of soldiers in the imperial army over the 1021 roster, from 432,000 to 826,000 men, with a concomitant increase in military expenditures. Although peace allowed reductions of some two hundred thousand men, the number of local militia recruits stationed along the northern borders increased.[46] By far the greatest contribution to military expenses was the cost of provisioning the armies, which soared from less than 1 percent of total state expenditures in 1007 to 36.5 percent of total state expenditures in 1048—four years after the end of the war![47] Perhaps most troubling, government expenditures as a percentage of total government income increased dangerously after the war, from 91.2 percent in 1048 to 100 percent (no surplus) in 1049, and then—after a modest drop to 98.5 percent in 1064—to 113 percent and a deficit in 1065.[48] In response to the postwar economic stresses, serious efforts were made to reform the state monopolies in tea and salt that were directly tied to military provisioning, and many of the leading public figures of the day submitted memorials and treatises on how to solve the looming fiscal crisis and "enrich the realm" (*fuguo*).[49]

If Wang's focus on the economy was in keeping with the temper of the times, his approach to economic revival bucked conventional wisdom. Whereas most prescriptions for achieving economic and fiscal health stressed the need to curtail state spending, especially on the surfeit of officials, in his 1058 memorial Wang denied that the national payroll was large enough to account for the fiscal crisis. The root cause of the nation's economic distress was not the number of officials, but rather their failure to understand the art of "managing fiscal resources" (*licai*); that is, to "utilize the productive forces of the world to generate wealth for the world, and use the wealth of the world to meet the needs of the world."[50] In more practical terms, over the course of the next decade Wang came to argue that the inflexible command structures the state employed to extract resources from a buoyant commercial and agrarian economy—especially its local-product quotas and its monopolies—had allowed the great guild merchants and wealthy traders to usurp the fiscal prerogatives of the state. The state depended on these merchants to transport goods to where they were needed and convert monopoly commodities to cash. The key to enriching the state while also stimulating the economy, then, was to suppress these so-called engrossers (*jianbing*)—a class that also included the rich landowners—by augmenting the capacity of the financial administration to participate directly in the market economy.[51] Thus the bureaucratic rejuvenation Wang called for in the Myriad Word Memorial was crucial precisely because only by training, recruiting, and empowering a cadre of financial specialists could the state recoup its economic authority from the engrossers. But to effectively pit specialized agents of the state against these powerful economic magnates required *increasing*—not decreasing—the size of the bureaucracy. For "only with many officials can [essential] tasks be accomplished. So long as these tasks are accomplished, there is nothing wrong with great [official] activity. And large expenditures will stimulate increasing prosperity. So long as they stimulate prosperity, then what is the harm in great expenditures?"[52] True to his word, under Wang's direction the number of qualified officials registered the greatest increase of the entire dynasty, jumping 41 percent from 24,000 men in 1067 to over 34,000 men in 1080.[53]

COMPARING THE REFORM MEASURES

Fan Zhongyan's and Wang Anshi's reform measures are summarized in tables 4.1 and 4.2. Although there was substantial overlap between the views of Fan and Wang on the crises of their day, it was the differences that sent their reform agendas in different directions. The points of agreement and divergence may be distilled as follows:

POINTS OF AGREEMENT

There were two main points of agreement: military affairs and government officials. Both Fan and Wang agreed that by segregating military and civil affairs and denigrating military matters and men in the aftermath of the Chanyuan agreement, the defense of the realm was placed in jeopardy. Both also agreed that too many officials looked on office as a way to get ahead rather than serve the common good. They concurred as well on the sources of that deterioration: an examination-oriented curriculum that stressed frivolous literary learning rather than moral values and the arts and (for Wang) the specialized expertise of governance; and a system of assigning men to office based on seniority rather than on demonstrated moral (for Fan) and professional (for Wang) merit, exacerbated by the excessive conferral of *yin* privileges on the kin of high officials.

POINTS OF INCIPIENT DIVERGENCE

Fan and Wang began to diverge over the two remaining features of professional culture: the right kind of men to employ and support. With regard to government employment, Fan sought to employ dedicated public servants imbued with the Confucian ideals needed to excel in an *extensive* career path through all aspects of the civil service hierarchy, with special focus on the local level. Wang's ideal official, by contrast, was the functional specialist in possession of the skills and experience needed to excel in an *intensive* career path marked by long tenures in positions matched to the incumbent's

TABLE 4.1. Fan Zhongyan's ten reform initiatives, 1043–1045

Reform Initiative/Dates	Objective
1. Clarify Standards for Promotion and Demotion (明黜陟) 1043/10–1045/2	Make merit and the challenges of each post rather than time in office the basis for genuine *mokan* (磨勘) personnel reviews, in order to encourage service in the provinces, break the monopoly of well-connected young men over choice positions in the capital, and advance the careers of young men of talent dedicated to "advancing the public good."
2. Restrain Nepotism (抑僥倖) 1043/11–1045/2	Limit the number and scope of allowable nepotism (蔭) appointments in order to reduce the glut of expectant officials drawing salaries. The three academic institutes and imperial archives (館閣) would be barred from nepotism appointments and open to merit alone.
3. Redefine Examination Curriculum (精貢舉) 1044/3–1045/3	Improve the link between exams and an ability to address the critical challenges of the day by emphasizing the Six Classics over poetry and literary prose, stressing the character and conduct of the candidates, and establishing an empire-wide system of schools.
4. Carefully Select Local Officials (擇官長) 1043/10–1045/10	Renew (or purge) local government by reviewing and where needed replacing all circuit intendants, prefects, and county magistrates. Responsibilities assumed by the surveillance investigators.
5. Equalize the Amount of Land Attached to Local Posts (均公田) 1043/11–1044?	Rationalize the publicly owned office-land system to generate funds for improved stipends so that accomplished officials will be eager to serve in the provinces and thus "deeply understand the suffering of the people, which is the foundation of transformative governance."
6. Promote Agriculture (厚農桑) 1044/1/28–?	Charge circuit officials with improving irrigation works, especially in Jiangnan, and with encouraging agricultural improvement, in order to cope with soaring grain prices and "strengthen the nation" (強國力).
7. Improve Military Preparedness (修武備) Never enacted	Recruit 50,000 able-bodied men from the metropolitan region to serve in a militia modeled after the Tang *fubing* (府兵) system, farming for three seasons and training for one.
8. Reduce Corvée (減徭役) 1044/5–?	In areas where population has fallen, consolidate administrative units by reducing superfluous counties to *zhen* (鎮) status, in order to lessen overall corvée burdens on the local population.
9. "Spread Beneficence and Trust" (覃恩信)	Forgive tax arrears to reestablish trust between the sovereign and the people. No details on enactment.
10. Stringently Enforce Imperial Decrees (重命令)	Severely punish officials who do not rigorously implement imperial orders. No details on enactment.

Sources: "*Da shouzhao tiaochen shishi* 答手詔條陳十事," *Fan Zhongyan quanji*, vol. 1:473–87; dates based on Jin Zhongshu, "Fan Zhongyan de gexin zhengce kao," *Fan Zhongyan yiqian-nian danchen*, vol. 2:961–1027.

TABLE 4.2. Ten major New Policies measures of Wang Anshi

Reform measure and date	Objectives
1. Tribute Transport and Distribution (均輸法) 1069/7	Replace the command requisition of government-needed goods with a market-oriented procurement system that authorized the circuit supply commissioner (發運使) to buy necessities and sell surpluses on the market, thereby reducing the power of "wealthy merchants and great traders" and other engrossers.
2. Green Sprouts Rural Credit (青苗法), aka Ever-Normal Granaries (常平法) 1069/9	Create a state-run rural credit system capitalized by liquidating reserve grain stocks in the Ever-Normal and Universal Charity granaries, managed by the new Circuit Intendants for Ever-Normal Granaries (提舉常平使) supervising county magistrates and local village officers. Intended to free poor households from dependence on usurious rural moneylenders or putative engrossers and thereby unleash rural productive capacity, but transformed instead into a robust government revenue stream.
3. Agricultural Land and Irrigation (農田水利法) 1069/11	Productivity-oriented measure that initiated 10,793 water-control and land reclamation projects empire-wide (1070–1076), reclaiming almost 39 million acres of agricultural land and remedying conservancy and flood control problems along the Yellow River and Bian Canal under the Directorate of Waterways (都水監).
4. Mutual Security System (保甲法) 1070/12	Organize local residents as a banditry and social control measure. In five northern circuits add drill and review (教閱), culminating in the complete militarization of the *baojia* system and its incorporation into the defense network of North China from 1076 on.
5. Revised Examination Curriculum (修經義) and Three Hall System (三舍法) 1071/2, 1071/10	Reform government school curriculum to focus on classics and policy issues.

particular expertise. And although Fan and Wang agreed that incumbents required adequate salaries and official recognition, only Wang was provoked enough by the issue of support to articulate a systematic model of personnel motivation and control.

POINTS OF SUBSTANTIAL DIVERGENCE

Fan and Wang diverged most sharply over whether the principal challenges of the day lay in the realm of political culture (for Fan) or the political economy (for Wang). For Fan, the main foe of change was *internal*, in the form of self-serving careerists who exercised oligarchical power through their monopoly over access to choice offices for themselves and their kin; control of the upper reaches of government, through their creation of

Reform measure and date	Objectives
6. Service Exemption (免役) (aka Hired Service [募役]) 1071/10	Relieve the often-ruinous burden on middle- and rich-peasant households of conscription into subbureaucratic functions at the village, county, and prefectural level (the "drafted service system" [差役法]) by replacing conscripts with volunteers paid for by a tax broadly imposed on all but the poorest rural and urban propertied households, including those (such as ranked officials and temple households) previously exempt from service.
7. State Trade Policy (市易法) 1072/3	Break the monopoly over trade in the capital held by rich monopoly merchants by creating a Metropolitan State Trade Bureau (市易務) to make commercial loans and buy and sell commodities. In 1073/10 provincial branches were created throughout the empire, financed by occasional investments from Shenzong himself, and all engaged in actively buying and selling a wide array of provincial commodities and generating interest-bearing commercial loans.
8. Local Horse Pasturage System (保馬法) 1072/5	Give militia and *baojia* households collective responsibility for raising horses in return for stipends and tax exemptions.
9. Land Survey and Equitable Tax Measure (方田均税法) 1072/8	Equalize the tax burden in the five circuits of North China by pushing through new cadastral surveys. Uncovered some 34.7 million acres of untaxed land and may have ameliorated some of the tax and labor burdens imposed on northern households by militarization of the north.
10. Create Prototype of the Superintendency for Tea and Horses (都大提舉茶馬司) 1074 (THA)	Officials buy tea in Sichuan to exchange for horses purchased from Tibetan traders in Qinghai, Shaanxi, and Gansu. The THA dominated the economy of Northwest China and the Upper Yangzi, generating substantial revenues for reform projects and the imperial war chest.

Source: Smith, "Shen-tsung's Reign."

extensive patron-client networks composed of slick-tongued sycophants; and strangle-hold on the flow of information to the emperor, by constricting the rights to memorialize on public affairs and letting positions in the Censorate and Bureau of Policy Criticism go unfilled. For Wang, bureaucratic rejuvenation depended on training, recruiting, and mobilizing a cadre of financial experts, or bureaucratic entrepreneurs, who could take on the real foes of good governance, who were *external* to the state: the agrarian and commercial magnates Wang labeled the engrossers.

It was these points of divergence, especially over whom to identify as the principal enemy of change, that propelled Fan's and Wang's reforms in different directions. The ten articles of Fan's reform blueprint of 1043/9 and ten of the major New Policies measures promulgated under Wang are itemized in tables 4.1 and 4.2. Because both reform programs have been extensively analyzed elsewhere, here I focus on comparing the two clusters. As shown in table 4.3, Fan's blueprint recapitulated the thrust of his prewar memorials, and was heavily weighted toward revitalizing the political culture. Thus the focus of his reforms was on privileging proven merit over either notional seniority or family connections in the selection and promotion of officials (items 1 and 2); redefining the examination curriculum to stress substance and moral deportment over literary prowess (item 3); improving local governance by vetting the entire provincial field administration, from the circuit down to the county level, and purging or demoting those deemed deficient (item 4); and enhancing personnel control by both improving official salaries *and* tightening performance accountability (items 5 and 10). This is not to say that the blueprint ignored military or economic concerns, on both of which Fan was quite expert. But there is little evidence that enactment edicts were drawn up for article 7, on recruiting militia for the capital region, or articles 6 and 9 on irrigation and tax amnesties. Article 8, on reducing corvée burdens, prompted just one legislative action, consolidation of the number of counties in Henan *fu* to dispense with an array of labor-service positions. The overall objective of Fan's blueprint was clearly political: that is, to liberate governance from the stranglehold of the same nepotistic oligarchs and self-serving careerists he had been denouncing for some two decades.[54]

Wang's focus, by contrast, was squarely on finance and the economy.[55] As Wang stressed to Shenzong in 1071, "The reason we have not yet begun our great enterprise is because our financial resources are inadequate. That is why I say that the management of resources is our most urgent priority."[56] And he promised the emperor that by dispatching "men good at finance" throughout the empire to wrest control of commodities transport and frontier provisioning, rural credit, and wholesale and even retail commercial sales from the so-called engrosser elements of society, he could "multiply the state's revenues without adding to the people's taxes."[57] Wang certainly fulfilled the first part of his vow, for it was not long before the green sprouts, service exemption, and state trade measures joined the Sichuan tea monopoly and the newly commoditized wine and ferry franchise fees as robust engines of revenue generation. In 1075 conscript *baoding* guardsmen at the bottom of the mutual security organizational apparatus were designated as the primary tax collection agents of the state, allowing New Policies planners to divert the service exemption fees meant for the hiring of service professionals into an enlarged state-run interest-bearing loan fund and to increase state trade purchases of commercial goods from around the country for resale in the

TABLE 4.3. The Qingli and Xining reform policies compared

Fan Zhongyan's Qingli Reforms	Wang Anshi's New Policies
Professional/Political Culture	*Professional/Political Culture*
1. Clarify Standards for Promotion and Demotion. Selection and promotion. Aimed at oligarch privileges.	5. Revised Examination Curriculum and Three Hall reform. Instruction.
2. Restrain Nepotism. Selection and promotion. Aimed at oligarch privileges.	*Economy*
3. Redefine Examination Curriculum. Instruction.	1. Tribute Transport and Distribution. Aimed at commercial engrosser class.
4. Carefully Select Local Officials. Appointments and employment. Animates the reformers' purge of local officiary.	2. Green Sprouts Rural Credit, starts as redistributive credit-relief measure aimed at rural engrosser moneylenders, becomes robust revenue generator.
5. Equalize the Amount of Land Attached to Local Posts. Support/salaries.	3. Agricultural Land and Irrigation measure. A successful irrigation and land reclamation measure.
10. Stringently enforce imperial decrees.	6. Service Exemption or Hired Service measure. Starts as progressive attempt to professionalize and spread costs of subbureaucratic service, ends up as widespread tax increase and robust revenue generator.
Economy	
6. Promote Agriculture. Productivity measure with focus on irrigation.	7. State Trade Policy. Aimed at commercial engrosser class of monopolistic merchants, turns government into the biggest single wholesaler and provider of commercial credit, yielding substantial returns to the state.
8. Reduce Corvée Burdens. Local relief.	
9. "Spread Beneficence and Trust." Local relief through tax forgiveness and amnesties.	9. Land Survey and Equitable Tax Measure. Redistributive intent meant to uncover agricultural lands hidden by rich and powerful families of North China.
Military	10. Superintendancy for Tea and Horses. Created to exchange Sichuan tea for Tibetan horses, but parallels State Trade to dominate entire economy of Northwest China and the Upper Yangzi.
7. Improve Military Preparedness via militia recruitment in the capital region.	
	Military
	4. Mutual Security System. Starts as Kaifeng then empire-wide banditry and social control measure but by 1076 is militarized and incorporated into defense network of all of North China.
	8. Local Horse Pasturage System. Grafts war-horse pasturage duties onto the militia and *baojia* organizations of North China.

capital.[58] By 1077, state trade monopoly profits, green sprouts interest payments, and the panoply of new service exemption fees had added an extra 18 million strings of cash to the 54 million strings obtained through traditional currency sources.[59]

THE INSTITUTIONAL FOUNDATION OF POLITICAL SUCCESS

Wang Anshi fulfilled his promise to Shenzong to multiply state revenues, but not without adding to the burdens on the people. On the evidence of one-time supporters of the New Policies as well as their critics, the hunger for funds transformed the redistributionist economic measures into relentless engines of revenue extraction, driven by implacable and well-rewarded bureaucrats. Yet the New Policies endured. By contrast, Fan's reforms, which might have accomplished their goal of creating a more effective, transparent, and merit-based civil service, were abolished and the reformers cashiered in little over a year. How can we account for the difference in outcomes? I argue that the triumph of the New Policies as a political campaign can be attributed to Wang's greater success in five domains: capturing key institutions of government, creating powerful new reformist organizations, neutralizing political foes, mobilizing bureaucratic followers, and—above all—retaining the unwavering support of his emperor for the reforms.

CAPTURING KEY GOVERNMENT INSTITUTIONS AND CREATING NEW REFORMIST ORGANIZATIONS

Fan Zhongyan

The comparative success of Fan and Wang in these five domains is summarized in table 4.4 and illustrated in figures 4.1 and 4.2. Outside of the emperor, the most important Northern Song political institution was the Council of State, the principal legislative body of the government. The Council was headed by one or two grand councilors, who also headed the Secretariat-Chancellery; and they were joined by the director of the Bureau of Military Affairs as well as one to three assistant civil and assistant military councilors.[60] The power of the Council and its heads could be offset by the Censorate and the Bureau of Policy Criticism, two separate remonstrance agencies that were gradually merged by the end of the eleventh century. Each agency had the authority to comment on and criticize policy and personnel decisions, to investigate and impeach individual officials, and to serve as counterweights to the grand councilors.[61]

As depicted in figure 4.1, Fan Zhongyan's reform coalition achieved only a fragile presence on the Council, although initially their prospects looked good. As of 1043/8, Fan Zhongyan held one of the two assisting civil positions, Han Qi and Fu Bi were the two assistant military councilors, and the elder sympathizers Yan Shu and Du Yan occupied one of the grand councilor positions and the military directorship.[62] But in fact their hold on power was precarious: Yan and Du were politically impotent and were soon disaffected by the reformers; Han Qi was immediately dispatched back to the Shaanxi warfront as military high commissioner (*xuanfushi*); Fan Zhongyan's influence was checked by his antireform co-councilor Jia Changchao (998–1065); and both Fan and Fu Bi spent their time in the capital in terror of political reprisals, begging to be sent out to the provinces.[63] Throughout this period the Council was controlled by the long-serving grand councilor Zhang Dexiang (978–1048, grand councilor from 1038/3–1045/4), who dismissed the reformers "as children jumping up and down in play. [Although I know] I can't make them stop, once they bounce into the walls they'll cease on their own."[64]

Early reformer influence over the remonstrance agencies also proved ephemeral. In 1043/3 Renzong, seeking to hasten a transition from war to peace, increased the number of critics in the Bureau of Policy Criticism to four and quickly filled the posts with the fervent reformers Ouyang Xiu, Yu Jing, Cai Xiang, and (somewhat later) Sun Fu. Shortly thereafter the power of the policy critics was expanded to include policy-making as well as critique, when (in 1043/8) they were authorized to attend the daily meetings of the inner court in response to a recommendation by their compatriot, Tian Kuang (1005–1063).[65] But their relentless attacks against senior ministers and the mainstream bureaucracy shattered what remained of the wartime political unity.[66] More damagingly for the reform cause, their political campaigns soon drew counterattacks from influential members of the Censorate, whose accusations of factionalism and abuse of power turned Renzong against the reformers by early 1044.

Almost as important as capturing key positions at the top of the government was controlling existing or creating new line agencies. Here too Fan's reformers fared poorly. Their one possible success was an order of 1044/3 to every prefecture and county to create new reform-oriented schools, but it appears that this produced a glut of schools for which there were insufficient students, necessitating a retrenchment.[67] But there was a bigger disappointment. The reformers, led chiefly by Ouyang Xiu, insisted that fully eight or nine of every ten prefectures and counties were misgoverned by superfluous officials (*ronglan*)—the old and debilitated, the timorous and inept, and

TABLE 4.4. The five imperatives of reform success: The Qingli And Xining reforms compared

	Fan Zhongyan's Qingli Reforms, 1043–44	New Policies under Wang Anshi, 1069–76
	Council of State	
Capture key government institutions	Qingli reformers a temporary and fragile presence in Council, with real power in the hands of the long-serving antireform grand councilor Zhang Dexiang.	Xining reformers take full control of Council, as Wang Anshi (grand councilor 1070 to 1076) and his hand-picked lieutenants overwhelm the few remaining antireformers.
	Censorate 御史台 and Bureau of Policy Criticism 諫院	
	Reformers gain temporary control of Bureau of Policy Criticism but are attacked by censors.	Reformers gain full control of both Censorate and Bureau of Policy Criticism.
Create reform-centered government agencies	Qingli reformers enjoy only modest success reshaping government to meet their objectives, by expanding the local school system and tasking fiscal intendants with monitoring and impeaching local officials.	New Policies leadership creates a new array of reform-centered institutions that in their unprecedented penetration of society and the economy anticipate the early modern fiscal-military state.
Neutralize political opponents	After some initial success neutralizing foes, reformers overplay their hand and are attacked as factionalists by censors, state councilors, and finally the emperor.	Wang's ouster of reform foes complete; after 1070 his biggest problem comes from internal not external criticism by senior lieutenants who bridle under Wang's tyrannical ways.

(continued)

the rapacious and corrupt. To remedy the situation, Ouyang called for a thoroughgoing rectification of the territorial bureaucracy. This wholesale vetting was to be entrusted to twenty specially designated, free-standing surveillance investigators assigned to cover every circuit of the empire, and charged with personally evaluating the honesty, diligence, physical fitness, and abilities of each prefectural and county official in their jurisdiction.[68] Ouyang hoped that autonomous surveillance investigators could purge circuit and local government of the plague of parasitic officials who occupied these desirable bureaucratic positions, and thus create vacancies for "those [virtuous] men awaiting appointments who would no longer be resentful over their blocked careers."[69] But rather than create a new free-standing post, the councilors simply grafted the investigator's title onto that of the circuit fiscal intendants.[70] The result, according to the censor and future judicial icon Bao Zheng (999–1062), was disastrous, as investigators ignored men with

	Fan Zhongyan's Qingli Reforms, 1043–44	New Policies under Wang Anshi, 1069–76
Mobilize followers	The Qingli reformers comprised a fervent group of political activists, most of them born around the Chanyuan Covenant of 1005 and linked by their loyalty to Fan Zhongyan and their shared political ideals. Though a tight-knit fraternity, their self-righteous contempt for their colleagues as a whole antagonizes and repels many members of the civil service.	Once in power recruits ambitious new examination graduates and low-ranked finance experts for influential New Policies posts that match their skills, earning him the reputation of "exclusively employing mean and petty men" 專用小人. At every level, reform and mainstream officials are "incentivized" with generous promotions or symbolic and material rewards for meeting New Policies goals.
Retain imperial support	Renzong tolerates Fan's reforms in the hope they will end an unwanted war of necessity. Imperial support was eroded by the reformers' insistence on continuing the war after Yuanhao had offered terms in late 1043; turmoil caused by the Surveillance Investigator program as of 1044; and the reformers' ill-judged acknowledgment of their status as a "faction" or "party" (朋黨) in 1044/4, which infuriates the emperor. Following completion of a peace treaty with Yuanhao in 1044/12, the reformers are quickly purged and the reform measures aborted.	Shenzong actively promotes Wang's reforms in order to ready his realm for irredentist wars of choice. Shenzong ascends the throne committed to repudiating the Chanyuan covenants in favor of pursuing irredentist wars, and to generating the revenues those wars would require. Wang Anshi's reforms provide exactly the military and economic mobilization the emperor desires. Shenzong has momentary doubts about green sprouts and state trade after public demonstrations in 1074, and tires of Wang's histrionic tantrums. But after accepting Wang's resignation in 1076 Shenzong personally assumes control of government, intensifying revenue-generation and militarization as preparation for his longed-for (and disastrous) invasion of the Xi Xia domain in 1081–82.

influential backers while harassing the unprotected with unsubstantiated charges in order to meet court expectations and advance their own careers.[71] Concerned about this investigative reign of terror, Renzong restricted the surveillance program in 1044/8 and then abolished it altogether in 1045.[72]

Wang Anshi

As shown in figure 4.2, the contrast between Fan and Wang's control of government could not be more dramatic. On his appointment as assistant civil councilor in 1069/2, Wang complained that those on the council only wanted to avoid offending the "conventionalists" and had no interest in reform.[73] In

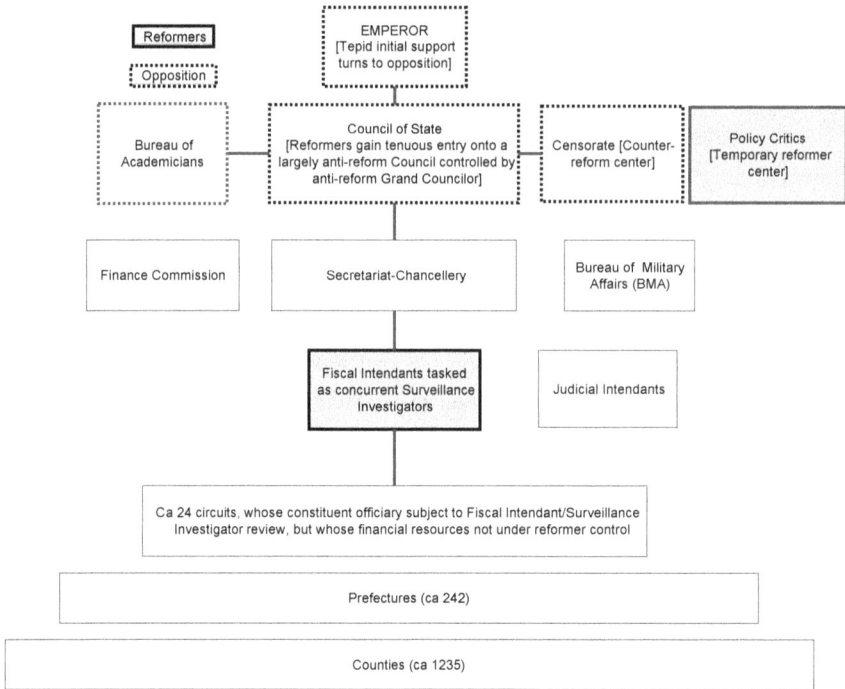

FIGURE 4.1. Qingli reformers' control of state institutions

little over a year Wang successfully replaced all green sprouts foes on the council with his own lieutenants. From 1071 to his first resignation in 1074 and then final exit in 1076 Wang was the unrivaled chief of government, opposed only by an ineffective Feng Jing (1021–1094) and an emasculated Wen Yanbo (1006–1097), whose power as military director was nullified by Wang's transfer of military financing, personnel, war-making, and even control over the *baojia* organization to new or revived reform organizations.[74]

Wang launched the same uncompromising attack against reform foes in the Censorate and Bureau of Policy Criticism. Although censorial exposés of reform excesses sometimes shook Shenzong's resolve, Wang persuaded the emperor that the role of remonstrance officials was to uphold court policies, not oppose them. Because Shenzong's revanchist dreams were so dependent on Wang's fiscal measures, he came, like Wang, to see the censorial bureaus as an administrative arm of the court rather than an independent political entity and censorial opposition to any regime decisions as grounds for dismissal. Thus between mid-1069 and mid-1071 Wang—with his emperor's backing—ousted seventeen censors, four policy critics, and (for good mea-

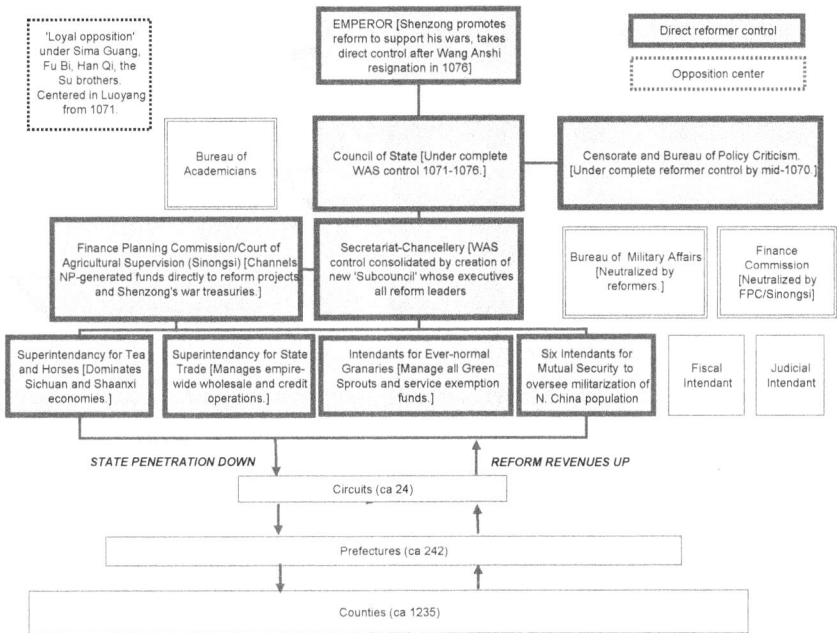

FIGURE 4.2. Xining reformers' control of state institutions

sure) three drafting officials (*zhizhigao*), silencing in-house opposition to the reforms during their crucial probationary phase.[75]

Beyond ousting foes from existing nodes of power, Wang created an integrated network of new organizations to craft, implement, and monitor his reform program. At the executive level, Wang established a Subcouncil for the Compilation of Secretariat Regulations (Bianxiu Zhongshu Tiaoli Si) answerable directly to Wang Anshi and staffed by an array of examiners (*jianzheng zhongshu wufang gongshi*) who could be dispatched as watchdog investigative commissioners (*chafangshi*) to the provinces.[76] Fiscal matters were consolidated in the new Finance Planning Commission (Zhizhi Sansi Tiaolisi), headed directly by Wang and his closest associates Han Jiang (1012–1088) and Lü Huiqing (1032–1111). The Finance Planning Commission and its successor the Court of Agricultural Supervision (Sinongsi) were staffed by an executive secretariat in the capital and a contingent of special commissioners who traveled throughout the empire, all chosen largely for their expertise in agriculture, water control, and finance.[77]

At the operational level, Wang created an army of new circuit intendants to administer the reform measures, including Intendants for Ever-Normal and Universal Charitable Granaries (Tiju Changping Guanghui Cang); Intendants for Militia and Mutual Security in the capital and (between 1075 and 1080) the five northern circuits (Tiju Yiyong Baojia); Superintendents for State Trade (Dutiju Shiyisi), to preside over state wholesale and credit operations in the capital and the provinces east of Sichuan and Shaanxi; and Superintendents for Tea and Horses (Duda Tiju Chamasi).[78] Not only did this new organizational network provide the administrative reach and extractive capacity of an incipient fiscal-military state, but it also created a cadre of ambitious but low-ranked bureaucrats—the legions of "petty men" denounced by Wang's critics—grateful to the reformers for their positions.[79]

NEUTRALIZING OPPONENTS, MOBILIZING FOLLOWERS, AND GAINING IMPERIAL SUPPORT

Wang also outperformed Fan in the next three categories: neutralizing opponents, mobilizing followers, and gaining imperial support. Among the Qingli reformers, no one attacked political and ideological foes more tenaciously than Ouyang Xiu. Not long after his appointment as policy critic in 1043/3, Ouyang singly or in concert with his colleagues engineered the demotions or blocked the advances of five men seen as obstacles to the reform agenda, including a sitting assistant state councilor whose dismissal paved the way for Fan Zhongyan's own promotion as civil councilor.[80] Fan Zhongyan himself was no less zealous in ousting line officials he saw as obstructive, even horrifying Fu Bi at the cavalier way he struck circuit intendants from the roster, unmoved at the thought of "the cries of their families."[81] Perhaps the reformers' most notorious success was in blocking the appointment of the former Shaanxi Military Pacification Commissioner Xia Song (985–1051) as Bureau of Military Affairs Commissioner. In a rare collaboration between remonstrance agencies, Ouyang Xiu and Yu Jing (1000–1064) joined with counterparts in the Censorate to denounce Xia as cowardly in the war zone but so corrupt and mean-spirited at court that even Lü Yijian feared him. Shi Jie's (1005–1045) poem celebrating the ouster of Xia Song and the elevation of Fan and his allies made him a hero among the reformers.[82] But the more reformer attacks came to resemble orchestrated factional politics, the more Renzong—for whom factionalism was the most heinous of political transgressions—threw his support behind the reformers' opponents. Within the year following the announcement of the reforms in 1043/9, Renzong personally warned reformer policy critics that his appointment of a reform foe (Chen Zhizhong, 990–1059) to the state council was none of their concern. Renzong then stood by as Censorial officials impeached Fan's followers as a way of implicating Fan and the reform leadership. When a peace treaty with the Tanguts was completed in late 1044 the reform leadership itself was opened to attack, as the still-seething Xia Song wrought revenge on Fu Bi and the now-deceased Shi Jie while grand councilors Zhang Dexiang and Jia Changchao encouraged censorial officials to oust Fan Zhongyan, Ouyang Xiu, and Han Qi.[83] Thus by inciting foes to fury without successfully ousting them, the Qingli reformers overplayed their hand, catalyzing a counterattack that resulted in their complete ouster by early 1045.[84]

Wang Anshi was even more fanatical about dislodging foes than his Qingli predecessors, but—perhaps learning from Fan's mistakes—he was far more successful. Even the reform consigliere Lü Huiqing wondered if Wang thought he could "really silence all under heaven."[85] In early 1070 Shenzong reluctantly let the much-admired Sima Guang go, after Sima protested that there was no point in remaining at court when the emperor would neither heed his advice nor give him real power.[86] From this point until his own resignation in 1076 Wang's most significant opposition came internally, from other reformers like Zheng Xia (1041–1119), Zeng Bu (1036–1107), and Lü Huiqing who bridled at Wang's tyrannical ways.

With respect to mobilizing followers, Fan's small group of reform partisans could not have been more fervent. But they formed a closed fraternity animated by self-righteous contempt for their colleagues. In making a case for the surveillance investigators, for example, Fan Zhongyan was even more derisive than Ouyang Xiu had been, declaring that "among the officials of the realm very few indeed are enlightened and wise, while the vast majority are idiots."[87] This scorn by reform leaders for officialdom as a whole so antagonized and repelled their civil service colleagues that one former supporter accused them of "stirring up shameful personal secrets as acts of loyalty, recommending callow nobodies to the institutes, and gathering together in poetry sessions to fan support for their faction."[88] Given their fragile hold on the key institutions of government and a core following numbering no more than twenty men at most, Fan Zhongyan and his faction stood little chance in their unequal war with a mainstream bureaucracy that resented both the reformers' ad hominem attacks and their claims of moral superiority.

Wang Anshi, by contrast, was far less judgmental than Fan and the Qingli reformers, and he favored practical skills over moral fervor. Once in power he staffed his panoply of reform agencies with ambitious new examination graduates and low-ranked finance experts, all of them eligible for generous career and material incentives for meeting reform objectives. Though critics denounced Wang's "exclusive employment of mean and petty men," observers found it hard not to marvel at how Wang created a vast, empire-wide cadre of followers. According to the memoirist Wei Tai (ca. 1050–1110), for example,

> Wang [Anshi] grasped the reins of state and dedicated himself to transforming the world. Since through their memorials and opinions the old men of accumulated virtue refused to cooperate with Wang, he instead reached down to employ men newly advanced [into the civil service], appointing them to posts without regard for formal rank. Thus in no time at all the policies that were to characterize the entire period were all launched, and in the forbidden recesses of the Hanlin Academy, the halls of the Censorate, and in the strategic positions at court and in the provinces, there were no vacancies that were not filled by these newly advanced scholars.[89]

Moreover, by establishing an extensive network of bureaucratic functionaries dependent on the New Policies for their professional and economic well-being, Wang ensured that the reforms would continue well past his own resignation in 1076. Bi Zhongyou (1047–1121) made this point to his mentor Sima Guang in 1086, when Sima was triumphantly summoned to court to head a conservative restoration of the prereform order in the aftermath of Shenzong's death: "When Wang Anshi was in charge there was no one in office at court or in the provinces who was not his follower, and that is why he could enact his policies. Although we now wish to undo the shortcomings of those days, seven or eight of every ten senior court officials, circuit intendants, departmental directors, and military officers are still Wang Anshi's followers."[90] As a result, just as Bi Zhongyou predicted, the key elements of the New Policies were retained during the seven-year conservative regency, and were revived in full once Zhezong assumed his majority in 1093.[91]

The emperors were also a part of the equation. Wang Anshi could not have mobilized his army of bureaucrat-specialists without the support of his emperor—support that Fan Zhongyan lacked. Renzong wanted one thing above all from Fan's reforms: a definitive end to a humiliating and expensive war of necessity. When Fan and the reformers sought to prolong a war of necessity into a war of choice, by continuing to push for a chance to attack the Tanguts at home after Yuanhao offered terms for peace, Renzong and even the reformers' sympathizers in the state council lost patience with them.[92] This miscalculation was compounded by a famous exchange at court in 1044/4, when Fan and Ouyang Xiu infuriated the emperor even further by acknowledging that the reformers were indeed a faction, though a faction of the virtuous. Although Ouyang's contribution to the exchange, his "Discourse on Factions" (Pengdang lun), was destined to become a model of political prose, it was so glaring an example of political imprudence that Ouyang recanted his views within a year.[93] But at that point it was too late to regain the favor of an emperor constitutionally opposed to the open exercise of factional politics, and who in 1044/10 had obtained the peace agreement with Yuanhao he had long sought.[94] The next month Renzong issued an edict denouncing the partisanship that had overtaken court politics in terms that left no doubt he was singling out the reformers:

> We exert ourself to approximate the governance of old. But it is the shortcoming of this era of peace that all grasp for power and influence. People devote their energies to building a circle of associates who [gather at] home to tear down others; they rely on one another to purchase reputations, even to the point that they solicit bribes in secret, then recommend one another as worthies in public. Then there is the case of the Surveillance Investigators, who use their orders as an opportunity for unrestrained meanness. . . . [We] hereby authorize the Secretariat-Chancellery and the Censorate to investigate these matters and report.[95]

With this Fan Zhongyan begged to be relieved of his post as state councilor.[96]

Shenzong also wanted one thing from reform: the financial and military capacity to pursue offensive wars of choice against the Tanguts and then recapture the Sixteen Prefectures from the Kitan. For as Shenzong put it to his reluctant war minister Wen Yanbo, "If we are to raise troops for our frontier campaigns then our treasuries must be full."[97] Thus Wang's activist economic vision exactly matched Shenzong's irredentist zeal, earning Wang a level of imperial support that transcended momentary crises and doubts. In the view of the senior minister Zeng Gongliang (999–1078), "the emperor and Wang Anshi are like one man; that is simply Heaven's doing."[98] So allied were the ambitions of Wang and Shenzong that even after Wang's resignation in 1076 the emperor promoted the reforms on his own. If anything Shenzong intensified the revenue-gathering propensity of Wang's economic measures, for with Wang out of office the emperor was even freer to pursue his irredentist dream, whose origins he attributed to his forbear and Song founder Taizu.[99] In like fashion Shenzong's sons, Zhezong and Huizong, assumed the charge of pursuing their father's dream, propelling both the New Policies economic measures and an obsession with wars of choice through the second decade of the twelfth century, weaving both activist reform and irredentist expansion into the narrative if not the fact of the fall of the Northern Song.

CONCLUSION

The Qingli and Xining reforms represented a multigenerational response to a shared and abiding sense of crisis in the Song polity. That sense of crisis, in turn, reflected the confluence of two trends. In the domestic sphere, the unparalleled social and political ascent of the exam-educated literati in the decades following the Chanyuan covenant of 1005 produced an elite class that quickly outgrew the only employment opportunity that social esteem deemed worthwhile: that is, a position in the civil service. As a result, proposals to address problems anywhere in the social and political order were typically inaugurated with calls to reform the training, selection, and promotion of the civil servants themselves, in order to fill government posts with "the right kind of men"—that is, men after the reformer's own heart. This is precisely where Fan and Wang's early visions began.

But demoralization of the political elite was not enough to generate reforms. As demonstrated by the Qingli and Xining reform movements, a second catalyst was needed to prod the political system into action: threats—real or imagined—from abroad. Were it not for the Tangut invasion of Shaanxi in 1040, Fan Zhongyan and his followers might well have languished in political limbo following Fan's expulsion from the capital in 1036. But a war of necessity obliged Renzong to mobilize men based on their skills rather than their ideological or factional affiliations, resuscitating the career of Fan and his *guwen* disciples. Similarly, it was a desire to end the war that prompted Renzong to support Fan's reform agenda, support that he promptly withdrew once a truce was achieved. But peace brought no end to territorial ambitions, and continued skirmishing between Song and Tangut forces throughout the 1050s and 1060s persuaded a new emperor, Shenzong, that the only way to secure his borders was to pursue a war of choice that would extirpate the Xi Xia state and then recover the Sixteen Prefectures from the Kitan Liao. So once again war catalyzed a reform program that not only transformed the structure of government, but also radically extended the reach of the state in society and the economy. In the aftermath of the traumatic fall of the Northern Song, however, political thinkers repudiated the large-scale state-directed reform programs that many blamed for the disaster, a story Jaeyoon Song takes up in his chapter in this volume.

It has not been my goal to define or assess the outcomes of either set of reform programs, but rather to identify the principal reasons Wang's reforms were successfully enacted while Fan's reforms were not. Although the five imperatives of capturing key institutions of government, creating reformist organizations, neutralizing political foes, mobilizing bureaucratic followers, and retaining the support of the emperor by no means exhaust the factors that account for their success or failure, they have the advantage of being analytically clear and hence applicable to other cases. It may be that the fifth imperative—support of the emperor—should be expanded to "support of the actual head of government." This would accommodate those cases where a junior or otherwise infirm or inconsequential sovereign is eclipsed by a de facto regent. In that case the model employed here could be extended to the 1898 reforms, for example, where support of the Guangxu emperor was overturned by opposition from the real ruler of the realm, his formidable aunt the Dowager Empress Cixi.

But the very possibility of extension raises its own questions. Would one really want to apply a model of institutional reforms in the mid-eleventh century to a case in the late-nineteenth? Are internally generated reform movements over the past millennium really as rare as I have suggested, or the very concept of institutional reform a productive category of historical analysis? Because there does seem to have been significant continuity in the structure of the Chinese political order over the last thousand years, I believe the answer to all of these questions is positive. From the eleventh through the twentieth centuries, and very likely well into the twenty-first, China has been governed by autocrats at the head of a state supported by a ruling class defined by membership in an exclusive order—be it the imperial civil service or the Chinese Communist Party—that aimed to monopolize political and economic power along with social esteem. One consequence of this precocious and persistent "single-party state" has been the repetition of calls to reform the personnel system as a prelude to initiating changes in the larger social, political, and economic order. In his famous 1980 speech on "the present situation and the tasks before us," Deng Xiaoping, like Fan Zhongyan, Wang Anshi, and the self-strengtheners of the late-nineteenth century, focuses on rejuvenating the political class—in his case the Party cadre—as the key to solving the problems of the day. Among some of his statements are the following:[100]

- "The problem [today] is that the composition of our cadre force is irrational: there are too many people who are not professionally competent and too few who are."

- "The current problem, in a nutshell, is not that we have too many cadres but that their training does not match their work, and that too few of them have specialized training in their particular field of endeavor."
- "Economic construction involves a large number of trades and fields of expertise, each one requiring specialized knowledge and the constant accumulation of new knowledge. . . . Therefore, we need to build up a huge contingent of cadres who combine an unswerving socialist orientation with professional knowledge and competence."

Nowhere does Deng cite Wang Anshi, let alone Fan Zhongyan. But as of 1980, at least, it appears that a leader of the communist single-party state, seeking to revive China's strategic and economic position, could still unconsciously draw on the reformist rhetoric of the traditional Chinese bureaucracy in ways that seemed fresh and even radical.

NOTES

1   Characterization of the two reform movements as minor and major is associated with James T. C. Liu, one of the earliest scholars to write about both reforms in English. See "An Early Song Reformer"; *Reform in Sung China*; and *Ou-yang Hsiu*. The single most focused anthology of articles on Fan Zhongyan's reforms in particular and his life and thought in general is *Fan Zhongyan yiqiannian danchen guoji xueshu yantaohui lunwen ji*. For sources on Wang Anshi's reforms see Smith, "Shen-tsung's Reign and the New Policies of Wang An-shih, 1067–1085." I draw heavily on that chapter and on a forthcoming essay entitled "A Crisis in the Literati State: The Sino-Tangut War and the Qingli-era Reforms of Fan Zhongyan, 1038–1045." Although the Qingli era spanned 1041–1048, Fan's reforms were enacted and rescinded between 1043 and 1045. Wang's New Policies were promulgated at the start of Emperor Shenzong's Xining reign period (1068–1077) then perpetuated under imperial direction through the Yuanfeng reign period (1078–1085), despite Wang's own resignation in 1076.
2   R. Bin Wong puts the stability of Chinese political institutions into comparative perspective in *China Transformed*.
3   Lü Zhong, "Zhiti lun," in his "Leibian huangchao dashiji jiangyi xulun," *QSW* 346:155. Li Huarui analyses Lü Zhong's observations in his *Wang Anshi bianfa yanjiu shi*, 93–99.
4   Wang Anshi, "Ji Fan Yingzhou wen," *Fan Zhongyan quanji* 2:959; Wang Anshi, "Shang Renzong Huangdi yanshi shu," *QSW* 63:341.
5   Based on a tabulation of the men identified as belonging to Lü's coalition by Wang Zhishuang, of twenty identifiable members, nineteen were northerners and fourteen were self-identified (through the use of choronyms) as descendants of illustrious lineages. Wang Zhishuang, "Bei Song Renzong chao Lü Yijian jituande zucheng jiqi xingzhi," as interpolated against the Chinese Biographical Database (http://isites.harvard.edu/icb/icb.do?keyword=k16229). Although Wang's list may not be exhaustive, the results suggest the orientation and high status of the Lü coalition. For Fan's campaign against

Lü Yijian, see Wang Deyi, "Lü Yijian yu Fan Zhongyan"; Fang Jian, *Fan Zhongyan ping-zhuan*, 46–67; and McGrath, "The Reigns of Jen-tsung (1022–1063) and Ying-tsung (1063–1067)," esp. 289–300. For more recent studies of the political climate of the 1030s, see Skonicki, "Employing the Right Kind of Men," and Lamouroux, "Song Renzong's Court Landscape."

6   Li Huarui, *Song-Xia guanxi shi*, chaps. 1 and 2; Li Fanwen, *Xi Xia tongshi*, chaps. 3 and 4; and Dunnell, "The Hsi Hsia."

7   Tsang, "War and Peace," chaps. 6 and 7.

8   See Smith, "Shen-tsung's reign," 348–53.

9   The exchange is recorded in *CBBM* 59.1094–95. The key document, included in full, is Wang Anshi's answer to Shenzong's query about why disaster has not yet occurred, "Benchao bainian wushi zhazi."

10   "Zouzhang shiwu shu" (1025), *Fan Zhongyan quanji* 1:172–80; "Shang zhizheng shu" (1027), *Fan Zhongyan quanji* 1:182–200; "Shang zizheng Yan Shilang shu" (1030), *Fan Zhongyan quanji* 1:201–7; and a quartet of essays in 1036, plus a "Chart of the Hundred Offices" that demonstrated how all the officials who advanced most rapidly through the ranks were members of Lü Yijian's clientele (*men*): *Fan Zhongyan quanji* 1:129–36 and *Fan Wenzheng gong nianpu, Fan Zhongyan quanji* 2:730–31. For discussions, see Liu, "An Early Sung Reformer," 123; Skonicki, "Employing the Right Kind of Men," 60–66; and Bol, *This Culture of Ours*, 166–75.

11   Wang, "Shang Renzong Huangdi yanshishu," *QSW* 63:328–43. For analysis and sources see Smith, "Shen-tsung's reign," 358–60. The complete memorial is translated in Williamson, *Wang An Shih,* vol. 1:48–84.

12   "Shang zhizheng shu," *Fan Zhongyan quanji* 1:184.

13   "Shang Renzong yanshi shu," *QSW* 63:339; *CBBM* 59.1042–44.

14   "Zou shang shiwu shu," *Fan Zhongyan quanji* 1:173–74; repeated in 1027, in *QSW* 63:192–93.

15   "Shang Renzong yanshi shu," *QSW* 63:334.

16   "Shang Renzong yanshi shu," *QSW* 63:329.

17   *Fan Zhongyan quanji* 1:183 (1027); *QSW* 63:330.

18   *Fan Zhongyan quanji* 1:172–73 (1025); Bol, *This Culture of Ours*, 167.

19   CB 147.3563; Thomas Lee, *Government Education and Examinations in Sung China*, 175; Ge Shao'ou, "Fan Zhongyan dui Songdai difang jiaoyu de gongxian."

20   *QSW* 63:333, 336–37.

21   The numbers of both prefectural-level units (*fu, zhou, jun,* and *jian*) and counties varied somewhat over the course of the Northern Song. The *Yuanfeng jiuyu zhi* of 1085 cites 1235 counties (*xian*) and 297 prefectural-level units, 242 of them ordinary prefectures (*zhou*): *Yuanfeng jiuyu zhi*, 1. Each unit required multiple appointments from the regular bureaucracy, making the territorial administration a major source of employment for the civil service.

22   *Fan Zhongyan quanji* 1:184–87 (1027), items 3 and 4.

23   *Fan Zhongyan quanji* 1:176 (1025).

24   *Fan Zhongyan quanji* 1:195–96 (1027).

25   I address this in greater detail in "A Crisis in the Literati State."

26   *QSW* 63:337.

27 *Fan Zhongyan quanji* 1:134–35, "Tuiwei chenxia lun" (1936); *QSW* 63:331–32, 336–37.

28 I elaborate on Wang's personnel policies in *Taxing Heaven's Storehouse.*

29 *Fan Zhongyan quanji* 1:196 (1036).

30 See Max Weber, *Economy and Society*, chaps. 11 (Bureaucracy) and 12 (Patriarchalism and Patrimonialism). See especially pp. 1047–51 for his remarks on China.

31 *QSW* 63:338.

32 *QSW* 63:332, 338. On the New Policies application of these precepts, see Smith, *Taxing Heaven's Storehouse* and "Shen-tsung's reign."

33 *Fan Zhongyan quanji* 1.132 (1036), "Jin ming lun"; Reforms 5 and 10.

34 *QSW* 63:331, 334–35. For a classic formulation of organizational control theory that resonates with Wang's notions of bureaucracy see Amitai Etzioni, "Organizational Control Structure."

35 *QSW* 63:334–35. Wang estimates that officials in lower-tier counties and prefectures were paid a monthly salary of between four to five thousand cash to eight to nine thousand cash. But given gaps in service they typically just amassed three years of active-duty pay every six or seven years, reducing their total monthly average to less than four or five thousand cash at the top and three or four thousand cash at the bottom. Out of this must come expenses for studies, funerals, weddings, and so on.

36 Smith, *Taxing Heaven's Storehouse*, 177–90 on "Motivating Personnel."

37 For the politics of the post-Chanyuan era see Olsson, "The Structure of Power Under the Third Emperor of China"; Liu Jingzhen, *Bei Song qianqi huangdi he tamende quanli*; Lau and Huang, "Founding and Consolidation of the Sung Dynasty"; McGrath, "The Reigns of Jen-tsung (1022–1063) and Ying-tsung (1063–1067)."

38 Fan complains about both the restrictions on political memorializing and the suppression of the oversight agencies in 1025, 1027, and 1036. For overviews see Kracke, *Civil Service*, 34–37; James Liu, *Ou-yang Hsiu*, chap. 5; and Jia Yuying, *Songdai jiancha zhidu*, especially chaps. 3 and 4.

39 These oft-made points are all recapitulated in the four essays submitted in 1036 as part of Fan's open attack on Lü Yijian. Besides *Fan Zhongyan quanji* vol. 1.129–36, see Skonicki, "Employing the Right Kind of Men," 60–65.

40 *Fan Zhongyan quanji* 1.205–06 (1030).

41 *QSW* 63:341.

42 *QSW* 63:328.

43 State Council incumbents and their dates of tenure for the reigns of Renzong through Shenzong are tabulated in *SS* 211.5459–94; they are also reproduced in Higashi Ichio, *Ō Anseki jiten*, 211–20. On Northern Song factionalism see Levine, *Divided by a Common Language.*

44 *CB* 121.2851 (1038).

45 Wang Anshi to Shenzong, 1070/7, *CB* 213.5169.

46 Wong, "Government Expenditures in Northern Sung China (960–1127)," 5, 7, tables 1 and 3.

47 Wong, "Government Expenditures," 157, table 23. On provisioning the military in Shaanxi and the greater northwest, see Cheng Long, *Bei Song Xibei zhanqu liangshi bugei dili*, chaps. 6 and 7.

48 Wong, "Government Expenditures," 161–62, table 25.

49   Among those with significant economic discussions are Fan Zhongyan, Ouyang Xiu, Zhang Fangping, Sima Guang, Li Gou, and Cai Xiang. See Robert Hartwell, *A Guide to Sources of Chinese Economic History*, 14–45.

50   *QSW* 63:336.

51   As Li Huarui shows in his chapter, Wang Anshi is following Mencius in his condemnation of engrossers.

52   Wang Anshi, "Kanxiang zayi: Yiyue fei dushuijian," *QSW* 64:58; Smith, *Taxing Heaven's Storehouse*, 111–18, "Wang Anshi's theory of bureaucratic entrepreneurship."

53   Based on Chaffee, *The Thorny Gates of Learning*, 27, table 4.

54   Although *CB* 143.3444 claims there are no details on the enactment of articles 6, 7, 9, and 10, Jin Zhongshu, "Fan Zhongyan de gexin zhengce kao," 992–93 cites *SHY* Shihuo 1.25b–26b, as evidence that promotional incentives were offered to officials who could improve hydrology and land reclamation, increase their populations, and promote agriculture, as specified in article 6. On the consolidation of Henan *fu*'s counties see *CB* 149.3617, and Mostern, *"Dividing the Realm in Order to Govern,"* 176–77. For positive evaluations of the *potential* economic contributions of Fan's blueprint, see Song Xi, "Lun Fan Zhongyan zhi fuguo ce"; and Wang Shengduo, *Liang Song caizheng shi*, 40–42. On Fan's military contributions see Tsang, "War and Peace," chaps. 7 and 8; and Don Wyatt, "Unsung Men of War,"192–218.

55   For two recent studies of Song political economy that focus wholly or in part on Wang Anshi's fiscal reforms see William Liu, "The Making of a Fiscal State in Song China, 960–1279"; and Luo, "Ideas in Practice."

56   *CB* 220.5351.

57   As stated in a debate with Sima Guang before the emperor, recorded by Sima Guang in "Erying zoudui," *Sima wenzheng gong chuanjia ji*, 42.543–45.

58   Smith, "Shen-tsung's reign," 426–28.

59   Miyazawa Tomoyuki, "Hoku-Sō no zaisei to hakei keizai," table 300. On licensed purchases (*chengmai*) of the wine and ferry franchises, see *Wenxian tongkao* 19.186b-c.

60   Most officials in the top tiers of the Bureau of Military Affairs were civilians, especially after Chanyuan. See Chen Feng, "Cong Shumiyuan zhang'er chushen bianhua kan Bei Song 'yi wen yu wu' fangzhen de yingxiang," 56–71.

61   Jia Yuying, *Songdai jiancha zhidu*, highlights the contribution of the policy critics to Fan Zhongyan's rise and the subsequent reforms in chap. 4, 168–76.

62   State Council incumbents are tabulated in *SS* 211 (*zaifu* 2), 5465–68 for the Qingli reform years.

63   "Fan Wenzheng gong nianpu," *Fan Zhongyan quanji* 2:746–47; Fu Bi, "Xushu qianhou cimian enming yi bian chanbang zou," *QSW* 28:358, a retrospective assessment composed in 1068 for emperor Shenzong in which he describes his sense of fear throughout the reform year.

64   Recorded by Wang Su's son Wang Gong, in his *Wenjian jinlu*, 23b–24a.

65   *Sushui jiwen* 4.66; *CB* 140.3359–60; *CB* 142.3415–17.

66   Wang Deyi, "Fan Zhongyan yu Lü Yijian," 108–11. Skonicki discusses Ouyang's attacks on Lü Yijian associates in ""Employing the Right Kind of Men," 87–88.

67   *CB* 147.3564; Lee, *Government Education and Examinations*, 175. The evidence of both enactment and retrenchment is not completely clear.

68   *CB* 141.3374–75. The principal documents on the surveillance investigators are antholo-gized in *CBBM* 41.721–731. Deng Xiaonan puts the Qingli surveillance inspectors in historical context in "Cong 'ancha' kan Bei Song zhidu de yunxing," especially 77–88.

69   *CB* 143. 3466.

70   *CB* 141.3375; *SHY* Shihuo 49.13b–14a. Judicial intendants were also charged with assum-ing surveillance responsibilities, but without an additional title. This 1043/5 edict pro-vided the legislative authorization for a surveillance system whose first incumbents were appointed in 1045/10.

71   Bao Zheng, "Qing buyong kenue zhiren chong jiansi zou," *QSW* 25:350.

72   *CB* 151.3689–90, 157.3803.

73   *CBBM* 58.1032.

74   Smith, "Shen-tsung's reign," 373.

75   *SS* 327.10546; Smith, "Shen-tsung's reign," 373–78.

76   Higashi, *Ō Anseki jiten*, 79–81; Smith, "Shen-tsung's reign," 378–84.

77   Higashi, *Ō Anseki shimpō no kenkyū*, 264–363.

78   Smith, "Shen-tsung's reign," 382–83; Smith, "State Power and Economic Activism Dur-ing the New Policies."

79   *CBBM* 64.1133–44 anthologizes documents on "Wang Anshi's exclusive use of petty men." Mark Knights writes that "a fiscal-military state was one capable of sustaining large-scale warfare through taxation and fiscal innovation, such as the creation of a national debt or credit-providing institutions." He provides a brief introduction to the concept of and recent literature on the fiscal-military state in the online *Oxford Bib-liographies*, at www.oxfordbibliographies.com/view/document/obo-9780199730414/obo-9780199730414-0073.xml. See also William Guanglin Liu, "The Making of a Fiscal State in Song China, 960–1279."

80   Skonicki, "Employing the Right Kind of Men, 87n140; *Song zaifu biannian lu jiaobu* 5.248.

81   "Fan Wenzhenggong nianpu," *Fan Zhongyan quanji* 2:745–46.

82   For the appointment and its reversal, *CB* 140.3364–5. Shi Jie's poem and the reac-tions to it are described in "Shi Jie nianpu," *Songren nianpu congkan* 2:884–85. When Fan Zhongyan and Han Qi learned of the poem, entitled "The Divine Virtue of the Qingli Era (Qingli shengde)," while en route back to the capital from Shaanxi, Fan was appalled, telling Han, "Because of this demon we will be destroyed" ("Shi Jie nianpu," 885). Fan would later reject Shi Jie as a candidate to join the four activists in the Policy Criticism Bureau on the grounds that he was too disputatious: "Shi Jie buyi wei jian-guan," *Fan Zhongyan quanji* 2:802. For the entire poem and preface see *QSW* 29.184–7. *Changbian* entries on Xia Song's ouster and later revenge are anthologized in *CBBM* 37.654–62.

83   Sources on these counterattacks against the reformers are anthologized in *CBBM* 38. The events are summarized in McGrath, "The Reigns of Jen-tsung (1022–1063) and Ying-tsung (1063–1067)," 321–23.

84   Fan Zhongyan and Fu Bi were ousted from the state council in 1045/1 (*CB* 154.3740–41; "Fu Bi nianpu," *Songren nianpu congkan* 2:924); Han Qi was reassigned to a provin-cial post in 1045/3 (*Han Weigong jiazhuan, Han Weigong ji* 13, 195–96; *CB* 155.3758–59); and Ouyang Xiu was arrested in 1045/8 on the order of antireform chief councilor Jia

Changchao, on charges of committing incest with his widowed sister's daughter by a previous, non-Ouyang marriage. This "Case of Niece Zhang" is well told by Liu, *Ouyang Hsiu*, 65–69. See also *CB* 157.3798–99; "Ouyang Xiu nianpu," *Songren nianpu congkan* 2:1084–85.

85 *CB* 268.6574.

86 The following year Sima retired to Luoyang, which became the opposition capital for the next fourteen years (Freeman, "Loyang and the opposition to Wang Anshi"). For Sima Guang's special role as a counterweight to the reformers see Ji, *Politics and Conservatism in Northern Song China*, chap. 7.

87 *CB* 141.3374–75; *CB* 151.3671.

88 Investigative Censor Liu Yuanyu, in *CB* 154.3744.

89 Quoted in *CB* 260.6336. *CBBM* 64 is dedicated to "Wang Anshi's exclusive use of mean and petty men."

90 *SS* 281.9525–26.

91 For the full revival of the New Policies under Zhezong see Ari Levine, "Che-tsung's reign (1085–1100) and the Age of Faction."

92 I develop this point more fully in "A Crisis in the Literati State."

93 The events are narrated in *CB* 148.3580–82, which reproduces the text of the "Discourse." For two recent studies of the 1044 factionalism debate and Ouyang Xiu's "Discourse" see Ari Levine, "Faction Theory" and *Divided by a Common Language*, especially 48–49. See also James Liu, *Ou-yang Hsiu*, 52–55; and Wang Deyi, "Lü Yijian yu Fan Zhongyan," 110–13. For Ouyang's about-face see *CB* 155.3763–66, analyzed and partially translated by Liu, *Ou-yang Hsiu*, 54–55.

94 *CB* 152.3706–07 for the exchange of oath letters.

95 *CB* 153.3718.

96 Before being allowed to resign from the council, Fan (and Fu Bi) were subjected to further humiliation at the hands of Zhang Dexiang and the new policy monitor Qian Mingyi, as recorded in *Song zaifu biannian lu jiaobu* 5.259–62.

97 Wenxian tongkao, 24.232c.

98 *CB* 215.5238–39.

99 *CB* 295.7192.

100 Deng Xiaoping, "The Present Situation and the Tasks Before Us," 248–49.

REFERENCES

PRIMARY SOURCES

Fan Zhongyan quanji 范仲淹全集, compiled by (Qing) Fan Nengjun 范能濬. 2 vols., Nanjing: Fenghuang chubanshe, 2004.

Han Weigong jiazhuan 韓魏公家傳, author unknown, in *Han Weigong ji* 韓魏公集, *juan* 10–19. Reprint of the *Congshu jicheng chubian* (1936) edition.

Huang Song Zizhitongjian changbian jishibenmo 皇宋資治通鑑長編記事本末, by Yang Zhongliang 楊仲良 (fl. ca. 1170–1230). Harbin: Heilongjiang renmin chubanshe, 2006.

"Kanxiang zayi: Yiyue fei dushuijian" 看詳雜議：議曰廢都水監, by Wang Anshi. In *QSW* 64.58.

Quan Song wen 全宋文, edited by Zeng Zaozhuang 曾枣庄 et al. Shanghai: Shanghai cishu chubanshe, 2006.

"Shang Renzong Huangdi yanshi shu" 上仁宗皇帝言事書, by Wang Anshi 王安石. In *QSW* 63:328–42.

Sima wenzheng gong chuanjia ji 司馬文正公傳家集, Sima Guang's 司馬光 collected works as compiled by (Qing) Chen Hongmou 陳弘謀 (1696–1771). Shanghai: Shangwu yinshuguan, 1937.

Song huiyao jigao 宋會要輯稿, compiled by Xu Song 徐松 (1781–1848) et al. Taibei: Shijie shuju, 1964.

Song zaifu biannian lu jiaobu 宋宰輔編年錄校補, by Xu Ziming 徐自明 (*jinshi* 1178). 4 vols. Beijing: Zhonghua shuju, 1986.

Songren nianpu congkan 宋人年譜叢刊, compiled by Wu Hongze 吳洪澤 et al. 12 vols. Chengdu: Sichuan daxue chubanshe, 2003.

Song shi 宋史, edited by Tuo Tuo 脫脫 (1313–1355) et al. Beijing: Zhonghua shuju, 1977.

Sushui jiwen 涑水記聞, by Sima Guang 司馬光 (1019–1086). Beijing: Zhonghua shuju, 1997.

"The Present Situation and the Tasks Before Us," by Deng Xiaoping. In his *Selected Works of Deng Xiaoping*, 224–58. Beijing: Foreign Languages Press, 1983.

Wenjian jinlu 聞見近路, by Wang Gong 王鞏 (fl. 1070s). E-SKQS ed.

Wenxian tongkao 文獻通考, by Ma Duanlin 馬端臨 (1254–1323). Shitong ed., Shanghai: Shangwu yinshuguan, 1939.

"Xushu qianhou cimian enming yi bian chanbang zou" 敘述前後辭免恩命以辯讒謗奏, by Fu Bi 富弼. In *QSW* 28:357–62.

Xu zizhi tongjian changbian 續資治通鑑長編, by Li Tao 李燾 (1115–1184). Beijing: Zhonghua shuju, 1985.

Yuanfeng jiuyu zhi 元豐九域志, by Wang Cun 王存 (1023–1101). Beijing: Zhonghua shuju, 1984.

"Zhiti lun" (治體論), by Lü Zhong 呂中. In his "Leibian huangchao dashiji jiangyi xulun" 類編皇朝大事記講義序論, *QSW* 346:152–55.

SECONDARY SOURCES

Bol, Peter K. *"This Culture of Ours": Intellectual Transition in T'ang and Sung China*. Stanford: Stanford University Press, 1992.

Chaffee, John W. *The Thorny Gates of Learning in Sung China*. Cambridge, UK: Cambridge University Press, 1985.

Chen Feng 陈峰. "Cong Shumiyuan zhang'er chushen bianhua kan Bei Song 'yi wen yu wu' fangzhen de yingxiang 从枢密院长贰出身变化看北宋以文驭武方针的影响. In his *Songdai junzheng yanjiu* 宋代军政研究, 56–71. Beijing: Zhongguo shehui kexue chubanshe, 2010.

Cheng Long 程龙. *Bei Song Xibei zhanqu liangshi bugei dili* 北宋西北战区粮食补给地理. Beijing: Shehui kexue wenxian chuban she, 2006.

Deng Xiaonan 鄧小南. "Cong 'ancha' kan Bei Song zhidu de yunxing" 從'按察'看北宋制度的運行. In *Jinshi Zhongguo zhi bian yu bubian* 近世中國之變與不變, edited by Lau Nap-yin 柳立言, 53–104. Taibei: Zhongyan yanjiu yuan, 2013.

Dunnell, Ruth. "The Hsi Hsia." In *The Cambridge History of China*, Vol. 6: *Alien Regimes and Border States*, edited by Herbert Franke and Denis Twitchett. Cambridge: Cambridge University Press, 1994.

Etzioni, Amitai. "Organizational Control Structure." In *Handbook of Organizations*, edited by James G. Marsh. Chicago: Rand McNally, 1965.

Fan Zhongyan yiqiannian danchen guojixueshu yantaohui lunwen ji 范仲淹一千年誕辰國際學術研討會論文集. 2 vols. Taibei: Guoli Taiwan daxue wenxueyuan, 1990.

Fang Jian 方健. *Fan Zhongyan pingzhuan* 范仲淹评传. Nanjing: Nanjing daxue chubanshe, 2001.

Freeman, Michael Dennis. "Loyang and the opposition to Wang Anshi: The Rise of Confucian Conservatism, 1068–1086." PhD diss., Yale University, 1973.

Ge Shao'ou 葛紹歐. "Fan Zhongyan dui Songdai difang jiaoyu de gongxian" 范仲淹對宋代地方教育的貢獻. In *Fan Zhongyan yiqiannian danchen*, vol. 2:1151–84. Taibei: Guoli Taiwan daxue wenxueyuan, 1990.

Hartwell, Robert M. *A Guide to Sources of Chinese Economic History, A.D. 618–1368*. Chicago: Committee on Far Eastern Civilizations, 1964.

Higashi Ichio 東一夫. *Ō Anseki jiten* 王安石事典. Tokyo: Kokusho Kankokai, 1980.

———. *Ō Anseki shimpō no kenkyū* 王安石新法の研究.Tokyo: Kazama Shobo, 1970.

Ji, Xiao-bin. *Politics and Conservatism in Northern Song China: The Career and Thought of Sima Guang (A.D. 1019–1086)*. Hong Kong: Chinese University of Hong Kong, 2005.

Jia Yuying 賈玉英. *Songdai jiancha zhidu* 宋代監察制度. Kaifeng: Henan daxue chuban she, 1996.

Jin Zhongshu 金中樞. "Fan Zhongyan de gexin zhengce kao" 范仲淹的革新政策考. In *Fan Zhongyan yiqiannian danchen*, vol. 2:960–1027. Taibei: Guoli Taiwan daxue wenxueyuan, 1990.

Kracke, Edward. *Civil Service in Early Sung China*, 960–1067. Cambridge, Mass.: Harvard University Press, 1953.

Lamouroux, Christian. "Song Renzong's Court Landscape: Historical Writing and the Creation of a New Political Sphere (1022–1042)." *Journal of Song-Yuan Studies* 42 (2012): 45–94.

Lau, Nap-yin, and Huang K'uan-chung. "Founding and Consolidation of the Sung Dynasty under T'ai-tsu (960–976), T'ai-tsung (976–997), and Chen-tsung (997–1022)." In *The Cambridge History of China*, Vol. 5, Part 1: *The Sung Dynasty and its Precursors, 907–1279*, edited by Denis Twitchett and Paul Jakov Smith, 206–278. Cambridge, UK: Cambridge University Press, 2009.

Lee, Thomas. *Government Education and Examinations in Sung China*. Hong Kong: Chinese University Press, 1985.

Levine, Ari Daniel. "Che-tsung's reign (1085–1100) and the Age of Faction." In *The Cambridge History of China*, Vol. 5, Part 1: *The Sung Dynasty and its Precursors, 907–1279*, edited by Denis Twitchett and Paul Jakov Smith, 484–555. Cambridge, UK: Cambridge University Press, 2009.

———. *Divided by a Common Language: Factional Conflict in Late Northern Song China*. Honolulu: University of Hawai'i Press, 2008.

———. "Faction Theory and the Political Imagination of the Northern Song." *Asia Major, Third Series* 18, no. 2 (2005): 155–200.

Li Fanwen 李范文. *Xi Xia tongshi* 西夏通史. Yinchuan: Ningxia renmin chubanshe, 2005.

Li Huarui 李華瑞. *Song-Xia guanxi shi* 宋夏关系史. Baoding: Hebei renmin chubanshe, 1998.

———. *Wang Anshi bianfa yanjiu shi* 王安石變法研究史. Beijing: Renmin chubanshe, 2004.

Liu, James T. C. "An Early Sung Reformer: Fan Chung-yen." In *Chinese Thought and Institutions*, edited by John K. Fairbank, 105–131. Chicago: University of Chicago Press, 1957.

———. *Ou-yang Hsiu: An Eleventh-century New-Confucianist*. Stanford: Stanford University Press, 1967.

———. *Reform in Sung China: Wang An-shih and his New Policies*. Cambridge, Mass.: Harvard University Press, 1959.

Liu, William Guanglin. "The Making of a Fiscal State in Song China, 960–1279." *Economic History Review* (2014): 1–31.

Liu Jingzhen 劉靜貞. *Bei Song qianqi huangdi he tamende quanli* 北宋前期皇帝和他們的權力. Taibei: Daoxiang chubanshe, 1996.

Luo, Yinan. "Ideas in Practice: The Political Economy of Chinese State Intervention during the New Policies Period (1068–1085)." PhD diss., Harvard University, 2015.

McGrath, Michael. "The Reigns of Jen-tsung (1022–1063) and Ying-tsung (1063–1067)." In *The Cambridge History of China*, Vol. 5, Part 1: *The Sung Dynasty and its Precursors, 907–1279*, edited by Denis Twitchett and Paul Jakov Smith, 279–346. Cambridge, UK: Cambridge University Press, 2009.

Miyazawa Tomoyuki 宮澤知之. "Hoku-Sō no zaisei to hakei keizai" 北宋の財政と貨幣經濟. In *Chūgoku sensei kokka to shakai tōgō* 中國專制國家-社會統合. Kyoto: Bunrikaku, 1990.

Mostern, Ruth. *"Dividing the Realm in Order to Govern": The Spatial Organization of the Song State (960–1276 CE)*. Cambridge, Mass.: Harvard University Asia Center, 2011.

Olsson, Karl F. "The Structure of Power under the Third Emperor of China: The Shifting Balance after the Peace of Shan-yüan." PhD diss., University of Chicago, 1974.

Skonicki, Douglas. "Employing the Right Kind of Men: The Role of Cosmological Argumentation in the Qingli Reforms," *Journal of Song-Yuan Studies* 38 (2008): 39–98.

Smith, Paul Jakov. "Shen-tsung's Reign and the New Policies of Wang An-shih, 1068–1085." In *The Cambridge History of China*, Vol. 5, Part 1: *The Sung Dynasty and its Precursors, 907–1279*, edited by Denis Twitchett and Paul Jakov Smith, 347–483. Cambridge, UK: Cambridge University Press, 2009.

———. "State Power and Economic Activism during the New Policies, 1068–1085: The Tea and Horse Trade and the Green Sprouts Loan Policy." In *Ordering the World: Approaches to State and Society in Sung Dynasty China*, edited by Robert Hymes and Conrad Schirokauer, 76–127. Berkeley: University of California Press, 1993.

———. *Taxing Heaven's Storehouse: Horses, Bureaucrats, and the Destruction of the Sichuan Tea Industry, 1074–1224*. Cambridge, Mass.: Harvard University Asia Center, 1991.

Song Xi 宋晞. "Lun Fan Zhongyan zhi fuguo ce" 論范仲淹之富國策. In *Fan Zhongyan yiqiannian danchen* (1990), Vol. 2:1029–42.

Tsang, Shui-lung 曾瑞龍. "War and Peace in Northern Sung China: Violence and Strategy in Flux, 960–1104 A.D." PhD diss., University of Arizona, 1997.

Wang Deyi 王德毅. "Lü Yijian yu Fan Zhongyan" 呂夷簡與范仲淹. *Shixue huikan* 4 (1971): 85–119.

Wang Shengduo 汪聖鐸. *Liang Song caizheng shi* 兩宋財政史. 2 vols. Beijing: Zhonghua shuju, 1995.

Wang Zhishuang 王志双. "Bei Song Renzong chao Lü Yijian jituande zucheng jiqi xingzhi" 北宋仁宗朝呂夷簡集團的組成及其性質. *Xingtai xueyuan xuebao* 18, no. 3 (2003): 40–44.

Weber, Max. *Economy and Society*. Edited by Guenther Roth and Claus Wittich. 3 vols. New York: Bedminster Press, 1968.

Williamson, H. R. *Wang An Shih, a Chinese Statesman and Educationalist of the Sung Dynasty*. 2 vols. London: Arthur Probsthain, 1935–1937.

Wong Hon-chiu. "Government Expenditures in Northern Sung China (960–1127)." PhD diss., University of Pennsylvania, 1975.

Wong, R. Bin, *China Transformed: Historical Change and the Limits of European Experience*. Ithaca: Cornell University Press, 1997.

Wyatt, Don J. "Unsung Men of War: Acculturated Embodiments of the Martial Ethos in the Song Dynasty." In *Military Culture in Imperial China*, edited by Nicol Di Cosmo, 192–218. Cambridge, Mass.: Harvard University Press, 2009.

5 Bureaucratic Politics and Commemorative Biography

The Epitaphs of Fan Zhongyan

CONG ELLEN ZHANG

IN HIS FAMOUS "RECORD OF THE YUEYANG TOWER" (YUEYANG LOU JI), Fan Zhongyan penned one of the most frequently quoted sayings concerning the political ideals of the Chinese literati. Writing in 1046, immediately after the failure of the Qingli reforms (1043–1045), of which he was the leader, Fan Zhongyan (989–1052) drew inspiration from the deeds of the worthies from the past.[1] Paragons of humaneness, Fan wrote, "took no delight in external things, nor did they feel sorry for themselves. When they occupied a high position at court, they felt concern for the people. When banished to distant rivers and lakes, they felt concern for their sovereign." Through the mouths of the ancients, Fan called on himself and his fellow scholar-officials to "be first in worrying about the world's worries and last in enjoying its pleasures."[2]

In a powerful way, Fan Zhongyan rearticulated the classical Confucian vision of the gentleman serving as the loyal advisor to the emperor and being the devoted guardian of the welfare of the people. In a long career in the government, he tried to live up to these ideals. For approximately three decades, Fan occupied multiple positions in the central and local governments and was an instrumental force in the first major Song war with the Tangut Xi Xia (1038–1044). His concern for the key issues of the time, including personnel management, the examination system, border affairs, and other social and economic problems, were reflected in a large number of memorials and local initiatives and, ultimately, in the reform programs of the Qingli reign period (1041–1048).[3] Fan Zhongyan's ascendancy at the court was counterbalanced by political setbacks, especially in terms of his multiple clashes with the grand councilor Lü Yijian (978–1044). During a fifteen-year period (1029–1045), Fan was demoted four times.[4] The last demotion occurred in the beginning of 1045, when Emperor Renzong

(1022–1063) withdrew his support for the reform, resulting in Fan Zhongyan's ouster from the court.[5]

Not only did politics and court service remain central to Fan's life and career, they also deeply affected the way he was remembered. This can be seen in the backstory to the writing of Fan Zhongyan's two epitaphs: a *muzhiming* (tomb or funerary inscription) by Fu Bi (1004–1083) and a *shendaobei* (spirit path stele) by Ouyang Xiu (1007–1072).[6] Points of contention included two turning points in Fan Zhongyan's life and career, his exile in 1036 and reinstatement in 1040.[7] Both were politically charged events and closely connected to the powerful grand councilor Lü Yijian. Fan Zhongyan's case illustrates a major change in epitaph writing in the Northern Song. As epitaphs became increasingly lengthy and more biographical in focus, multiple parties, including the author and the deceased's family and close associates, became more attentive to their content. This change created much tension among people of diverse interests and had especially far-reaching consequences when factionalism plagued politics.

WRITING FAN ZHONGYAN'S *MUZHIMING*

Whoever was entrusted with authoring the epitaph of such a prominent political and literary figure as Fan Zhongyan would know that his work, upon completion, would come under close scrutiny. In Fan's long career as an accomplished writer, scholar, statesman, and reformer, he had gathered a large following as well as formidable enemies, all of whom were stakeholders in his legacy.

Among Fan's closest supporters were Yu Jing (1000–1064), Yin Zhu (1001–1047), Fu Bi, Ouyang Xiu, Han Qi (1008–1075), and Cai Xiang (1012–1067). All shared Fan's idealistic vision of a morally charged government and remained Fan's closest associates in the unfolding of partisan politics in the 1030s and during the Qingli reforms. Of these followers, Fu Bi, Ouyang Xiu, and Han Qi played especially important roles in the writing of Fan's epitaphs. Fu Bi had been a long-time disciple of Fan Zhongyan and later became very close to Fan's second son, Fan Chunren (1027–1101). In addition to authoring Fan Zhongyan's *muzhiming*, Fu also wrote Fan Chunyou's (Fan Zhongyan's eldest son) *muzhiming*; Fan Chunren later composed Fu's *xingzhuang* (record of conduct).[8]

Both at the court and while dealing with border troubles, Han Qi remained Fan Zhongyan's steadfast friend and colleague.[9] He and Fan worked especially closely during the Song–Tangut border troubles in the early 1040s. Han authored neither of Fan's epitaphs, but as I will show, he was actively involved in the writing process. Moreover, at the request of Fan Chunren, Han Qi wrote a preface to the collection of Fan Zhongyan's memorials, in which he praised Fan for being extremely loyal to Emperor Renzong and for sparing no effort in fulfilling his official duties.[10]

Even more than Fu Bi and Han Qi, Ouyang Xiu was an active leader of the reforms.[11] Along with Fan, Ouyang was demoted in 1036 as a result of their confrontation with Lü Yijian. When Fan Zhongyan provocatively defended factions in front of Emperor Renzong in 1044, Ouyang in turn defended Fan in his famous "Discourse on Factions" (Pengdang lun). In a memorial that influenced the discourse on factions for the rest of the Northern Song and beyond, Ouyang "reimagined factions as inherently ethical affiliations of superior men who selflessly served the public good, whereas cliques of petty men were just self-serving."[12]

Of Fan Zhongyan's enemies, no one was more intimidating than the three-time grand councilor Lü Yijian (1029–1033, 1033–1037, and 1040–1043).[13] In fact, two of Fan's demotions directly resulted from his opposition to Lü. It was only with Lü's dismissal in 1043 that the Qingli Reforms began, and the short-lived reform ended partially because Lü's supporters successfully rallied against it. As recent scholarship has shown, however, the relationship between Lü and Fan was actually a complicated one. Fan and Lü had known each other for a long time before their face-off in court politics. When Fan charged Lü with nepotism and abusing personnel management policies in 1036, Lü in turn accused Fan of forming a faction and had Fan exiled. Lü too was soon demoted. Both were recalled to the court in 1040. Their official responsibilities necessitated that they cooperate with each other. At Lü's death in 1044 in the midst of the Qingli reforms, Fan Zhongyan composed an elegy in which he commended Lü for being a competent, even accomplished, grand councilor.[14] However, when the reforms ended the next year, Lü's former disciples returned to occupy influential positions. Almost all the reformers were ousted from the capital. Fan Zhongyan would be posted in several local positions until the end of his life.[15]

Fan Zhongyan died on 1052/5/20 in Xuzhou (in Jiangsu). In the next two and a half years, his supporters and families collaborated and fought with each other over the portrayal of Fan in the *muzhiming*, completed by Fu Bi in 1052/10, and the *shendaobei*, completed by Ouyang Xiu in the second half of 1054. Their main disagreement was whether Fan had reconciled with Lü in 1040. While Ouyang Xiu clearly stated that there was a compromise between Fan and Lü, Fu Bi and Fan Zhongyan's sons vehemently denied its possibility.

Since Fu Bi eventually wrote Fan's *muzhiming* and Ouyang Xiu Fan's *shendaobei*, both traditional and modern scholars have taken it for granted that this had been the original arrangement. But a close reading of the extant material reveals that Ouyang had initially been chosen to be Fan's *muzhiming* writer by Fan's family and friends. That Ouyang did not author the *muzhiming* as planned was probably due to a combination of factors, with the difficulty of writing Fan's epitaph in a precarious political atmosphere being an important consideration.

Three letters to and from Ouyang Xiu strongly suggest that Ouyang had initially been designated to write Fan's *muzhiming*. In the first letter, from Du Yan (978–1057) to Ouyang Xiu, Du explicitly says: "Xiwen [Fan Zhongyan's literary name] is wise, unique, and outstanding. Even a hundred people combined could not be compared with him. Only a great master capable of using beautiful words could fully bring honor to his accomplishments. You are a person with outstanding vision and have agreed to write Mr. Fan's [*muzhi*]*ming*. This must also have been the result of his accumulated virtue. Knowing this, I cannot stop sighing with emotion."[16] In the letter, Du acknowledges what a formidable task it would be to perpetuate Fan's legacy and his belief in Ouyang's ability to do justice to Fan's life and accomplishments. Du's use of *ming*, instead of *beiming*, which was often used generically in discussions of epitaph writing, leaves no doubt that Ouyang had been chosen as the author of Fan's *muzhiming*. If Du knew about this arrangement, it was very likely common knowledge among Fan's close associates.

Two letters dated 1052 from Ouyang Xiu himself, to Han Qi and Sun Mian (996–1066), also refer to Fan Zhongyan's sons entrusting Ouyang with Fan's *muzhiming*.[17] In the letter to Han Qi, Ouyang writes, "All under Heaven has been saddened by the news of Mr. Fan's death. Earlier, his family entrusted me with his [*muzhi*]*ming*. Even though I am in mourning [for my mother], I could not possibly have rejected the request."[18] Ouyang's letter to Sun Mian specifically mentions the same request, adding that, since Fan Zhongyan had been an intimate friend, he would of course do his best. This letter alludes specifically to writing Fan's *maiming* or "interred epitaph," a term that could not possibly have been used interchangeably with *bei* or *shendaobei*.[19] If there were lingering doubts about Ouyang being the original *muzhiming* writer, his letter to Sun Mian sufficiently proved them groundless.

Why then did Ouyang fail to produce Fan's *muzhiming*? In both letters cited here Ouyang Xiu notes two difficulties of the task, which eventually led to a change in authorship. The first is that Ouyang Xiu's mother had died in

1052/3, two months before Fan Zhongyan passed away. Ritual stipulations required that Ouyang concentrate on grieving and preparing for her burial instead of being preoccupied with other activities. The other difficulty, according to Ouyang, was that Fan's virtues and talents were not easily put into words. Fan's active involvement in court politics from the late 1020s onward, particularly his confrontation with Lü Yijian in 1036, made writing his *muzhiming* an especially daunting task. The hostility between the two began when Fan criticized Lü for showing favoritism in official evaluations and promotions. Within several days of the attack, Fan Zhongyan and his supporters, including Ouyang Xiu, were condemned for forming factions and exiled to remote regions throughout the country.[20]

Ouyang Xiu took it for granted that his portrayal of Fan would have to address this episode in Fan's life and the larger issues of factions and factionalism. But he would have to handle them with care. Not only did many of Lü Yijian's supporters remain influential, but Fan's epitaph also had to be written in a way that would not damage the reputation of Emperor Renzong, who had apparently sided with Lü in 1036 and withdrew his support of Fan's reform in 1045. With all these in mind, Ouyang exclaimed, "How difficult the task is!"[21] Ouyang nonetheless made it clear that he was not trying to get out of writing Fan Zhongyan's *muzhiming*. In the letter to Sun Mian, the author of Fan Zhongyan's record of conduct, Ouyang wrote, "As soon as I receive the record of conduct, I will do my best to write the *ming*."[22]

In the end, however, it was Fu Bi who authored Fan Zhongyan's *muzhiming*.[23] Because I have found no explanation for this change in the extant sources, some speculation is in order. It is very possible that, since he had been in mourning, Ouyang was slow in completing Fan's *muzhiming*. At the same time, Fan Zhongyan's sons wanted a prompt burial for their father. Fan died in 1052/5 in Xuzhou and was buried near Luoyang (Henan) in 1052/12. In fact, Fu Bi's *muzhiming* indicated that Fan Zhongyan's family had planned an even earlier burial date, 1052/11/1.[24] Either way, the time it took for Fan to be buried was significantly shorter than the average time a burial took in the Northern Song, which, based on my preliminary calculations, was around a year and a half to two years.

It is also possible that both Ouyang's failure to complete the epitaph in time for the originally scheduled burial and the Fans' decision to hold a very quick burial might have been motivated by political considerations. For Fan Zhongyan's sons, with their father's opponents in power, it would have been desirable to have Fan Zhongyan laid to rest as soon as he was given a posthumous title. It appears that that process went rather smoothly, even though no extant sources provide a date for the granting of the title, Wenzheng (Literary and Upright). It is quite possible that Fan's family proceeded with his burial as soon as the title was secured. Indeed, if we take into account the long distance traversed in transporting Fan Zhongyan's body from Xuzhou to Luoyang, we cannot help but be impressed by the speed that arrangements were made and plans carried out.

From the perspective of Ouyang Xiu, given his mother's death and his concern for the political situation, he simply could not have been able to supply Fan's epitaph in the time required. A decision to replace him followed. This explains why Ouyang either completely distanced himself or was excluded from Fan's burial. In a letter to Cai Jiao, Fan Zhongyan's son-in-law, dated 1053, Ouyang confessed that, since he had been in mourning, he had not heard about Fan Zhongyan's funeral and burial and was grateful that Cai sent him a copy of Fan's *muzhiming* by Fu Bi.[25] The only plausible explanation for why Ouyang, one of Fan Zhongyan's closest friends and supporters, lost touch with the planning of Fan's burial, is that the Fans were disappointed in Ouyang's failure to complete the *muzhiming* on time and consequently turned to Fu Bi.

Further evidence supports these hypotheses. In a letter to a man named Yao, dated 1053, Ouyang wrote, "With Xiwen having received a fine posthumous title, it would have been all right even if he did not have a *muzhiming*. Now that Mr. Fu has written him one, he will be guaranteed immortality for sure."[26] Here Ouyang implies that given the political atmosphere of the time, Fan's family and friends, including himself, had been genuinely worried about whether Fan would be granted an appropriate posthumous title and what title it might be. That concern, more than who was going to author Fan's *muzhiming*, determined the date of Fan's burial. In other words, as soon as Fan had received the title, his family was ready to have him laid to rest. When Ouyang proved unable to deliver the *muzhiming* on time, the Fans turned to someone else.

If Ouyang had been offended in being passed over, he did not show it. With a fine title and a *muzhiming* by Fu Bi, Ouyang declared, Fan would certainly be assured of immortality. In a different letter Ouyang praises Fu's *muzhiming* as "detailed and factual. It is very good."[27] Fu Bi, in contrast, seemed to have felt somewhat awkward about replacing Ouyang. In a long letter, dated 1053, Fu first criticizes his fellow scholar-officials for lacking the courage to promote the deeds of the virtuous and condemn the evil in their epitaph work. He then continues,

The task of elevating the good and diminishing the evil and perpetuating the name of the good and ending that of the evil should start with us. We should not be afraid [of any repercussions in doing so], remain silent, or suffer from the frustrations [of not writing truthfully]. When I wrote Xiwen's *muzhiming* I used exactly this method. But I hated the fact that I had the intention [of elevating Xiwen], but could not find the [right] words. [Even so,] I feel that [my *muzhiming* for him] has slightly promoted the goodness of Xiwen and exposed the evil of the wicked. Yongshu [Ouyang Xiu's literary name] has said, "If there is something that one wants to say, he should not refrain from saying it. He should express it clearly. This way, one can release the indignation of the loyal and the righteous [toward the wicked]. Would that not be pleasing?" It seems that you approve of my thinking. In Xiwen's *muzhiming*, my denigration of the wicked was all based on facts that everyone under Heaven has heard of or known about. I did not fabricate anything. Several sons of the [Lü] family are all in influential positions. They will not spare us any slander.[28]

This long letter first and foremost shows that Fu Bi, generally considered a lesser writer and definitely a less prolific *muzhiming* author than Ouyang, was a bit anxious about Ouyang's reaction to his work. He made sure to mention that he and Ouyang shared the same high standards when it came to promoting the worthy and braving potential attacks from the wicked and powerful. In this context, Fu Bi humbly declared that, even though he might have failed to find the right words, he had played a small part in promoting Fan's life and deeds by speaking out candidly in an adverse political climate.

Fu's letter can also be read in another way. Despite their shared concern for Fan's legacy, Fu implied that he, not Ouyang, was the courageous one in glorifying Fan's virtues and deeds. Indeed, as our discussion will shortly demonstrate, Fu vehemently defended Fan, especially in Fan's clashes with Lü Yijian. In not writing the *muzhiming*, Ouyang might very well have lost the opportunity to prove his devotion to Fan Zhongyan and his commitment to writing epitaphs with honesty and courage. But Fan's *shendaobei* provided the perfect platform.

WRITING FAN ZHONGYAN'S *SHENDAOBEI*

Given their close relationship, the commemoration of Fan Zhongyan would not have been complete without a major piece from Ouyang Xiu. Since he did not get to author Fan Zhongyan's *muzhiming*, which was needed for the burial, it was only natural that Fan's family turned to Ouyang for Fan's *shendaobei*, which could be and was installed much later. Ouyang Xiu would have wanted nothing else. In the letter to Cai Jiao, dated 1053, Ouyang promised that, even with the time constraints he was under due to mourning duties, he would finish the *shendaobei* by the end of the year at the latest. He added, "I will write the *shenke* according to your suggestions. How would I dare not to do my best? Although I am clumsy and slow, I have written for so many famous worthies of the time. How could I possibly decline to author this one?"[29] Note here that Ouyang used *shenke* instead of *ming* or *maiming*, as he did in letters dated to 1052, further indicating that he was originally designated to write Fan's *muzhiming* and was only asked to author the *shendaobei* after the original plan fell through.

In the letter Ouyang also appears to be assuring Cai of his commitment to the task, even insinuating that there might have been doubts about his willingness to write it. Contemporary sources indeed give the impression that Fan's sons and friends had grown a bit impatient with Ouyang.[30] Du Yan, for example, pushed Ouyang about the progress of the *shendaobei* through a Mr. Yao. In response to Yao's inquiry, Ouyang acknowledged that "Mr. Du esteems the virtuous and is eager to transmit Mr. Fan's deeds." The reason he had taken the time, Ouyang explained, was that he wanted to be sure of the wording and to "be ready to fight off any enemies." Ouyang further stated, "I have tens of thousands of things to express and am not afraid of recording them. . . . [The only problem is that] this epitaph is completed fifteen months later [than it should have been]. When this piece comes out, slander from the wicked and the evil cannot possibly get close to me [because every fact in the biography is verifiable]. If one wants to stand firm, one must be reasonable and principled."[31]

Note that in this letter Ouyang did not list mourning his mother as a reason for not completing Fan's *shendaobei* more quickly. Rather, he emphasized that he was taking the time to make every word solid so that Fan's enemies would have no further opportunity to slander Fan nor to find fault with himself. If we take Ouyang's words literally, that he would finish the *shendaobei* by the end of 1053 and this epitaph would have been completed fifteen months later than originally scheduled, Ouyang would have been expected to finish an epitaph for Fan in 1052/9 or 1052/10, in time for the burial planned for 1052/11/1. This is yet further indication that Ouyang had originally been designated Fan's *muzhiming* writer.

Very soon after he promised to deliver the *shendaobei* at the end of 1053, however, Ouyang decided to have his mother buried with his father in their native place in Jiangxi, instead of in Yingzhou (Fuyang, Henan), as he had originally planned and where he had remained in mourning.[32] As a result, Ouyang traveled with his mother's coffin to Jiangxi. It was not until the end of 1053 that he returned to Yingzhou. Consequently, the *shendaobei* for Fan was not finished until the second half of 1054.[33]

Ouyang's trip to Jiangxi aside, his letter to Yao provides ample evidence of his continual concern for repercussions that might come from writing Fan's epitaph. This may very well have explained his initial procrastination in completing Fan's *muzhiming*. Anticipating a fight, Ouyang was very careful in drafting the *shendaobei*. Two letters from Ouyang to Han Qi, both dated 1054, provide us with solid evidence in this respect. In the first letter, Ouyang referred to meeting with Fan Chunren and reading the preface Han Qi had composed for the collection of Fan Zhongyan's memorials.[34] He then mentioned having studied Fan's *muzhiming* by Fu Bi, praising it again for being detailed and honest. In addition, Ouyang had gone through the many eulogies in Fan's honor. After all this research and preparation, he concluded, "It is really hard for me to add any more [to everything that has been said about Mr. Fan]. Ever since I ended mourning for my mother, I have put in my best effort. But my work has not taken into account even one or two percent of Mr. Fan's worthy deeds."[35]

The main purpose of this letter to Han Qi, however, was to ask for Han's feedback on a draft of the *shendaobei*. Ouyang wrote, "I now have it delivered to you from afar for your inspection. The friendship between you and Mr. Fan is most profound. Both at court and away, the two of you spared no effort in fulfilling your duties. I secretly worry that there are errors or things that I have not recorded in enough detail. I plead that you please enlighten me [so that I can make corrections accordingly]. I dare to make this request because this is a matter concerning the fair and honest assessment of someone at the court and under Heaven."[36] Because none of Han Qi's letters to Ouyang have survived, we have no way of knowing what specific advice Han gave Ouyang. We do know that Ouyang wrote back with gratitude, saying that he had corrected everything that Han had suggested and was waiting to hear about one particular memorial by Fan Zhongyan.[37] The very fact that Han seemed to have made multiple suggestions also indicates that both were extremely cautious about Fan's *shendaobei*. Indeed, it took Ouyang Xiu over two years to craft it. And this was far from the end of the story.

THE CONTROVERSY OVER FAN ZHONGYAN'S *SHENDAOBEI*

Despite the concerns of Ouyang Xiu, Fu Bi, and others regarding possible attacks from Fan's enemies when his funeral inscriptions were completed, neither Ouyang nor Fu Bi experienced any setbacks in their careers as a result. Nor have I found any contemporary source that contains any reactions from Fan's former opponents. As far as we are concerned, with the end of the Qingli reforms, the court "backed away from an activist, programmatic administration with its attendant factional conflict and turned instead to a leisurely form of 'cultural glamour.'" For this reason, it was characterized by "institutional stability combined with steady turnover of smaller numbers of chief officials."[38] In the mid-1060s, there is evidence that even Ouyang Xiu and Lü Yijian's sons got along.[39]

What instead had taken Ouyang Xiu by surprise was the strong reactions from Fan's family and friends. To put their concerns and Ouyang's remark on the differences between the two epitaphs into context, it is necessary to compare them very briefly. First and foremost, we should note that Fan Zhongyan's *shendaobei* (at approximately 2,200 characters) was only half the length of his *muzhiming* (approximately 4,000 characters).[40] But the major differences between the two epitaphs are in their portrayal of two major events in Fan Zhongyan's life and career. The first concerned Fan's exile in 1036 and the second his recall in 1040.

Both epitaphs refer to Fan's exile in 1036 as a result of his offense against the then grand councilor Lü Yijian and identify Fan as representing the loyal and upright side. Fu's *muzhiming* used about 350 characters to represent the moment in an extremely emotional way. Fan was said to have directly confronted Lü with regard to Lü's abuse of personnel policies. "The grand councilor became increasingly angry and urged his followers [*dang*] to criticize Mr. Fan in front of the emperor. Mr. Fan in turn kept vilifying [*di*] the grand councilor's unethical deeds [*budao*]. This developed to the point that their dispute would never stop if Mr. Fan did not leave the court." In addition to the clash between Fan and Lü, Fu Bi referred to many rallying to support Fan. "Those who said that Mr. Fan should not be punished for being loyal and upright were all heroes [*yinghao*] of the age. The grand councilor called them a faction. All were exiled soon thereafter."[41]

In contrast to Fu's lengthy, dramatic portrayal of the face-to-face conflict at the court, Ouyang's *shendaobei* was much more concise. Ouyang first quoted Fan's memorial to the court, in which Fan identified the key to proper personnel management: "Appoint people according to their talent and officials will [turn to] study and cultivate themselves [in the hope for promotions]. The reigns of Yao and Shun did not go beyond this practice." Ouyang, like Fu, went on to include Fan's criticism of Lü's personnel policies: "The grand councilor Lü became so angry [*nu*] that he and Mr. Fan argued in front of the emperor. Mr. Fan requested to respond to Lü. Their debate became very keen. In punishment, Mr. Fan was demoted to Raozhou."[42]

An immediately noticeable difference in these two narratives is that Fu Bi's version is more strongly worded than Ouyang's. In contrast to Ouyang, who only used "angry" (*nu*) in the text to describe Lü's reactions to Fan's criticism, Fu Bi used "follower" (*dang*), "vilify" (*di*), and "unethical" (*budao*) to demonize Lü and "heroes" (*yinghao*) to glorify Fan's supporters. An equally important if not more provocative gesture is that throughout Fu's *muzhiming*, Lü was only referred to as the grand councilor (*chengxiang*). Out of spite, Fu Bi mentioned neither Lü's personal nor his family name. Ouyang, in contrast, specifically referred to Lü Yijian as Mr. Lü (Lügong) or Grand Councilor Lü (Lü Chengxiang).

Ouyang did not stop at showing more respect to Lü. He continued to directly address the issue of factionalism, as he did in the "Discourse on Factions," something that Fu chose to avoid. Ouyang writes, "Ever since Mr. Fan was exiled as a result of Mr. Lü's accusations, scholar-officials have disagreed with each other on who was right and who was wrong. Mr. Lü was worried. Subsequently, everyone who supported Mr. Fan was identified as members of a faction and demoted or exiled."[43] In contrast to Fu Bi reserving the term "faction" (*dang*) for Lü's followers, Ouyang clearly identified 1036 as the official beginning of a generalized era of factionalism. In Ouyang's telling, it was the heated debate between his own supporters and Fan's that had Lü Yijian worried that he might lose control.

If Fu's and Ouyang's depictions of the 1036 clash differed greatly in their tone and emphases, the two texts diverged even farther when dealing with Fan's reinstatement in 1040 and his role in dealing with the Tanguts. Without a doubt, 1040 marked a turning point in Fan's career. More importantly, his position and responsibilities also required that Fan work closely with Lü Yijian. In the *muzhiming*, Fu Bi attributed Fan's return to the court to Emperor Renzong. As he relates it, on hearing of the Song army's defeat by the Tanguts the shocked emperor declaimed, "'If only I could have the assistance of Fan, I would have no need to worry.' Several days later, when Mr. Fan's memorial arrived, the emperor was elated. He showed it to the grand councilor and said, 'I knew I could rely on Fan.'"[44]

Ouyang's narrative of this episode, however, credited both Lü Yijian and

Fan Zhongyan for their willingness to work together at a time of national crisis. In Ouyang's depiction, "When Mr. Lü was reappointed as the grand councilor [in 1040], Mr. Fan was also reinstated. The two reconciled and vowed to cooperate in dealing with the enemy [i.e., the Tanguts]. Scholar-officials under Heaven all praised them. But the allegations of factionalism had begun and could not be stopped."[45]

Thus whereas Fu attributed Fan's recall to Renzong's recognition alone, Ouyang implied that Lü at least acquiesced to Renzong's suggestion, if it was indeed Renzong who had proposed the idea. Ouyang even went on to say that Fan and Lü decided to cooperate in the face of border troubles, again implying that Lü had been more than willing to bring Fan back. In Ouyang's portrayal of the event, not only did Lü play a positive role in Fan's return to the court, but both he and Fan decided to cooperate with each other. For this, Ouyang said, both Fan Zhongyan and Lü Yijian, not Fan alone, earned the praise of their fellow scholar-officials.

Traditional and modern scholars have written extensively about whether Fan and Lü had compromised, which is not the primary concern of this study.[46] Our focus here is instead on the immediate reactions to Ouyang's portrayal of the Fan-Lü reconciliation and their significance to our understanding of the dynamics among Fan Zhongyan's supporters in the postreform era. Fu Bi seems to have been the first to react to Ouyang's *shendaobei*. That Fu would be interested in reading Ouyang's *shendaobei* and finding out the differences between the two epitaphs is completely understandable. After all, he was a surrogate for Fan's *muzhiming* and had been nervous about Ouyang's response. Now that Ouyang's epitaph for Fan was completed, Fu would have every reason to be an enthusiastic reader. In fact, he did have some reservations about the way Fan Zhongyan's life was treated in the *shendaobei*. We are not certain if Fu ever brought this up with Ouyang directly, but his opinion nonetheless reached Ouyang through a mutual friend, Xu Wudang (1024–1086), not long after the completion of the *shendaobai*. In a letter to Xu, dated 1054, Ouyang wrote,

> [In your letter], you referred to Mr. Fu Bi talking about Mr. Fan's *shendaobei*. When I was at Yingzhou, we had decided that this was the objective way [to represent Fan]. Portraying the episode that involved Mr. Lü this way would demonstrate that Mr. Fan's virtue and tolerance were so overwhelming that they could encompass the entire universe and that he was loyal and upright and always made the interest of the state his top priority. Recording this episode with Mr. Lü in a factual way would

guarantee that we earn the trust of tens of thousands of generations. If we described their relations as two enemies arguing with each other, each exaggerating his own case, the later generations would not believe us and would consider our words extreme. Generally speaking, my *shendaobei* of Mr. Fan uses plain language and stays away from emotional expressions, while Mr. Fu's *muzhiming* is filled with his strong hatred of that which is evil. Noticing the differences between these two biographies, people of later generations will not find it strange knowing [our different intentions]. [In addition] I did not get the sequence of the positions that Mr. Fan had held wrong. I only listed them briefly. I did explain later [in the *shendaobei*] that "I will not include the sequence of the positions that he held." This way, later generations will not seek information about Mr. Fan's record of positions in this biography. Please explain all these to Mr. Fu. If he thinks it necessary to make changes, please have him find others to do it.[47]

Ouyang's letter reveals once again that there had been extensive discussion, among Ouyang Xiu and others, regarding the way Fan's life was to be portrayed. There was no question whatsoever that the main concern had been potential attack and retaliation from Lü's supporters, for which everyone involved seemed to have prepared. What caused special unease among Fu Bi and others was Ouyang's treatment of the Fan-Lü conflict and their subsequent "reconciliation." For the purpose of the current study, however, the more important issue was how Fan Zhongyan's legacy could best be defined and preserved. In other words, while a defense of Fan's antagonism with Lü was necessary to elevate Fan's uprightness and to highlight the legitimacy of the Qingli reforms, would Fan's image and reputation in history have been greatly distorted or diminished if the episode about his compromise with Lü Yijian had been excluded?

This is where Ouyang Xiu, Fu Bi, and Fan Chunren fundamentally disagreed with each other. In the context of the current discussion, Fu Bi's reaction to Ouyang's treatment of the Fan- Lü compromise was not surprising. To Fu Bi, whether Fan and Lü had actually reconciled might have been less important an issue than Ouyang publicly admitting that Fan willingly cooperated with Lü Yijian. Moreover, by accepting Ouyang's narrative, Fu Bi would have to acknowledge that he had left out that episode on purpose and that Ouyang's epitaph of Fan was thus more significant and of higher quality.

At least superficially, Ouyang accepted Fu Bi's explicit expressions of hatred for evil in the *muzhiming*. But his letter strongly suggests that Ouyang did consider his *shendaobei* to be superior in more than one way. First,

Ouyang implied that he was more ready to face the "uncomfortable" truth than Fu, and hence was more courageous. More importantly, by including the reconciliation between Fan and Lü that many, including Fu, avoided addressing, Ouyang actually established Fan as a generous and open-minded person. This was completely in line with Fan's aspirations, as articulated in the "Record of the Yueyang Pavilion," that a gentleman should not worry about his own gain or loss—in this case, Fan's exiles as a result of opposing Lü Yijian. His focus should instead be on the welfare of his sovereign and of the state. To Ouyang Xiu, Fan Zhongyan's collaboration with Lü was an indication that Fan was willing to go beyond a selfish concern for his own reputation in the interest of the empire. As for failing to present Fan's service record in chronological order, which Fu had identified as a problem, Ouyang replied that he had already included an explanation in the *shendaobei* so that later generations would not rely on his work in this respect.

Ouyang's emotional defense of his *shendaobei* in his letter to Xu Wudang suggests that he was offended by Fu Bi's implied criticisms. Ouyang was especially unhappy with the fact that Fu Bi had positioned himself to be the authoritative figure in the portrayal of Fan Zhongyan's legacy. He did not even try to spare Fu's feelings when he said that he was not willing to modify the completed *shendaobei*. If Fu Bi wanted anything changed, he would have to find another writer.

Fu Bi was not the only one who challenged Ouyang's writing. The inclusion of the Fan-Lü compromise also upset Fan Zhongyan's sons, who did not believe that their father had reconciled with Lü Yijian. By contrast, no contemporary source implies that Fan's sons had reservations about Fu Bi's *muzhiming*. For one thing, Fan Chunren might have blamed Ouyang for showing too much respect for Lü Yijian by addressing him as Mr. Lü, which Fu Bi did not. Most likely, what led to the confrontation between Ouyang and Fan Chunren was the way Ouyang characterized the outcome of the 1036 incident: even though Fan and Lü later reconciled, "allegations of factionalism had begun and could not be stopped." [48] As much as Ouyang was a strong supporter of Fan Zhongyan and the author of the most famous essay on factions, his writing nevertheless acknowledged that Fan was the original factionalist. Fan Chunren was unlikely to have welcomed this claim, to say nothing of its permanent and public circulation through the medium of an epitaph. [49]

Fan Chunren's denial of the Fan-Lü cooperation might also have had much to do with his own personal experience. Wang Ruilai has recently argued that since Fan Zhongyan's family went to Raozhou with him in 1036 and suffered greatly on the road, it would have been particularly difficult for Fan Chunren to accept the possibility of his father later reconciling with Lü. Even if Chunren knew that Ouyang had told the truth, he might not want the episode to be included in his father's epitaph. After all, there were plenty of other aspects of Fan Zhongyan's accomplishments that Ouyang could have highlighted. Even Ouyang himself admitted that he had only been able to include one to two percent of Fan's worthy deeds in the *shendaobei*.

The disagreements between Ouyang and Fan's sons are not preserved in any direct correspondence. There might not have been any in the first place, given the way important messages were relayed by such middlemen as Du Yan, Fu Bi, and Xu Wudang, as discussed earlier. But multiple Song *biji* (miscellaneous writings) recorded the drama, and all sided with Ouyang. Sima Guang (1019–1086) even went so far as to identify Lü Yijian as the one who proposed Fan Zhongyan's recall and promotion. In a conversation between the two, Fan Zhongyan was said to have expressed his gratefulness to Lü by saying, "Previously, I offended you due to our differences on governmental affairs. I did not expect that you would reward me by giving me a promotion." To this Lü replied, "How dare I still think about what happened in the past?" indicating a full reconciliation between Fan and Lü.[50] Sima did not provide a source for this episode, but Su Che (1039–1112) did. In his *Longchuan biezhi*, Su testified that he initially doubted that Fan Zhongyan had actually reconciled with Lü Yijian. But after consulting Zhang Fangping (1007–1091), who was of the same age as Ouyang Xiu and a witness to court politics of the time, Su concluded that "the younger generations [Fan Zhongyan's sons] did not know the truth. All instead blamed Ouyang."[51]

Anecdotes contained in other *biji* confirm that the clash between Ouyang and Fan's sons was rather intense. According to Ye Mengde (1077–1148), the author of *Bishu luhua*, Fan Zhongyan's sons not only denied the trustworthiness of Ouyang's writing but also asked Ouyang to make changes. Ouyang, however, stood by his work, insisting to Fan Chunren that "I personally witnessed it [the reconciliation]. You were still young at the time [Chunren was fourteen in 1040]. How could you have possibly known [that your father and Lü did settle their differences]?" But Chunren and his brothers remained adamant about their request and deleted the reference to the reconciliation when having the *shendaobei* inscribed in stone. The Fans' audacity offended Ouyang so much that, when they had a rubbing of the inscription delivered to Ouyang, Ouyang replied, "This is not my writing," and specifically instructed that later generations should instead refer to the *shendaobei* in his collected work.[52]

In the midst of the factional struggles of the second half of the Northern Song and during the Southern Song, the Qingli reforms and reformers came to be seen in an increasingly positive light. As a result, stories about Ouyang's *shendaobei* for Fan were further used to highlight Ouyang's as well as Fan's outstanding virtues. In *Mozhuang manlu*, Zhang Bangji (active in the twelfth century) celebrated Ouyang's courage in restoring the historical truth. Zhang recorded that when Fan Zhongyan's sons insisted that "Our father did not forget his enemies until his death," Ouyang tried to reason with them. Ouyang's logic was that since he himself had suffered from the factional struggles, he would have had no reason to defend Lü. Yet, Ouyang insisted that "One must be impartial when it comes to leaving trustworthy records to posterity." In other words, as much as Ouyang disliked Lü Yijian and endured exile for opposing him, he still considered it his responsibility as a biographer and a historian to be honest about the relationship between Lü and Fan.

From Ouyang's perspective, the fact that Fan was willing to work with Lü in the face of national crisis demonstrated Fan's generous and upright nature. The selfish and narrow-minded refusal of Fan's sons to believe that their father could forgive Lü for obstructing his career caused Ouyang to ask, "How could the nature of father and son be so far apart?"[53] Equally important, by refusing to believe Ouyang's narrative, not only did the sons mistake Fan's strength and high-mindedness for a weakness, but they also failed to appreciate the trouble Ouyang had gone to in promoting Fan's legacy.[54] As far as we can tell, Ouyang never came to terms with the way he was treated by Fan Zhongyan's sons. Years after their encounters he was still emotional about the incident. In a letter dated 1057, after bringing up Fan Chunren's deletion of part of the *shendaobei*, Ouyang Xiu commented, "From this incident, it can be seen that friends, disciples, and former colleagues and filial sons often have different intentions [when it comes to commemorating the deceased]. How could I ever turn my back on such an intimate friend [as Fan Zhongyan]!"[55]

It is important to note that, in addition to the two epitaphs and the extant material contained in Song *biji*, two more biographies of Fan, one by Zhang Tangying (1026–1068), very likely written for the long-lost *State History of the Renzong Reign*, and the other by the compilers of the Song dynastic history, completed in the fourteenth century, also differed from one another in their portrayal of Fan's 1036 exile and 1040 reinstatement.[56] Zhang's biography for Fan is the shortest of the four and recorded the confrontations between Fan and Lü without singling out either Lü Yijian or factionalism. Instead, it simply states, "Because Fan repeatedly accused officials of not

following the law, the court remonstrators thought that he was sowing dis-
cord between the emperor and his officials. Fan consequently was demoted
to Raozhou." And in the midst of the Song-Tangut war, "Fan was recalled
because the emperor knew he was equally talented in civil and military
affairs."[57] Fan Zhongyan's official biography in *Song shi* is the longest of all
four biographies. Its depiction of the 1036 event included specific reference
to Lü's favoritism in official evaluations and promotions, the opposition of
Fan and his supporters to Lü's policies, and the accusation by Lü's supporters
that Fan was guilty of faction formation. What especially distinguishes this
biography from the other three is its reference to Renzong's fixation about
the spread of factionalism and its consequences. For this reason, Fan was
"not pardoned [by the emperor] and was demoted." The narrative of this
incident was immediately followed by Fan's recall in 1040 and his willingness
to cooperate with Lü Yijian. "The emperor asked Zhongyan to forget previous feelings of animosity. Zhongyan prostrated to thank the emperor and
said: 'The previous disagreements I had with Yijian concerned state affairs. It
had nothing to do with Yijian personally.'"[58] These two biographies are not
the main focus of this study. Suffice it to say that, in addition to portraying
Emperor Renzong as a more tangible presence in the Fan-Lü antagonism,
the authors of Fan Zhongyan's *Song shi* biography found a middle ground
between Fu Bi's and Ouyang Xiu's representation of Fan's achievements and
the evolution of factionalism in the pre-Qingli era.

CONCLUSION

This discussion of the drama surrounding the writing of Fan Zhongyan's
epitaphs has first and foremost revealed the central place court politics
occupied in the lives of Song literati. Fan Zhongyan's life and legacy were
largely defined and complicated by his official career, especially his role
in the emergence of factionalism in the 1030s and in the Qingli reforms.
And the controversy over his *shendaobei* centered on these same issues.
This is hardly surprising. As Paul Smith's essay in this volume argues,
intense competition for the limited positions in the civil service, "the only
employment opportunity that social esteem deemed worthwhile," meant
that "proposals to address problems anywhere in the social and political
order were typically inaugurated with calls to reform the training, selection,
and promotion of the civil servants themselves."[59] Indeed, the showdown
between Fan Zhongyan and Lü Yijian took the form of Fan's criticism of
Lü's mismanagement of personnel policies. And recruiting "the right kind

of men" for service remained a central goal of the Qingli and later the New Policies (1068–1085) reformers. In this sense, factionalism was an inevitable outcome of literati politics.

Not only did factionalism have long-term institutional and ideological implications, it also had a large impact on the cultural life of the literati. Compared to power struggles in the earlier periods, writing played an especially prominent role in the partisan politics of the Northern Song. This was especially evidenced by the development of "Discourses on Factions" into a literary subgenre in its own right.[60] On a broader level, political struggles not only affected what got written but also how certain records were received and interpreted. Charles Hartman's essay in this volume, for example, has demonstrated how the changing political and intellectual atmosphere in the late Northern and early Southern Song shaped the transmission and reframing of the meaning of the legend about Taizu's oath. Epitaph writing, or biographical writing in general, also became more intricately connected with contemporary politics. Granted, funerary inscriptions continued to be a literature of commemoration. And Fu Bi and Ouyang Xiu, as friends and fellow-reformers of Fan Zhongyan, surely intended for their work to perpetuate Fan's name and legacy. But the two authors were also motivated by political considerations. In other words, while putting Fan Zhongyan to rest necessitated preparing his epitaphs, the consensus among Fan's family and friends was that Fan's *muzhiming* and *shendaobei* should make a political point. What is striking in this case is that the point the two authors strived to make differed. Fu Bi's epitaph for Fan can be best characterized as a tool of political contestation, aiming to continue the political battle of the previous decades. Ouyang's biography was less partisan, representing a more matter-of-fact portrayal of the antagonism between the reform and the antireform camps and its consequences. His writing, while less emotionally charged in tone, was nonetheless political in nature. Seen from another perspective, despite Ouyang's confessed concern for potential attack from Fan Zhongyan's opponents, it was possible that what had really worried him was hostile reactions from Fan's family and friends, who were as large stakeholders as Lü's followers in Fan's epitaphs.

Whichever case it might have been, Fan Zhongyan's epitaphs marked the beginning of the politicization of commemoration and epitaph writing in the Northern Song. The escalation of court politics in the second half of the Northern Song would further strengthen this trend. With the old and new parties making increasingly "polemical and contending claims to political authority, positing rigid ethical distinctions between themselves and their adversaries," both the epitaph author and the deceased's family exercised more caution in working with each other.[61] Out of concern for the political ramifications of epitaph writing, some elite families chose to put off a burial or to go without an epitaph for the deceased. Epitaph writers from the late Northern Song avoided writing for controversial figures for fear of political consequences. When they did write, their work was often rampant with factional language.[62] In retrospect, the compromise between Fan and Lü, whether it had actually happened or not, and the extended exchanges between Fan's family and supporters concerning Fan's involvement in factionalism would have been politically and ideologically inconceivable in the New Policies period and its aftermath.

This utilization of epitaph writing for political purposes occurred at a time when epitaph writing itself was undergoing major changes from the second half of the Tang (617–907) to the Northern Song. Although it continued to be an integral component of the burial ritual, Northern Song epitaphs became increasingly lengthy and more biographical in focus.[63] In addition to such staple components as the deceased's family background and his outstanding deeds, an elite man's epitaph typically concentrated on his examination experience, official service record, and political and social associations. All suggested a close relationship between the literati and the state. Especially relevant to the current study is the growing visibility of the epitaph author in his work. In addition to being compensated for his time and to fulfilling his obligation as a friend, disciple, or acquaintance, the epitaph writer increasingly identified himself with his work and with the social and political affiliation of the deceased. The controversy over Fan Zhongyan's epitaphs certainly had much to do with Fan's politically-charged career. Equally important was the fact that both Fu Bi and Ouyang were eager to establish their relationship with Fan and make themselves a presence in his biography. In the end, Fu demonstrated his loyalty to and admiration for Fan by using highly militant rhetoric, while Ouyang elevated Fan's image through his honest testimony of the Fan-Lü reconciliation.

The case of Fan Zhongyan's epitaphs also confirms that, despite the fact that both the funerary biographer and the deceased's family aimed to celebrate Fan's life, their interests differed greatly. The most important concern of the filial child and his family was to glorify their ancestors. This meant they would be more than willing to neglect what they considered to be unworthy deeds or uncomfortable truths, a trend that caught the attention of many contemporary epitaph writers.[64] The biographer's position differed significantly. On the one hand, he was obligated to promote the words and deeds of the deceased as well as the filial devotion of the deceased's sons and grandsons. After all, this was the task he was commissioned to do. On the other hand, Northern Song epitaph writers agreed that they were also responsible to write truthfully, as historians did, a topic about which Ouyang himself felt strongly. This means that just as historians would have to sort out a vast amount of sources in their construction of a reliable historical narrative, epitaph writers were in the position to choose, as Ouyang called it, "the one to two percent" of a person's character and accomplishments in their representation of the deceased. The epitaphs for politically prominent people would have involved the collaboration of other nonfamily members. In the case of Fan's epitaphs, in addition to the *xingzhuang* by Sun Mian, the *muzhiming* by Fu Bi, and the *shendaobei* by Ouyang Xiu, many others, such as Han Qi, Du Yan, and Xu Wudang, were active participants and contributors.

In the end, Fan Chunren and his brothers did not seem to have been in a position to determine the content of the epitaphs in any meaningful way. This tension between the writer and his collaborators on the one hand, and the deceased's family on the other, was certainly not limited to the writing of Fan Zhongyan's epitaph or that of the biographies of politically or literally prominent figures. More than anything, that tension was a manifestation of the inherent conflict between the epitaph author's interest in controlling his work and the deceased family's commitment to shaping their ancestor's image.

NOTES

1   Fan Zhongyan has been the subject of many scholarly works. The Qingli reforms were a series of political, social, and economic programs initiated by Fan and his supporters during Emperor Renzong's Qingli reign. For more information about Fan's life and career, especially his reform programs in the 1040s, see James Liu, "An Early Song Reformer"; Peter Bol, *"This Culture of Ours,"* 166–75; Chen Rongzhao, *Fan Zhongyan yanjiu*; Fang Jian, *Fan Zhongyan pingzhuan*; and Paul Jakov Smith, "Anatomies of Reform," in this volume.

2   Fan Zhongyan, *QSW* 18:420–21. The first half of the translation is by Richard Strassberg and the second by William Theodore de Bary. See Strassberg, *Inscribed Landscapes*, 159; de Bary, *Sources of Chinese Tradition*, 596.

3   For a list of these initiatives, see table 4.1 in Smith's chapter in this volume.

4   Fan was demoted to Hezhongfu (Yongji, Shanxi) in 1029 for his opposition to Empress Dowager Liu's regency; to Muzhou (Jiande, Zhejiang) in 1033 for his opposition to the dismissal of Empress Guo; to Raozhou (in Jiangxi) in 1036 for his opposition to Grand Councilor Lü Yijian; and to Binzhou (in Shaanxi) in 1045 at the end of the Qingli reforms.

5   For a general discussion of Emperor Renzong's reign, during which Fan Zhongyan served, see Michael McGrath, "The Reigns of Jen-tsung and Ying-tsung," 279–334.

6   The largest difference between *muzhiming* and *shendaobei* is that *muzhiming* were interred with the dead and *shendaobei* were erected next to the deceased's tomb. In the Song, *muzhiming* and *shendaobei* were often composed based on factual information provided in the deceased's *xingzhuang* (record of conduct), which was required of all ranking officials after death. For two excellent discussions of *muzhiming* writing in the Tang and Song periods, see the introductions to Beverly Bossler's *Powerful Relations* and Nicolas Tackett's *The Destruction of the Medieval Chinese Aristocracy.*

7   For a study of Ouyang Xiu's epitaph writing in English, see Ronald Egan, *The Literary Works of Ou-yang Hsiu*, 49–63. Ouyang Xiu's epitaph writing has been the subject of many studies in Chinese, all focusing on his insistence that epitaphs include only factual, reliable information. See Li Guiyin, "Lun Ouyang Xiu yi shibi wei beizhi de chengjiu," 199–201; Wang Shuizhao, "Ouyang Xiu suozuo *Fanbei Yinzhi* beiju zhi yin fafu," 176–83; Xu Hairong, "Ouyang Xiu beizhi zuopin de shizhuan tedian," 66–69; Zhu Shangshu, "Chuan Shiqian zhi fengshen," 79–94.

8   Fu Bi, *QSW* 29:66–68; Fan Chunren, *QSW* 71:311–26. For a close examination of the relationship between Fan Zhongyan and Fu Bi, see Zhang Xiqing, "Fan Zhongyan yu Fu Bi guanxi kao," 197–203. Fu Bi's official biography can be found in *SS* 313.10249–56. His *muzhiming* and *shendaobei* were authored by Han Wei (1017–1098) and Su Shi (1037–1101), respectively. Han, *QSW* 49:227–42, Su, *QSW* 92:27–40.

9   Han Qi's official biography can be found in *SS* 312.10221–30. His *xingzhuang* was composed by Li Qingchen (1032–1102) and can be found in *QSW* 79:38–53, his *muzhiming* by Chen Jian (1016–1084) in *QSW* 48:334–44, and his *shendaobei* by Fu Bi in *QSW* 29:47–51.

10 Han Qi, *QSW* 40:20–21. The collection, according to Han Qi, had nineteen chapters. Han's preface is about 400 characters long.

11 Ouyang Xiu's *muzhiming* by Han Qi can be found in *QSW* 40:115–20. His official biography can be found in *SS* 319.10375–82. For Ouyang Xiu's role in the Qingli reforms, see James Liu, *Ou-yang Hsiu.*

12 Ari Levine, *Divided by a Common Language*, 43. Levine provides a much more detailed discussion of Fan and Ouyang's faction theory in "Faction Theory," 172–83. For some comprehensive studies of factions and faction theory in the Northern Song, see also Luo Jiaxiang, *Beisong dangzheng yanjiu*, and Douglas Skonicki, "Employing the Right Kind of Men," 39–98.

13 Lü's official biography can be found in *SS* 311.10206–10.

14 Yao Hong's recent study has shown Lü as an accomplished grand councilor and documented a more positive evaluation of Lü by the Southern Song historian Li Tao (1115–1184). Yao is among several modern scholars who argue that Lü and Fan reconciled. Yao Hong, "Bei Song zaixiang Lü Yijian jianchen xianyi," 188–92.

15 Wang Deyi, "Lü Yijian yu Fan Zhongyan," 85–119.

16 Du Yan, *QSW* 15:371.

17 Ouyang Xiu, *QSW* 33:191; Ouyang Xiu, *QSW* 33:219.

18 Ouyang Xiu, *QSW* 33:191.

19 Ouyang Xiu, *QSW* 33:219.

20 Fu Bi, *QSW* 29:58; Ouyang Xiu, *QSW* 35:223–24.

21 Ouyang Xiu, *QSW* 33:219.

22 Ouyang Xiu, *QSW* 33:219. Sun's *xingzhuang* for Fan Zhongyan did not survive.

23 Fu Bi, *QSW* 29:56–62.

24 Fu Bi, *QSW* 29:56; Ouyang Xiu, *QSW* 35:222.

25 Ouyang Xiu, *QSW* 33:357.

26 Ouyang Xiu, *QSW* 33:354.

27 Ouyang Xiu, *QSW* 33:270.

28 Fu Bi, *QSW* 29:20–21.

29 Ouyang Xiu, *QSW* 33:357.

30 Ye Mengde, *Bishu luhua*, shang.51a–b.

31 Ouyang Xiu, *QSW* 33:354.

32 Yan Jie, *Ouyang Xiu nianpu*, 177–78.

33 Ouyang Xiu, *QSW* 35:222–26. During this time, Ouyang authored funerary biographies for his parents, two wives, and two other people. Yan Jie, *Ouyang Xiu nianpu*, 177–78.

34 Han Qi, *QSW* 40:20–21.

35 Ouyang Xiu, *QSW* 33:191.

36 Ouyang Xiu, *QSW* 33:191.

37 Ouyang Xiu, *QSW* 33:192.

38 Michael McGrath, "The Reigns of Jen-tsung and Ying-tsung," 323–24.

39 Xia Hanning, "Zhu Xi, Zhou Bida guanyu Ouyang Xiu *Fangong shendabei* de zhenglun," 228.

40 Ouyang's *shendaobei* for Fan Zhongyan was among the longest funerary biographies he authored. Ouyang insisted, on several occasions, that this type of text should be concise and only include the most important information. When discussing Du Yan's *muzhiming* with Du's son, Ouyang wrote that his writing "is brief and only records the important affairs in a person's life." In the same letter, Ouyang also mentioned that, because his *muzhiming* for Yin Zhu was too brief, Yin's sons eventually asked Han Qi to write a *mubiao*, an above-ground stele inscription. Ouyang Xiu, *QSW* 33:108.

41 Fu Bi, *QSW* 29:58.

42 Ouyang Xiu, *QSW* 35:224.

43 Ouyang Xiu, *QSW* 35:225.

44 Fu Bi, *QSW* 29:58.

45 Ouyang Xiu, *QSW* 35:225.

46 The general consensus has been that Fan and Lü did reconcile. Wang Ruilai's recent study has meticulously documented the entire process. A major exception was Zhou Bida (1126–1204), the compiler of Ouyang Xiu's collected works, who insisted that the 1040 compromise did not happen. For this reason, Zhou and Zhu Xi (1130–1200) had a debate through correspondence. Wang, "Fan Lü jiechou gong'an zai tantao," 54–67; Xia Hanning, "Zhu Xi, Zhou Bida," 222–29.

47 Ouyang Xiu, *QSW* 33:344.

48 Ouyang Xiu, *QSW* 35:225.

49 As far as we know, copies of many Northern Song epitaphs, especially those by established political and scholarly figures for their peers, enjoyed wide circulation among the educated elite as models of literary and artistic composition. Fan Zhongyan, for example, once wrote to a Tian, thanking him for sending Fan copies of three epitaphs. So

did Ouyang Xiu. Fan Zhongyan, *QSW* 18:382; Ouyang Xiu, *QSW* 33:109, 33:331. Huang Tingjian mentioned that copies of Sima Guang's *xingzhuang* could be purchased for dozens of cash. Huang Tingjian, *QSW* 105:124–25.

50 Sima Guang, *Sushui jiwen* 8.162.

51 Su Che, *Longchuan biezhi* shang.83.

52 Ye Mengde, *Bishu luhua* shang.51a–b.

53 Zhang Bangji, *Mozhuang manlu* 8.236–37.

54 Some modern scholars hold the same view, seeing Fan's reconciliation with Lü Yijian as an indication of Fan's lofty virtue. Fang Jian, "Cong Fan Zhongyan de jiaoyou kan pengdang zhizheng," 90–95.

55 Ouyang Xiu, *QSW* 33:108.

56 For emperor Renzong's reign, the compilation project began in 1063 and was completed in 1069. Cai Chongbang, *Songdai xiushi zhidu yanjiu*, 79.

57 Zhang Tangying, *QSW* 70:286.

58 *SS* 314.10269–70.

59 Smith, "Anatomies of Reform," chap. 4, this volume.

60 Levine, "Faction Theory," 169. See also Shen Songqin, *Beisong wenren yu dangzheng*.

61 Levine, "Faction Theory," 155.

62 For this reason, Liu Chengguo cautions that modern scholars be very careful in using epitaphs as historical sources. Liu, "Bei Song dangzheng yu beizhi xiezuo," 35–42.

63 Fu Bi's *muzhiming*, for example, is over 7,000 words. Han Wei, *QSW* 49:227–42.

64 Zeng Gong, for example, wrote extensively on this topic in a letter to Ouyang Xiu, dated in the mid-1040s. Zeng, *QSW* 57:246–47.

REFERENCES

PRIMARY SOURCES

Bishu luhua 避暑錄話, by Ye Mengde 葉夢得 (1077–1148). Siku quanshu edition.

Longchuan biezhi 龍川別志, by Su Che 蘇轍 (1039–1112). Beijing: Zhonghua shuju, 1982.

Mozhuang manlu 墨莊漫錄, by Zhang Bangji 張邦基 (12th century). Zhonghua shuju, 2002.

Quan Song wen 全宋文, edited by Zeng Zaozhuang 曾棗莊 et al. Shanghai: Shanghai cishu chubanshe, 2006.

Song shi 宋史, edited by Tuo Tuo 脫脫 (1313–1355) et al. Beijing: Zhonghua shuju, 1977.

Sushui jiwen 涑水紀聞, by Sima Guang 司馬光 (1019–1086). Beijing: Zhonghua shuju, 1989.

SECONDARY SOURCES

Bol, Peter K. *"This Culture of Ours": Intellectual Transitions in T'ang and Sung China*. Stanford: Stanford University Press, 1992.

Bossler, Beverly. *Powerful Relations: Kinship, Status, & the State in Sung China (960–1279)*. Cambridge, Mass.: Harvard University Council on East Asian Studies, 1998.

Cai Chongbang 蔡崇榜. *Songdai xiushi zhidu yanjiu* 宋代修史制度研究. Taibei: Wenjin chubanshe, 1993.

Chen Rongzhao 陳榮照. *Fan Zhongyan yanjiu* 范仲淹研究. Hong Kong: Sanlian shuju Xianggang fenshe, 1987.

de Bary, William Theodore. *Sources of Chinese Tradition*, vol. 1. New York: Columbia University Press, 1999.

Egan, Ronald. *The Literary Works of Ou-yang Hsiu (1007–1072)*. Cambridge, UK: Cambridge University Press, 1984.

Fang Jian 方健. *Fan Zhongyan pingzhuan* 范仲淹評傳. Nanjing: Nanjing daxue chubanshe, 2001.

———. "Cong Fan Zhongyan de jiaoyou kan pengdang zhizheng" 從范仲淹的交遊看朋黨之爭. *Suzhou daxue xuebao* 4 (1998): 90–95.

Levine, Ari Daniel. *Divided by a Common Language: Factional Conflict in Late Northern Song China*. Honolulu: University of Hawai'i Press, 2008.

———. "Faction Theory and the Political Imagination of the Northern Song." *Asia Major*, Third Series, 18, no. 2 (2005): 155–200.

Li Guiyin 李貴銀. "Lun Ouyang Xiu yi shibi wei beizhi de chengjiu" 論歐陽修以史筆為碑志的成就. *Shehui kexue jikan* 4 (2011): 199–201.

Liu Chengguo 劉成國. "Bei Song dangzheng yu beizhi xiezuo" 北宋黨爭與碑志寫作. *Wenxue pinglun* 3 (2008): 35–42.

Liu, James T. C. *Ou-yang Hsiu: An Eleventh Century Neo-Confucianist*. Stanford: Stanford University Press, 1967.

———. "An Early Song Reformer: Fan Chung-yen." In *Chinese Thought and Institutions*, edited by John K. Fairbank, 105–31. Chicago: University of Chicago Press, 1957.

Luo Jiaxiang 羅家祥. *Beisong dangzheng yanjiu* 北宋黨爭研究. Taibei: Wenjin chubanshe, 1993.

McGrath, Michael. "The Reigns of Jen-tsung (1022–1063) and Ying-tsung (1063–1067)." In *The Cambridge History of China*. Vol. 5, Part 1: *The Sung Dynasty and Its Precursors, 907–1279*, edited by Denis Twitchett and Paul Jakov Smith, 279–346. Cambridge, UK: Cambridge University Press, 2009.

Shen Songqin 沈松勤. *Bei Song wenren yu dangzheng* 北宋文人與黨爭. Beijing: Renmin chubanshe, 1998.

Skonicki, Douglas. "Employing the Right Kind of Men: The Role of Cosmological Argumentation in the Qingli Reforms." *Journal of Song-Yuan Studies* 38 (2008): 39–98.

Strassberg, Richard, trans. *Inscribed Landscapes: Travel Writing from Imperial China*. Berkeley: University of California Press, 1994.

Tackett, Nicolas. *The Destruction of the Medieval Chinese Aristocracy*. Cambridge, Mass.: Harvard University Asia Center, 2014.

Wang Deyi 王德毅. "Lü Yijian yu Fan Zhongyan" 呂夷簡與范仲淹. *Shixue huikan* 4 (1971): 85–119.

Wang Ruilai 王瑞來. "Fan Lü jiechou gong'an zai tantao" 范呂解仇公案再探討. *Lishi yanjiu* 1 (2013): 54–67.

Wang Shuizhao 王水照. "Ouyang Xiu suozuo *Fanbei Yinzhi* beiju zhi yin fafu" 歐陽修所作《范碑》《尹志》被拒之因發覆. *Jiangxi shehui kexue* 9 (2007): 176–83.

Xia Hanning 夏漢寧. "Zhu Xi, Zhou Bida guanyu Ouyang Xiu *Fangong shendaobei* de zhenglun" 朱熹周必大關於歐陽修《范公神道碑》的爭論. *Jiangxi shehui kexue* 3 (2004): 222–29.

Xu Hairong 徐海容. "Ouyang Xiu beizhi zuopin de shizhuan tedian" 歐陽修碑志作品的史傳特點. *Dongguan ligong xueyuan xuebao* 13, no. 2 (2006): 66–69.

Yan Jie 嚴傑. *Ouyang Xiu nianpu* 歐陽修年譜. Nanjing: Nanjing chubanshe, 1993.

Yao Hong 姚紅. "Bei Song zaixiang Lü Yijian jianchen xianyi" 北宋宰相呂夷簡奸臣獻疑. *Renwen zazhi* 3 (2008): 188–92.

Zhang Xiqing 張希清. "Fan Zhongyan yu Fu Bi guanxi kao" 范仲淹與富弼關係考. *Zhongzhou xuekan* 3 (May, 2010): 197–203.

Zhu Shangshu 祝尚書. "Chuan Shiqian zhi fengshen, neng chushen er ruhua: Lun Ouyang Xiu beizhiwen de wenxue chengjiu" 傳史遷之風神, 能出神而入化: 論歐陽修碑誌文的文學成就. In *Songdai wenhua yanjiu* 宋代文化研究, vol. 8:79–94. Chengdu: Bashu shushe, 1999.

PART 3

Statecraft Theory

6   Northern Song Reformist Thought and Its Sources

Wang Anshi and Mencius

LI HUARUI

FROM THE ZHOU AND QIN PERIODS ON, THE RULING CLASS HAS taken Confucian principles of governing seriously, a phenomenon that should be considered in historical context. While he was alive, Confucius proposed only vague ideas regarding how to administer the country. After he died, his school of thought soon split apart. In the ideas of Mencius and Xunzi, we can see the sharp divergences that appeared within the over-arching philosophy of Confucianism. From then on, a distinctive feature of Confucian political thought has been the diversity of ways that have been proposed to implement and interpret Mencius's and Xunzi's political positions and programs, all claiming the mantle of Confucius. Although thinkers and political figures alike claimed to be followers of Confucius, some paired him with the Duke of Zhou, others with Mencius or Yan Hui.[1] With the turn from the Han-Tang reverence for the Five Classics to the Song reverence for the Four Books, Confucian governance entered the stage of "the Way of Confucius and Mencius."

It is true that contemporary scholars have extensively studied the Tang-Song "movement to promote Mencius," the creation of the Four Books, and the development of Mencian thought in the Song. In all these areas, scholars have reached some basic shared understandings.[2] However, as these com-mon understandings are mostly limited to intellectual history and political culture, other questions remain. What were the similarities and differences between Han and Tang scholar-officials' approaches to political theory and those of Song scholar-officials? What kind of relationship was there between Song scholars' esteem for Mencius and their ambitious plans to construct the social order? How were Mencius's political ideals put into practice by Song scholar-officials? On these issues, there is room for further investigation. Although both the political reformer Wang Anshi (1021–1086) and the philosopher Zhu Xi (1130–1200) played crucial roles in the Song promotion of Mencius as the "Second Sage," the focus of this chapter is on Wang Anshi.

WHY DID WANG ANSHI HOLD MENCIUS IN ESTEEM?

Why did Wang Anshi hold Mencius in esteem? Both Song and modern scholars have looked into this question. The evidence for Wang Anshi's esteem for Mencius is of two sorts. First, no one influenced Wang Anshi's words and deeds more than Mencius. Wang's biography in the *Veritable Records* states, "[Wang] Anshi early on had a great reputation, and in his studies he judged himself against the standard of Mencius. As for Xunzi and Han Yu (768–824), he did not speak of them."[3] Once, after Wang presented a memorial, Cai Bian (1058–1117) commented, "Generations will say his words rank with Mencius's."[4] His student Lu Dian (fl. eleventh century) wrote, "[Wang Anshi's] words are like those of the *Odes* and *Book of Documents*, his actions on par with Confucius or Mencius." Even Sima Guang (1019–1086), who strongly opposed Wang's reforms, wrote: "[Wang Anshi] has read everything, but he is especially fond of the writings of Mencius and Laozi."[5] In the Southern Song, Luo Congyan (1072–1135) wrote, "Wang Anshi's learning was brilliant and his deeds unsurpassed. [Since] there were no ancients in front of him [to emulate], he judged himself against Mencius. Viewing him as a man of his time, it can be said that he was a literatus of a brilliant age."[6] It is a fact that Wang Anshi had a less lofty opinion of Confucius, but this refers to Confucius as he was depicted by earlier classicists. He admired the Confucius described by Mencius as putting it all together.[7] Wang wrote that the real Confucius "exceeded even Yao and Shun in combining the ideas of earlier sages and planning how to have lasting achievements."[8] Wang even expressed his esteem for Mencius in his poems: "Confucius and Mencius are like the Sun and the Moon, turning in the blue sky."[9] In Wang Anshi's eyes, Mencius was the greatest sage after Confucius. "Sinking spirits and floating souls cannot be summoned, but once you read the words of Mencius, you will imagine the virtue and lifestyle of Mencius. What harm is there that the whole world dislikes my impractical views? I am comforted by this man of ancient times."[10] Here Wang looks on Mencius as his soulmate. He also said, "Although my wish to transmit the moral heart-and-mind remains strong, my studying and writing are in decline. If someday I am able to catch a glimmer of Mencius, for the rest of my life how dare I long for Mr. Han [Yu]?"[11] These examples express Wang Anshi's desire to follow Mencius with his whole heart and soul.

The second sort of evidence of Wang Anshi's esteem for Mencius is Wang's role in bringing the *Mencius* to prominence in government schools and getting the court to recognize the *Mencius* as a classic. Because Wang at that time held important positions at court and Emperor Shenzong had confidence in him, the movement to promote Mencius gained the court's vigorous support. Under Wang's guidance, scholars of the New Learning camp for the most part had a high regard for Mencius. Among them were some who wrote interpretations of the *Mencius*. For example, Wang Anshi composed the *Mengzi jie*, Wang Pang (1044–1076) the *Mengzi zhu*, Xu Yuncheng (fl. eleventh century) the *Mengzi xinyi*, Wang Ling (1032–1059) the *Mengzi jiangyi*, and Shen Gua (1029–1093) the *Mengzi jie*. The letters between Wang Anshi and Wang Ling often touch on Mencius. Additionally, Mencius received a title of nobility and his statue was placed in the Confucian Temple, paired with the statue of Confucius. At the same time, the *Mencius* was added to the classical canon and tested in the civil service examinations. As a recent scholar put it, "Wang Anshi is the official who most deserves credit in the 'movement to promote Mencius.'"[12] Whereas the court affirmed Yan Hui's position as Second Sage at the founding of the Song, under Shenzong in 1074, Wang Anshi told his friend and well-known classical scholar Chang Zhi (1019–1077), among others: "I request that images of Mencius and Yang Xiong (53 BCE–18 CE) be placed in the Confucian Temple and titles of nobility be bestowed on them. I also request that we use the term 'emperor' [*di*] as Confucius' posthumous title. Inform the ritual officials to deliberate and determine the right way to handle these matters."[13] The modern scholar Zhu Weizheng writes, "This is the first record of a medieval court's formal discussion of replacing Confucius and Yan Hui with Confucius and Mencius and regarding them as the two principle masters of the teaching that reaches Heaven. . . . Although at that time the advocates did not achieve their goal, after this eulogies for Confucius and Yan Hui gradually grow rarer in Song official documents."[14]

Why did Wang Anshi have so much respect for Mencius? Han Yu wrote, "Only after I began to read Mencius's work did I learn to treat the Way of Confucius with respect."[15] He added, "Those who seek to observe the Way of the Sages must start with Mencius."[16] These two sentences are also crucial for understanding Wang Anshi's esteem for Mencius. It is true that Wang sometimes wrote dismissively of Han Yu, saying, for instance, "How dare I long for Mr. Han for the rest of my life?" and "Mr. Han has already departed. How can I follow him?" However, Han Yu's quotations above clearly express the attitude of Wang Anshi, who wrote, "Mencius has returned and I did not resist."[17] Mencius borrowed the words of Confucius to express what he referred to as taking the government of the Former Kings as a model and implementing the Way of the Sages. In this way, Neo-Confucians of the mid-Northern Song like Wang Anshi advocated using what they called the "intentions" of the sages, both to refute the tradition of annotating the "words" of the sages and to demand changes to the existing social order.[18]

Wang Anshi, in venerating Mencius, wanted to measure himself against Mencius and to become the Mencius for the new age. In one of his earliest extant writings, Wang wrote:

> In the age of Yang [Zhu] and Mo [Di], Mencius was the only one who refuted them. In the age of Sakyamuni and Laozi, Han Yu was the only one who refuted them. It can be said that Mencius and Han Yu had established methods and fixed ambitions, and did not let the times overpower their Way. Because they unfortunately did not find a ruler through whom they could achieve their ambitions, the efficacy of true Confucianism was not demonstrated. . . . When I was posted to Yangzhou, I became friends with Sun Mou (1019–1084). He carries out the Way of antiquity, and he also is good at ancient style prose. I know that he is capable of taking the hearts of Mencius and Han Yu as his own.[19]

The key element here is taking the stance of not letting the times overcome the Way but rather firmly holding on to the Way and not letting oneself be buffeted by the waves. This spirit of taking on responsibility for the Way came from Mencius, who said: "When the Way exists in this world, the Way must follow one's person. When the Way does not exist in this world, one's person must follow the Way. I have never heard of the Way following other people" (*Mencius* 7A.42).[20]

In terms of personality, Wang Anshi was similar to Mencius. In the Xining period (1068–1077), Wang's opponents circulated a pithy critique of him, drawing attention to the three things he refrained from: he did not stand in awe of Heaven-sent calamities, he did not value following the ways of earlier Song emperors, and he did not fear gossip.[21] The modern historian Deng Guangming thinks that this saying conveys Wang Anshi's undaunted spirit.[22] His spirit was very similar to the heroic spirit Mencius displayed when he discussed problems of administering the state with his disciples, claiming, "If it [Heaven] wanted to bring peace to the world, who is there in the present age apart from me?" (*Mencius* 2B.13). In terms of "setting forth" and "carrying out," Wang was further imbued with Mencius's teachings.

Once he gained the emperor's trust and implemented his policies, he was unwavering. Therefore, he regarded Mencius's "talk of [accomplishing] great deeds" as the spiritual pillar of his reforms (*Mencius* 2B.2). We can see this in an anecdote involving the Southern Song official Ni Si (1147–1220). When someone asked Ni Si why Sima Guang had written a piece titled "Doubting Mencius," Ni replied that Wang Anshi's use of Mencius's talk of great deeds had created doubts in Sima Guang's mind.[23]

Mencius lived during the Warring States period, when the rulers of each state fought to expand their territory. As Mencius put it, "Wars that arise from territorial contests kill so many people that the fields are packed with corpses; wars that arise from contests over cities kill so many people that the cities are packed with corpses" (*Mencius* 4A.14). Internally, rulers taxed heavily and were oppressive. Mencius observed that while the palace is well-supplied with food, "the people have a hungry look and, out beyond, in the more wild regions, lie the bodies of those who have died of starvation" (*Mencius* 1A.4). Another way to put this is that the discrepancies between society and the ruling class were worsening. While the Warring States period was rife with hardships, it was also the age that gave birth to China's unification. Mencius advanced a theory of humane government, which involved the well-field system as a way to ensure the people's livelihoods as well as policies to lighten punishments, reduce taxes, and avoid making demands on farmers during their busy seasons. Although at that time his policy proposals were considered impractical and were not adopted, they can still be considered both a prescription for alleviating social problems and a vision for reform. In later generations, when social conflicts intensified, some reformers still found Mencius's approach quite attractive. For example, at times when land was being voraciously bought up by "engrossers" (*jianbing,* referring to landlords avidly expanding their holdings), people often longingly turned to the well-field system as a solution. In one poem Wang Anshi wrote, "So long unbearable, we wish to see the well-fields regulated," evidence that he thought highly of the well-field system. Another poem by Wang has the lines, "In the past when I lived in the countryside, I pitied the common people. If they cannot eat their fill in a bumper year, what will they have when floods and droughts strike?"[24] This resembles Mencius's description of the people's suffering in the Warring States period: "Even in years of prosperity their lives are bitter, while in years of dearth they are unable to escape starvation" (*Mencius* 1A.7). Thus, it is entirely possible that Mencius's political thought inspired Wang Anshi, and that he regarded Mencius's ideas as both the starting point and the theoretical basis from which to survey society and carry out reforms.[25] Mencius promoted taking the Way of the Former Kings as a model, and he regularly praised Yao and Shun. Wang likewise advised Shenzong to model himself on Yao and Shun and to consider the "government of the Former Kings" as a catchphrase and a model for reform. In his famous "Ten Thousand Word Memorial" (1058), Wang cited *Mencius* 4A.1 on the king's needing to pattern himself on the Way of the Former Kings in order for the common people to benefit. He then went on,

> The application of what Mencius said to our own failure in the present is obvious. Now our own age is far removed from that of the ancient kings, and the changes and circumstances with which we are confronted are not the same. Even the most ignorant can see that it would be difficult to put into practice every single item in the government of the ancient kings. But when your servant says that our present failures arise from the fact that we do not adopt the governmental system of the ancient kings, he is merely suggesting that we should follow their general intent. Now the Two Emperors were separated from the Three Kings by more than a thousand years. There were periods of order and disorder, and there were periods of prosperity and decay. Each of them likewise encountered different changes and faced different circumstances, and each differed also in the way he set up his government. Yet they never differed as to their underlying aims in the government of the empire, the state, and the family, nor in their sense of the relative importance and priority of things [as set forth in the *Great Learning*, chapter 1]. Therefore, you servant contends that we should follow only their general intent. If we follow their intent, then the changes and reforms introduced by us would not startle the ears and shock the eyes of the people, nor cause them to murmur. And yet our government would be in accord with that of the ancient kings.[26]

In this passage, taking the government of the Former Kings as a model means striving to carry out the political ideals of Mencius and thus govern effectively and rebuild society. After he came to power, many of the New Policies and administrative theories that Wang adopted were, at their core, Mencius's political ideals.

When discussing Wang Anshi and his reforms, we should consider the implementation of his policy measures not only during Shenzong's reign, but also during Zhezong's (r. 1085–1100) and Huizong's reigns (r. 1100–1125). In this way, we can get a complete picture of how Wang Anshi's school carried out Mencius's political ideals. Following the antireform regency of Empress

Dowager Gao (1032–1093), Zhezong came of age and ruled on his own. The reform faction returned to power, and the position of Wang Learning rose accordingly. During the Chongning period (1102–1106), Huizong energetically promoted Wang Learning. An edict issued during that period asserted:

> The methods of the Way were divided among the Hundred Schools, and crude scholars corrupted them for a thousand years. Literati, accustomed to [the pettiness of] commentary writing, let their intelligence become disordered. For a long time, they saw neither the entirety of Heaven and Earth nor the main principles of the ancients. Therefore, Wang Anshi, Duke of Jingguo, due to his perceptive wisdom, transmitted the Classics of the Sages, explained the subtleties of human nature, joined together the scattered remnants of the Way and its power, explained hidden meanings, opened the minds of scholars, and linked everything together through a single principle. . . . Like a sage on the inside and a king on the outside, he was fully prepared for everything. Heaven conferred on him this heavy responsibility so that he could make this culture of ours flourish. Since Mencius, he has had no equal.[27]

Such high praise reflects Wang Anshi's lifelong wish "to glimpse Mencius." For a time Wang was treated as a successor to Mencius, and later he was ranked as a great Confucian master who was paired with Confucius in the Confucian Temple.

MENCIUS'S IDEAS ON THE WELL-FIELD SYSTEM AND WANG ANSHI'S IDEAS ON "SUPPRESSING THE ENGROSSERS"

Humane government and the Kingly Way form the nucleus of Mencius's political theory. To him, the Way of the Former Kings lay in striving for the happiness and benefit of the people. This meant the state definitely had to be founded on a sound economic base. Because Chinese thinkers had always considered agriculture to be the primary economic base, land was a key issue. Therefore, it was natural for Mencius to assume that the economic base of the Kingly Way depended on the equitable distribution of land. His ideal land system is the famous well-field system.

To understand Mencius's intention in advocating the implementation of the well-field system, we need to understand his proposed "theory of the constant means of livelihood." Mencius said to King Xuan of Qi and Duke Wen of Teng:

It is only a gentleman who will be able to have a constant mind despite
being without a constant means of livelihood. The people, lacking a
constant means of livelihood, will lack constant minds, and when they lack
constant minds there is no dissoluteness, depravity, deviance, or excess
to which they will not succumb. If, once they have sunk into crime, one
responds by subjecting them to punishment—this is to entrap the people.
With a person of humanity in a position of authority, how could the
entrapment of the people be allowed to occur? Therefore, an enlightened
ruler will regulate the people's livelihood so as to ensure that, above, they
have enough to serve their parents and, below, they have enough to support
their wives and children. In years of prosperity they will always have
enough to eat; in years of dearth they are able to escape starvation. Only
then does he urge the people towards goodness; accordingly, they find it
easy to comply. At present, the regulation of the people's livelihood is such
that, above, they do not have enough to serve their parents and, below,
they do not have enough to support wives and children. Even in years of
prosperity their lives are bitter, while in years of dearth they are unable
to escape starvation. Under these circumstances they only try to save
themselves from death, fearful that they will not succeed. How could they
spare the time for the practice of rites and righteousness? (*Mencius* 1A.7)

In Mencius's opinion, guaranteeing the peasants' source of livelihood
was the way to resolve their land issues, and this was a key element for
safeguarding social stability. Without a constant means of livelihood, peasants had "no dissoluteness, depravity, deviance, or excess to which they will
not succumb," and many had "sunk into crime" (*Mencius* 1A.7). In order to
help the peasantry avoid such a fate, Mencius demanded that the rulers of
Qi, Liang, and other states "return to the root of the matter" (*Mencius* 1A.7)
and carry out humane government. Furthermore, he presented them with a
concrete proposal of how to stabilize the people's livelihoods: "Let mulberry
trees be planted around households of five *mu*, and people of fifty will be able
to be clothed in silk. In the raising of chickens, pigs, dogs, and swine, do not
neglect the appropriate breeding times, and people of seventy will be able to
eat meat. With fields of a hundred *mu*, do not interfere with the appropriate
seasons of cultivation, and families with several mouths to feed will be able
to avoid hunger" (*Mencius* 1A.3). These are the specific details of Mencius's
theory of the constant means of livelihood. When replying to King Hui of
Liang and King Yi of Qi regarding how to manage government affairs, he
consistently expounded upon this idea. Mencius several times emphasized

this position using the story of King Wen "who was good at caring for the old, [and thus] humane persons would all turn to him" (*Mencius* 7A.2).

In order to implement his proposal to stabilize the people's livelihoods, Mencius suggested using the Western Zhou's well-field system and refining it to fit the circumstances of the Warring States period. This was called "correcting the boundaries and equalizing the well-fields." He added: "Now, humane government must begin with the setting of boundaries. If the boundaries are not set correctly, the division of the land into well-fields will not be equal, and the grain allowances for official emoluments will not be equitable. This is why harsh rulers and corrupt officials are prone to neglect the setting of boundaries. Once the boundaries have been set correctly, the division of the fields and the determination of emoluments can be settled without difficulty" (*Mencius* 3A.3). As for what Mencius referred to as "correcting the boundaries" and "the division of fields and the determination of emoluments," Zhu Xi explains in his commentary: "*Jing jie* [or "setting the boundaries"] refers to ordering the land and dividing the fields, and *jing* is drawing the borders of channels and roads to set and confer [the fields]." Zhu added that if the model is not corrected, the fields would not be clearly divided and thus taxation and official grain emoluments would be inequitable, all of which would be to the advantage of engrossers.[28] Zhu Xi's explanation is right. When Mencius put forward concrete measures to correct the setting of boundaries, equalize the well-fields, and make the grain emoluments equitable, his goal was to guard against overbearing engrossers and protect the peasants' "fields of one-hundred *mu*" against encroachment.[29]

In the Qin and Han there was the military merit field system, during the Western Jin there was the occupy-and-tax field system, and from the Northern Wei through the Tang there was the equal-field system. In each system, the state conferred fields on the common people, an idea inherited from Mencius's promotion of the well-field system. As Ye Shi (1150–1223) wrote, "From the Han to the Tang, when land conferral systems were in place, rulers had ways to forge relationships with their subjects; when there were policies of assigning corvée, then the people had a way to serve their rulers." From the middle of the Tang until the Song, Ye noted, "The system of conferring fields came to an end. From then on the people bought and sold on their own privately."[30] Because of the division of rich and poor exacerbated by the engrossers, social contradictions grew progressively worse. Su Xun (1009–1066) wrote, "After the well-field system was abolished, those who tilled did not own fields, while those who owned fields did not till." The rich, getting richer, got the landless to till for them and treated them like slaves.

At harvest time, Su noted, the landowners got half the crop, the tillers the other half. This was bad enough, but in addition the wealthy continually complained about having to pay taxes. The only solution, in Su's view, was to reestablish the well-field system.[31]

Like Li Gou (1009–1059), Zhang Zai (1020–1077), and the Cheng brothers Hao (1032–1085) and Yi (1033–1107), Wang Anshi in his early years yearned for the ancient well-field system. Before coming to power, Wang indeed regarded the restoration of the well-field system as the fundamental solution to land inequality problems. However, after assuming power, Wang's view of the system diverged sharply from that of Zhang and the Chengs. Wang not only abandoned the idea of equalized well-fields but also considered the well-fields that Zhang Zai and others advocated to be "the Way to disorder." Two dialogues between Wang and Emperor Shenzong in 1070 and 1071 reveal their attitudes regarding the well-field system.

In the first exchange, Shenzong asked Wang Anshi about Zhang Zai's student Fan Yu (fl. eleventh century), telling him that Fan Yu had said their first priority should be "putting the field system in order." Wang Anshi replied that Cheng Hao had advocated implementing the ancient well-field system, and Shenzong commented that that would only create chaos. He added that while it was acceptable for the emperor to establish rules that limit people, taking away fields that people already own was unacceptable. Wang Anshi concurred.[32] In the second exchange, Shenzong and Wang discussed the Tang equal-field system with its *zu yong diao* taxes. After Shenzong spoke positively of the system, Wang Anshi said it was close to the well-field system and achieved the goals of the Former Kings, but did not see it as something they could quickly implement. When Shenzong asked why, Wang replied:

> Ordinary commoners own fields, and some of them accumulate fields. We cannot snatch them away and impose something like the *zu yong diao* tax policy, with limits on the size of fields. But if the ruler can truly recognize which policies people like and dislike, he can build disadvantageous policies into the laws he applies to engrossers. As a consequence, the people themselves will not dare protect their excessive fields. If he builds incentives into the law that he applies to ordinary farmers, then people will persuade themselves to take up tilling and land ownership will not go beyond the limit. However, this must be done gradually before it becomes required by law. When the ruler truly understands policies' advantages and disadvantages and makes known his own preferences, he need not fear that the people will fail to adopt what they like and avoid what they dislike.[33]

Why did Wang Anshi shift from advocating implementation of the well-fields to repudiating it? To answer this, we need to discuss the development of Wang's idea of "restraining the engrossers." As already seen, when Wang served in prefectural and county posts in his early career, he expressed the idea of suppressing engrossers in his poems and essays. Wang sought to crack down on engrossers because he believed that their power was the source of the state's impoverishment and the people's destitution. He wrote, "Later generations did not return to antiquity, and the poor had to treat the engrossers as their masters." Therefore, he wanted to end the impoverishment of the state and the people by suppressing the engrossers. To do this, he, like Li Gou, longed for the well-field system of antiquity and "wished to see the well-fields equalized." After he assumed power, however, Wang changed from an immature, idealistic poet to a realistic politician who recognized that restoring the well-field system was impossible. Not only did he himself stop discussing the well-field system, but he also regarded the discussions of it by Cheng Hao, Zhang Zai, and others as "the Way to disorder." In place of the well-field system, Wang adopted the policy of imposing restrictions on overbearing engrossers.[34] Qi Xia writes, "He introduced policies that could be feasibly implemented, such as the Green Sprouts, Hired Service, and State Trade policies. Although it was not possible to even out differences in wealth, he could somewhat check the development of the overbearing engrossers' power and slightly lessen the peasants' burden, thus improving the social relations of production. Wang Anshi's reversal on the well-field system suited the objective situation."[35] In other words, given the historical conditions, Wang Anshi did not blindly restore Mencius's well-field system; rather, by grasping the essence of Mencius's well-field system and carrying out specific New Policies measures, he improved ways to "regulate the people's livelihoods." Thus, he truly realized Mencius's ideal society in which "above, they have enough to serve their parents and below, they have enough to support their wives and children. In years of prosperity they always have enough to eat; in years of dearth they are able to escape starvation" (*Mencius* 1A.7).

Of course, after coming to power, Wang Anshi was unable to restore the well-field system easily since he could not "hastily snatch the people's fields" to give to the poor. This does not mean that Wang ignored the social phenomenon of unfair land ownership. In his New Policies, he inherited the "square the fields and equalize the tax policy" of the "thousand-pace square fields policy" proposed by Guo Zi (fl. eleventh century) and others during Renzong's reign (r. 1022–1063). The square field policy instituted by Shenzong is described in the *Changbian* as follows: "Divide the fields, measure them, and using the registers of the area's villages, inspect the land quality ratings. . . . When the area's measurements are completed, calculate their fertility, set their quality ratings, divide them into five grades, and use the grades of land to make the tax burden fair. . . . When [families] divide, pawn the fields, partition them, or move away, officials will provide a receipt and record the transaction in the ledgers, taking the present situation as the baseline."[36] To a certain degree this is the implementation of Mencius's assertion that "humane government must begin with the setting of boundaries" (*Mencius* 3A.3).

THE RELATIONSHIP BETWEEN MENCIUS'S COMMISERATING GOVERNMENT AND WANG ANSHI'S RECONSTRUCTION OF THE SOCIAL ORDER

The contemporary historian Meng Wentong writes, "Mencius's learning was primarily about 'having a commiserating mind, and implementing a commiserating government' (*Mencius* 2A.6). When Han Confucians spoke of government, many focused more on the political system than on society. Song Confucians did the opposite." Meng further notes that Song Confucians preferred to focus on personnel management over reforming laws and emphasized moral cultivation over fiscal and military concerns.[37] Indeed, Wang Anshi had a profound understanding of Mencius's concept of commiserating government. In an afterword, Wang wrote:

> Mencius said that the Former Kings had a commiserating mind, and they had a commiserating government. I read *Efficacious Prescriptions* and sighed to myself saying, this could be called a commiserating government. In general, rulers are those who issue commands, and ministers those who implement the commands. If neither the ruler nor the ministers neglect their duties, then the world will be well-governed, and we can say that they truly have a ruler. The virtue that is fostered would spread to the Four Seas and reach the Man and Yi [barbarians], curing illnesses thought to be incurable and saving lives. Although my rank is low, were I really to receive a command to govern the people, it would be unforgivable of me not to extend Your Majesty's grace to the people.[38]

Wang Anshi's policies reflected Mencius's idea of commiserating with the common people in three principal realms: farmers' welfare, charity for the poor, and education. In an article on the development of disaster relief in the Song, I wrote that if we considered Wang Anshi's reforms from the perspective of the politics of famine relief, their ultimate objective was to establish a rational social relief system and to cultivate the peasants' ability to resist natural disasters.[39] Famine relief policies were thus issued in the context of a new age and closely linked to the suppression of engrossers. Cheng Bi (1162–1242) wrote, "To promote abundance and minimize want by taking from those who have more than enough to give to those without enough is to govern in the Kingly way."[40] The regulations of the Green Sprouts policy says: "The principle behind this is the same as that of the Former Kings when they dispersed favor and extended benefits as assistance during planting and harvesting, that is, by taking from those with plenty to aid those with little and restraining those who take by force. . . . It was not enough to wait until a famine."

As for the Hired Service policy, it states, "In general, when distributing money first consider the number of counties in the prefectures and how many people they have to hire and assess it according to the household grades. If there was more than enough to pay for hiring laborers, also increase the rate to two-tenths and save it to cover shortfalls when there are floods and droughts. Do not raise it beyond two-tenths. Refer to it as 'Hired Service surplus money.'"[41] Wang wrote of the Hired Services policy, "Those whom it lets off are the simple poor people of the countryside who are not able to survive on their own; those who are assigned obligations are only the officials and engrossers whom people refer to as powerful households."[42]

In 1082, Shenzong expressed this sentiment in the palace examination's policy question:

> We heard that the Kingly Way begins with taking agriculture as the foundation. Therefore, we instituted the ever-normal granaries, and they caused an accumulation [of grain] in the granaries so that farmers could eat their fill. We created the Hired Service policy so that the corvée labor imposed by the government would not impede the efforts of the farmers. Nevertheless, among the people today, those who exert themselves in agriculture dwindle, while those who turn to commerce increase. As soon as they encounter a flood or a drought, then the strong scatter to the four directions, and the weak will wander off and end up in the gullies. Grieved as we are by this, we ponder ways to strengthen agriculture at the expense of commerce. However, we have not yet found a good way to do this. Alas! The well-field system was abolished, replaced by the unrestricted buying and selling of land, which we need not discuss further. [The equal field

system,] with its fields that were distributed according to household size and passed down for generations, fell into decay and engrossers got the land. Ordering limits on landholding is no longer possible. [We want to] encourage city dwellers to go back to the fields, to reduce the number of [homeless] people roaming about the world, and strengthen people's ties to the land. In years of bountiful harvests they will have enough for family celebrations, and in years of bad harvest, they will not freeze or starve. What do you gentlemen think is the way to achieve these goals?[43]

In the latter half of Zhezong's reign, although each of the New Policies was slightly altered, the practices of Shenzong's era were largely followed. In 1100/1, Zhezong died of illness, and Shenzong's eleventh son Zhao Ji ascended the throne as Song Huizong. On the whole, Huizong continued Zhezong's New Policies. He particularly developed aspects of the social relief system initiated in the reigns of Renzong, Yingzong (r. 1063–1067), and Shenzong, a subject that warrants its own book.

During Renzong's reign, the government first set up eastern and western relief offices in the capital to care for widowers, widows, orphans, the childless, and other people who were not able to survive on their own. However, the scale was small: "They supplied grain to the old, the sick, the orphaned, the poor, and the beggars. Afterward only twenty-four people were given money and grain." Under Yingzong, the state expanded the scope of the eastern and western relief offices to "daily supply three hundred people. At harvest time, [the government] issued five million cash from the Palace Storehouse to cover their expenses, and then switched to using Sizhou's *shili qian* [money intended for building and maintaining Daoist and ancestral temples], increasing the amount to eight million." At the same time, they added southern and northern relief offices. In addition to setting up relief offices at the capital, the emperor also decreed, "When there is heavy rain or snow, prefects and magistrates should provide three days of rent money for free to a maximum of nine days in the year. [Publicly] announce this decree."[44]

From 1069 on, the court ordered the Chancellery that during the winter in the capital region, the relief offices would support "the old, the ill, the orphaned, the poor, and the beggars," and no longer rigidly restrict the number of people: "If you hear that the four relief offices have more people than budgeted for, give money to support them until the spring." In 1076, Shenzong further accepted the proposal of the Taiyuan prefect Han Jiang (1012–1088) to extend the legal period for providing assistance to the elderly

NORTHERN SONG REFORMIST THOUGHT

and ill during the winter in the Hedong region. At that time, according to the *Song shi*, "The prefectures gave rice and beans from the first of the eleventh month until the end of the third month of the following year." Han proposed to extend this period: "[We should] begin to support them from the first of the tenth month until the end of the second month of the following year. If there is a surplus, extend it to the end of the third month." He added, "Those unable to survive on their own, including widowers, widows, orphans, the childless, the infirm and old, and the sick and abandoned, ought to be given shelter and support. Let them occupy the abandoned homes of households that died out. If none are available, then use government offices to shelter them and the property of extinct households to cover their expenses, with no restrictions on the number of months. Supply them with rice and beans according to the law on beggars. If those funds are short, then use the interest from the ever-normal granaries." During Zhezong's reign, Shenzong's policies were continued, and poorhouses were established in each region one after another to support the old and weak.[45]

Under Shenzong, the Song court not only supported helpless and impoverished people during the winter through local authorities, but also ordered those authorities to assist temples in burying the bodies of those who died without anyone to inter them. In 1079/3/2, "it was decreed that within Kaifeng prefecture, in the cases of travelers whose coffins are stored in monasteries and of the poor unable to afford burial, the government should assign three or five *qing* of barren official land where burials will be permitted, with monks to handle the matter."[46]

In Huizong's reign, Cai Jing (1047–1126) was in charge of the government, and the social relief system underwent significant development. He used the state's administrative power to extend the existing capital and regional relief organizations to the whole country. In 1102, "Cai Jing, then in charge, established poorhouses and charity clinics. He distributed several times as much ever-normal granary rice than before. He dispatched officials and soldiers to serve as commissioners with instructions to provide stoves, food and drink, and padded clothing and blankets. The prefectures and counties went overboard; in some cases, they provided bed curtains and hired wet nurses and maids. They were wasteful and lacked regulations, running up expenses. The poor were happy while the rich were upset."[47] Among these institutions, the poorhouses were based on the relief offices but expanded. The charity clinics treated illnesses and were similar to modern hospitals.

In 1104, under the direction of Cai Jing, the court also set up paupers' graveyards, systematizing the practice dating to Shenzong's reign of assisting the monasteries in properly burying the dead: "Cai Jing expanded [the burial plots] into cemeteries, set up registers of those buried, and placed [the bodies] side by side at a depth of three *chi* so that they would not be exposed. The circuit intendants inspected the charity clinics and recruited monks to take charge of them."[48] In the Daguan (1107–1110) and Zhenghe (1111–1118) periods, further orders were issued:

> For walled stockades and market towns of one thousand or more households, those which have supervising officials should turn to the county government to set up more poorhouses, charity clinics, and paupers' graves. For those lying by the side of the roads as well as beggars who lack clothing, you are permitted to send them to a nearby poorhouse for relief money and rice. Teachable poor and orphaned children should be sent to primary school. Pay for their clothes with money from the ever-normal granaries' *touzi qian* and exempt them from school fees. In the case of foundlings, hire wet nurses to care for them [in infancy] and as before let Buddhist and Daoist temples raise them as novices.[49]

In 1120, an edict was issued that curtailed the program, indirectly showing how extensive it was:

> The poorhouses, charity clinics, and paupers' graveyards should be scaled back to the level of the old Yuanfeng policies. For people needing shelter and support, give one *sheng* of polished rice and millet and ten cash daily, and a supplement of firewood, charcoal, and five cash from the eleventh to first months, with children at half rations. The charity clinic's cash and grain will follow the poorhouse policy, and its medicine follow the old precedents. The paupers' graveyards should cease holding Buddhist and Daoist ceremonies and only handle burials according to the regulations now implemented.[50]

As can be seen, poorhouses, charity clinics, and paupers' graves had been widely established in major prefectures and counties across the country.

Mencius said, "Old men without wives are called widowers; old women without husbands are called widows; the elderly without children are called desolates; the young without parents are called orphans—these four, the most destitute and the voiceless among the people, King Wen made his first concern, displaying humaneness in his conduct of government" (*Mencius* 1B.5). He also said, "Making it possible for them to nourish their lives, bury their dead, and be without rancor is the beginning of kingly government" (*Mencius* 1A.3). Although earlier and later dynasties cited these sayings of Mencius, none of them implemented social relief to the degree that the mid- to late-Northern Song did.

However, these efforts—evening out differences in wealth, providing a constant means of livelihood, and relieving the needy—are merely the "beginning" of the Kingly Way. Because they only provide an economic base, one still needs to "attend carefully to the education provided in the schools, which should include instruction in the duty of filial and fraternal devotion" (*Mencius* 1A.3). Only by teaching everyone the principles of human relations can the Kingly Way be achieved. When expounding on the problem of education, Mencius took the education of the ancient monarchs as a model. It had two components: the first was technical skills, and the second was interpersonal ethics, which emphasized honoring those worthy of honor and holding relatives dear. Mencius said:

> Hou Ji taught the people to sow and to reap and to cultivate the five grains. When the grains ripened, the people had their nourishment. It is the way of human beings that when they have sufficient food, warm clothing, and comfortable dwellings, but are without education, they become little more than birds and beasts. It was the part of the sage to grieve anxiously over this. He appointed Xie as minister of education in order to teach the people about human relations: that between parents and children there is affection; between ruler and minister, rightness; between husband and wife, separate functions; between older and younger, proper order; and between friends, faithfulness (*Mencius* 3A.4).

Mencius also said, "Attend carefully to the education provided in the schools, which should include instruction in the duty of filial and fraternal devotion" (*Mencius* 1A.3).

Wang Anshi had a profound understanding of Mencius's ideas on education, which he developed in several ways. He wrote, "The world cannot go a day without government instruction, nor a day without schools. The ancients divided the fields of the world into the shape of the character for "well" [井], and ward schools, district academies, and the national university were set up among them." Wang added, "Although I wish to reform the affairs of the world so that they conform to the intentions of the Former Kings, the circumstances make it impossible. Why is this? The reason is that there are not enough well-trained people in the world yet." He further wrote, "What is meant by 'molding and perfecting them'? The only way is to instruct them, support them, select them, and appoint them."[51]

After Wang Anshi came to power, he employed three approaches in his efforts to reform education, following Mencius's train of thought. His first approach was actively setting up prefectural and county schools—the "Way of instructing them." Here, instruction primarily refers to education in schools under the government's direction. In this regard Wang wrote:

> The sages served as the government for the world. In the beginning, it was as if they did nothing about the world, and yet everything in the world ended up in good order. This was due to the sincere cultivation of their policies. Therefore, in the system of the Three Dynasties, schools were established at the ward level, academies at the district level, and the university at the countrywide level. They exhausted their Way in order to educate gentlemen. Worthy men not yet employed continued to be supported and respected. This was the way the Duke of Zhou treated gentlemen.[52]

Wang looked upon education at government schools as the basis for cultivating and training talented individuals, and he advocated regulating private schools as well. He believed that after the Three Dynasties, private schools led to disorder; the inundation of private schools made unhelpful learning flourish and created a divergence of opinions on matters of morality. For the sake of "uniting the Way and virtue in order to make the customs of the world the same," he wanted to restrict private schools and promote government schools under the direct control of the state.

Wang Anshi's second approach was to reform the civil service exam system and make schools the main channels for educating and selecting officials.[53] Schools set up by the Song government hit two peaks during the sixty years when Wang Anshi's New Learning was popular, the first during the Xining period, and the second during Huizong's reign. From Shenzong's through Huizong's reigns, the Song dynasty implemented the Three Halls policy at the Imperial University, a system of ascending grades from the Outer Hall to the Inner Hall to the Upper Hall. This was the first appearance of the modern system of grade levels, one of China's contributions to the world history of education.

Wang Anshi's third approach to education was to go beyond earlier practice in dividing education into subjects. Besides the Imperial University, the Song government established schools for the military, law, medicine, mathematics, calligraphy, and painting, one after the other. Even though the government did not attach enough importance to these other branches of learning, there is no doubt that this was the beginning of implementing separate subjects in higher education. In these ways, Wang Anshi developed Mencius's philosophy of education, which already stressed both nurturing human relations and cultivating practical work skills. Wang wrote: "Education is the basis for so many governmental tasks—carrying out village archery and drinking ceremonies, performing music in spring and autumn, supporting the elderly and toiling farmers, honoring the worthies and employing the talented, testing skills and selecting wording, even receiving reports, reporting victory, and checking on prisoners. In this way, they supported the world's wise and humane, sagacious and righteous, and loyal and harmonious officers but did not neglect narrow specialists. All were supported."[54]

ADDITIONAL REMARKS

Shenzong's promotion of Wang Anshi's reforms was a major event in the history of the Northern Song. The reforms were both a top-down attempt by the rulers to alter the long-term decline in state power and alleviate social problems and a social reform movement by scholar-officials who wanted a return to the political ideals of the Three Dynasties.

The intellectual basis of Wang Anshi's ideas have usually been analyzed in terms of his use of the *Rites of Zhou* or the influence Legalism had on him. The *New Meanings of the Three Classics*, promulgated by Shenzong in 1075, was the cornerstone for the philosophy behind Wang's reforms. As the editors of the *Siku quanshu* wrote, the *New Meanings of the Three Classics* "were based entirely on Wang Anshi's theories of the Classics. The Three Classics were the *Book of Documents*, the *Odes,* and the *Rites of Zhou*." "The only one that Wang Anshi wrote himself was the one on the *Rites of Zhou*."[55] After Wang's reforms were rejected, scholars and officials said he used the *Rites of Zhou* to bring disorder to the Song. This was a common opinion of scholars who over the centuries criticized Wang Anshi. By contrast, Deng Guangming contends that Wang Anshi was an innovator influenced by pre-Qin Legalist thought. He cites a conversation Wang Anshi had with Shenzong in which he said: "Your majesty observes that [all we have for] Shang Yang's (d. 338) agricultural and military institutions are a few lines written by Sima Qian. If the laws are simple and important, then it is easy for those below to follow them; if they are confused and petty, then it is difficult for those below to follow them, and it is also difficult for those above to monitor them."[56] Speaking to Shenzong, Wang Anshi also cited the famous reformer Wu Qi in the state of Chu during the Warring States of whom it was said, "Trying to enrich the state and strengthen the troops, they destroyed the wandering persuaders who spoke of vertical and horizontal alliances."[57] These two examples, Deng Guangming argues, illustrate that Wang's proposals for enriching the state and strengthening the troops came directly from pre-Qin Legalist methods for ordering the country and bringing peace and stability.[58] By contrast, what I have shown in this chapter is that under the specific historical conditions of the Song, Wang Anshi's reforms embodied Mencius's political thought and ways of creating the ideal social order.

How can we explain these three somewhat contradictory interpretations of Wang Anshi's philosophy? I think we should not assume that a statesman employs only one kind of conceptual model, because outstanding statesmen choose strategies and tactics according to changing circumstances. Wang Anshi himself said "taking the government of the Former Kings as a model" meant taking their intentions as a model. Given that Wang esteemed Mencius and the desire to suppress engrossers permeated his administration, it is not an exaggeration to say that the ideas behind his reforms came from Mencius, or even that he put into practice Mencius's political ideals. Wang did manage finances according to the *Rites of Zhou*,[59] but in his view Mencius's thought and the Zhou institutions (as depicted in the *Rites of Zhou*) both could be traced to the same source.[60]

Wang Anshi praised the Legalists' "enriching the state and strengthening the army" as a tactic to gain the emperor's trust in order to carry out his policies. If he could not cater to the desires of the ruler to reform real problems, his efforts to gain the ruler's trust and implement his policies would fail. This is precisely the difference between Wang Anshi and Zhu Xi, who also revered Mencius. Wang was both a major thinker and a major statesman. In the Qing period, Lu Xinyuan (1834–1894) wrote, "Since the Three Dynasties, there has been the study of statecraft, the study of the Classics, and the study of literary works. Those who attain competence in even one of these can be considered Confucians. Learning has been unenlightened for a long time because there are differences in what people want, what they have the strength to do, and what the times make important. In the worst cases, people ridicule each other. From the Han to the Song, for more than one thousand years, few people were equally competent in statecraft, classical studies, and literary works, but Wang Anshi was such a person."[61] Zhu Xi, by contrast, was only a great thinker. His repeated attempts to convince Xiaozong (r. 1162–1189) to heed his advice failed.

In the middle of the Northern Song, a group of scholar-officials active in political circles became key political actors. Wang Anshi, the Cheng brothers, and Zhang Zai were among this group's "creative minority" (to borrow Yu Yingshi's term).[62] Wang's school of thought differed from the Cheng-Zhu school (which later became the Learning of the Way) in ideas about the mind and the nature. However, in their esteem for Mencius they largely agreed. Why was this? Academic circles up to now have not given a fully satisfactory explanation. From the Southern Song to the late Qing, the struggle between Wang Learning and the Cheng-Zhu Learning of the Way was complicated by such issues as their positions in the transmission of the Way, heterodoxy, and orthodoxy. Since the late Qing, scholars have analyzed Wang Anshi's ideas and reforms in terms of Western evolutionary theory and the Marxist theory of class struggle, asking whether or not they were progressive and whose class interest they represented. As Zhu Weizheng notes, more recently scholars have paid particular attention to Song scholars who rejected Wang Anshi's political practices, from Cheng Yi to Zhu Xi, and shown that in their efforts to reinvigorate the dominant cultural traditions, they in fact became the executors of the reform movement's will.[63] In the Southern Song, Zhu Xi and his contemporaries continued the political culture of the New Policies era. In this sense, the age of Zhu Xi can be called the post–Wang Anshi age.[64]

NOTES

Translated by Peyton Canary

1   Zhu Weizheng, *Zhongguo jingxue shi shijiang*, 46–47.
2   For details, see Wang Zengyu, "Mengzi zai Songdai Yasheng diwei zhi queli ji qi yingxiang"; Zhou Shuping, *Liang Song Mengxue yanjiu*; and Zhu Hanmin and Xiao Yongmin, *Songdai "Si shu" xue yu lixue*.
3   This biography is preserved in the *Wanyan ji shancun*.
4   *Junzhai dushu zhi jiaozheng*, "Wang Jiefu Linchuan ji," 19.1000.
5   Zhou Shuping, *Liang Song Mengxue yanjiu*, 56.
6   *Yuzhang wen ji*, "Zun Yao lu," 7.1135–706.
7   Referring to *Mencius* 5B.1.
8   *Wang Wengong wenji*, "Fuzi xian yu Yao Shun," 28.323.
9   *Wang Wengong wenji*, "Yang Xiong san shou," 38.447.
10 *Wang Wengong wenji*, "Mengzi," 73.775.
11 *Wang Wengong wenji*, "Feng chou Yongshu jian zeng," 620.
12 Zhou Shuping, *Liang Song Mengxue yanjiu*, 56–57.
13 *SS* 105.2548.
14 Zhu Weizheng, *Zhongguo jingxue shi shijiang*, 23.
15 *Wubai jia zhu chang li ji*, "Du Xunzi," 11.1074–232.
16 *Wubai jia zhu chang li ji*, "Song Wang Xun Xiucai xu," 20.1074–348.

17 *Wang Wengong wenji*, "Qiu huai," 51.573.

18 See Yu Yingshi, *Zhu Xi de lishi shijie*, 122. Yu points out that the *daoxue* thinkers, although politically opposed to the New Policies, derived their arguments on reconstructing the social order from the *Mencius*.

19 *Wang Wengong wenji*, "Song Sun Zhengzhi xu," 36.433.

20 Unless otherwise noted, all translations of *Mencius* are from Bloom, *Mencius*.

21 This saying was a clever play on the line in *Analects* 16.8 that the gentleman has three things he stands in awe of: Heaven, important men, and the words of the sages.

22 Deng Guangming, *Bei Song zhengzhi gaigejia Wang Anshi*, 2–5, 92–111.

23 *Zhanyuanjing yu*, 2.866–309.

24 *Wang Linchuan ji*, 12.60–61.

25 See Yang Zhijiu, "Wang Anshi yu Mengzi."

26 *Wang Wengong wenji*, "Shang Huangdi wanyan shu," 1.1–2; trans. de Bary and Bloom, *Sources of Chinese Tradition*, 1:613–614.

27 *Song dazhaoling ji*, 156.584.

28 *Sishu zhangju jizhu*, 256.

29 Li Yan and Zhang Feng, "Mengzi de 'Jingtian shuo' yu 'Hengchan lun' qianxi." Also see Li Yan, "Mengzi de jingtian shuo he fengong lun," and Li, *Buzixiaozhai wencun*, 141–53.

30 Ye Shi ji, "Bieji" "Minshi shang," 652. The history of and debates about systems for redistributing land are taken up again in Jaeyoon Song's chapter in this volume.

31 *Jiayou ji jianzhu*, "Tianzhi," 5.135.

32 *CB* 213.5181.

33 *CB* 223.5419.

34 Qi Xia, "Songdai jingji shi," 1129.

35 Qi Xia, "Songxue de fazhan yu yanbian," 378–80.

36 *CB* 237.5783.

37 Meng Wentong, *Ruxue wulun*, 131.

38 *Wang Wengong wenji*, "Shan jiu fang hou xu," 36.432.

39 Hao Chunwen and Li Huarui, *Zhongguo gudaishi lunwen xuancui*, 497–524.

40 *Mingshui ji*, "Mi tao jiu huang," 5.1171–282.

41 Qi Xia, "Wang Anshi bianfa," 268.

42 *SS* 177.4299–4300.

43 *Wang Weigong ji*, "Yuanfeng wunian dianshi jinshi cewen," 4.1100–40. In addition, *Houshan ji*, 14.1114–649~650, and *Daoxiang ji*, 29.1121–420~421, also record this question.

44 *SS* 178.4338.

45 *SS* 178.4338.

46 *SHY* Shihuo 68.128.

47 *SS* 178.4339.

48 *SS* 178.4339.

49 *SS* 178.4339–40.

50 *SS* 178.4340.

51 *Wang Wengong wenji*, "Mingzhou Cixi xian xue ji," 34.405.

52 *Wang Wengong wenji*, "Zhou gong," 26.302.

53 Qi Xia, "Wang Anshi bianfa," 92–98, and Yuan, *Songdai jiaoyu*, 26–43.

54 *Wang Wengong wenji*, "Mingzhou Cixi xian xue ji," 34.405.

55 *Siku quanshu zongmu* 19.149–50.

56 *Siming zun Yao ji*, "Lun dao men," 3.448–373.

57 *CB* 250.6092.

58 Deng Guangming, *Bei Song zhengzhi gaigejia Wang Anshi*, 72.

59 Wang Anshi's policies had a significant connection with the *New Meanings of the Three Classics*, especially the *Rites of Zhou*. Recently, some scholars compared the New Policies measures one by one —the Green Sprouts, State Trade, Hired Service, and *baojia* policies—with the *Rites of Zhou's quanfu* rank (*quanfu* consisted of officials in charge of financial matters like taxation) and found each one's corresponding source. See Yu Jinghui, "Wang Anshi zhi 'Jingshu zhengzhi' yu Xining bianfa."

60 See *Wang Wengong wenji*, "Da Han qiu ren shu," 7.76.

61 *Yigu tang ji*, "Shu Linchuan ji shu hou," 8.

62 Yu Yingshi, "Zhengtong yu daotong zhijian," 98–99.

63 Zhu Weizheng, *Zhongguo jingxue shi shijiang*, 24.

64 Yu Yingshi, *Zhu Xi de lishi shijie*, 893–97.

REFERENCES

PRIMARY SOURCES

Daoxiang ji 道鄉集, by Zou Hao 鄒浩 (1060–1111). Siku quanshu ed.

Han shu 漢書, by Ban Gu 班固 (32–92 CE). Beijing: Zhonghua shuju, 1962.

Houshan ji 后山集, by Chen Shidao 陳師道 (1053–1101). Siku quanshu ed.

Jiayou ji jianzhu 嘉祐集箋注, by Su Xun 蘇洵 (1009–1066). Shanghai: Shanghai guji chubanshe, 1993.

Junzhai dushu zhi jiaozheng 郡齋讀書志較證, by Chao Gongwu 晁公武 (d. 1171). Shanghai: Shanghai guji chubanshe, 1990.

Mingshui ji 洺水集, by Cheng Bi 程珌 (1164–1242). Siku quanshu ed.

Siku quanshu zongmu 四庫全書總目. Beijing: Zhonghua shuju, 1987.

Siming zun Yao ji 四明尊堯集, by Chen Guan 陳瓘 (1057–1122). Xuxiu sikuquanshu ed.

Sishu zhangju jizhu 四書章句集注, by Zhu Xi 朱熹 (1130–1200). Beijing: Zhonghua shuju, 2005.

Song dazhaoling ji 宋大詔令集. Beijing: Zhonghua shuju, 1962.

Song huiyao jigao 宋會要輯稿, compiled by Xu Song 徐松 (1781–1848) et al. Beijing: Zhonghua shuju, 1957.

Song shi 宋史, edited by Tuo Tuo 脫脫 (1313–1355) et al. Beijing: Zhonghua shuju, 1977.

Wanyan ji shancun 琬琰集刪存. Shanghai: Shanghai guji chubanshe, 1990.

Wang Linchuan ji 王臨川集, by Wang Anshi 王安石 (1021–1086). Taibei: Shijie shuju, 1966.

Wang Weigong ji 王魏公集, by Wang Anli 王安禮 (1034–1095). Siku quanshu ed.

Wang Wengong wenji 王文公文集, by Wang Anshi 王安石 (1021–1086). Shanghai: Shanghai renmin chubanshe, 1974.

Wubai jia zhu Chang li ji 五百家註昌黎集, by Han Yu 韓愈 (768–824), annotated by Wei Zhongju 魏仲舉. Siku quanshu ed.

Xu zizhi tongjian changbian 續資治通鑑長編, by Li Tao 李燾 (1115–1184). Beijing: Zhonghua shuju, 1985.

Ye Shi ji 葉適集, by Ye Shi 葉適 (1150–1123). Beijing: Zhonghua shuju, 1983 ed.

Yigu tang ji 儀顧堂集, by Lu Xinyuan 陸心源 (1834–1894). Guojia tushuguan cang bajuanben.

Yuzhang wenji 豫章文集, by Luo Congyan 羅從彥 (1072–1135). Siku quanshu ed.

Zhanyuanjing yu 湛淵靜語, by Bai Ting 白珽 (1248–1328). Siku quanshu ed.

SECONDARY SOURCES

Bloom, Irene, trans. *Mencius*. New York: Columbia University Press, 2009.

de Bary, Wm. Theodore, and Irene Bloom, eds. *Sources of Chinese Tradition*. New York: Columbia University Press, 1999.

Deng Guangming 鄧廣銘. *Bei Song zhengzhi gaigejia Wang Anshi* 北宋政治改革家王安石. Beijing: Sanlian shudian, 1997.

Hao Chunwen 郝春文 and Li Huarui 李華瑞, eds. *Zhongguo gudaishi lunwen xuancui* 中國古代史論文選萃. Beijing: Zhongguo shehui kexue chubanshe, 2013.

Li Yan 李埏. *Buzixiaozhai wencun* 不自小齋文存. Kunming: Yunnan renmin chubanshe, 2001.

———. "Mengzi de jingtian shuo he fengong lun—du 'Mengzi' zhaji" 孟子的井田說和分工論—讀'孟子'札記. *Shehui kexue zhanxian* 1 (1991): 155–60.

Li Yan 李埏 and Zhang Feng 章峰. "Mengzi de 'Jingtian shuo' yu 'Hengchan lun' qianxi" 孟子的'井田說'與'恆產論'淺析. *Yunnan xueshu tansuo* 2 (1996): 20–24.

Meng Wentong 蒙文通. *Ruxue wulun: Song-Ming zhi shehui sheji* 儒學五論: 宋明之社會設計. Guilin: Guangxi shifan daxue chubanshe, 2007.

Qi Xia 漆俠. "Songdai jingji shi" 宋代經濟史. In *Qi Xia quanji* 漆俠全集. Baoding: Hebei daxue chubanshe, 2008.

———. "Songxue de fazhan yu yanbian" 宋學的發展與演變. In *Qi Xia quanji* 漆俠全集. Baoding: Hebei daxue chubanshe, 2008.

———. "Wang Anshi bianfa" 王安石變法. In *Qi Xia quanji* 漆俠全集. Baoding: Hebei daxue chubanshe, 2008.

Wang Zengyu 王曾瑜. *Diandi bian* 點滴編. Baoding: Hebei daxue chubanshe, 2010.

———. "Mengzi zai Songdai Yasheng diwei zhi queli ji qi yingxiang" 孟子在宋代亞聖地位之確立及其影響. In *Qingzhu Deng Guangming jiaoshou jiushi huadan lunwen ji* 慶祝鄧廣銘教授九十華誕論文集, edited by Tian Yuqing 田餘慶, 491–98. Shijiazhuang: Hebei jiaoyu chubanshe, 1997.

Yang Zhijiu 楊志玖. "Wang Anshi yu Mengzi" 王安石與孟子. *Shehui kexue zhanxian* 3 (1979): 142–46.

Yu Jinghui 俞菁慧. "Wang Anshi zhi 'Jingshu zhengzhi' yu Xining bianfa—yi 'Rites of Zhou' jingshiwei zhongxin" 王安石之'經術政治'與熙寧變法—以'周禮'經世為中心. PhD diss., Beijing daxue, 2013.

Yu Yingshi 余英時. "Zhengtong yu daotong zhijian: Zhongguo zhishifenzi de yuanshixingtai" 政統與道統之間: 中國知識份子的原始形態. In *Shi yu Zhongguo wenhua* 士與中國文化, edited by Zhou Gucheng 周谷城, 84–112. Shanghai: Shanghai renmin chubanshe, 1987.

———. *Zhu Xi de lishi shijie: Songdai shidafu zhengzhi wenhua de yanjiu* 朱熹的歷史世界: 宋代士大夫政治文化的研究. Beijing: Sanlian shudian, 2004.

Yuan Zheng 袁征. *Songdai jiaoyu: Zhongguo gudai jiaoyu de lishixing zhuanzhe* 宋代教育: 中國古代教育的歷史性轉折. Guangzhou: Guangdong gaodengjiaoyu chubanshe, 1991.

Zhou Shuping 周淑萍. *Liang Song Mengxue yanjiu* 兩宋孟學研究. Beijing: Renmin chubanshe, 2007.

Zhu Hanmin 朱漢民 and Xiao Yongmin 肖永民. *Songdai "Si shu" xue yu lixue* 宋代"四書"學與理學. Beijing: Zhonghua shuju, 2009.

Zhu Weizheng 朱維錚. *Zhongguo jingxue shi shijiang* 中國經學史十講. Shanghai: Fudan daxue chubanshe, 2005.

7 Debates on Just Taxation in Ma Duanlin's *Comprehensive Survey*

JAEYOON SONG

LIKE MOST OTHER AGRARIAN EMPIRES, THE SONG GOVERNMENT depended on farmers for much of its revenue. But how could taxes be levied on farmers in a fair and efficient way? Should they be levied per capita or on the basis of property? Should the government step in to redistribute land when inequalities became too great? For Confucian scholars, offering answers to these questions was not easy. Not only were they committed to the validity of the Classics, but they also aspired to ideals of benevolent government, epitomized for many by the well-field (*jingtian*) system mentioned in the Classics, which provided land for every family. And, of course, some also worried about the government's need for revenue in order to perform such basic functions as defense of borders. Consequently, Song scholars and officials reached a variety of conclusions about the best way to collect revenue from farmers. At one extreme were classicists who advocated reviving the well-field system in all particulars. At the other extreme were pragmatists who hesitated to disturb the existing power structure. Many writers fell somewhere in the middle, some seeing advantages in the early Tang "equal field" system (*juntianfa)* with its standard taxes on every household, others proposing ways to improve the fairness of the Song tax system by resurveying land.

An excellent source for these debates during the Southern Song is Ma Duanlin's (ca. 1254–1323) *Comprehensive Survey of Literary Remains* (Wenxian tongkao; hereafter *Survey*), which devotes its first seven chapters to "land taxes." Although at first glance the discussion seems to focus on interpreting somewhat cryptic passages in the classics, Ma is well-aware of the consequences of these interpretations for policies in his own day. By highlighting Southern Song calls for a retreat of the state, Ma Duanlin proclaimed his own faith in the legitimacy of private ownership, which he believed should form the basis of good government in his day.

Born into a prominent scholar-official family in Yaozhou, Jiangxi, Ma

Duanlin studied under a follower of Zhu Xi (1130–1200) and entered officialdom through the *yin* (protection) privilege.[1] After the capital Lin'an fell to the Mongols in 1276, he declined an offer to serve the Yuan government and returned home. Thereafter, in self-imposed isolation, he devoted his energies to compiling the *Survey*, finishing this massive work at the age of fifty-three in 1307.[2] The *Survey* was brought to the court for the emperor's review, and then published by imperial decree in 1322 when Ma was in his late sixties.

Ma Duanlin was committed to showing that government institutions were products of history. As he saw it, the institutions which stand the tests of time evolve through trial and error in real historical situations. And institutions, however well-designed in the beginning, come to an end when they no longer serve human communities. He thus had little use for those who proposed reviving the Tang equal-field system with its standard per household taxes, much less the ancient well-field system. Recognizing the unbridgeable differences between "antiquity" and "modernity," he sought to articulate a realistic alternative for his own time. Throughout the *Survey*, Ma favors the political virtues of prudence, moderation, and skepticism.

Ma Duanlin's survey of land taxes traverses three different periods: classical antiquity; later history (from the Qin through the Tang and the Five Dynasties); and the recent past (Northern and Southern Song). As his source for the institutions of classical antiquity he draws primarily on later commentaries on the Classics; for the study of the institutions of the Qin through Five Dynasties he employs memorials by influential statesmen and scholars; and for a close review of the politics of the recent past he uses both the historical and the political-philosophical writings of Southern Song authors. Throughout Ma Duanlin consistently prioritizes Southern Song thinkers.

THE *COMPREHENSIVE SURVEY OF LITERARY REMAINS*

In its time, Ma Duanlin's *Survey* was perhaps the most important work of its kind to have ever been written. In terms of scale and thoroughness, it remained unmatched for centuries to come. Though classified as an encyclopedia (*leishu*), this work systematically organizes cumulative debates on major institutions of the state, most of which emerged in antiquity and evolved throughout history down to Southern Song. In the preface to the *Survey*, Ma writes that "the investigation of institutions and the inquiry into statutes and charters" should be the tasks of "all-embracing Confucians" (*tongru*). Although *wenxian* is loosely translated by Hok-lam Chan as "literary remains," Ma Duanlin himself is much more precise. For him, *wen* refers to historical documents of various sorts such as classics, histories, collected essential documents (*huiyao*) of dynasties, and the writings of the "hundred schools," including commentaries and records. *Xian* refers to the debates on state affairs encapsulated in ministers' memorials and contemporary Confucians' (*zhuru*) arguments and comments, to the leisurely conversations of luminaries, as well as to the records of petty officials who collected popular stories (*baiguan*).[3]

As a comprehensive history of institutions across the dynasties, the *Survey* takes its cues from Du You's (735-812) *Comprehensive Statutes* (Tongdian) and Zheng Qiao's (1104–1162) *Comprehensive Treatises* (Tongzhi).[4] The model of Du You was particularly strong. As Edwin G. Pulleyblank noted decades ago, Du You's views "have a refreshing down-to-earthness and practicality combined often with a clear insight into the nature of contemporary problems and their historical background.[5] Nevertheless, as Hok-lam Chan aptly points out, Ma's *Survey* is superior to both the *Comprehensive Statues* and *Comprehensive Treatises* in that it provides more "judicious documentation and evaluation of the source materials" on the political, social, and economic institutions of Chinese empires.[6] For this reason, the *Survey* would be taken seriously by statesmen and statecraft thinkers throughout the Ming and Qing, as attested to by the publication of sequels as late as 1921.[7]

Like Du You, Ma Duanlin begins with fiscal issues. He devotes the first seven chapters of his *Survey* to tracing changes in land-tax policy from the earliest historical records down to the Southern Song. A close reading of these chapters shows that Ma's statecraft thought was heavily influenced by four Southern Song thinkers in particular: the early Neo-Confucian scholar Hu Yin (1098–1150), the Southern Song Neo-Confucian leader Zhu Xi (1130–1200), and the Yongjia statecraft thinkers Ye Shi (1150–1227) and Chen Fuliang (1137–1203).

The way in which Ma Duanlin engages Zhu Xi and the Yongjia thinkers, the leaders of the two most important Southern Song schools of statecraft, reflects a new intellectual trend that arose in the 1230s.[8] As James Liu argues, when the Mongols conquered the Jurchen Jin and directly confronted the Southern Song, "the political competition at the cultural level between the Mongols and the Southern Song" resulted in the ascendancy of the Learning of the Way (Daoxue) school.[9] But around this same time some literati took it upon themselves to reconcile the tension between Zhu Xi's Learning of the Way school and the Yongjia statecraft schools. This intellectual synthesis would evolve over the last several decades of the Southern Song and continue into the early Yuan.[10] The *Survey* seems to exemplify this trend, yet Ma's intention was not simply to reconcile the two schools, but to highlight the tensions between them. At the same time, Ye Shi's writings seems to have had the most direct influence on his thought.

THE SIGNIFICANCE OF LAND TAXES

The issue of land taxes was made all the more pressing by the social and economic transformation of the countryside between the Tang (618–907) and Song periods. The Tang equal-field system, enforced by the imperial will against increasing calls for the recognition of the private ownership of land, could not stand the test of time.[11] Its collapse in mid-eighth century has generally been viewed as marking the beginnings of vast socioeconomic changes some historians have dubbed "the medieval economic revolution."[12] By legalizing the private ownership of land, the Tang imperial state gave up standard per household taxes in favor of taxing property.[13] As the state abandoned its ambitions to redistribute land a class of large-scale estate-owners emerged.[14] As the commercial economy grew, private land transactions in the countryside grew apace, without much state interference. The modern Chinese historian Qi Xia writes rather cynically that the Song dynasty had "no land policy whatsoever" while "land-engrossing intensified without interruption." He argues that officials, landlords, and wealthy merchants whose households accounted for around 0.5 to 0.6 percent of the total household population formed a triad of wealth.[15] As land engrossing increased, the economic gap between rich and poor grew wider. The Japanese historians of the Tokyo school have presented a similar picture, with a large portion of the population forced to work as hired laborers or tenants while the wealthy landowners, many of whom were officials, sought to build up large estates for economic security as well as social prestige.[16]

Wang Anshi tried to alleviate economic inequality through his interventionist, state-directed New Policies.[17] This approach was widely rejected during the Southern Song. But while united in their opposition to the New Policies model of income equalization, Southern Song observers counseled a variety of solutions of their own. These ranged from reinstating the Tang equal-field system, to imposing limits on the size of landholdings, to clarifying farm boundaries. Some even downplayed the problem by emphasizing the mutual reliance between rich and poor, or even urging a retreat of the state by emphasizing the positive functions of the wealthy as the natural pillars of society.[18]

These historical developments helped shape Ma Duanlin's understanding of land taxes. In his preface he begins with the ancient Three Dynasties (Xia, Shang, and Zhou) when the lands of all-under-heaven were regarded as communal property and the vassal lords shared them with the population in accordance with the well-field system. These vassal lords formed an organic whole with those under them; they "regarded the lands as their own, they treated the people as their children, and their descendants received those lands generation after generation."[19] Residing in their fiefs, the vassal lords were able to respond to the needs of the farmers because they knew the local environment. However, with the Qin unification, Ma argues, the earlier patrimonial bond between the government and the people was supplanted by the absolute monopoly of power by one man at the top and the privatization of land. The spread of private property proved irresistible, despite concerted attempts to reinstate the regulations of the Three Dynasties during the Northern Wei (386–534) and early Tang (618–907) through the equal-field system. Those efforts failed "because the well-field system was impossible to revive in the absence of the classic enfeoffment system" (in other words, hereditary lords).[20] Ma Duanlin concludes:

> During the Three Dynasties era, the Son of Heaven could not treat the realm as his private possession. [By contrast], the Qin abolished the enfeoffment system, and put all-under-heaven in the service of one man. During the Three Dynasties, commoners could not take private possession of landed property. But the Qin abolished the well-field system and did away with [equitably] granting land to ordinary people [the "hundred names"]. [Instead], the Qin seized lands from those who deserved them and granted lands to those whose lands should have been seized. Because [unification and privatization] have continued for so long, attempts to restore antiquity will [always] prove difficult. Restoring the enfeoffment system would encounter resistance over the dividing up of lands, while reinstating the well-field system would fan grievances over the forcible confiscation of people's land. That is why I argue that [a restoration of the ancient systems] would not work. Taxing people's farm lands without trying to control their size began with Shang Yang (390–338 BCE); taxing the amount of land owned by the people with no distinction between adult males and others began with Yang Yan (727–781). The well-field system, the fine institution of the Three Dynasties periods, was destroyed by Shang Yang, and the per household tax system, the fine institution of the Tang, was destroyed by Yang Yan. Although gentlemen condemn these two men's

actions, the rulers of later periods have to a man abided by their laws. *Any attempt at reforming these laws ended up making things worse and the state and the people had to suffer the bad consequences together. This is because ancient times and present times are of necessity different.* I have thus put my "Inquiry into Land Taxes" first. In it I describe land tax regulations through the ages, with the supplementary [observations] on water management, military colonies, and state-owned land, for a total of seven chapters. [Emphasis added].[21]

This passage encapsulates how Ma Duanlin views the history of land taxes. He begins by idealizing the institutions of the Three Dynasties period before private property existed. Instead of monopolizing the wealth of all-under-heaven, the sage rulers shared it with the people through a hierarchically organized feudal network of numerous semiautonomous polities, captured by the well-known phrase "one thousand eight hundred states" (*qian babai guo*), each of which secured the communal ownership of land for the people in accord with the well-field system. With the rise of the Qin empire, private ownership of land grew apace. As a result, the people of the realm, who had once been linked organically to the lords of their own states, came to "serve" (or pay taxes to) one man on top. In Ma Duanlin's view, the golden times of the Three Dynasties gradually declined to reach the abysmal low with the advent of the unified Qin empire. By adopting the field-boundary (*qianmo*) system, the Qin empire recognized private ownership of land. This lasted until the Northern Wei reinstated public ownership of land though the equal-field system. In less than two hundred years, by mid-Tang, however, these efforts succumbed to the irresistible trend of privatization.

Although Ma Duanlin idealizes the Three Dynasties period, he credits both Shang Yang and Yang Yan for having reformed land taxes in keeping with the changed conditions of their times. Ma's view of history seems neither progressive nor regressive. While praising the Three Dynasties era, he scorns any fundamentalist attempt to restore the ancient institutions. As a historian he was pessimistically aware of the differences between "antiquity" and "modernity."

ANTIQUITY: TAX JUSTICE AND LAND REDISTRIBUTION

In the history of Chinese political thought, antiquity—that is, the institutions of the ancient sage rulers as presented in the Classics—provided the idealized normative models of good government. Unlike traditional classicists, who tended to idealize the ancient institutions, Ma Duanlin describes the institutions of antiquity in a matter-of-fact tone. Although he does point to some general principles of land taxation that might be considered applicable for his time, he is consistently skeptical about the restorability of the ancient institutions for later periods. By historicizing antiquity, he illuminates the objective conditions that held together the ancient institutions of government. His survey of ancient land taxes focuses on three topics in three important classic texts: the principles of tax justice in "The Tribute of Yu" chapter of the *Book of Documents*; the ideal of a tithe tax in the *Mencius*; and the land redistribution model in the *Rituals of Zhou*.

THE PRINCIPLES OF TAX JUSTICE IN "THE TRIBUTE OF YU"

Most chapters in the *Survey* begin with descriptions of ancient institutions. Ma Duanlin begins his survey of land taxes by introducing "The Tribute of Yu" chapter of the *Book of Documents*. "The Tribute of Yu," one of the earliest sources showing the geographic ideas of ancient China, describes the primordial process of state-making through the imposition of just taxation based on a precise cadastral survey and accurate geographical information. We are told in the *Book of Documents* that, having controlled the floods at King Yao's order, Yu divided the whole territory into the Nine Provinces and imposed the Five Tenures, the concentric squares of the administrative boundaries of King Yao's government.[22] Although the historicity is debatable, traditional exegetes inferred from it the principles of just taxation. Ma begins by presenting the geography of the ancient Nine Provinces as given in "The Tribute of Yu," as shown in table 7.1.

"The Tribute of Yu" describes soil types, the grades of arable land based on soil productivity, tax rates, and tribute items. One issue is perplexing: the grades of lands do not seem to correspond to the grades of taxes. The soil productivity of Jizhou and Yuzhou are graded as the fifth and the fourth, respectively, whereas the highest rates of taxes are imposed on both. The soil productivity of Yongzhou is highest, yet the taxes there stand only at the sixth grade. The land taxes of the Tribute of Yu thus seem inconsistent.

Ma Duanlin begins his discussion of this issue with the view of the Tang classicist Kong Yingda (574–648). Kong explains the inconsistency by saying that the apparent discrepancy of tax rates applied to different regions stems from the density of the labor force: where labor density is high, even lower quality land should have higher rates of taxation, and vice versa.[23] According to this view, one might think that the sage kings of antiquity counterintuitively endorsed, and even legislated, regional inequities.

TABLE 7.1. The nine provinces in "The Tribute of Yu"

Province	Soil Types	Soil Productivity	Rates of Taxation	Tribute Items
Jizhou 冀州	White/soft	Fifth	First/second	Leather
Yanzhou 兖州	Black/fertile	Sixth	Ninth	Paint, silk thread
Qingzhou 青州	White/fertile	Third	Fourth	Salt, hemp, seafood
Xuzhou 徐州	Red and muddy	Second	Fifth	Silk
Yangzhou 揚州	Mostly mud	Ninth	Sixth/seventh	Clothes
Jingzhou 荊州	Mostly mud	Eighth	Third	Feathers, oxtail hair, ivory, leather
Yuzhou 預州	Soft/fertile and black underneath	Fourth	First, second	Paint, ramie cloth, hemp, cotton thread, whetstone
Liangzhou 梁州	Blue-black	Seventh	Seventh, eighth, ninth	Gold, iron, silver, steel, animals
Yongzhou 雍州	Yellow and soft	First	Sixth	Marble, jade

Note: Both arable land and taxes are graded based on a scale of one (highest) to nine (lowest).

To solve this puzzle, Ma Duanlin turns next to the influential Southern Song classicist Lin Zhiqi (1112–1176), who argues that grades of taxation specified in "The Tribute of Yu" varied with the actual agricultural output in each province.[24] As Lin interpreted it, tax grades corresponded to the overall level of production in each region based on three combined factors: soil productivity, the area of land under cultivation, and the size of the population.[25] In Lin's view, the nine grades of taxation corresponded to the actual agricultural output calculated ex post facto in each province. In other words, the sagely ancient government imposed taxes based on its precise knowledge of the rural socioeconomic realities.

By citing Lin Zhiqi's comment, Ma Duanlin affirms the need for in-depth cadastral surveys to minimize the discrepancy between state tax registers and actual landholding, a chronic problem for the imperial state throughout the ages. In the following chapters on the land taxes of later periods, Ma documents the Land Survey and Equitable Tax Policy (Fangtian Junshui Fa), the state-initiated cadastral survey and land redistribution that was enforced in the five northern circuits during the 1070s under Wang Anshi's

New Policies.[26] He even praises the expansion of farm lands through state-led land reclamation projects during this period.[27] In the following chapters, he also cites "the boundary measure" (*jingjie fa*) of the early Southern Song, another attempt by the state to realize tax justice in rural society.[28] But despite being well disposed to large-scale cadastral surveys, Ma is no supporter of other forms of state activism. That may be why of the three hundred and more commentaries on the *Book of Documents* published throughout ages down to the end of Southern Song, Ma Duanlin cites only Lin Zhiqi's comments in addition to Kong Yingda's.[29] Indeed, Lin demonstrated his antistatist orientation by opposing a court attempt to revive Wang Anshi's *New Commentaries on the Three Classics* (Sanjing xinyi), the state orthodoxy of the New Policies government, on the grounds that Wang misused the Classics.

Among Lin's disciples was Lü Zuqian (1137–1181), one of the most influential Neo-Confucian scholars of the day. Not surprisingly, Ma Duanlin cites Lü Zuqian to spell out the implications of Yu's administration. "The institutions of taxes and corvée labor," writes Lü, "are visible for the first time in 'The Tribute of Yu.'" Ma goes on to cite Lü's summary of the governmental structure outlined in "The Tribute": tribute (local products) and land taxes (grain) were convertible; land taxes (grain) were collected only from within the Royal Domain (Wangji) in Ji province; all the other provinces in the outer Four Domains sent up tribute, not grain; the royal court exchanged tribute from the provinces for grain at the market; as "the unity of soldiery and farming" incurred no extra expenditure for defense, it was sufficient for the court to collect taxes only from within the Royal Domain; and because military expenditures were modest, low rates of taxation were possible in antiquity.[30] The main point for Ma here, as throughout the *Survey*, is that because the underlying system of government is now fundamentally different from that in "The Tribute of Yu," it would be impossible to reinstate the attendant institutions of antiquity.

THE IDEAL OF A TEN-PERCENT TAX

On land taxes in "the Tributes of Yu," Ma Duanlin turns to Zhu Xi's commentary on the *Mencius*. Among the Confucian Classics, the *Book of Documents*, the *Mencius*, and the *Rituals of Zhou* all idealized a tax-rate of ten percent (or a tithe). The state should first distribute a portion of land to the people before collecting at most one-tenth of its produce. Ma points to the relevant phrase in the *Mencius* and Zhu Xi's commentary on it.

Mencius: The sovereign of the Xia dynasty enacted the fifty *mu* allotment, and the payment of a tax. The founder of the Yin enacted the seventy *mu* allotment, and the system of mutual aid. The founder of the Zhou enacted the hundred *mu* allotment, and the share system. In reality, what was paid in all these was a tithe.[31]

Zhu Xi's commentary: During the time of Xia, every male received a fifty *mu* allotment of land, from which each man calculated the output of five *mu* and submitted it as tribute. The Shang instituted the well-field system, according to which six hundred thirty *mu* of land were divided into nine units. Each unit was seventy *mu* with the middle reserved as communal land. Eight surrounding households each received one unit, providing their labor for the cultivation of the communal field in return for being exempted from taxes on their private land.[32]

During the Zhou an adult male received one hundred *mu* of land. The Districts organized ten men into one channel [*gou*] in accordance with the policy of tribute and taxation [*gongfa*].[33] The Inherited Region used the policy of mutual aid [*zhufa*], and organized eight households with a common well [*tongjing*].[34] As they tilled the land together and shared the burdens of taxation in proportion to the number of *mu* each held, it was called the share system [*che*]. In fact, all of these were a tithe system.[35]

Zhu Xi's commentary specifies the rates of land taxes in the Three Dynasties period as not exceeding one-tenth of the grain production of each well-field plot. Having invoked Zhu's description of the ancient tithe tax Ma Duanlin shifts attention to the well-field system. In Zhu Xi's view, the principle of low taxation in Chinese antiquity presupposed the redistribution of land to the people. Ma Duanlin pays special heed to the well-field system precisely because it provided the ancient reference for the state-led redistribution of land, an issue that was still alive in Southern Song. By citing Zhu Xi's commentary, Ma acknowledges Zhu's influence during the late Southern Song and early Yuan. But far from fetishizing Zhu Xi, Ma puts Zhu Xi to the test over interpretations of the well-field system.

THE WELL-FIELD SYSTEM

Unlike modern historians, Ma Duanlin's interest in the well-field system was not primarily with its historicity.[36] His primary goal is to show how canonical references to the well-field system generated a sustained public debate on social equity and tax justice. The well-field system represents the ancient method of land redistribution whereby the state could secure a stable source of revenue from a population of self-reliant small landholders. Traditional political thinkers and classicists generally believed that with the rise of the Qin empire, the time-honored well-field system was abolished for good. The equal-field system of the Northern dynasties and early Tang dynasty represented yet another state-initiated attempt to nurture a population of landed farmers; yet by the mid-Tang the privatization of land had gone too far to be reversed. Fiscally hard pressed, the state decided to acquiesce to the growing private commercial economy by accepting "the Twice-a-Year Tax" proposed by Yang Yan, who in Ma's iconoclastic view "pacified the people by reforming" the traditional laws of the Tang founders.[37]

It is with this grand historical change in mind that Ma Duanlin introduces Southern Song debates on the well-field system found primarily in Southern Song commentaries to the *Rituals of Zhou*. As the "constitution" of state activism, Wang Anshi's (1021–1086) commentary on the *Rituals of Zhou* rose to preeminence during the New Policies government.[38] Struggling with Wang Anshi's legacy, Southern Song literati redefined the fundamental implications of the *Rituals of Zhou* for their time.[39] As a result, at least five generations of Southern Song scholars wrote close to one hundred commentaries on this rather controversial classic, many of which Ma Duanlin appears to have read.

Ma Duanlin's first concern is the extent to which the well-field system was applied in antiquity. Following the Han classicist Zheng Xuan (127–200), Zhu Xi believed that during the Zhou, the well-field system was enacted only in the Inherited Region in the Royal Domain; in the Districts of the regional states, the population was organized in accordance with the policy of tribute and taxation. But by way of contrast, Ma Duanlin cites Chen Jizhi (ca. twelfth century), one of the less renowned Yongjia statecraft thinkers, who argues that the well-field system would have been implemented everywhere, regardless of the distinction between the Royal Domain and the regional states. Chen argues that the two famous phrases, "ten men have a channel" and "one hundred men have a brook," which for Zhu Xi designates the separate units of local organizations in the regional states, should be regarded as a network of waterways dividing the basic units of rural communities. Therefore, they are not in conflict with the well-field system itself.[40] Chen Jizhi's view is supported by another prominent Yongjia thinker, Chen Fuliang, who deems Zhu Xi's interpretation misleading. In Chen Fuliang's reading, the *Rituals of Zhou* describes the well-field system for the Inherited Region because the area, allotted as fiefs to the royal kin and ministers, had mountains and forests; in contrast, as the Districts outside the Royal Domain were presumably "spacious open fields," the *Rituals of Zhou* remains silent as to the well-field system in those areas.[41]

To settle the disagreement between Zhu Xi and the Yongjia scholars, Ma Duanlin cites Mencius's famous phrase: "in the remoter districts, observe the nine-squares division and reserve one division to be cultivated on the system of mutual aid; in the more central parts of the kingdom, make the people pay for themselves a tenth part of their produce."[42] The system of mutual aid is based on "the policy of giving the land" (*shoutian zhi zhi*), whereas the system of "paying a tenth part of their produce in the kingdom" refers to "the system of taxing the people" (*qumin zhi zhi*). The system of mutual aid, though seemingly more burdensome, only requires the people to till the public field regardless of soil productivity or the quality of the harvest. The system of tribute and taxation, though seemingly less onerous, requires the people to submit one-tenth of their produce, for which the taxpayers might be forced to take a loan. Ma concludes: "Since the system of mutual aid was abolished completely, it soon turned into the system of tribute/taxation. Therefore, the people tilled their private lands and submitted their public rents. Even though the productivity of the land was not fixed, the amount of taxation was, so despite limiting the tax rate to ten percent the people were seriously harmed. What then need be said about rates of taxation above one-tenth!"[43] Ma again takes the opportunity to argue that the well-field system could only work under the classic enfeoffment (*fengjian*) system of antiquity; any attempt at restoring the well-field system in the centralized bureaucratic (*junxian*) administration of later periods was doomed to fail.[44]

THE VICISSITUDES OF LAND TENURE: QIN (221–206 BCE) THROUGH TANG (618–907)

With only a few exceptions, political thinkers and classical scholars regarded the shift away from the well-field system as a historic decline. One exception was Liu Zongyuan (773–819), who in his influential essay "On the Classic Enfeoffment System," conceptualized the rise of empire as an ascent of human society from scattered savage communities to villages, then chiefdoms, tribal states, city-states, regional states, territorial states, and finally one unified and politically and culturally integrated empire.[45] Ma Duanlin does not directly cite Liu Zongyuan, but he finds a parallel formulation in

Liu's contemporary Du You, the Tang grand councilor and author of the *Comprehensive Statutes*.

In the *Comprehensive Statutes*, Du You praised Shang Yang's adoption of the field boundary system: "When serving the Duke of Xiao in Qin, Shang Yang observed that the land of the Three Jin (Han, Wei, and Zhao) was cramped and the people poor, whereas the land of Qin was extensive but the population sparse." Because the land had not been fully opened, the advantages of extensive land had not yet been exploited. "Thereupon, [Shang Yang] enticed the people of the Three Jin with offers of land and houses, returning to the Three Dynasty's innocence of war, and focusing [their attention] on domestic matters. Meanwhile he had the Qin folk respond to the enemies without. He abolished the well-field system, enforced the field-boundary system, and assigned [the populace] land for farming without fixed limits. Within a few years, the state became wealthy and the military strong, no other state its equal."[46]

Next Ma Duanlin quotes Zhu Xi's essay "on implementing the field-boundary system" (*kai qianmo bian*). In it Zhu Xi first cites the "Treatise on Food and Commodities" of the *Han shu,* which states: "the Duke of Xiao in Qin had Shang Yang abolish the well-field system, and implement the field-boundary system."[47] Traditionally, the word *qianmo* was interpreted as "crisscrossing small pathways" between the fields, *qian* as vertical aisles and *mo* as horizontal gangways.[48] Following this view scholars generally thought that under the Qin, Legalists' boundaries were systematically rearranged into a crisscrossing network, giving rise to the notion that "*field-boundary* is the Qin institution and the well-field the ancient institution."[49] Zhu Xi thinks such conventional wisdom misunderstands the ancient realities. In his view, the ancient model of the field-boundary system is actually shown in the organization of the fields in the *Rituals of Zhou*, whose "Artificers' Records" describes the well-field system as a nested hierarchy of precisely defined crisscrossing boundaries: *sui* (the width of two *chi*), *gou* (four *chi*), *xu* (eight *chi*), and *kuai* (two *xun*). "As the Former Kings grieved over losing the fields adjacent to the wet marshes," Zhu Xi reasons, they "corrected the boundaries of the fields, put a stop to land disputes, managed waterworks, and prepared for flood or drought" to get ready for the future.[50]

Zhu Xi makes this point in order to criticize Shang Yang's short-sighted implementation of the field-boundary system, which he believes failed to maximize both man-power and land productivity.[51] But Zhu Xi also condemns Yang Yan's later effort to offset the concentration of landed wealth and attendant shrinkage of state income by introducing the twice-a-year system of taxation. For Zhu Xi, Yang Yan's strategy was a makeshift policy that destroyed the economic basis of self-sufficiency for the people.[52] Based on this reasoning, Zhu Xi argues that to think of "the implementation of the field boundary system" as Shang Yang's invention is historically unfounded; contrarily, as the ancient institution of the Three Dynasties, the field-boundary system should be closely linked with the well-field system itself. Zhu Xi opposes the conventional view that the field-boundary system was purposely invented. Rather, as an ideal model, it legitimizes "the boundary measure." Given the aggravated conditions of the time, determining the boundaries of fields helped both the government and the people. At least in the way in which Ma presents Zhu Xi's view of land tenure in history, Zhu should be viewed as in favor of state intervention on some matters.

The field-boundary system marked the beginning of state recognition of the privatization of land. Critics of the Qin empire remembered it as the beginning of a steady downward spiral. Ma Duanlin takes a more contingent view. To be sure, the abolition of the well-field system in the Qin also destroyed the tithing system in taxation, which led to exorbitant tax rates.[53] The early Han policies of laissez-faire offered a brief moment of respite for the people, but a prolonged period of noninterventionism coupled with very low tax rates exacerbated the polarization of wealth through land-engrossing.[54] In the late fifth century Northern Wei implemented the equal-field system, which the Northern Qi (550–577), Northern Zhou (557–581), Sui (581–618), and Tang continued. Although many conservative radicals praised the equal-field system, Ma Duanlin shows no such idealism; instead he closely observes the break up of the equal-field system in the wake of the An Lushan Rebellion (755–763). As to Yang Yan's twice-a-year tax system, Ma Duanlin states:

> In general, to impose taxes, one should observe the size of landholdings; this is an unchangeable principle, ancient or modern. The payment [*gong*], mutual aid [*zhu*], and share [*che*] systems of the Three Dynasties were imposed based only on land, without imposing a separate household tax. Generally speaking, the Three Dynasties gave land to the people without imposing a separate household tax; the two Han dynasties lowered the rates of taxation without distributing land to the people. In the period from Northern Wei to mid-Tang, the state increased the household tax on the grounds that it granted land, but even when it did not grant land, the taxes could not be reduced, causing the people enormous harm. With the implementation of the twice-a-year system these chronic problems were removed. How could we slight this measure just because it came from Yang Yan?[55]

Ma Duanlin endorses the twice-a-year system based on a pragmatic response to the mid-Tang crisis. In the aftermath of the An Lushan rebellion, "the masses scattered," "the state ledgers became empty documents," and "only unkempt fields remained."[56] Given the conditions of the time, Ma concludes that "although the twice-a-year system was not a far-reaching plan, it was a decent policy for remedying the problems."[57]

Ma Duanlin's positive evaluation of Yang Yan's policy flies in the face of many moralist thinkers whom Ma also quoted in the *Survey*. Hu Yin (1098–1150) eulogizes the standard per household tax system as the best policy since the Northern Wei and laments its demise.[58] Zhu Xi criticizes Yang Yan's abolition of the per household system as but a fleeting effort to avoid the impending crisis, and laments that "the profound and subtle intent of the sages and worthies of high antiquity was thereby curtailed."[59] Ma also cites Lü Zuqian, who judges Yang Yan as being "a sinner against high antiquity."[60] It would be hasty to draw any meaningful conclusions from these three Neo-Confucians' shared elegy for the break up of the early Tang tax system. It seems obvious, though, that Ma Duanlin was fundamentally opposed to the then-prevalent moralist reading of early Tang fiscal history. For Ma a more penetrating understanding was provided by the Yongjia statecraft thinker Ye Shi, who endorsed Yang Yan's measure as a practical solution that acknowledged the irreversibility of land privatization.[61]

CLARIFYING THE BOUNDARIES OF FIELDS

Ma Duanlin's differences with Zhu Xi are further developed in his critique of "the boundary measure" (*jingjie fa*) first enacted in 1142. Mencius famously stated: "Now, the first step towards a benevolent government must be to lay down the boundaries." Because allowing boundaries to be poorly defined abets corrupt taxation, "oppressive rulers and impure ministers are sure to neglect this defining of the boundaries."[62] Invoking Mencius, Southern Song statesmen and literati demanded that the state adopt the appropriate boundary measures for the time. Ma notes that in 1132 the vice director in the Department of Works, Li Zhuo (*js.* 1100; fl. 1130), proposed that the state give vagrants incentives to reclaim land, return deserters to work within two years, remove uncultivable lands from the register, and reduce taxes. Ma dates the Southern Song boundary reforms to this.[63] In 1142, the vice director at the Left Office of the Department of State Affairs, Li Chunnian (*js.* 1118), argued for the necessity of adopting what then became the new boundary measure. Li identified ten problems caused by unclear boundaries: (1) the illegal and untaxed encroachment on others' lands leading to social unrest and lawsuits; (2) obsolete official ledgers causing the unlawful imposition of taxation; (3) yamen clerks siphoning off the state treasury by bribing market intendants; (4) village tax collectors' manipulation of the tax rates; (5) claims made on unregistered properties through the fabrication of titles; (6) widespread public distrust of the cadastral registers; (7) the government's unlawful acquisition of the uninherited properties of fugitives and the deceased; (8) both public and private transactions burdened by obscure taxes; (9) false reporting of their landholdings by cunning people; and (10) exorbitant rates of taxation impeding the people from cultivating abandoned lands.[64] Li predicted substantial benefits from enacting a new boundary measure, including: (1) the transparent division of the public and private sectors; (2) the equitable imposition of taxes without relying on official ledgers; (3) the prevention of false reports by locals; (4) the prevention of manipulation by tax collectors; (5) collection of the due amount based on the actual value of the land; (6) the settling of legal disputes; (7) the deterrence of corrupt behavior; (8) the imposition of a set rate without incurring surcharges; (9) benefits to the destitute; and (10) the utilization of abandoned lands through sales to local buyers.[65]

As Ma Duanlin notes, Zhu Xi endorsed Li Chunnian's plan, which he himself implemented in 1190 when he served as prefect of Zhangzhou (Fujian). After conducting a survey, Zhu confirmed that the boundary measures implemented in the 1140s had benefitted both the public and private sectors, and he urged Emperor Guangzong to allow the policy to be reinstated in Zhangzhou.[66] In this way Zhu Xi joined a line of Southern Song thinkers who invoked Mencius's goal of achieving a just tax system based on precise information about public and private landholdings. Unfortunately, Ma Duanlin chooses not to express his own views on the boundary measure. But because he endorses Shang Yang's and Yang Yan's policies rather than Zhu Xi's moralistic critique of them, it seems obvious that he remains skeptical toward any such later statist attempts to redress the problems of landlordism. Ma's take on this issue will be shown more clearly with his endorsement of Ye Shi's call for the expansion of local autonomy.

THE PRIVATIZATION OF LAND AND SOCIAL INEQUALITY

As we have seen, Ma Duanlin opens his *Survey* by presenting a range of views of the ideal world of antiquity and the post-Qin world of putative historical decline. Up to this point, Ma has associated himself with thinkers like Du

You who favored policies that accepted the irreversibility of the privatization of property as opposed to the moralists like Zhu Xi who favored the state-enforced redistribution of land. This serves as prelude to the main issue for Ma: how to manage the social inequalities arising from the privatization of land.

Ma Duanlin employs the Han Dynasty usurper Wang Mang (c. 45 BCE–23 CE) as critic of the Qin system of land privatization. Having seized the Han throne, Wang Mang issued an edict that indicted the Qin for creating an unbridgeable gap between the rich few (the land engrossers) and the poor masses. Powerful families were able to take advantage of Qin's low tax rates (one thirtieth) on owners and high rents on tenants to acquire more land. The hard-pressed farmers tilled the land of the rich and paid half the harvest as rent. Wang's radical land redistribution system, known as the Royal Field (Wangtian) system, was designed to nationalize all land and to ban land sales. But as Ma notes, it led to total chaos. Ma stresses Wang Mang's case as an abortive attempt to restore the well-field system through the coercive power of the state.[67]

Ma Duanlin also cites the Later Han historian Xun Yue (148–209), who like Wang Mang also reveals the downside of low rates of taxation, but unlike Wang Mang, calls for a restoration of the well-field system as the only solution to social inequality. In Xun's formulation, even with the lowest rate of land taxation (sometimes as little as 1 percent) in the early Han, the rich reaped the benefits at the expense of the poor masses: "The benevolence extended by the state might have been superior to the Three Dynasties, yet the ferocity of the wealthy and powerful was even more severe than during the failed Qin."[68] Xun Yue holds the Han state to blame for failing to protect the populace from the exploitation of land engrossers. In his view, it was precisely during the founding of both the Eastern and Western Han, when the population was small, that it would have been relatively easy to reinstate the well-field system. Since that was not done, the only realistic solution Xun Yue could propose was to put a ceiling on land ownership, a similar plan to the one proposed by Dong Zhongshu (179–104).[69]

Ma Duanlin deploys Xun Yue as a bridge to the pragmatic Northern Song statecraft thinker Su Xun (1009–1066). In the passages Ma excerpts, Su Xun argues that the economic gap between rich and poor intensified with the abolition of the well-field system. In graphic language, he indicts the unequal realities in which "one man with land has ten tillers. Whereas the landlord hoards up to the half of [the land's output] and becomes rich, the tillers share the other half among themselves to become destitute and hungry without anyone to rely on."[70] Moreover, because the landlords only pay taxes on the grain paid to them as rent, their rate of effective taxation is even lower than the one-tenth rule of the Zhou dynasty. Therefore, Su Xun reasons, the actual Northern Song tax rate was lower than one-twentieth of the yield. Su Xun saw no easy solution to the structural gap between rich and poor caused by abolition of the well-field system. Reinstating the well-field system itself was doomed to failure, because the state-enforced confiscation of all land would constitute an all-out class war against the wealthy, a radical idea Su Xun opposed. Nor could the state force wealthy families to donate their lands to form a pool of public property. Noting that the well-field system as described in the *Zhouli* presupposes a grid of concentric squares divided by a network of waterways, Su Xun concludes that any attempt to restore the well-field system along classical lines would be undone by changes in the geographic terrain over the vast span of time.[71] But he does identify a way to achieve the same effect in his day, by imposing limits on the amounts of land individuals could own. This, he argues, would be the only way to enjoy the benefits of the ancient well-field system without enforcing it in practice.[72]

HISTORICAL CHANGE AND SEARCH FOR A NEW ORDER: YE SHI'S ARGUMENT

As prelude to his own conclusions, Ma Duanlin turns to the Yongjia statecraft thinker Ye Shi's views of historical change and social justice. Ye was probably the most systematic Southern Song critic of the New Policies. By reflecting on the work of government in a new light, he proposed ways in which the state could retrench its administrative structures and become stronger and wealthier.[73] Ye forcefully argues that in a post-Qin world the foundation of government has already changed: with the growth of a private commercial economy, the state can no longer control society to redress economic inequalities; the elite, as the pillars of society, should be given more leeway.

> For a long time now the people of all-under-heaven have been unequal. The powers of "opening and closing [of the market], collecting and distributing [goods], and deciding prices" no longer emanate unitarily from the king. Rich people and big merchants share those powers. We do not know for how many thousand years long it has been so. If we took [those powers] from them all of a sudden, would it work? Would it be right to hate the private interests of those people and try to turn them into

national interests? Alas! If the Duke of Zhou were here today, he would not have used such laws.[74]

In a changed post-Qin world, Ye Shi argues, the emergence of a large private sector in society and the economy has nullified the traditional conceptions of the king as an all-caring patriarch. As a result of privatization, the organic integration of the people with the government based on land redistribution and corvée labor collapsed. In this context, any attempt at restoring land redistribution, that is, the well-field system of antiquity, should be considered an unrealistic and irresponsible anachronism. Instead of competing with merchants and large landowners, the government should rely on them as they have become active partners of governance in the multiple centers of all-under-heaven. In short, Ye endorses the rise of commerce and a burgeoning private economy as the positive engine of economic growth.

Then what is Ye Shi's solution to the land problems of the day? Ye Shi denies two extreme answers widely adopted by "vulgar officials" (shuli) and "Confucians" (ruzhe). Vulgar officials simply suppress land engrossing by force in order to support the weak and the poor. Despite the well-meaning intention of vulgar officials, suppression is not a reliable strategy for the emperor. In the elite-dominated socioeconomic realities of the day, he cautions, suppression of the large landowners would result in an unmanageable wave of lawsuits. Besides, magistrates no longer possessed the powers of "nurturing the people," which had long since been assumed by the wealthy. Furthermore, landless people rent land from the wealthy; those who have land but no money to buy seedlings borrow money from the wealthy; those who are in dire straits turn to the wealthy; tenants belong to the wealthy; traveling actors and acrobats sponge on the wealthy; even the subofficials who could not meet their quotas turn to the wealthy. Having recognized the practical powers of the wealthy in society, Ye Shi matter-of-factly concedes:

> Then the wealthy are the base of prefectures and counties, upon whom both the high and the low depend. The wealthy nurture the commoners for the Son of Heaven, and send tribute for the emperor's use. Although they might take an ample amount of profit and increase their interest, if we consider their diligence and effort, it could be considered roughly what they deserve. Only those who are extremely violent and who exploit ceaselessly should be guided and exhorted by the officials. If it is impossible to guide and exhort them, officials should address [the problems] on a

case by case basis, and have them change [their disruptive behavior] by themselves; then [those disruptions should] cease. Officials should not preemptively harbor grievances toward [the wealthy] or seek fame by wielding authority. Since the sovereign cannot nurture the commoners by himself, it is not a good policy for officials to take it upon themselves to destroy the wealthy and foment mutual hatred between landlords and tenants as well as general unease.[75]

In short, Ye Shi proposes that the emperor ally with the wealthy, who as the backbone of the state "nurture" poor peasants on behalf of the emperor. Ma Duanlin also cites Ye's conclusion:

> Therefore, your minister considers that the Confucians' theory of restoring the well-field system can be discarded, and the crude officials' will to suppress the land-engrossing wealthy can also be dropped. If we extend wisdom grounded on our own time, observe the world [as the basis for] establishing laws, and sincerely allow institutions to be decided by Your Highness, within ten years there will be neither extremely rich nor extremely poor people. Land engrossing will disappear on its own accord without suppression. To have all-under-heaven immediately gain the benefit of life is what the Son of Heaven should do in consultation with numerous ministers. Otherwise, not only will the ancient well-field system not work but [appropriate] institutions for the present will not be established. Only empty talk will pervade as the high will deceive and the low disobey. Crude officials will regard baseness as real and Confucians will regard loftiness as honor. [In that case], on what basis could all-under-heaven be governed![76]

In Ye Shi's view, as the ancient visions of good government could no longer work, the emperor should base himself on the existing order of society. Instead of disrupting entrenched socioeconomic realities, the government should try to alleviate the tax burdens of the wealthy. Unlike Northern Song conservatives, Ye defends the wealthy. The new definition of the wealthy as the engine of economic growth fits well into his overall constitutional vision of reforming the Southern Song state: to relieve fiscal pressure, he calls for decreasing the size of the military, which according to his calculation, occupied more than 80 percent of the overall state income. Ma Duanlin found this political vision of Ye Shi's particularly persuasive.

MA DUANLIN'S VIEWS OF LAND TAXES AND SOCIAL JUSTICE

Ma Duanlin's historical survey leads him to his own conclusions about the relationship between land taxes and social justice:

> Ever since the Qin abolished the well-field system, the gentlemen of later generations all lamented that their rulers could not benefit the population by restoring the institutions of the Three Dynasties, but instead allowed the wealthy and powerful to seize the advantage through land engrossing. Their arguments are indeed correct. When it comes to reflecting on [the institutions of] antiquity and the present and investigating their benefits and harms, Su Xun's and Ye Shi's arguments are the most correct ones. I would like to argue yet further by adding to Ye Shi's theory: "It is not easy to speak of the well-field system."[77]

As Ma Duanlin understands it, the Zhou could enforce the well-field system because of their precise survey of geography and terrain, population, and even farmers' behavior patterns and work habits. "Only when the ruler is fully informed of all aspects of village life can the redistribution of land be implemented without causing trouble."[78] But because Ma deems this an unattainable goal for the present, he adopts Ye Shi's argument that the institutions of antiquity cannot be restored:

> In general, when the emperors and kings of antiquity divided the land and governed, without there were dukes, marquis, counts, earls and barons, while within there were the three ministers and grand masters. The land they governed was confined to an area of no more than one hundred *li* square; they ruled their fiefs on a hereditary basis and treated the people as their children. Thereupon, they organized the fields they received in a crisscross manner, [so that] the boundaries of the fields were correct and the grain salaries they received were stable. Greedy persons and powerful people could not exert all their strength to violate laws and institutions, nor could corrupt officials and sly clerks play tricks with the documents to create havoc with the records.[79]

Like Ye Shi, Ma Duanlin praises the great achievements of the ancient sage rulers. But he analyses the principles of government that held together the systems holistically: the well-field system presupposed the systematic division of government into a collection of self-governing community-like states whose rulers collected precise data on the geography, demographics, local customs, and culture of their jurisdictions. And this gets us to the main objective of Ma's historical survey: his goal is not to reinstate the institutions of antiquity but to oppose adventurist attempts to bring them back. In this regard, both Ye Shi and Ma Duanlin were conservative realists. His conditional endorsement of the Qin field boundary institution reflects this view:

> In Qin times, the Qin rulers put an end to the well-field system, assigned the people to the land they tilled, and taxed them in accordance with the amount of land they occupied. Cai Ze [of the state of Yan] said: "The lord of Shang broke apart the well-field and destroyed the field boundaries, and thereby stabilized the people's livelihoods and unified their intentions." That he said the words "stabilize" and "unify" suggests that the land redistribution system of the Zhou must have become disorderly and inequitable by Qin times. (Zhu Xi's *Dialogues* says: from Cai Ze's saying we can see that the Zhou institutions had become dysfunctional by Qin times).[80]

By the Han through Tang period, according to Ma, it had become impossible to restore the institutions of the Three Dynasties. This was especially true with respect to the equal-field system, which some recent thinkers including Zhu Xi enthusiastically praised. He notes that in the fourteen hundred years from the Qin to the present, a land distribution system had only been enacted for a mere two hundred years from the Northern Wei through the early Tang. How then had a land-redistribution system endured over the one thousand years of the Three Dynasties? Ma's answer repeats the argument he proclaims in his "Preface": "In general, the enfeoffment system was why it was possible to maintain the well-field system. . . . Restoring the enfeoffment system would encounter resistance over the dividing up of territory, while reinstating the well-field system would fan grievances over the forcible confiscation of people's land. To restore the enfeoffment system would cause conflict from the very process of dividing the land. To restore the well-field system would raise grievances as it should involve confiscating the people's fields. This is why those bookish arguments [in favor of restoring the well-fields] would be impossible to put into practice."[81]

Among the thinkers cited in the first seven chapters of the *Survey*, Ye Shi seems to have exerted the most direct influence on Ma Duanlin. Taking Ye's view a step further, Ma constructs a principled defense of Yang Yan's twice-a-year system. By endorsing Yang Yan's plan as a reasonable way to meet the mid-Tang crisis, Ye and Ma accept the positive aspects of private landhold-ings. Despite the rising gap between rich and poor, Ye and Ma emphasize the productive roles of the wealthy in rural socioeconomic realities.

CONCLUSION

Ma Duanlin's contemporary Liu Yin (1249–1293), an icon of Confucian eremitism in the Yuan period, devoted his life under Mongol rule to Daoist self-cultivation through the practice of such traditional cultural activities as painting, poetry, and calligraphy.[82] Unlike Liu Yin, Ma Duanlin dedicated his eremitism to the completion of an encyclopedic book with a strong political agenda. Was he, like Huang Zongxi (1610–1695), "waiting for the dawn" with his plans for the prince?

The contents of the *Survey* show that his intention was not simply to draw from literary remains to document the past. Rather, through an in-depth study of the existing sources on government, he formulated his own constitutional agenda. Throughout the *Survey*, he seeks to place the evolving social, economic, and political institutions of the imperial state in their own historical context. His intention was to lay out the central elements of the positions of influential thinkers on major issues of statecraft. He included conflicting voices from earlier periods, but his main interest seems to have been to represent the voices of the Southern Song statecraft thinkers. On the issue of land taxes, we have seen that Ma introduces the writings of such significant thinkers such as Lin Zhiqi, Hu Yin, Zhu Xi, Lü Zuqian, Chen Fuliang, Ye Shi, and many others of lesser renown. After letting these figures speak, Ma Duanlin draws a series of conclusions on various smaller topics related to land tenure.

Although the seven chapters of the *Survey* on "Land Taxes," discussed here are but a part of Ma Duanlin's constitutional agenda, we can draw some meaningful conclusions from a close reading of them. As regards the issue of land taxes, Ma makes some important political claims for his own time. In order to deny the restorability of a land-redistribution system, for example, he musters relevant sources to critique the myths of antiquity that permeated the intellectual culture of the day.

With respect to the institutions of Qin and post-Qin empires, Ma Duanlin takes a provocative, yet balanced, position, by casting both Shang Yang's abolition of the well-field system and Yang Yan's abolition of the equal-field system in a positive light. He recognizes as historical reality the irreversible tendency toward the privatization of landholdings. From this perspective,

Ma Duanlin endorses the retreat of the state from the economic realities of the time. Further, he invokes Ye Shi's powerful argument that the wealthy are productive mediators between the state and the populace.

Because of the enormous standing of Zhu Xi in post-Southern Song intellectual history, we tend to dismiss the influence of statecraft thinkers on the making of social and political institutions in later imperial China. As we have seen, the Neo-Confucians like Zhu Xi and Lü Zuqian were to some extent contradictory: devoted as they were to moral self-cultivation, they generally viewed the morally autonomous local elite as the self-motivated agents of good government.[83] For the past two decades, modern scholars have held up Zhu Xi and other Neo-Confucians' social and political agendas as epitomizing Southern Song elite activism. But Southern Song Neo-Confucians still idealized the equal-field system of the early Tang Empire and condemned Yang Yan's introduction of the twice-a-year tax system. Ma Duanlin seems to consider their positions inconsistent at best.

A Marxist historian like Qi Xia might detect in Ma's position the expression of the landlords' class biases. Shigeta Atsushi might find in Ma's views the precursor to what he calls "gentry rule," the symbiotic partnership between the state and gentry-landlords, in which "the state protected the rights of landlords to collect rent from their tenants."[84] From a world historical perspective, historians who regard the private ownership of land as a sign of progress might point to Ma's explicit defense of the wealthy as an expression of early modernity.[85]

My own interest in Ma Duanlin stems from a larger intellectual historical question regarding the relationship in history between ideas and political order. I look on Ma Duanlin's *Survey* as a history of political thought on social, economic, political, and military institutions. Ma highlights the tensions between Zhu Xi and the Yongjia statecraft thinkers. By putting their views of government on an equal footing, Ma reconstructs a history of Southern Song political and institutional thought that not only decenters Zhu Xi's views but in fact favors the Yongjia thinkers. Scornful of the moral teachers who would pass all-too-hasty judgments on historical experience, Ma Duanlin sometimes promotes his political claims in a provocative manner. Building on Ye Shi's argument, he envisions a social order in which the landed gentry represent themselves as the mainstay of good government. In this sense, Ma Duanlin explicitly calls for the economic freedom of the independent, propertied social elite. Ma's *Survey* reveals a vivid stream of intellectual undercurrents that converged to form the brimming river of statecraft traditions in Ming and Qing times.

NOTES

1   His teacher was Cao Jing (1234–1315), from Xiuning, Anhui.

2   Chan, "Ma Tuan-lin's Historical Thought," 35.

3   Ma Duanlin, *WXTK*, "Zixu," 3. *Wenxian* is taken from Confucius's comment in the *Analects* 3.9: Zhu Xi glosses *xian* as "worthies" (*Sishu zhanggou jizhu*, 74). For a specific analysis see Chan, "Ma Tuan-lin's Historical Thought," 48.

4   On the *Tongdian*, see Pulleyblank, "Neo-Confucianism and Neo-Legalism," 97–106, and McMullen, *State and Scholars in T'ang China*, 203–5. On the *Tongzhi*, see Lee, "History, Erudition, and Good Government."

5   Pulleyblank, "Neo-Confucianism and Neo-Legalism," 100.

6   Chan, "Ma Tuan-lin's Historical Thought," 46–47.

7   Endymion Wilkinson surveys all ten of the comprehensive encyclopedia, or *Shitong*, in *Chinese History*, 646–48.

8   For an introduction to the rivalry between the Yongjia school and the Learning of the Way (Daoxue) school in the Southern Song period, see de Weerdt, *Competition over Content*, especially chap. 1.

9   Liu, "How Did a Neo-Confucian School Become the State Orthodoxy?" 502–3.

10 Wang Yuzhi's *Corrected Meanings of the Rituals of Zhou* (Zhouli dingyi), compiled during the 1230s, was a typical case. This book with Zhen Dexiu's preface was submitted for the emperor's view in 1243 (Jaeyoon Song, "Afterward" in *Traces of Grand Peace*). The *Detailed Study of Institutions throughout All Ages*, attributed to Lü Zuqian (1137–1181), contains an early Yuan (1326) preface which makes an explicit argument that Lü Zuqian meant to harmonize Zhu Xi and the Yongjia statecraft thinkers through a study of institutions (*Lidai zhidu xiangshuo*, 1–2).

11 For the over-rigid land tenure system of the early Tang and its breakdown, see D. C. Twitchett, *Financial Administration under the T'ang Dynasty*, chap. 1.

12 Miyazaki, *Chūgokushi* vol.1, chap. 5; Sudō, *Chūgoku tochi seido shi kenkyū*, chap. 1; Elvin, *The Pattern of the Chinese Past*. For an introduction to social and economic changes since the mid-Tang, see Twitchett, "Introduction," 22–31.

13 Twitchett, *Financial Administration under the T'ang Dynasty*, chaps. 1–3; Pulleyblank, *The Background of the Rebellion of An Lu-shan*, chap. 2; for a classic Japanese study of the Tang land tenure system and its collapse, see Hori Toshikazu, *Kindenseino kenkyū*, chaps. 4 and 6; for a more recent Chinese work, see Yang Jiping, *Beichao Sui Tang juntianzhi xintan*, esp. chaps. 3 and 4.

14 For the development of estates in the late Tang onward, see Sudō, *Chūgoku tochi seido shi kenkyū*, chaps. 2–3, and Zhao Gang and Chen Zhongyi, *Zhongguo tudi zhidushi*, chap. 6; for the rise of estates in the mid-Tang, see the *Cambridge History of China*, vol. 3:26–27.

15 Qi Xia, *Zhongguo jingji tongshi*, 263–64, 290–94.

16 Golas, "Rural China in the Song," 300–301.

17 See the chapters by Smith and Li in this volume.

18 For the descriptions of general Southern Song opposition to state activism and elite voluntarism, see von Glahn, "Community and Welfare," Hymes, "Moral Duty and Self-Regulating Process," and "Introduction," in Hymes and Schirokauer, *Ordering the World*. For literati voluntarism and community-building from Southern Song to Ming, see Bol, *Neo-Confucianism in History*, chap. 7.

19 *WXTK*, "Zixu," 3–4.

20 *WXTK*, "Zixu," 3–4.

21 *WXTK*, "Zixu," 3–4.

22 *WXTK* 1.1; *Shangshu zhengyi* 6.132–71.

23 *WXTK* 1.1.

24 The editors of the *Song History* included Lin Zhiqi in the "Confucian Grove" (Rulin) section of the biographies (SS 433.12861).

25 *WXTK* 1.1–2. This passage is derived from Lin Zhiqi's *Comprehensive Interpretation of the Book of Documents* (Shangshu quanjie; extant in full), one of the most influential books of Southern Song classical learning.

26 Smith, "Shen-tsung's Reign," 393; Higashi Ichio, *Ō Anseki Shinpō no Kenkyū*, 815–28.

27 *WXTK* 4.100–02.

28 *WXTK* 5.119.

29 Zhu Yizun, in his *Jingyikao, juan* 72–85, lists more than two hundred titles of Song commentaries on the *Book of Documents*.

30 *WXTK* 3.63.

31 Legge, *The Works of Mencius*, book 3, part 1.6.

32 *WXTK* 1.2.

33 "The Districts" here refer to the state-controlled local organizations outside of the Royal Domain (one thousand *li* square) under the king's direct rule in the *Rituals of Zhou*.

34 "The Inherited Region" here refers to the area allotted as fiefs to the royal kin and ministers within the Royal Domain.

35 *WXTK* 1.2–3.

36 Most Western scholars hold that the well-field system was but a utopian ideal reimagined by political thinkers like Mencius: von Faulkenhausen, *Chinese Society in the Age of Confucius*. In contrast, a group of PRC scholars have made a case for its existence in ancient China, using scattered evidence to argue that something akin to the well-field system as the communal ownership of land could have existed in Chinese antiquity. See Xu Yizhen, *Jingtian zhidu yanjiu*; Jin Jingfang, *Lun jingtian zhidu*; and Zhao Gang and Chen Zhongyi, *Zhongguo tudi zhidu shi*.

37 *WXTK* 3.59.

38 Bol, "Wang Anshi and the *Zhouli*."

39 Song, "Tension and Balance."

40 *WXTK* 1.4–5.

41 *WXTK* 1.4–5.

42 *Sishu zhangju jizhu*, 5.298. Legge's translation, *The Works of Mencius*, 3.3.15.

43 *WXTK* 1.7.

44 *WXTK*, "Zixu," 4.

45 Song, "Redefining Good Government," 301–5.

46 *WXTK* 1.13.

47 *Hanshu* 24 *shang*.1126.

48 *WXTK* footnote 1: Yan Shigu's definition.

49 *WXTK* 1.13–14.

50 *WXTK* 1.14.

51 *WXTK* 1.14.

52 *WXTK* 1.14.

53 *WXTK* 3.64.

54 *WXTK* 3.64.

55 *WXTK* 3.64.

56 *WXTK* 3.65.

57 *WXTK* 3.65.

58 *WXTK* 2.46.

59 *WXTK* 1.14.

60 *WXTK* 3.64.

61 *WXTK* 2.49.

62 *Sishu zhangju jizhu*, 5.292. Legge's translation, *The Works of Mencius*, 3.3.14.

63 *WXTK* 5.117–18.

64 *WXTK* 5.118.

65 For a detailed study see Wang Deyi, "Li Chunnian yu Nansong tudi jingjie."

66 *Zhu Xi ji* 21.16.873–874; *WXTK* 5.126–27; Wang Deyi, "Li Chunnian," 468.

67 *WXTK* 1.21.

68 *WXTK* 1.22. For Xun Yue's life and thought, see Chen, *Hsün Yüeh (A.D. 148–209)*.

69 *WXTK* 1.22.

70 *WXTK* 1.22.

71 *WXTK* 1.22–23.

72 *WXTK* 1.22–24; Hatch, "Su Hsun's Pragmatic Statecraft," 70–71.

73 For an introduction to Ye Shi's political career and thought, see Lo, *The Life and Thought of Yeh Shih*; For a close analysis of Ye Shi's political thought, see Bol, "Reconceptualizing the Nation in Southern Song," 33–64; and Song, "Critical Confucianism."

74 *Ye Shi ji* 659; *WXTK* 20.566.

75 *WXTK* 1.25.

76 *WXTK* 1.26.

77 *WXTK* 1.26.

78 *WXTK* 1.26.

79 *WXTK* 1.26.

80 *WXTK* 1.27.

81 *WXTK* 1.28.

82 Tu Wei-ming, "Towards an Understanding of Liu Yin's Confucian Eremitism," 233–77.

83 Bol, *Neo-Confucianism in History*, chap. 7.

84 Kamachi, "Feudalism or Absolute Monarchism," 340–43.

85 For a description of the implications of the Korean debate on the private ownership of land, see Palais, "Land Tenure in Korea," 73–74.

REFERENCES

PRIMARY SOURCES

Hanshu 漢書, by Ban Gu 班固 (32–92). Beijing: Zhonghua shuju, 1964.

Jingyikao 經義考, compiled by Zhu Yizun 朱彝尊 (1629–1709). Beijing: Zhonghua shuju, 1998.

Liji jijie 禮記集解, by Sun Xidan 孫希旦 (1736–1784). Beijing: Zhonghua shuju, 1989.

Lidai zhidu xiangshuo 歷代制度詳說, by Lü Zuqian 呂祖謙 (1137–1181). SKQS ed. Taibei: Shangwu, 1983–86.

Song shi 宋史, by Tuo Tuo 脫脫 (1313–1355) et al. Beijing: Zhonghua shuju, 1977.

Shangshu quanjie 尚書全解, by Lin Zhiqi 林之奇 (1112–1176). SKQS ed. Taibei: Shangwu, 1983–1986.

Shangshu zhengyi 尚書正義, by Kong Yingda 孔穎達 (574–648) et al. Beijing: Beijing daxue chubanshe, 1999.

Sishu zhanggou jizhu 四書章句集註, by Zhu Xi 朱熹 (1130–1200). Shanghai guji chubanshe, 2001.

Wenxian tongkao 文獻通考, by Ma Duanlin 馬端臨 (ca. 1254–1323). Beijing: Zhonghua shuju, 2011.

Ye Shi ji 葉適集, by Ye Shi 葉適 (1150–1223). Zhonghua shuju, 1961.

Zhouli dingyi 周禮訂義, by Wang Yuzhi 王與之 (ca. 13th century). SKQS ed. Taibei: Shangwu, 1983–86.

PRIMARY SOURCES IN TRANSLATION

Li Ki, translated by James Legge. Oxford: Clarendon, 1885.

The Works of Mencius, translated by James Legge. New York: Dover Publications, 1970.

SECONDARY SOURCES

Bol, Peter K. *Neo-Confucianism in History*. Cambridge, Mass.: Harvard University Asia Center, 2008.

———. "Reconceptualizing the Nation in Southern Song: Some Implications of Ye Shi's Statecraft Learning." In *Thought, Political Power, and Social Forces*, edited by Ko-wu Huang, 33–64. Taibei: Institute of Modern History, Academia Sinica, 2002.

———. "Wang Anshi and the *Zhouli*." In *Statecraft and Classical Learning: The Rituals of Zhou in East Asian History*, edited by Benjamin Elman and Martin Kern, 229–251. Leiden: Brill, 2010.

Chan, Hok-lam. "Ma Tuan-lin's Historical Thought." In *Yüan Thought: Chinese Thought and Religion under the Mongols*, edited by Hok-lam Chan and Wm. Theodore de Bary, 27–87. New York: Columbia University Press, 1982.

Chen, Chi-yun. *Hsün Yüeh (A.D. 148–209): The Life and Reflections of an Early Medieval Confucian*. Cambridge, UK: Cambridge University Press, 1975.

De Weert, Hilde. *Competition over Content: Negotiating Standards for the Civil Service Examinations in Imperial China (1127–1279)*. Cambridge, Mass.: Harvard University Asia Center, 2007.

Elvin, Mark. *The Pattern of the Chinese Past*. Stanford: Stanford University Press, 1973.

Golas, Peter J. "Rural China in the Song." *Journal of Asian Studies* 39, no. 2 (1980): 291–325.

Hatch, George. "Su Hsun's Pragmatic Statecraft." In *Ordering the World: Approaches to State and Society in Sung Dynasty China*, edited by Robert Hymes and Conrad Schirokauer, 59–75. Berkeley: University of California Press, 1993.

Higashi Ichio 東一夫. *Ō Anseki Shinpō no Kenkyū* 王安石新法の研究. Tōkyō: Kazama Shobō, 1970.

Hori, Toshikazu 堀敏一. *Kindensei no Kenkyū: Chūgoku kodai kokka no tochi seisaku to tochi shoyūsei* 均田制の研究: 中国古代国家の土地政策と土地所有制. Tōkyō: Iwanami Shoten, 1975.

Hymes, Robert. "Moral Duty and Self-Regulating Process in Southern Song Views of Famine Relief." In *Ordering the World: Approaches to State and Society in Sung Dynasty China*, edited by Robert Hymes and Conrad Schirokauer, 280–309. Berkeley: University of California Press, 1993.

Hymes, Robert, and Conrad Schirokauer, eds. *Ordering the World: Approaches to State and Society in Sung Dynasty China*. Berkeley: University of California Press, 1993.

Jin Jingfang 金景芳. *Lun jingtian zhidu* 論井田制度. Jinan: Qi Lu shushe, 1982.

Kamachi, Noriko. "Feudalism or Absolute Monarchism? Japanese Discourse on the Nature of State and Society." *Modern China* 16, no. 3 (1990): 330–70.

Lee, Thomas H. C. "History, Erudition, and Good Government: Cheng Ch'iao and Encyclopedic Historical Thinking." In *The New and the Multiple: Sung Senses of the Past*, edited by Thomas H. C. Lee, 163–200. Hong Kong: Chinese University Press, 2004.

Liu, James T. C. "How Did a Neo-Confucian School Become the State Orthodoxy?" *Philosophy East and West*, 23, no. 4 (1973): 483–505.

Lo, Winston. *The Life and Thought of Yeh Shih*. Gainesville: University Presses of Florida, 1974.

McMullen, David L. *State and Scholars in T'ang China*. Cambridge, UK: Cambridge University Press, 1988.

Miyazaki Ichisada 宮崎市定. *Chūgokushi* 中国史. Tōkyō: Iwanami Shoten, 1977.

Palais, James B. "Land Tenure in Korea: Tenth to Twelfth Centuries." *Journal of Korean Studies* l, no. 4 (1982–83): 3–72.

Pulleyblank, Edwin. *The Background of the Rebellion of An Lu-shan*. Westport, Conn.: Greenwood Press, 1982.

———. "Neo-Confucianism and Neo-Legalism in T'ang Intellectual Life, 755–805." In *The Confucian Persuasion*, edited by Arthur F. Wright, 77–140. Stanford: Stanford University Press, 1960.

Qi Xia 漆俠. *Zhongguo jingji tongshi: Songdai Jingji juan* 中國經濟通史: 宋代經濟卷. Beijing: Jingji ribao chubanshe, 1999.

Smith, Paul. "Shen-tsung's Reign and the New Policies of Wang An-shih, 1067–1085." In *The Cambridge History of China*, vol. 5, part 1, edited by Denis Twitchett and Paul Smith, 347–483. Cambridge, UK: Cambridge University Press, 2009.

Song, Jaeyoon. "Critical Confucianism: Ye Shi's Constitutional Vision." *Journal of Confucian Philosophy and Culture* 22 (2014): 27–47.

———. "Redefining Good Government: Shift Paradigms in Song Dynasty (960–1279) Discourse on *Fengjian*." *T'oung Pao* 97 (2011): 301–43.

———. "Tension and Balance: Changes of Constitutional Schemes in Southern Song Commentaries on the Rituals of Zhou." In *Statecraft and Classical Learning: The Rituals of Zhou in East Asian History*, edited by Benjamin Elman and Martin Kern, 252–76. Leiden, Boston: Brill, 2010.

———. *Traces of Grand Peace: Classics and State Activism in Imperial China*. Cambridge., Mass.: Harvard University Asia Center, 2015.

Sudō Yoshiyuki 周藤吉之. *Chūgoku tochi seido shi kenkyū* 中国土地制度史研究. Tōkyō: Tōkyō Daigaku Shuppankai, 1954.

Tu Wei-ming. "Towards an Understanding of Liu Yin's Confucian Eremitism." In *Yüan Thought: Chinese Thought and Religion under the Mongols*, edited by Hok-lam Chan and Wm. Theodore de Bary, 233–77. New York: Columbia University Press, 1982.

Twitchett, Denis C. *Financial Administration under the T'ang Dynasty*. Cambridge, UK: Cambridge University Press, 1970.

———. "Introduction." In *The Cambridge History of China*. Vol. 3, Part 1: *Sui and T'ang China, 589–906*, edited by Denis C. Twitchett and John K. Fairbank, 1–47. Cambridge, UK: Cambridge University Press, 1979.

Von Faulkenhausen, Lothar. *Chinese Society in the Age of Confucius (1000–250 BC): The Archaeological Evidence*. Los Angeles: Cotsen Institute of Archaeology, UCLA, 2006.

Von Glahn, Richard. "Community and Welfare: Chu Hsi's Community Granary in Theory and Practice." In *Ordering the World: Approaches to State and Society in Sung Dynasty China*, edited by Robert Hymes and Conrad Schirokauer, 221–54. Berkeley: University of California Press, 1993.

Wang Deyi 王德毅. "Li Chunnian yu Nansong tudi jingjie" 李椿年與南宋土地經界. *Songshi yanjiu ji* 宋史研究集 7, 441–80.

Wilkinson, Endymion. *Chinese History: A New Manual*. Cambridge, Mass: Harvard University Asia Center, 2012.

Xu Yizhen 徐喜辰. *Jingtian zhidu yanjiu* 井田制度研究. Changchun: Jilin renmin chubanshe, 1984.

Yang Jiping 楊際平. *Beichao Sui Tang juntianzhi xintan* 北朝隋唐均田制新探. Changsha: Yuelu shu she, 2003.

Zhao Gang 趙岡 and Chen Zhongyi 陳钟毅. *Zhongguo tudi zhidu shi* 中國土地制度史. Taibei: Lianjing chubanshiye gongsi, 1982.

PART 4

State Power in Practice

8 Soldier Mutinies and Resistance during the Northern Song

ELAD ALYAGON

IN THE GOVERNMENT YARD OF LINHAI, AN ARCHER IN THE LOCAL militia was shouting drunkenly. District Defender Shu Dan (1042–1104) flogged the drunken soldier with a bamboo rod, yet the soldier did not submit. The heavy cane was brought out and the flogging recommenced. With a voice growing sterner and sterner the soldier stated he was willing to have his back flogged as well. Shu Dan shouted at the clerks, ordering them to flog the man's back. The soldier cried out again with a loud voice, "You dare not behead me!" Shu Dan lifted his blade and beheaded the soldier. This impromptu execution impressed Shu Dan's superiors who recommended him when the court called for new talent. Even the great minister Wang Anshi (1021–1086) was delighted with this official who was stern in appearance, of broad learning, and eloquent in speech. Shu Dan was promoted.[1]

This anecdote paints the picture of a man who functioned in two separate kingdoms. One is the kingdom of elite men. In that kingdom Shu Dan was a learned and eloquent individual. The other kingdom was that of the military camp where violence reigned supreme; instead of eloquence there were shouts and curses. Learned though he was, Shu Dan educated the soldier with the bamboo rod, the heavy cane, and, finally, the blade.

The army is one of the most prominent manifestations of state power, both as a reflection of the state's strength, as well as an organization that regulates almost every aspect of soldiers' lives. Yet the Song penal-military complex was also a space where the authority of officials was met with defiance by members of the Song's biggest underclass, its soldiers. This chapter studies the limits of state power and the points where those who dwelled in the social and spatial margins of the state resisted it. Modes of resistance carried out by Song soldiers included resistance to conscription, desertion, insubordination, and mutiny.

THE SONG MILITARY

The Northern Song penal-military complex was a huge and elaborate organization that had many functions: it was a military force, an organization for extraction of labor, a correctional institution for convicts, and a space for the poor and the homeless. The men in it numbered in the hundreds of thousands, peaking at 1.4 million soldiers.[2] At the top were the imperial armies (*jinjun*), the elite fighting forces of the Northern Song state. Below them were the prefectural armies (*xiangjun*). The prefectural soldiers provided various labor duties for the state but also participated in warfare and law enforcement when necessary. The imperial and prefectural troops were paid professional soldiers. Many of them spent a lifetime in the army, followed in many cases by their sons. There were also other paths for entry into the regular armies: volunteering, the assignment of refugees and convicts to military service, conscription of non-Han groups, and press gangs.

The third main tier of the Song military was the local militias (*xiangjun*). The local militia soldiers were in charge of local defense and providing logistical support for the regular army; they could be transferred to the regular armies when need arose.[3] Most of the local militias were concentrated in the north and northwestern border circuits to aid in the defense against the Northern Song's two great enemies, the Kitan Liao dynasty (916–1125) to the north and the Tangut Xia dynasty (1038–1227) to the west. Conscription to the local militias was based on the number of adult males in each household, and militia soldiers numbered in the hundreds of thousands at the very least.

Under Song law convicts were assigned to military service, usually to the prefectural armies where they did hard labor. According to need, convicts could also be assigned to the imperial armies. In some cases, convicts were promoted from the prefectural armies to the imperial armies.

One of the unique aspects of the Song military was the practice of tattooing soldiers on the face or arms. A Northern Song military tattoo was usually composed of characters denoting the name and number of the soldier's unit. When a soldier was transferred, the transfer was registered on his skin. Convicts and deserters were marked with special tattoos. Tattooing was one of the most feared and hated aspects of military service.

The pouring of resources and men into the border areas created a highly militarized border zone, with great numbers of regular troops (imperial and prefectural) and local militias. Many of the events that are related here took part in the northern and western border zones, but at certain points the story moves to other parts of the empire. Prefectural soldiers, for example, were also stationed in great numbers elsewhere, where they were put to hard labor.

The use of the term resistance needs little explanation when describing soldier mutinies, that is, organized armed actions that have relatively clear goals. Still, resistance carries a broader meaning here, similar to the way James C. Scott uses the term. These were the acts of everyday violence where peasants attempted to avoid direct conflict with the state and its agents. Such actions stemmed from the peasants' own world of values and traditions.[4] Peasants and soldiers in the Song resisted in similar ways.

The numbers and circumstances of troops varied over time. The burden of service in the local militias was especially heavy along the border with the Xia during great military campaigns. Life grew tougher for soldiers in the final years of the Northern Song as the military system fell into a state of disrepair. Still, some broad generalizations can be made. While there were many kinds of units and troops, soldiers were regarded as a distinct social group that occupied a very low place in the social hierarchy. Their life was extremely tough; they were treated badly; they resisted. This situation persisted throughout the Northern Song.

ESCAPING THE REGISTRY: LOCAL MILITIAS AND RESISTANCE TO REGISTRATION AND CONSCRIPTION

One of the initial points of resistance to the Song's military policies came even before an individual was made a soldier in the local militias. This took place when the state went about conscripting into its army large numbers of commoners. In the northern and western circuits, where there was a heavy burden of service in the local militias, the people found a variety of ways to evade conscription.

In 1047 the official Zhang Fangping (1006–1091) spoke of the impact of the war with the Xia on the militarization of the Song-Xia border and the steep rise in the overall number of Song troops:

> Since the Xia savages have been disobeying the imperial order, [we] have
> begun to register local soldiers. Suddenly the command came to tattoo
> them in order to reinforce the registers of the [regular] armies. . . . In the
> inner and outer prefectures over 420,000 men were added to the imperial
> armies. This is nearly a million more than in the previous three reigns. This
> number does not include the local militias of *yiyong*, the prefectural armies
> of all prefectures, the small detachments of reserve soldiers in all armies,

and other units. The soldiers in the endless string of army camps increase every day, while the number of people working the fields decreases every day.[5]

The military policies put a heavy burden on the shoulders of the border zone residents. In addition to the usual tax burden, they had to support large numbers of troops, and also provide men to serve in the local militias. At times the local militia troops were sent to provide logistical support, carrying supplies to the regular units in the border zones. A return journey home was not assured, given the hardships of the journey and the possibility of a sudden transfer into the regular armies.

The local people did not go into the army peacefully. In 1039 the official Fu Bi (1003–1083) reported on the fear among people of the western border since the beginning of the war with the Xia: "The village people are terrified, saying this is registration for the local armies, leading them to flee and hide in the mountains and forests. They drill holes in their limbs and bodies, not caring if they injure themselves, seeking a moment's reprieve from tattooing."[6] The government failed to compensate the peasants for the disruption conscription caused to their lives. In 1039 the official Song Qi (997–1061) described the financial straits of peasants conscripted to the prefectural armies: "The prefectural armies of the world do not choose from among the weak and the lame, but tattoo [and conscript] all of them, only planning [to use them] for supplying labor. [The conscripts] originally have no knowledge of the military arts. Beyond that, [based on the] monthly expense of grain from the storehouse, and the yearly payment of cloth from the storehouse, a family of a few people cannot care for itself. Therefore, those who support each other in flight and then become bandits are too many to count."[7]

The military burden caused many peasants to abandon their lands, but the Song state did not rely solely on registration of lands for social control. It targeted the bodies of its subjects and used tattooing as a technology for registering and controlling people in the border zones. This made them highly resentful and reluctant to cooperate. In 1040 Han Qi (1008–1075) reported a state of great trepidation among the people of Shaanxi who feared that conscription into the "strong and robust" (*qiangzhuang*) local militias meant tattooing and conscription into the regular army. As a result of the peasants' opposition, Emperor Renzong (r. 1022–1063) ordered that Han Qi avoid tattooing the arms and faces of the peasants who were to be conscripted to the militias.[8]

The fear that conscription into the local armies was just one phase of a process that led to service in the regular armies was not unjustified. Once men appeared in the military registers, the state often used them to fill its missing quotas in the regular armies. A transfer into the regular armies included a tattooing of the face, one of the most hated and feared symbols of conscription. Here too the state was willing to compromise at times. In 1041, after Li Zongyi (*jinshi* 1019) reported that many men of the local militias fled in order to avoid having their faces tattooed, it was decided to only tattoo the hands of the "strong and robust" militia members of Hedong circuit when conscripting them into the regular army.[9] So close was the link between tattooing and conscription that the government had to make sure its tattooing policies would not undermine its military objectives.

In 1042 Han Qi asked to reinforce the army under his command in Qinzhou (in modern Gansu) with more regular troops. He laid out the various strategies commoners used to avoid military service:

> It reaches the point where father and son, older and younger brother, drift apart and join their wives' kin. Some hire people to assume their names, and they trade identities with each other, so that the officials cannot distinguish between them. Whenever there is need for them to go to the prefectural seat to aid in defense, they usually all gather together and flee. . . . Now if we only tattoo the back of their hand, and have them put under the name of *baoyi gongjianshou* local militias, then that would eventually make them no different from commoners. I ask to have them tattooed on the face and made into imperial soldiers. Each person would receive 2,000 cash compensation for the face tattoo. There would be no need for other gifts. [10]

The power of the popular mood was also reflected in the issue of the gifts given for tattooing. Later on, fearful of the anger of tens of thousands of people, Han Qi reversed his position regarding the gifts.[11] Later that year (1042) the fiscal commission reported that altogether 125 commands of *baojie* ("safeguarding victory") were tattooed (fifty to sixty thousand men).[12]

Han Qi was concerned that the peasants were able to make use of the government's difficulties in mapping out the human geography of the border zones. The state used the family unit as a way of binding the peasant to the army. Family members could be taken in to replace a militia member who was sick or fled. The peasants, however, had their own countermeasures to these policies and they continued to use them for decades to come. In 1070 the military commissioner's office at Qinfeng[13] reported on men from the *baoyi* local militias whose children and grandchildren divided up their plots, assumed other surnames, and hardly ever held on to their true identities.[14]

The militarized border zones were places where the central government's violent policies only underscored the limits of state power. When peasants refused to cooperate, how could the government know who was who? How could it successfully register and manage the local population? Controlling the land was not enough. Tattooing the face was viewed as a solution to the problem of registering and controlling the local people, but that too had to be done with caution. The central government tried to fathom public opinion before and during the implementation of conscription policies in the northwest. Mass resistance to government military policies, or the specter of such resistance, was an important topic in policy discussions at court.

Another wave of unrest in the border regions was reported after the beginning of the New Policies. This comprehensive program of reform included a restructuring of the Song's military organization. An important part of the reform was the organization of the entire Song population into *baojia* (mutual surveillance units). All male adults of appropriate age were to serve in the *baojia* on a part-time basis. The *baojia* were to take charge of local law enforcement, but in the northern and western borders they were to go through combat training with the goal of eventually replacing the regular armies.

Resistance of peasants to the *baojia* policy was a topic of conversations between Emperor Shenzong (r. 1067–1086) and Wang Anshi, the mastermind behind the reform plan. When the emperor asked in 1071 about disturbances caused by the reform, Wang Anshi explained that the people were merely afraid of being tattooed for the *yiyong* local militias.[15] In another conversation Shenzong and Wang Anshi discussed reports of people who had cut off their own fingers in order to avoid the *baojia*. While Wang Anshi agreed there might have been some isolated cases of self-injuries, here too he pointed to the past and argued that the true reason for alarm was the trauma of past conscription policies, namely, the conscripting and tattooing of the men of Shaanxi and Hedong for the *yiyong* local militias and the *baojie* imperial armies.[16]

Wang Anshi was wary of arousing the people's suspicion and so in 1072 he objected to changing the cycle of the *baojia* service. He feared that any change in government policies would validate the peasants' fears that this was nothing but a ruse leading to the tattooing of the arm and conscription into the army.[17] As another measure meant to alleviate some of the people's fears, Wang Anshi suggested using the Ministry of Agriculture rather than let the Ministry of War to administer the *baojia*. Wang believed that this way the people would not suspect they would be tattooed and conscripted for the army.[18] Wang Anshi was well aware of the distrust and fear peasants felt toward the government, and understood how the government's constantly shifting policies contributed to these sentiments.

In a retort to Wang Anshi, the official Wang Yansou (1043–1093) described the daily hardships of commoners in the *baojia*: physical abuse, destruction of their livelihood, and extortion. He explained that as a result some drove their adopted children and their son-in-laws out of their homes, some re-wed their mothers, brothers split their houses, some poisoned their own eyes, cut their fingers, and burned their skin in order to exempt themselves. Those who escaped sentenced their families to fines and themselves to hardship. Owners of horses had to lend their animals for official use.[19]

Despite Wang Yansou's claim, these patterns of behavior were not new. This can be seen in the words of Sima Guang, a leader of the opposition to the New Policies, who noted in 1064, before the beginning of the reforms, that once men were tattooed for the militias they were forever exposed to conscription. Sima argued that if there was a flood or a famine they would want to split their households, sell their fields, and drift away and work as tenants, since they all worried that the officials would suddenly enlist them.[20]

Elsewhere in this volume, Paul Smith scrutinizes in detail state policy debates in the imperial court. This study suggests that no matter the outcome of debates and the reversals of factional politics at the court, there was a continuity in the impact of state policies on those at the lowest rungs of Song society. From the peasants' point of view the traumas of conscription formed a pattern: appearing on any kind of military registry could be disastrous. No matter where the political wind shifted, the men appearing on the military registers would be the first candidates for shuffling, transferring, or reinforcing wherever they were needed. The political pendulum swayed between reform and counter-reform, reformers and conservatives, but all roads led the peasants in the border regions toward the army. The main goal of the peasants was, therefore, to avoid the registry, whether by changing their identity, hiding, or self mutilation.

HARDSHIP, SELF-MUTILATION, AND DESERTION

Once a commoner became a soldier in the army, his life could become bitter and short. One of the most dangerous and terrible duties in the prefectural armies was work on the Song's waterways. Accounts of the working condi-tions of these soldiers reveal a brutal and deadly existence. In 1016 Emperor Zhenzong (r. 997–1022) ordered medical treatment for the soldiers in Hang-zhou after great numbers of them who were working in the water contracted a foot disease and many of them died.[21] In 1023, great numbers of soldiers working the rivers in the height of summer died of thirst.[22] Emperor Shen-zong spoke in 1076 of large numbers of soldiers who were digging a canal in Huainan. The southern men working there were too weak to handle the daily work load. Many of the soldiers became very ill but they still had to be carried to the work place for inspection; many died on the way.[23]

Hard labor was often accompanied by serious instances of abuse. In 1080 the censor Man Zhongxing reported that in the units working on the dikes clerks were taking bribes from the staff of the moat forts and the soldiers. According to Man: "[The soldiers all had to] give money, and it was referred to as the norm. If [the money] was slightly short, they would nitpick and harass [the soldiers] for their mistakes, and would then cane and flog them. [The soldiers] suffered from the beatings and the extortion, and they had to resort to borrowing money from the officials in order to be able to satisfy [their demands]."[24] In other cases, there were severe arrears in soldiers' pay. In 1080 Lü Wenqing (d. 1099) warned that there were problems with pay for soldiers in 216 commands of imperial soldiers in the Kaifeng area as well as River Clearing and postal station units. According to the account, this situation continued for years without being investigated.[25]

The soldiers on the waterways resisted in a variety of ways. Self-mutilation was one way of escaping a harsh location. In 1012 there were reports that River Clearing soldiers were using sickles and axes to cut off their own toes in order to gain a transfer to a neighboring prison citadel.[26] Another edict from the same year addressed the problem of soldiers who were breaking their own arms and legs in order to avoid corvée or to gain a transfer to a better location.[27]

The most common mode of resistance, though, was most likely deser-tion. In 1076 Emperor Shenzong commented on the groups of bandits troubling Hebei and Jingdong that were often composed of deserters from river control units.[28] In 1089 the secretariat looked into the matter of the soldiers sent to work for the Yellow River Conservation Office. Of these soldiers, 1,319 had died and 3,691 had fled.[29] These were great numbers even considering the size of the Song army.

Prefectural armies assigned other work also suffered from large-scale desertion. That was the case in the year 1070 when the Song mobilized great numbers of prefectural soldiers in order to repair a series of forts in the Shaanxi border area. So many soldiers fled from Shaanxi circuit that the remaining manpower was not enough to handle the transport of grain and fodder.[30]

If viewed from the angle of their work conditions, desertion was merely an act of self-preservation and resistance, perhaps the only recourse soldiers had. Yet when they acted, they proved themselves to be criminals and worthy of their place at the bottom of society. They were then branded accordingly with a special tattoo that marked them as captured deserters.[31] The military system transformed men in two opposite directions. It turned convicts into soldiers, but it also turned soldiers into convicts when despair and suffering drove them to desertion. By creating such terrible working and living conditions, the state participated in and contributed to the criminalization of its soldiers.

The marking of the soldiers' faces left them with very limited options, and rejoining society was hard. One of the only options left for deserters was banditry. This meant that the problem of large numbers of deserters brought about the problem of large numbers of bandits.

Putting a stop to desertion was further complicated by another choice that deserters had: joining the ranks of a different military unit. The meeting of manpower quotas was one of the standards according to which officials were assessed and then rewarded or punished. The great scholar-official Ouyang Xiu (1007–1072) reported that "the clerks who recruited many men would get a reward."[32] Therefore, many officials allowed deserters from other units to join their own unit, thereby granting them both refuge and material support. Soldiers deserted from their units in order to join other units in situations when such a move meant a more preferable duty or location. They could also use it to gain an additional "signing bonus" when they joined the new unit.[33] The state regarded this phenomenon as "illegal transfer."

The scale of illegal transfers was a cause for concern for officials. In 1082 the Kaifeng superior prefecture's administrative assistant Du Chang (d. 1104) asked that soldiers in Shaanxi who were transferred between units illegally be tattooed and placed in the local prefectural armies. His request was approved and extended to all circuits.[34] In 1083 the prefect of Ansu military prefecture (in modern Hebei) Pan Xiaochao supported Du Chang's proposal: "When imperial soldiers desert, those who turn themselves in can do an illegal transfer, thus escaping penal servitude. The prefectural soldiers who commit a crime and desert can transfer illegally without being caught. To escape hard labor, they go to a place where the labor is lighter. To escape harsh and distant places, they transfer to closer locations. The payment and grain given to them are wasted. This results in growing shortages of artisans in the construction forts."[35] Repeated attempts to address this problem reveal that it was not solved. In 1091 the Ministry of Justice reported a request by the Bureau of Military Affairs that the soldiers of the Fengxiang Superior Prefecture (in modern Shaanxi) *jian zhong baoning* military units were forbidden to transfer to other units and have their tattoos altered.[36] In a 1097 memorial, Jingyuan circuit (in modern Gansu and Ningxia) military commissioner Zhang Jie (1027–1102) criticized the practice of illegal transfers of deserters. According to Zhang, men moved freely back and forth between being bandits and being soldiers according to their economic needs. Zhang even reported the capture of a spy who took advantage of this to enter service in a Song fort. He also told the story of Li Fu, a non-Han officer from the Weizhou (in modern Gansu) twentieth command who was caught replacing a government horse with a sickly horse. He fled and became an officer in a different unit. As a result of Zhang Jie's request, it was decreed that the newly built forts and outposts of Shaanxi and Hedong circuits would not accept deserters as transfers.[37]

In 1106 the eunuch general Tong Guan (1054–1126) argued that officials in Shaanxi summoned deserters and allowed them to turn themselves in without questioning. They then gave them money and had them return to their original camp. Tong Guan asked that soldiers who deserted outside the time limit set by an imperial amnesty should not be shown any leniency. His request was approved.[38]

Attempts to approach the problem of illegal transfers differently met staunch opposition. In 1109 an official of the Bureau of Military Affairs warned of the many problems created by the law promulgated by Shaanxi circuit penal superintendent Wu Anxian (b. 1043). The law allowed deserters from the imperial and prefectural armies to move to a different unit and have their tattoos altered accordingly. The official warned that the law allowed officials to compete for the soldiers, artisans, and craftsmen of another unit or agency. It also allowed some units to cover up the true numbers of deserters in their ranks by assigning them names of soldiers missing from their own unit: "Not only do [the deserters] escape punishment, they also take money on false pretense. Seniors and subordinates cover for each other, and none can put a stop to it. This causes the soldiers to indulge in dreams of flight and bettering their lot by taking over a plot of land." Instead, the official asked for a stricter implementation of rewards and punishments in order to prevent illegal transfers. His request was approved.[39]

The competition between different units over human bodies continued to be fierce until the end of the Northern Song. In 1120 Tong Guan spoke on the need to forbid deserters who turned themselves in from joining a different unit; rather they should be sent back to their original unit.[40]

The assessment of officials according to how they met manpower quotas created a loophole that soldiers used to their advantage. And so, "superiors and subordinates covered for each other."[41] No matter how many times officials called for a stricter enforcement of the laws, the system offered contradictory incentives. Many continued to object to the legalization of "illegal transfers" and by so doing demonstrated their uncompromising attitude toward crime and mismanagement, even though their stance meant the problem was left unresolved.

DEFYING HUNGER

Northern Song reports about the living standards in the military camps reveal a social landscape marked by misery, poverty, and hunger. In 1032 the attendant censor Li Hong (*jinshi* 1008) spoke of the bad state of the soldiers from Chuanxia (in modern Sichuan and Shaanxi) who were sentenced to serve in the border area in Shaanxi. They were old and sickly and many of them were lame and thin. Li added, "They share a single room with their wife. They do not have enough food to last through the day. That is truly pitiful."[42] In a similar report from the year 1048 Zhang Fangping warned that a soldier's salary was hardly enough to cover even his uniform costs. Therefore, the soldiers' wives and children went cold and hungry. Zhang Fangping warned: "When the wives and children cannot escape cold and hunger, how can the feelings of the petty people not turn in anger against their superiors? That is why the situation in the army turns easily to turmoil."[43] Soldiers did whatever they could to survive. Some soldiers sold their clothes in order to support themselves. Wang Anshi spoke of the problem of soldiers who wore clothes made of paper underneath their armor.[44]

A shortage of food stood at the heart of much of the discontent and bitterness of army life. Problems with food supply and quality were also a result of the huge logistical challenges the Song army faced. Most of the armies were stationed around the capital and in the northern and western border regions, and food had to be transported across great distances in order to feed these armies. Given delays, droughts, or any other possible interruptions to the food supply, food had to be stored in advance, generally enough to last two or three years.[45] The need to store food for such great lengths of time created its own host of problems. Natural disasters could destroy the supplies, such as an earthquake and rains in Hebei that destroyed a military granary.[46] Food could not keep forever, and wheat was especially hard to keep.[47] This meant that the old grain had to be distributed to the soldiers first. The daily meal of old grain was one of the most unbearable elements of military life.

The sequence of food distribution caused great tension within the military camp. The officials in charge had to strike the right balance between getting rid of the old food (by giving it to the soldiers) and distributing food of a reasonable quality. Some chose to quell dissent by being generous with the "good stuff." Guo Chengyou was demoted in 1050 for a variety of violations, including the giving of new grain to his soldiers in an attempt to raise morale among the troops.[48] The official Wang Deyong (987–1065) tried to come up with balanced formulas of 80 percent good food and 20 percent rotten food. When soldiers raised a clamor over the bad food they were getting, Wang Deyong went to the granary and scolded the clerks in charge of the distribution of the food for not following his orders. He resolved the situation by flogging both the person in charge of rice distribution and the soldiers who complained about it.[49]

Dissatisfaction with food could trigger a full blown mutiny. Sima Guang's *Sushui jiwen* provides an account of a mutiny in Guanghua (in modern Hubei) military prefecture in 1043. The official in charge was Han Gang, a harsh and impatient man. When his soldiers were given hard dry bread, they suspected that Han Gang was giving away food, drink, and pay that was theirs by right and began tossing the dry bread at the official's quarters. When Han Gang responded in brute force, the unrest turned into a mutiny, and Han Gang fled for his life. Eventually, the mutiny was suppressed after the rebels went on a round of pillaging.[50] In this case, the relationship between officials and soldiers was made worse by Han Gang's strict, even cruel, style of management. Though this is a story of a military unit on a combat mission (defense against bandits), the soldiers had to break into the storehouse and steal weapons in order to rise against their superiors. So great was the distrust of soldiers that access to weapons had to be limited. The soldiers were constantly watching the actions of their superiors. The distribution of food, drink, and pay was the prism through which the superiors' conduct was measured. The distribution of food was also that highly volatile moment when tensions exploded, and dry bread became both a symbol of dissatisfaction and a weapon to hurl at their superiors.

After Emperor Shenzong ascended the throne in 1067, he set about reforming the military system. The rotation system was replaced with the "area generals system" system or *jiangbingfa*. Soldiers were no longer to be rotated between different camps and officers. Instead, they were to be attached to the same officer for an extended period of time. The imperial armies were hit hard by the reform. In 1081 Shenzong remarked:

> I have heard that in the various circuits of the southeast, since we established the "area generals system," the military men train every day. They no longer have time to use old skills to supplement their income. As for the imperial armies that are under the jurisdiction of the patrolling inspectors, precedent was that they be given an increase in their income. If they could catch bandits, they would also get a reward. These days, local soldiers have been recruited. The armies no longer travel in and out, and that has also drained their income for clothing and food. As a result of this, within the army there is great poverty, and soldiers cannot even get enough food to carry them through the day.[51]

The final years of the Northern Song were also years of growing military decline. The bad state of the army is reflected in reports of the declining living standards of soldiers. Many of the soldiers had to find ways to earn enough to survive. According to an account from 1126, soldiers had to take on additional duties and even among the imperial armies there were men who had to leave the camp and rent out their strength to pay for clothing and food.[52] Others traded their equipment for food. In the spring of 1126 there were reports of soldiers who traded their weapons, shields, and body armor in the marketplace in exchange for cooked food. The government succeeded in confiscating over 4,200 military items from the commoners who had purchased them.[53]

Much of the violence employed by soldiers was a reaction to the harsh living conditions within the army. The military was a system that could alleviate some temporary forms of poverty during famines, but it was also a producer of poverty. It is ironic that despite the army being part of the penal-judicial system, a space for the containment and correction of criminals and other marginal populations, it was also an important generator of violence and disorder.

DEFYING ORDERS

Food was not the only cause of strife in the Song armies. Soldiers had many bones to pick with their superiors, and the authority of officials was constantly tested. Drilling was one of the routine burdens of military life in the combat-ready units, and soldiers sometimes refused to take part in it. That was the case in 1075 when *guangyong* imperial unit soldiers Dou Yuan and Li Xiu led other soldiers in leaving the training grounds and refusing to participate. Dou and Li were beheaded, and the other nine soldiers were flogged and sent to a prison citadel in Guangnan.[54]

Another main concern of the military was the organization of labor. Here too soldiers could refuse to work, but with dire consequences. In 1077 Wang Xiu and another nine soldiers from the Ballista *xiongwu* second command were accused of inciting the soldiers to refuse to go and transport wheat.[55] The deputy troop commandant Niu Sui was accused of not having tried to stop them. It was decreed that Wang Xiu should be beheaded at the camp's gate. The other nine were to be banished to an island or to Guangnan. Niu Sui was to be flogged a hundred times and demoted to the Caozhou (in modern Shandong) clerk reserves (*yuanliao shengyuanzhi*).[56]

Refusal to work could include large numbers of soldiers, as seen in a case from 1079. Over a thousand corvée soldiers laboring in Heyang (in modern Henan) tried to flee rather than report for duty. The prefect Lü Gongru (1030–1100) got them to return to work with a combination of mercy, threats, and severe punishments. The ringleader and his associates were tattooed and exiled. The rest were escorted back to the work site.[57]

The soldiers on the waterways, many of them convicts, could be very hard to control. In 1091 the judicial commission of Hedong East circuit listed crimes committed by soldiers working on the dikes. These crimes reveal some of the problems officials dealt with in management of these soldiers: robbery, theft, murder, arson, breaking inmates out of prison, hiding criminals, providing assistance to passing bandits, giving bandits weapons, and leaking information about plans to capture bandits.[58]

STOPPING TROUBLE AT ITS ROOT: THE POLICY OF ZERO TOLERANCE

In the Song penal-military complex, tensions ran high. The soldiers were rotated between camps and worked to exhaustion with the declared intention of keeping them weak and reforming them through hard work. Poverty was the norm. Morale was low. How, then, could one prevent the soldiers from rising up in mutiny? One approach was that of zero tolerance to any possible discipline problem.

A policy of zero tolerance could be deemed more important than upholding the law. An officer in Bingzhou (in modern Shanxi) flogged a soldier to death who was not under his command. Zhang Yong (945–1015) warned that if the officer were to be executed over the matter of one soldier, the soldiers would slight their superiors and cause trouble. He added that it was even more dangerous since they had thousands of soldiers stationed there in a border area filled with tribal groups. Zhang suggested that the officer be beaten with a rod and transferred. Instead, the emperor had the officer executed. Some time later the soldiers there killed an officer, pulling out his heart and internal organs. According to the account, the court then realized Zhang had been right.[59]

The zero tolerance policy was clearly geared toward control of lower-ranking soldiers. The public harsh disciplining of soldiers created violent spectacles that reinforced the power hierarchy within the army. In the previous incident, the court followed the letter of the law and its decision was answered with the soldiers creating a violent spectacle of their own. The use of terror in the previous incident was deemed a shield for the official, alone and isolated, a jailer jailed, surrounded by his underlings who were in turn surrounded by a hostile non-Chinese population.

With a well-timed execution an official could gain both authority from below and appreciation from above. Zhang Yong himself had a clerk executed, thereby winning the obedience of the military officers.[60] Zhao Gai cemented his authority by having a soldier who ran away and broke into a private residence beheaded in the market place.[61] When Li Ji (960–1030) was appointed Qinzhou prefect, the officers there thought little of him until he had to decide the case of a soldier who had stolen silver hairpins from women in the marketplace in broad daylight. Li Ji, who was reading a book when the soldier was brought before him, ordered that the soldier be beheaded and continued reading. This gained him the respect of his officers, and his reputation even reached the court.[62] A garrison soldier in Shu (Sichuan) went on a crime spree during which he extorted valuable items from a wealthy family, climbed on the roof of an inn and set it on fire, and killed and wounded people. After he turned himself in, the official Xue Kui had him executed on the spot; his decision was allegedly praised by the public.[63]

Harsh laws and punishments employed in military life were important for the weeding out of potential troublemakers. Cao Wei (973–1030), the son of the celebrated general Cao Bin (931–999), executed an old soldier for arguing with him in a minor incident.[64] In 1052 Guo Shenxi (997–1074) was awarded for proving himself capable at suppressing soldiers who tried to instigate disorder in the ranks by executing one and tattooing two others.[65] Swift actions aimed at especially undisciplined soldiers could prevent problems before they started.

Strictness was also deemed necessary for the soldier's own good. Li Zhaoliang (993–1063) was another tough and resolved official. According to his biography, soldiers of the *wansheng* and *longmeng* imperial army units were gambling. The game ended in a fight with soldiers tearing apart roof beams to hit each other. There was panic among the troops, but Li Zhaoliang caught, arrested, and beheaded the unruly soldiers, flogging the ringleaders first. The entire army shook with fear as a result, we are told. In another instance, a cavalry soldier lost his bow. He was to be released due to an amnesty but Li Zhaoliang said, "A careless imperial guard cannot be pardoned." The soldier was demoted and sent to penal servitude. According to the account, the imperial army became disciplined from then on.[66] Here, Li Zhaoliang's harsh discipline was necessary not only for his own safety but also to protect the soldiers from their own unruly and violent behavior toward one another.

An official's state of mind could shape how he administered justice. An anecdote about two eminent officials, Han Qi and Wen Yanbo (1006–1097), contrasts their characters through their reactions to comparable cases of crime by soldiers:

> Han Qi and Wen Yanbo served one after the other at the North Gate garrison.[67] During Han Qi's tenure, the director of the walls was flogging a soldier. The soldier had only received two strokes when he began cursing incessantly. The director sent him to trial. Han Qi asked the soldier, "Did you in fact curse the director?" [The soldier] said, "I did." Han Qi said, "You are an imperial soldier. Since you had a duty to do in your subprefecture, then there is an order to follow." Han Qi then pronounced the sentence and had him taken to the marketplace where he was beheaded. [All this time] he was calm and relaxed as in normal times. When those around him saw him throw down his brush, only then did they know something was amiss. During Wen Yanbo's tenure, once again there was a soldier from another subprefecture who was delivered for trial, his crime similar to the previous one. Wen Yanbo shook with anger, and asked whether [the accusations] were true or false. The soldier replied truthfully. Wen Yanbo also had him sentenced and executed and threw down his brush. The two esteemed men responded differently. In the case of Han Qi, [he would have said,] "He was the one who committed the crime, so I have no [reason] to be angry." Wen Yanbo was heroic in a different manner. He could not tolerate wickedness.[68]

Officials were often praised for the bravery they demonstrated when they remonstrated with the emperor or when they spoke up against other powerful officials. For them the act of speaking up was a worthy one. Soldiers had no such recourse. The act of cursing was the common soldier's way of speaking up. The soldiers' courage and honesty were not praised, and instead were answered with a swift execution in the marketplace.

Stories of compassion and forgiveness exist as well. The *Sushui jiwen* tells of prefect Wang Huaji (944–1110) who summoned a passing soldier. As the soldier did not respond "Yes, sir," his officer wanted to whip him, but Wang Huaji convinced him to let it go, thereby making all admire his refined tolerance.[69] Another source records that when Han Qi was writing in his quarters, a soldier who held his candle burned his whiskers by mistake. Before long Han Qi noticed that the soldier was replaced. He feared the soldier might have been taken out for a flogging, and so he urgently called out: "Do not replace him. He now understands how to hold a candle properly!" According to the account, Han Qi's manner won over the entire army's staff.[70]

These examples of compassion and leniency are actually more telling of the harsh discipline and cruelty that were the daily bread of most soldiers. An insolent soldier could be beheaded. Flogging was the lot of those who failed to respond fast enough or took a misstep. As for compassion, those who recorded these anecdotes must have felt Wang Huaji's and Han Qi's behavior exceptional enough to make note of it.

SOLDIER MUTINIES

When despair and anger could no longer be tolerated, soldiers rose in mutiny against their superiors; the Song period is notable for the high frequency of such soldier mutinies. Though descriptions tend to be short, one soldier mutiny in Baozhou (in modern Hebei) received attention from a number of sources. The accounts of the mutiny in Baozhou as well as accounts of other mutinies will allow us to identify the main features of soldier mutinies during the Song period.

THE TRIGGER

The military garrisons at Baozhou had a long tradition of lawlessness. The imperial army unit stationed there was originally recruited from the bandits based on the river islets in Tongzhou (in modern Jiangsu), as well as pirates from the Liangzhe and Jiangnan circuits. It was later reinforced with deserters during the Duangong reign period (998–990). In the early Qingli reign period (1041–1049) it was elevated to the rank of an imperial army.[71] The military units in Baozhou gradually declined in status and began to suffer a reduction in income.[72] They were often at odds with the prefectural officials who slighted them. Before the mutiny, Controller General Shi Daiju (*jinshi* 1023) asked the fiscal commissioner to stop paying them the special bonus that they had received according to custom.[73]

The threat to the soldiers' income did not pass unnoticed. In 1044 when some soldiers began to talk about a mutiny, Xingzhou (in modern Shaanxi) prefect Liu Jizong was concerned and ordered that all the weapons used for practice be stored away. Shi Daiju was drinking and gambling with the supervisor of militia, Wei Gui.[74] The two began to quarrel in front of a displeased crowd of soldiers. Drunk, Wei Gui cursed Daiju: "The only achievement you can claim for yourself is reducing the soldiers' income!" This infuriated the soldiers.[75]

Much like the Baozhou mutiny, other soldier mutinies were also preceded by a perceived wrong, followed by a stage of anger and complaints. Such was the case in 1059 when soldiers in Jing (in modern Gansu and Ningxia) did not receive their pay. They cursed the controller–general and started complaining to each other, stirring up a riot.[76]

Overworking the soldiers was another cause for unrest. A soldier mutiny in Yizhou (in modern Guangxi) in 1007 was the result of the harsh working conditions. The prefect Liu Yonggui ordered his soldiers to go and cut wood in bad weather conditions, exposed to the rain and the wind. Those who failed to keep up were flogged. They even had to bring their wives and children to help them with the work.[77]

Incompetence could lead to mutiny. Wang Zhongzheng (1030–1101), an official in charge of one of the main military forces of the 1081 campaign against the Xi Xia, was inexperienced in military matters. Wang, lost and fearful in the wide open spaces of Tangut country, forbade starting fires after the second watch for fear of discovery by the enemy.[78] The rear guard's food had not been fully cooked by this hour and many of the soldiers who ate it fell ill. Once the army's food supplies had been exhausted, the angry soldiers began plotting to murder their commanding officers and scatter back.[79]

Soldiers and peasants were tied to the state in different ways. Peasants were indebted to the state through taxes, paying both in goods and in labor. Some of them had to join local militias on a part-time basis. Soldiers, however, though they were practically owned by the state, were also its paid employees. In the case of peasants, the government took on a parasitic role, claiming their crops and their labor without compensation. Soldiers, by contrast, were dependent on the state for their livelihood. The common soldiers of the Song armies did not only have duties, they also had things they perceived to be their "rights." These included food and payment.

INITIAL ROUND OF VIOLENCE

The trigger was followed by some kind of public outburst. A soldier shouted, a truth was revealed, a rumor was spread through the ranks. Soldiers complained out loud to one another. At that point, dissatisfaction became public. Not unlike the Maoist "speaking bitterness" campaigns, complaints and displays of public anger brought soldiers together with a common agenda and set them on a collision course with their superiors. The road to concerted violent action was clear, and once a violent course was taken, there was no going back, at least not for a while.

The Baozhou mutiny erupted on the day of the distribution of uniforms, always a dangerous moment in times of tension. Following the incident between Shi and Wei, the soldiers entered the officials' quarters with drawn blades. Daiju took his family and fled through the east gate into the Wudi camp. Liu Jizong also brought his family there. Together they used the Wudi troops to close the city, and then led the imperial army unit inside through the east gate to fight the rebels. When the tide turned against the officials, Shi Daiju and Liu Jizong climbed the town walls to flee the rebels. Liu Jizong tried to cross the moat and drowned. Shi Daiju hid within the abatis, where he was killed by the rebels.[80] The soldiers put Shi Daiju's head on a tree and shot arrows at it every morning until it there was no room left. At that point they would pull the arrows out and start shooting at it again.[81]

The soldiers then faced the task of choosing a leader. They first chose the official Wang Shouyi to lead them, but killed him when he refused.[82] They speared him through the heart and out his back. They then threatened Wei Gui who agreed to lead them on the condition that they listen to him. The soldiers agreed and made Wei their leader. Wei ordered that they not touch the granary or kill people without reason, and convinced them to return their loyalty to the Song. According to Sima Guang, Wei Gui had the soldiers' ears.[83]

The first round of violence between the soldiers and their superiors was an opportunity for the soldiers to carry out justice, usually targeting those perceived to be responsible for the unfairness but sparing potential allies. Shi Daiju's head became a target practice tool, but Wei Gui succeeded in moderating the rebels once he became their leader. In the Yizhou mutiny,

the soldiers killed the hated prefect Liu Yonggui and the supervisor of militia
Guo Jun, and chose Controller General Lu Chengjun to serve as their general.[84] The cruel official Li Ji was murdered in 1081 by Song soldiers while
they were all besieged by the Tanguts.[85]

The accounts of the initial round of violence contain some gruesome
details. A human head became a tool for target practice. Officials were running and hiding for their lives only to be dragged out of hiding by the rebels.
But was there room for action by the soldiers that would not be defined as
"chaos" (*luan*)? After all, the difference between the carrying out of justice
and the making of chaos is often a factor of power. As far as the soldiers were
concerned, their actions were the manifestations of justice.

NEGOTIATIONS

A mutiny, or even the prospect of one, could bring about a complete change
in attitude from the officials in charge. A policy of zero tolerance was not as
useful at this point. Some officials chose to negotiate with the soldiers and
either satisfy some of their claims or merely convince them to go back to the
fold of the Song state.

The initial round of violence in Baozhou was followed by a round of siege
and negotiations. According to the *Changbian*, officials who came to quell
the uprising spoke to the rebels on the walls. Some of the soldiers wanted
to surrender but, as more troops joined, the rebels stood firm in their
resistance.[86] According to Sima Guang, the court sent Drafter Tian Kuang,
who stood under the walls of the town and called out to the soldiers. Still,
the soldiers were suspicious and would shoot anyone who came near. Palace
eunuch Guo Kui called out to the soldiers: "Brethren! Lower a rope. I wish
to climb the wall and speak with you." Once the soldiers lowered a rope and
reeled him in, Guo Kui said: "Brethren! Do you not love yourselves? If you
were not sincere and faithful, would you come to this? The court knows
you find no joy in rebelling. The officials treated you unreasonably and
brought you to this point. Now we shall pardon your crime, and will award
you according to the set order. [Officials of] the Two Drafting Groups have
come here to speak with you, carrying an imperial edict, and you still suspect
them. Could it be that there is an imperial order that cannot be trusted? Are
the Two Drafting Groups deceitful?!"[87]

The eunuch Yang Huaimin took advantage of the negotiations to settle
an account with Fiscal Commissioner-in-Chief Zhang Wenzhi who tried to
take Yang's position and give it to a military official instead. Yang Huaimin
reported that the soldiers agreed to surrender in return for Zhang's head. The

emperor approved and sent an imperial commissioner to execute Zhang. Fu Bi ran into the imperial commissioner on his way there and sent him back, alerting the emperor to the fact that this was probably a personal grudge and also warning of the problems that could be created by executing a fiscal commissioner-in-chief in order to satisfy mutinous soldiers. Zhang Wenzhi was demoted instead.[88]

The *Song shi* contains another account of these negotiations in the biography of the official Li Zhaoliang. Here we are told that during the Baozhou uprising, the emperor sent Wang Guo to accept the soldiers' surrender. The soldiers clung to the wall and cried out: "If you bring infantry commander Li, we will surrender." Li Zhaoliang came with a few dozen of his entourage, none wearing armor or carrying a shield or bow. They knocked on the town gate and shouted to those on top: "For those who come to surrender, I guarantee that no harm shall come to them. Otherwise, no living creature will be left here." The soldiers began going down the rope from the wall and the next day the rest opened the gates and surrendered.[89]

Officials who were quick on their feet began negotiating with unruly soldiers before anger turned to bloodshed. The *Sushui jiwen* records how Wen Yanbo stopped a possible mutiny:

> As prefect of Yizhou (modern Chengdu), Wen Yanbo delighted in traveling and holding banquets. Once he entertained the military administrators in the government offices well into the night without ceasing. The soldiers escorting them started tearing down the stable to use it for firewood. They could not be stopped. When their commanders reported this to Wen Yanbo, the military administrators were shaking with fear, but Yanbo said, "The weather is cold. It is permissible to break it down and give it to them." His expression was carefree, and he enjoyed the banquet and drank just as before. This put a stop to the soldiers' anger, and they no longer had a reason to rebel.[90]

Anecdotes about the eminent official Wen Yanbo often portray him as a pleasure-seeker. In this story there is a powerful contrast between his lifestyle and that of the soldiers who served him. The extremely cold weather served as the trigger that made the banquet into a volatile situation. The military officials attending the banquet were already shaking, probably at the thought of their imminent death. Wen Yanbo saved the day by making a timely concession.

In 1064, upon Yingzong's (r. 1063–1067) ascension to the throne, gifts of silk were given to the officers in the prefectural armies in all prefectures. When the lower-ranking officers in Jingnan (in modern Hubei and Sichuan) discovered that they had received silk of inferior quality, the town stood on the brink of mutiny. The residents of the town began to flee. Only the excited plea of the patrolling inspector Zhang Shizheng convinced the officers to accept the gifts and prevented the outbreak of violence.[91]

In another instance, garrison soldiers barricaded themselves in the camp where arson and killings began to take place. The soldiers planned to kill the prefect and supervisor of militia, but when someone came to report the matter to these officials, they did not even dare to leave their quarters. Only the Hanzhou (in modern Sichuan) controller general Xue Changru (1000–1061) went to the military camp and told them: "'You all have parents, wives, and children. How can you do this? Those who did not initiate the plot should stand to one side.' None dared move, and only the eight ringleaders fled out the gate and scattered in the countryside where they were captured. At that time, without Changru a great disaster would have befallen all the people of the town."[92]

The Chinese empire was a highly hierarchical organization. In a local government, an official sat at the top of a local bureaucracy, with many clerks, servants, and soldiers under him. However, officials were not the only link that connected the imperial center and the provinces. Soldier mutinies reveal that soldiers did not necessarily see the pyramid in the same way and they could separate the local leadership from the high leadership at court. In the Baozhou mutiny, soldiers exacted their revenge on their superiors and made their requests of the political center. Suspicion was thick on both sides, but the soldiers had faith in the words of the emperor when carried by high enough officials. The emperor was willing to talk, even execute one of his own officials as a concession to the soldiers! In Jingnan the soldiers were disappointed that the gifts from their superior were insufficient to express the imperial act of grace. Rather than a pyramid-like hierarchy, it is possible to see here a few different players communicating directly with each other: the leaders of common soldiers, local administrators, and the central government.

AFTERMATH

After the Baozhou rebels surrendered, they left the town. The last to leave were caught and executed. Some of the officials were punished for reducing the unit's food rations and for not being on the alert for rebellious soldiers.[93] A few hundred soldiers were late to surrender, and were all buried alive;

the others were not investigated.[94] The *Changbian* notes that altogether 429 men were buried alive.[95] Li Zhaoliang divided the women of the mutinous Baozhou soldiers between the various armies, and took some of them into his own household.[96]

The punishing of mutinous soldiers' families was a standard practice. The punishments could be harsh. In 1071, following a soldier mutiny in Qingzhou (in modern Gansu), punishments allotted to the soldiers' families included the enslavement of the old, the sick, the young, and the women. Fathers and sons were tattooed and sent together to prison citadels. The old and sick were enslaved in their own circuit. All slaves were tattooed: the males on the left hand, the females on the right hand.[97]

Soldier mutinies ended in defeat, but that did not mean they failed completely. Soldiers who resisted sometimes had some of their demands met. Usually, a pardon was issued for most of the soldiers involved. At times the trigger for the violence was removed. In Jing, officials put a stop to the soldiers' riot by beheading two soldiers and tattooing three. The clerk responsible for delays in the soldiers' pay was also punished.[98] In another instance, the official Wang Deyong corrected the problems in the distribution of food.[99] But there could be no appearance of a rebel victory, and so the ringleaders were still heavily punished. The state did not stop with executing the mutiny leaders. Their families were punished heavily, tattooed and enslaved. It would seem that a mutiny had to be terminated with a moral spectacle of both grace and terror.

CONCLUSION

In his account of the Tang dynasty military, David Graff describes how during the eighth century there was a transition from rotating peasants in temporary military service to using full time professional soldiers. Graff argues that after the An Lushan Rebellion, Tang soldiers were developing a corporate identity of their own. Military service became the iron rice bowl of these men and they even refused to leave service, meaning many old men served in the ranks of the Tang military.[100] We can get a glimpse of the rank and file of this group in the tattooed military toughs and thugs that appear in the Tang miscellany *Youyang zazu*. Actions of resistance by Song soldiers show that this group continued to grow and develop and that it had claims, an awareness of what it deserved from the state, and its own ideas of justice and honor.

However, the Song state did not use only professional troops. In the northern border zones the Song state also continued the Tang practice of rotating peasants in service in local militias. It also made local militias likely candidates for conscription. This created a strong link between the criminal-martial culture of the professional troops and the culture and values of the border zones. The story of resistance is the story of regular troops and their families, but also of the local militias and the residents of the militarized border zones.

The Song's military policies were met with great resistance. Peasants did their best to avoid service by changing their names, fleeing their lands in order to join bandits, and even injuring themselves. Soldiers resisted the authority of their superiors through desertion, insubordination, and violence. These acts of resistance contributed to limiting and sometimes even reversing the state's policies.

The image of the Song as a Confucian age is no accident. Education based on classical texts became the highest social marker, and the scholar-official was the star and hero of the era. The examination system and the culture that grew around it are considered generators of a new elite that came to dominate the Chinese empire for close to a millennium.[101] In this volume Patricia Ebrey provides some support for the dynasty's Confucian image in her study of forced relocations. Ebrey finds that compared to other dynasties the Song state was more moderate when it came to the scale of forced relocations, and suggests that this could be explained in part by Confucian attitudes on the side of the rulers. This study of resistance suggests that state policies were also shaped by attitudes and activities at the bottom of society.

Soldier mutinies were often organized by common soldiers upset about concrete issues: their living conditions, the quality of their food, their pay, and their treatment. Their dissatisfaction was not toward the laws, but toward mismanagement by their superiors. The soldiers were angry that their superiors did not "play by the rules." Soldier mutinies were carried out for survival and for social justice as they understood it.

Unrest within the army was not the manifestation of hostility of the "military" (*wu*) toward the "civil" or "literary" (*wen*). It was the expression of the anger, despair, and hunger of the common soldiers. When they rose in mutiny, they did so against their superiors, both civil and military officials. It was the rising of the unprivileged against the privileged, the battle of the haves and the have-nots.

The material conditions in military camps turned them into volatile places. Soldiers were branded, separated, and enclosed in urban slums, brought together by labor, training, and abuse, all of this in close proximity to their superiors and the residents of the towns. Within this setting, anger and frustration could lead to sudden outbursts of violence. This vindicated, of course, the dangerous and unruly image of soldiers. The military system was officially a system of order and justice, but it was also a generator of disorder and unrest. Many of the soldiers who deserted and became bandits or rose up against their superiors did so because of the military system and not in spite of it.

The lone official, isolated and surrounded by the troops under his command, was situated in a peculiar position. Officially he was invested with much greater powers over his troops than a local official had over the peasants in his jurisdiction. After all, Song military laws were harsher than regular laws.[102] The social status of soldiers, much lower than that of regular commoners, also served to make them easier targets for victimization by their superiors. At the same time, when soldiers rose against their superiors, then the lives of these officials were in great jeopardy. Officials had to tread a fine line between ruthlessness and flexibility.

Soldiers were no admirers of the refined scholar-officials, nor did they follow them blindly. They complained, fought with their masters, and resisted authority time and again. Officials, for their part, were quick to turn to coercion, violence, and terror. The Confucian values they were so famous for were not for all to share. The meeting point between officials and soldiers was not one where values spread from above. It was a point of collision between two different worlds.

The huge economic growth that took place during the Song cannot be understood without considering the great amounts of labor carried out by soldiers in infrastructure development and manufacturing. The army was also a mass consumer of food, equipment, and money. Urbanization during the Song included the placing of large numbers of soldiers in towns and cities. Yet the soldiers' involvement in the Song's economic boom was violently coerced. The Song's economic development exacted a huge toll on the lower classes who met violence with violence.

The Mongol conquest led to the establishment of a new military system across the Chinese empire. The military institutions that gave birth to the tattooed soldiers of the Song ceased to exist.[103] This new social class, the tattooed soldiers, was forged through both exploitation and resistance within and against the Song army. With the collapse of the Song's military institutions, this social group was also to pass into darkness.

NOTES

1   *Pingzhou ketan* 1.118–19 (32).

2   Cheng Minsheng, *Songdai renkou wenti kaocha*, 99.

3   For more on Song military institutions see: Wang Zengyu, *Songchao junzhi chutan (zengding ben)*; Tan Su-cheng, "Songdai zhi jundui." For English language scholarship on the Song military see: Lorge, "War and the Creation of the Northern Song State"; Labadie, "Rulers and Soldiers"; McGrath, "Military and Regional Administration in Northern Sung China, 960–1126"; Chung, "Aspects of the Systems of Military Logistics During the Song Dynasty (960–1278 A.D.)."

4   Scott, *Weapons of the Weak*, 27–43.

5   *CB* 161.20.3897.

6   *CB* 124.13.2928.

7   *CB* 125.17.2942.

8   *CB* 126.37.2978–79.

9   *CB* 134.11.3189. Hedong circuit is in parts of modern day Shanxi and Shaanxi provinces.

10   *CB* 138.10.3311.

11   *CB* 138.10.3311–12.

12   *CB* 138.11.3312.

13   One of the three circuits bordering the Xia state in the northwest.

14   *SS* 191.4736.

15   *CB* 221.26.5375.

16   *CB* 221.64.5391–92.

17   *CB* 235.7.5697.

18   *CB* 235.29.5710.

19   *SS* 192.4783–84.

20   *CB* 203.2.4918.

21   *CB* 88.41.2019

22   *CB* 100.1.2324

23   *CB* 173.71.6688.

24   *CB* 303.54.7386.

25   *CB* 305.22.7418. The River Clearing army (Heqing) was in charge of maintaining dikes, river dredging, etc. on the Yellow River and Bian River.

26   *CB* 77.4.1755.

27   *CB* 78.26.1773.

28   *CB* 277.6.6768.

29   *CB* .422.12.10216–17.

30   *CB* 218.70.5309.

31   *CB* 467.30.11154.

32   *Ouyang Xiu quanji*, 422.

33   *CB* 334.13.8032.

34   *CB* 325.42.7823.

35   *CB* 334.13.8032.

36   *CB* 458.29.10961.

37   *CB* 493.7.11710–11.

38   *SS* 193.4812–13.

39   *SS* 193.4813.

40   *SS* 193.4815.

41   *SS* 193.4813.

42   *SHY* Xingfa 4.18b.6630.

43   *CB* 163.6.3928; *Lequan ji*, vol. 1104, 18.15a–b.151.

44   *SS* 194.4843–44.

45   *CB* 68.16.1527; 60.32.1341. *Lecheng ji*, 38.840.

46   *Pengcheng ji*, vol. 1096, 38.7a–b.372.

47   *Jile bian*, in *Quan Song biji*, vol. 7, part 4, 1.38.

48   *CB* 168.7.4046.

49   *Sushui jiwen*, in *Quan Song biji*, vol. 7, part 1, 4.46.

50   *SSJW* 11.133–34.

51   *CB* 312.6.7574

52   *Jingkang yaolu jianzhu* 7.792.

53   *SS* 197.4921.

54   *CB* 271.18.6636. Guangnan was a region consisting of modern Guangdong and Guangxi.

55   Ballista was a large weapon used to launch projectiles at distant targets. Its operation required a number of men.

56   *CB* 282.7.6900–01.

57   *CB* 299.27.7281.

58   *CB* 468.25.11186.

59   *Shengshui yantan lu*, 2.20–21.

60   *Qingxiang zaji*, 10.106–07.

61   *Huayang ji*, vol. 1093, 60.2b.442.

62   *SSJW* 6.79–80.

63   *Dongzhai jishi*, 4.35.

64   *SSJW* 2.25–26.

65   *CB* 173.9.4180.

66   *SS* 464.13563–64.

67   In the Northern Song capital, Kaifeng.

68   *Shaoshi wenjian houlu*, 20.155.

69   *SSJW* 8.97.

70   *Songren yishi huibian*, 8.356.

71   *SS* 187.4598.

72   *CB* 151.5.3676.

73   *SSJW* 4.50; 11.134–35.

74   Supervisor of militia according to Sima Guang. Military director-in-chief according to Li Tao.

75   *CB* 151.5.3676.

76   *CB* 190.5.4579.

77   *CB* 66.18.1472

78   Around nine o'clock at night.

79   *SSJW* 14.182–83.

80   An abatis is an obstacle made of sharp wood placed outside the walls.

81   *SSJW* 4.50.

82   *CB* 151.5.3676.

83   *SSJW* 4.50; 11.134.

84   *CB* 66.18.1472

85   *Shaoshi wenjian lu*, 10.101–02.

86   *CB* 5.3676–77.

87   The Two Drafting Groups were officials who worked under the grand councilors, in charge of drafting edicts.

88   *SSJW* 4.51; *CB* 152.3.3696–97.

89   *SS* 464.13563.

90   *SSJW* 10.118.

91   *Dongxuan bilu*, 11.123–24.

92   *Dongzhai ji shi*, 4.35–36.

93   *SSJW* 11.134–35.

94   *SSJW* 4.50–51: 11.134–35.

95   *CB* 151.35.3688.

96   *SS* 464.13563.

97   *CB* 221.49.5383.

98   *CB* 190.5.4579.

99   *SSJW* 4.46.

100   Graff, *Medieval Chinese Warfare*, 212, 216, 239.

101   For more on the Song's examination system see John Chaffee's *The Thorny Gates of Learning in Sung China*.

102   McKnight, "Law and the military in the Sung," 1.

103   Sogabe, "Sōdai no shi-hai ni tsuite," 21.

REFERENCES

PRIMARY SOURCES

Dongxuan bilu 東軒筆錄, by Wei Tai 魏泰 (active 11th–12th century). Beijing: Zhonghua shuju, 1983.

Dongzhai ji shi 東齋記事, by Fan Zhen 范鎮 (1007–1087). Beijing: Zhonghua shuju, 1980.

Huayang ji 華陽集, by Wang Gui 王珪 (1019–1085). Vol. 1093. Taiwan shangwu yinshu guan, 1983.

Jile bian 雞肋編, by Zhuang Chuo 莊綽 (b. 1078). In *Quan Song biji* 全宋筆記, part 4, vol. 7. Zhengzhou: Daxiang chubanshe, 2008.

Jingkang yaolu jianzhu 靖康要錄箋注, by Wang Zao 汪藻 (1079–1154). 3 vol. Chengdu: Sichuan daxue chubanshe, 2008.

Lecheng ji 欒城集, by Su Che 蘇轍 (1039–1112). 3 vol. Shanghai: Shanghai guji chubanshe, 1987.

Lequan ji 樂全集, by Zhang Fangping 張方平 (1007–1091). Vol. 1104. Taiwan shangwu yin shu guan 1983.

Ouyang Xiu quanji 歐陽修全集, by Ouyang Xiu 歐陽修 (1007–1072). Beijing: Beijing shi Zhongguo shudian, 1986.

Pengcheng ji 彭城集, by Liu Ban 劉攽 (1023–1089). Vol. 1096. Taiwan shangwu yinshu guan, 1983.

Pingzhou ketan 萍洲可談, by Zhu Yu 朱彧 (active 11th–12th century). Beijing: Zhonghua shuju, 2007.

Qingxiang za ji 青箱雜記, by Wu Chuhou 吳處厚 (*jinshi* 1053). Beijing: Zhonghua shuju, 1985.

Shaoshi wenjian houlu 邵氏聞見後錄, by Shao Bo 邵博 (d. 1158). 1983; Reprint, Beijing: Zhonghua shuju, 2006.

Shaoshi wenjian lu 邵氏聞見錄, by Shao Bowen 邵伯溫 (1057–1134). 1983; Reprint, Beijing: Zhonghua shuju 2008.

Shengshui yantan lu 澠水燕談錄, by Wang Pizhi 王闢之 (*jinshi* 1067). Beijing: Zhonghua shuju, 1981.

Song huiyao jigao 宋會要輯稿, compiled by Xu Song 徐松 (1781–1848) et al. Beijing: Zhonghua shuju, 1957.

Songren yishi huibian 宋人軼事彙編, edited by Ding Chuanjing 丁傳靖 (1870–1930). Beijing: Zhonghua shuju, 2003.

Song shi 宋史, edited by Tuo Tuo 脫脫 (1313–1355) et al. Beijing: Zhonghua shuju, 1977.

Sushui jiwen 涑水記聞, by Sima Guang 司馬光 (1019–1086). In *Quan Song biji* 全宋筆記, vol. 7, part 1, 2003. Reprint, Zhengzhou: Daxiang chubanshe, 2008.

Xu zizhi tongjian changbian 續資治通鑒長編, by Li Tao 李燾 (1115–1184). Beijing: Zhonghua shuju, 1985.

Youyang zazu 酉陽雜俎, by Duan Chengshi 段成式 (d. 863). Beijing: Zhonghua shuju, 1985.

SECONDARY SOURCES

Chaffee, John. *The Thorny Gates of Learning in Sung China: A Social History of Examinations*. Cambridge, UK: Cambridge University Press, 1985.

Cheng Minsheng 程民生. *Songdai renkou wenti kaocha* 宋代人口問題考察. Zhengzhou: Henan renmin chubanshe, 2013.

Chung, Alvin Chin-Wai. "Aspects of the Systems of Military Logistics During the Song Dynasty (960–1278 A.D.): The Procurement of Horses, Military Agricultural Colonies, and the Imperial Ordnance Industry." Master's thesis, McGill University, 1999.

Graff, David A. *Medieval Chinese Warfare, 300–900*. London: Routledge, 2002.

Labadie, John Richard. "Rulers and Soldiers: Perception and Management of the Military in Northern Sung China (960–ca. 1060)." PhD diss., University of Washington, 1982.

Lorge, Peter Alan. "War and the Creation of the Northern Song State." PhD diss., University of Pennsylvania, 1996.

McGrath, Michael C. "Military and Regional Administration in Northern Sung China, 960–1126." PhD diss., Princeton University, 1982.

McKnight, Brian E. "Law and the Military in the Sung." *International Conference on Sinology*, Academia Sinica, 1986.

Scott, James C. *Weapons of the Weak: Everyday Forms of Peasant Resistance*. New Haven, Conn.: Yale University Press, 1985.

Sogabe Shizuo 曽我部静雄. "Sōdai no shi-hai ni tsuite" 宋代の刺配について. *Bunka*, vol. 29, no. 1 (1965), 1–23.

Tan Su-cheng 譚溯澄. "Songdai zhi jundui" 宋代之軍隊. PhD diss., National Chengchi University, Taiwan, 1972.

Wang Zengyu 王曾瑜. *Songchao junzhi chutan (zengding ben)* 宋朝軍制初探 (增訂本). Beijing: Zhonghua shuju, 2011.

9 State-Forced Relocations in China, 900–1300

PATRICIA BUCKLEY EBREY

EXPELLING, DEPORTING, OR OTHERWISE FORCING PEOPLE TO move is an ancient practice that is still very much a part of the modern world. From ancient Assyria to Stalin's Soviet Union and beyond, governments have moved people to make them less of a threat or more of an asset. Those subjected to forced moves have faced hardships of many kinds, including inadequate access to food and shelter, and more than a few have died, even in modern times when the journey did not have to be made entirely on foot. A review of recent scholarship on forced migrations summed up the experience of being displaced this way: "People resent uprooting, find it traumatic, and in the long run look back in grief and with an anger that lasts longer than the wars or the dams that forced them out."[1]

Issues of interest regarding the use of deportations and forced relocations by the states of Liao, Song, Jin, and Yuan include the extent to which these states made use of forced relocations, how they organized them, how they conceived of them strategically, and what it was like to be on the receiving end, uprooted and transported far from home. Forced relocations let us view state power from both sides: from the perspective of those building states and from the perspective of those subject to coercive state actions. The multipower context of East Asia from 900 to 1300 led states to treat transferring populations as just another potential tool for state building. Those forced to move adjusted as best they could, sometimes perhaps even benefiting, but their welfare was rarely a key concern of state agents.

Forced relocations need to be distinguished from other sorts of government-managed migrations, intended for the good of the people moved. These would include moving people who had lost their homes to floods or earthquakes, or settling refugees fleeing wars in neighboring countries. Similarly, governments sometimes encouraged migration to thinly populated areas by offering assistance and other incentives, without compelling people to go. Another group not included in the analysis are soldiers whose commanders defected to the other side. Such soldiers were unlikely to have been asked if they wanted to fight on the other side, so their transfers were coerced, but here the focus is on civilians, generally moved with their families. At the same time, I do not try to distinguish forced relocations from mass enslavement followed by removal. Some deportees, on arrival, are set free and told to support themselves, generally a less bitter fate than those treated as slaves and closely watched to prevent their escape. Here I consider both ends of the spectrum of postrelocation liberty.

In Chinese there was no special term used to refer to forced relocations. Rather, the sources says that the government "moved" (*xi, qian, yi*) people, households, or families. When the parties were at war, which was often the case, the people involved were often referred to as captives (*fu*) or as being abducted (*lue*) or driven (*qu*).

The practice of transferring populations was not an innovation of the post-Tang period. In the Warring States period, as the state of Qin defeated one rival after another, it systematically transferred populations, moving sizable numbers of people out of the newly conquered territories and shifting comparable numbers of other people in from lands it already held.[2] After Qin's final victory over all its rivals in 221 BCE, it moved the richest and most powerful families out of the recently conquered states to its own new capital city, Xianyang. Reportedly, 120,000 families were moved, which would have equaled about 600,000 people.[3] Besides moving people to the political center, Qin also moved people to the frontiers, both north and south.[4]

Many of Qin's coercive measures were repudiated in subsequent centuries. Forced relocations, however, were not. In 198 BCE, when many people would have had personal knowledge of Qin's population transfers, an official warned the Han emperor that his new government was threatened by the power of the old ruling families of the east. Moving them to the capital, he remarked, would make it easier to keep them under scrutiny and add to the density of the capital region and thus "strengthen the trunk and weaken the branches." After the emperor agreed, reportedly more than 100,000 people were moved to the Chang'an region.[5]

In subsequent centuries, there were many further cases of the deportation of sizable civilian populations. Filling up a new city and its environs was one of the most common reasons. The short-lived regimes of the Sixteen Kingdoms moved people as a way to keep them under their power. The Northern Wei government not only moved Chinese farmers to the region of their capital in northern Shanxi, they also moved non-Chinese Rouran and Gaoche as well as people they had captured during campaigns against the Southern Dynasties.[6] After the collapse of the Northern Wei, in 528 Gao Huan reportedly compelled 400,000 families to leave Luoyang and move to his new capital of Ye in southern Hebei.[7] In the south in this era, the Southern Dynasties often inflicted forced moves on the non-Chinese people indigenous to the area (called most often "Man") who were captured and forced into the army.[8] In the late sixth century when the Sui had defeated the southern state of Chen to unify China, it destroyed the southern capital of Jiankang and forced its officials to move to its new capital Chang'an. Those making the trek reportedly formed a column 500 *li* long.[9] In the Tang, too, forced relocations are recorded. In 660 when Tang destroyed the Korean state of Paekche, its king and his son were brought to Luoyang. Reportedly more than 12,000 of its people were relocated to "the central plain."[10]

As a way states exerted power over populations, forced relocations can be compared to taxes, labor service, and conscription, all of which could be arbitrary and oppressive.[11] The Liao, Jin, and Yuan expected military service of their core population (that is, the Kitans, Jurchens, and Mongols), and all also drafted Chinese, usually to serve as foot soldiers or laborers. The most oppressive conscription was imposed by the early Mongols on newly subjugated people selected to serve as frontline troops, to be the first wave on the attack of the next city, forced to take the brunt of an attack on an enemy stronghold. Under these circumstances, being drafted was worse than being relocated, and was probably just as likely to result in never returning to one's home.[12]

Judged as burdens imposed on civilians, relocation stands out for being imposed on entire families. That is, women, children, and the elderly were not mobilized for labor service or military service but were subject to deportation. It also tended to be more arbitrary. In the case of taxes and labor service, it was generally recognized that the burden should be widely shared and imposed according to recognized rules, even if in reality varying degrees of irrationality or unfairness intruded into the system.[13] Forced relocations, by contrast, fell on only a small portion of the population, making their occurrence more like floods and earthquakes, seemingly arbitrary and unpredictable disasters.

THE KITANS AND THE STATE OF LIAO

Of the four states examined in this chapter, Liao was the most systematic in relocating people to places where they could help Liao's economy through their labor. The "Geographical Treatise" in the *Liao shi* reports nearly ninety places settled by captives in these ways.[14] Early in the rise of the Kitan state, as their armies defeated other Manchurian pastoral tribes (such as the Xi and the Shiwei), they made slaves of those they captured and in time absorbed many of them into the Kitan tribal structure.[15] This custom of taking captives carried over into the Kitans' military actions against settled populations, not only Han Chinese, but also Bohai and Korean.[16] Whether the rulers kept the captives for themselves or distributed them as booty to their followers, the captives commonly were resettled in Liao territory as subordinated groups under the ordo of a man of high rank.

The Liao founder, Taizu or Abaoji (d. 926), was especially active in relocating people (see tables 9.1 and 9.2). Liao conquered one place in Bohai after another in the 920s, in 926 bringing the state to an end and acquiring all of its territory. Rather than simply leave Bohai's settled population in place, sizable groups were uprooted and relocated to core Kitan areas, especially in what eventually was called the Supreme Capital circuit, most of it in current Inner Mongolia (see map 9.1). Bohai who were resettled in this period ended up in eleven different counties in the Supreme Capital, Eastern Capital, and Central Capital circuits.[17] People from a particular county in Bohai were normally kept together and a new county founded for them at their destination. For instance, the captives taken from Bohai's Long prefecture were moved about 800 kilometers west to the Supreme Capital Circuit's Zu prefecture, where their settlement was given the name Changba county.[18] Sometimes the name of their original county was retained: those captured in Bohai's Yong'an county in Qing prefecture were moved more than 800 kilometers to the Supreme Capital circuit's Longsheng prefecture, and their settlement given the name Yong'an county.[19] Raids into North China probably led to the taking of even more captives than the battles for Bohai, although numbers are far from precise. For instance, a 902 raid into northern Shanxi is said to have led to 95,000 people being taken captive, while a 912 raid into Hebei's You prefecture led to "huge numbers of captives" and another in 916 to Hebei and Shanxi also led to "innumerable captives."[20] Unfortunately, whether "innumerable" is closer to 5,000, 10,000, or 80,000 is not clear. Surviving records, probably reflecting a later date, show counties formed with these captives as rather small, most in the range of 1,000 to 5,000 households.[21]

After Taizu's death in 926, Liao continued to acquire captives and resettle them far from home. Like captives from Bohai, captives from North China were scattered quite widely in Liao territory, sometimes settled among groups of Bohai but more often by themselves. To give one example, Ding prefecture was raided several times and its residents ended up in the Eastern

TABLE 9.1. Places from which Chinese and Bohai were taken during Liao Taizu's reign (902–926)

Date	Place raided	Details about captives	Source
902	9 prefectures in 河東 Hedong and 代北 Daibei	95,000	LS 1.2, 34.396
903	河東懷遠 Hedong Huaiyuan		
903	薊 Ji	Returned with captives	LS 1.2
905	Several prefectures	Took all the people	LS 1.2
912	幽州 You	Huge numbers of captives	LS 34.396
916	振武 Zhenwu, 蔚 Wei, 新 Xin, 武 Wu, 媯 Gui, 儒 Ru, gaining all of 代北 Daibei, 河曲 Hequ, 陰山 Yinshan	Countless captives	LS 34.396
921	檀 Tan, 順 Shun, 安遠 Anyuan, 三河 Sanhe, 良鄉 Liangxiang, 望都 Wangdu, 潞 Lu, 滿城 Mancheng, 遂城 Suicheng, 定 Ding in Hebei	Took people captive and moved to Liao territory. Very large number from Ding	LS 2.17, 34.396
924	薊 Ji		LS 2.19
924	Bohai	Took Bohai people captive	LS 2.19, 34.396
925	Bohai	Tangut captives presented	LS 2.21, 34.396
926	Bohai	Bohai conquered	LS 2.22, 34.396

Capital circuit's Shuang prefecture (1,100 kilometers away), the Central Circuit's Yi prefecture (over 700 kilometers), and the Southern Circuit's Tan (300 kilometers), Ping (460 kilometers), and Ying prefectures (470 kilometers).[22] The casual way Liao moved people around can be seen in their role as part of the dowry for princesses. For instance, when Empress Dowager Chengtian (954–1009) of the Liao married her daughter Princess Chuguo, she had a city built for her dowry and moved 10,000 families to fill it.[23] As city dwellers, these captives probably plied a variety of trades. Yet in only a few cases is there any mention of Han captives as artisans (something the Mongols would do on a large scale).[24]

The demography of the Liao realm was dramatically altered when its rulers joined the fray in North China in the 930s. The puppet they set up as the ruler of the short-lived Later Jin recognized Liao suzerainty of Sixteen Prefectures in northern Hebei and Shanxi, with a settled population in the

TABLE 9.2. Places to which Chinese and Bohai captives were taken during Liao Taizu's reign

Circuit	Prefecture	County	Date	Details	Liao shi source
上京 Supreme	臨潢 Linhuang	臨潢 Linhuang	922–925	Captives taken in 燕 Yan and 薊 Ji prefectures.	37.439
		長泰 Changtai	926	Bohai captives taken from Bohai's 長泰 Changtai county lived mixed with Han settlers.	37.439
		定霸 Dingba		When Taizu took Bohai's 扶餘 Fuyu, the people moved here, to farm interspersed with Han.	37.439
		保和 Baohe		When Taizu defeated 龍州 Long prefecture, he moved people from 富利 Fuli county to create this county.	37.439
		潞 Lu	922	County created with the people from Youzhou's 潞 Lu county, taken when Taizu attacked 薊 Ji and raided 潞 Lu.	37.439
		宣化 Xuanhua		Taizu moved all of the people in Liaodong's 神化 Shenhua county when he defeated Bohai's 鴨淥府 Yalufu.	37.440
	祖 Zu	扶餘 Fuyu	926	Taizu moved captives from Bohai's 扶餘 Fuyu county here .	37.443
		顯理 Xianli	926	When Taizu captured the king of Bohai he moved his people here.	37.443
	永 Yong	長寧 Changning	926	When Taizu pacified Bohai, he moved its people here.	
	龍化 Longhua		902	When Taizu defeated 代北 Daibei, he moved its people here and built a city for them.	37.447
		龍化 Longhua		County set up with captives taken during Taizu's campaign against the Jurchen and his raids into Hebei's 燕 Yan and 薊 Ji.	37.447
	隆聖 Longsheng	永安 Yong'an		When Taizu pacified Bohai, he moved the people of 永安 Yong'an in 懷州 Huaizhou to this place.	37.447
	饒 Rao	長樂 Changle		When Taizu conquered Bohai, he moved its people here and established the county for them.	37.448
東京 Eastern Capital	瀋 Shen	樂郊 Lejiao		Established with captives Taizu took from Hebei's 薊州 Jizhou and 三河 Sanhe.	38.466
		嶺源 Lingyuan		Taizu moved captive commoners and officials from 薊 Ji in Hebei to set up this county.	38.466

Circuit	Prefecture	County	Date	Details	Liao shi source
	遼 Liao			東平府 Dongping fu was one of the first places taken by Taizu in his campaigns against Bohai, and he moved its people to fill 遼州 Liaozhou.	38.467
	祺 Qi			Taizu moved the captives he took in 檀州 Tanzhou here and called the place 檀州 Tanzhou, but later the name was changed.	38.467
		慶雲 Qingyun		Taizu created a 密雲 Miyun county with the captives he took from Hebei's 密雲 Miyun, but later the name was changed.	38.467
	銀 Yin	永平 Yongping		Taizu established it with captive households.	38.469
	歸 Gui			When Taizu pacified Bohai, he set this up with surrendered households.	38.475
中京 Central Capital	惠 Hui			Taizu built this city to settle several hundred Han captives.	39.483
	武安 Wu'an			Taizu built this city to house his Han captives.	39.483
	澤 Ze			Taizu built a camp for his captives from Hebei's 蔚州 Wei prefecture.	39.484
	興中 Xingzhong	興中 Xingzhong		Taizu settled Han he had captured here.	39.486
	黔 Qian	盛吉 Shengji		When Taizu pacified Bohai, the people captured in 興州 Xingzhou, 盛吉 Shengji county, were settled here.	39.487
	錦 Jin			Taizu set up the prefecture with Han captives.	39.487
	巖 Yan			When Taizu pacified Bohai, he moved Han households to 興州 Xingzhou.	39.488
南京 Southern Capital	檀 Tan	行唐 Xingtang		When Taizu raided 定州 Dingzhou and attacked 行唐 Xingtang, he drove all of its people north to 檀州 Tanzhou.	40.497
	平 Ping		922	Taizu settled captives from Hebei's 定州 Dingzhou here.	40.500
		安喜 Anxi		Taizu established it with captives from 定州 Dingzhou, 安喜 Anxi.	40.500
		望都 Wangdu		Taizu set it up with captives from 定州 Dingzhou, 望都 Wangdu county.	40.500
	灤 Luan			Taizu set it up with captives.	40.501
	營 Ying			Taizu set it up with captives from 定州 Dingzhou.	40.501

(continued)

TABLE 9.2. *(continued)*

Circuit	Prefecture	County	Date	Details	*Liao shi* source
西京 Western Capital	豐 Feng	振武 Zhenwu	916	On his way back from fighting the Tuhun, Taizu attacked this place and took all of its people east with him.	41.509
	蔚 Wei			When Taizu overcame 代北 Daibei, he made captives of the residents and took them away.	41.512
	東勝 Dongsheng		916	When Taizu defeated 振武 Zhenwu, the common people of 勝州 Shengzhou all rushed to 河東 Hedong, so this prefecture was abolished.	41.514

millions, mostly Han Chinese. Although Liao overlordship was rejected by the second Later Jin ruler and the state itself soon collapsed, Liao would retain the Sixteen Prefectures.[25]

Liao's biggest foray into North China was its southern campaign of 944 through 947, when Taizong and his armies reached Kaifeng and occupied it for three months. Many captives were taken on this campaign. Two Kitan princes, Bola and Ouliseng, founded counties with captives they acquired on these campaigns.[26] Being taken captive was, of course, not the worst possible fate. While on route back north from Kaifeng in 947, Liao forces retook Xiang prefecture from the petty warlord who had killed the recently installed Kitan commander. Reportedly when the Kitans returned, men and boys of all ages were killed, but girls and women were transported north. Groups composed solely of women would not have been told to start farming; presumably slavery was their fate.[27]

After Liao and Song signed a peace agreement in 1005, Liao no longer raided Song territory. It did, however, still sometimes relocate people for other reasons, such as to punish and weaken rebels. For instance, in 1029 a Bohai military officer named Da Yanlin rose in rebellion in the Eastern Capital. Descended from the Bohai royal family, he proclaimed himself emperor of a new dynasty. He must have had a sizable band of supporters, as he was able to hold the city against a siege for a year.[28] When Liao did regain the city, it moved the populace west to several different counties in the Supreme Capital circuit, such as Linhuang prefecture's Yisu county (500 kilometers).[29] A nearby city that had sided with the rebels, Nanhai, also held out for a year. After surrendering, all its residents were moved to the Supreme

Capital circuit, where a new county was set up for them (Qianliao county, about the same distance). To fill the now deserted Nanhai county, people from Ze prefecture were moved east (about 550 kilometers).[30]

The Liao seems generally to have moved captives far enough so that they could not easily return (see map 9.1). Even if a strong young man might succeed in making his way back when taken more than a few hundred kilometers from home, he would be less likely to try if he had small children or elderly parents with him. Carrying enough food for all of them would be nearly impossible. Probably as a consequence, few people who enter the historical record trace their families back to someone who returned to North China after they or their ancestors were forcibly moved to Mongolia or Manchuria by Liao. There are a few exceptions. One man who was captured at age six and kept as a house servant by the family of a future empress is recorded because his son was on close personal terms with Liao Taizu.[31] Several decades later, a boy captured in the Liao campaign of 1004, led by Empress Dowager Chengtian, was one of nearly one hundred captured boys under ten selected to be castrated for service as palace eunuchs. He gained favor with the boy emperor, who later gave him responsible positions.[32]

The highest-ranking group of forced migrants are also the ones whose journeys are recorded in the most detail: they are the royal establishment of the state of Later Jin. As a harbinger of the fate of the Northern Song court at the hands of the Jurchen in 1127, the Later Jin royal entourage was taken captive by Liao after they entered Kaifeng in 947. According to the two histories of the Five Dynasties, Liao ordered the imperial party to be moved north of the Liao Eastern capital, to Huanglong prefecture. The party included the deposed Later Jin ruler, his birth mother and his legal mother (that is, the empress of his father), his own empress, his younger brother, and two sons, along with fifty palace women, thirty eunuchs, fifty military and civil officials, a doctor, four guards, seven cooks, six miscellaneous palace workers, and twenty Later Jin soldiers, the whole group guarded by three hundred Kitan horsemen.[33] Several thousand officials were also moved north, accompanied by several thousand soldiers.[34]

The trip presented many trials. Richard Davis has translated the *New History of the Five Dynasties* account:

> The entourage, ten days after leaving You Prefecture, passed through Ping
> before departing via Yu Pass. Crossing a terrain of pebbles and stones
> and denied food when hungry, palace women and official companions
> were forced to forage for food, mostly tree fruits and wild plants. After

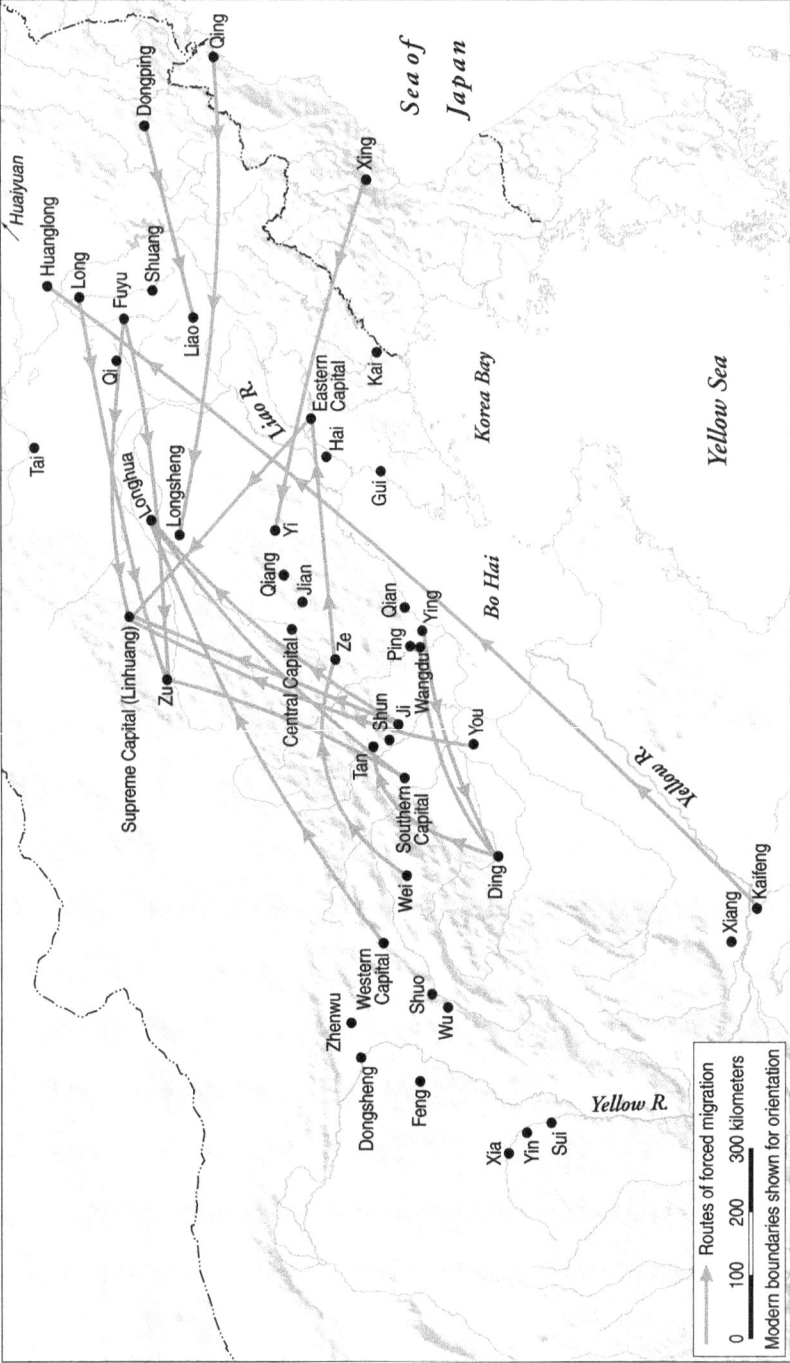

MAP 9.1. Points of origin and destination of forced migrants

another seven to eight days of travel, upon reaching Jinzhou, the barbarians coerced the Emperor and Empress Dowager to bow before a picture of [Kitan patriarch] Abaoji. The emperor could no longer bear the indignity and cried out, "By not allowing me to die, Xue Chao did me a profound disservice!" They crossed the Liao River ten days or so later, reaching Tiezhou, Bohai, before traversing Nanhai Prefecture for an additional seven to eight days to reach Huanglong Prefecture.[35]

After spending some time in Huanglong, the party was ordered to move to a very remote place 1500 *li* to the northwest, but en route a Kitan prince staged a coup and canceled the distant transfer, allowing the Jin deportees to move instead to Liaoyang, in one of the more densely settled parts of Liao territory. The prince saw them in Liaoyang and decided to claim some of the party, taking fifteen of the eunuchs, fifteen officials, and one of the deposed emperor's sons. The Kitan prince's brother-in-law asked for a young daughter of the former Jin ruler. Although the request was refused, the prince took her anyway. In 949, the deportees were moved again to Jian prefecture, said to be 1,200 *li* from Liaoyang, but more like 800 *li* (i.e., 400 kilometers) on modern maps (see map 9.1). In Jian prefecture the party was assigned fifty *qing* of land, which members of the party had to work to produce their own food.[36] It is unlikely that the group included many experienced farmers. Possibly as a consequence, by the late 950s, about a decade after they were first moved, half of them had died.[37]

There are only a few discussions of the pros and cons of moving people for state purposes in Liao sources. A memorial by a Kitan official advocating moving the Bohai people north argued that it was difficult to prevent them from causing trouble where they were, and that there was rich and fertile soil closer to the Kitan's Supreme Capital where they could be settled. "To take advantage of their weakness and to move the people back would be a permanent plan for ten thousand generations."[38] An argument against moving people was made a century later by a Chinese official serving Liao, Liu Shen (*jinshi* 1036), who was known for speaking up for the interests of the common people. He objected when the Liao emperor ordered that "rich people" be moved to fill the two prefectures of Chun and Tai near the border between the Supreme and Eastern Capital circuits.[39] Chinese officials were not always against forced relocations, however. Later in the eleventh century the Chinese official Liu Hui (*jinshi* 1079) proposed handling the problem of provisioning troops in the west by moving Han families to Yanluo Fort near modern Huhehot and having them grow food.[40]

One consequence of Liao's active practice of relocation was increased ethnic diversity and complexity. Liao seems to have made an effort to erase or at least weaken Bohai identity by moving large numbers of Bohai into regions where they would be in the minority (even if they lived with a few hundred families from the same place). They also tried intermixing Bohai and Han, and it was not uncommon for them to add other ethnic groups, such as Jurchen or Xi. In the case of both Bohai and Han, the long distances captives were moved also suggests that Liao wanted to weaken their social networks and make it more difficult for them to return home. Once Liao gained the Sixteen Prefectures in northern Shanxi and Hebei in the mid-tenth century, it had millions of Han, and does not seem to have tried to weaken Han identity. Still, thousands of Han Chinese were moved from the region of the Sixteen Prefectures into modern Inner Mongolia, Liaoning, and Jilin, adding to the ethnic complexity of those regions.

THE CHINESE AND THE STATE OF SONG

Although Song sources are much more abundant than Liao ones, they mention many fewer state-ordered forced relocations.[41] In the early Song, the government forced the moves of the royal houses they subjugated, in general moving them to the capital Kaifeng where it would be easier to keep an eye on them. After the surrender of the Southern Tang ruler Li Yu (937–978) in 976, he was brought to Kaifeng, along with a large group of his palace establishment and his high officials. Li was given a palace to reside in, and a stipend that supported him.[42] The ruler of Wuyue, Qian Chu (929–988), was invited to Kaifeng while he was still independent and shown how well the other former rulers were being treated to encourage him, too, to submit to Song. The early Song rulers regularly invited these former rulers to banquets and other events where they would be seen because their presence added to the glory of the Song court, showing that it attracted the allegiance of eminent personages from afar. Although these former rulers surely understood the coercion that had brought them there, they were not under the equivalent of house arrest, as the government no longer saw them as threats. Often their leading officials were taken into the Song civil service and some rose quite high.[43]

In the late tenth century, the Song government also used forced transfers to gain military advantage. In 969 the Song forced 10,000 families to move from territory in modern Shanxi held by the Northern Han south into Song-held territory in the vicinity of Luoyang. This was done to weaken the

Northern Han's resource base.[44] At least once, Song tried to bring civilians who had been moved into Liao-held territory back to Song territory. In 986, Song moved 500 Chinese households and 800 "tents" of Tuyuhun, Turks, and other tribes from four prefectures along the border with Liao (Yun, Ying, Huan, and Shuo). The families were described as suffering under the Kitans, welcoming the Song armies, and eager to return to their old lands.[45]

In 994, before a firm border had yet been established in the northwest, Taizong asked his councilors whether Xia prefecture, deep in the desert, was worth holding onto, and proposed that the city be razed and its Tangut residents moved to neighboring Yin and Sui prefectures within Song borders. His councilors noted that the prefecture had regularly caused trouble to the northwest, so destroying it would be beneficial. Taizong then issued the order that the residents be moved to nearby prefectures under Song control and be allotted government land.[46] The fears of Taizong's councilors were prescient, as the Xi Xia state forged out of this cluster of Ordos Desert prefectures emerged as the most powerful military competitor of the Song in northwest China.

In 1050, Renzong (r. 1022–1063) discussed the pros and cons of moving people with his councilors:

> [Renzong] said to his councilors: "In ancient times common people were sometimes moved to areas with ample land. Today, Min [Fujian] and Shu [Sichuan] are crowded. Should we move their people?" Ding Du answered, "That would be legal, but the authorities would not be able to carry it out. Taizu once moved more than a thousand families from Taiyuan to Shandong. Taizong also moved the common people from Yun, Ying, Huan, and Shuo prefectures to a number of prefectures in Jingxi. People from the northwest are hardworking and frugal. Today those known for their wealth in their villages are often the people who were moved there. But people definitely are 'contented in their old communities and dread moving.'"

Ding Du further elaborated that he was not against the poor moving to regions with more opportunity, but thought it should be done on a voluntary basis. Given the hardships faced by the poor, the government should encourage them to migrate to areas where they could be given uncultivated government land.[47]

I have found no records of forced relocations ordered by the Southern Song government. In part this was a reflection of its military weakness: it had not subjugated any other states whose ruling houses and palace establishments could be moved to its capital. Although there were a couple of periods of hostilities along the Song–Jin border after the peace treaty of 1141, Song does not seem to have set out to capture former Song subjects and bring them to Song-held territory. It faced enough of a challenge dealing with refugees, people who had fled on their own.

Thus, despite the fact that forced relocations had deep roots in Chinese statecraft, having been used so extensively by the Qin and Han governments, by Song times, the Chinese state of Song made relatively limited use of it. In its first half century, the Northern Song government moved people for military purposes a few times. Song statesmen did not think Song suffered a shortage of people—they wanted more land, not more people. In addition, they saw drawbacks to population transfers and sometimes explicitly argued that it was less disruptive to offer incentives to recruit volunteers rather than force unwilling people to move.

THE JURCHEN AND THE STATE OF JIN

In the early twelfth century, as the Jurchen took over all of Liao's former territory and about a third of Song's, they showed little reluctance to force people to move, generally taking them back to Jin territory. For instance, after taking Yanjing and the surrounding five prefectures in 1122, the Jurchen were said to have "exhaustively moved the rich and strong and those with skills to their home territory."[48] In 1130, after Jin took Jiankang and killed many of the residents, it took the survivors and forced them north.[49] Still, Jin relied less on moving people north than Liao had. They had gained millions of farmers and craftsmen when they gained control of North China. Rather than move large numbers of them north to fill the Jurchen homeland, the Jurchen moved south in large numbers.

What makes the Jin sources especially valuable is the survival of multiple sources on the Jin removal of over 15,000 people from Kaifeng in 1127. These give much more information on what it was like to be forcibly moved than the sources for the other dynasties.[50] This large forced move took place after the Jin capture of the Song capital, Kaifeng, near the end of 1126. Early in 1127, when the Jurchen were camped outside the city walls, they demanded that the Song government hand over a wide assortment of people, among them the royal family, imperial kinsmen, palace ladies, eunuchs, specific officials, and craftsmen of many sorts. Elsewhere I have described the experience of the retired emperor Huizong and those in his company.[51] Here let me look more closely at the experiences of the thousands of urban residents sought for their specialist skills.

Demands for urban specialists began not long after the Jurchen first gained control of the walls of Kaifeng. These demands for particular categories of people were widely publicized, so it is not surprising that many sources mention them, and that the totals and categories are not always consistent. In part this reflects the fact that the Jurchen did not make a single list and issue it once, but kept asking for additional people, sometimes with numbers attached, sometimes not.

One of the fuller lists is in the anonymous *Wengzhong renyu*. It reports that on 1127/1/25, the Jurchen demanded 600 maidservants, several hundred musicians from the Court Entertainment Bureau, and fifty inner retainers (most likely referring to eunuchs). On 2/1 they requisitioned all manner of artisans and craftsmen, and two days later male and female musicians and physicians. On 2/12 they demanded the clerks of the Six Boards and on 2/13 forty experts in the Classics. Two days later, perhaps after checking what specialists they already had, they issued a call for officials of the Astrological Service, eunuchs, Buddhists and Daoists, clerks of the directorates, tailors, dyers, carpenters, silversmiths, ironworkers, Yin Yang specialists, magicians, shadow puppeteers, string puppeteers, and singers, all of them along with their families.[52]

Other sources mention specialties not listed in *Wengzhong renyu*. For instance, one source records that on 12/13 a call was issued for twenty painters and fifty winemakers.[53] Another states that on 1/27, requisitioned workers included carvers of ivory and rhinoceros horn.[54] An order issued on 1/30, we are told, demanded 100 painters, 200 physicians, 100 miscellaneous entertainers, 400 musicians, fifty woodworkers, thirty each of bamboo, tile, plaster, and stone workers, ten saddle makers, 100 jade carvers, eighty gold and silver smiths, fifty clerks, and various attendants.[55] A National Academy student, Ding Teqi (d. ca. 1135), reported that when thirty experts in the Classics were sought, with promises of generous compensation, men readily volunteered.[56] Most of the time, though, being drafted into these levies was deeply dreaded. In response to a demand for more than a thousand craftsmen, one source notes, "Those selected to leave the city did so weeping, their relatives in tears parting from them at the city gate."[57] One source gives a rough figure of 3,000 families of craftsmen who were taken from the city.[58] This does not count all of the prostitutes and female musicians taken from the city, perhaps another three thousand.

The large numbers of women turned over to the Jurchens reflect the fact that the Jurchen had demanded a huge indemnity from Song, way beyond the capacity of the government to raise, and in the end the Jin let them pay it through women, each assessed a different amount depending on her status. Thus, to pay its indemnity, the Song had to supply more than 5,000 women, ranging from princesses and imperial consorts to low-status performers and prostitutes.[59] Within days, all the women of the entertainment quarters were rounded up, along with former palace ladies, even if they had already been married.[60] More than a thousand women were rejected by the Jurchen, who demanded that the Song send more suitable substitutes.[61]

No source describes conditions in the Jurchen camps where the urban specialists were kept for weeks, but they cannot have been very good because a great many people died there. The *Record of the Song Captives,* by a Jin author identified as Kegong, states that of the more than 16,000 people taken as captives into the Jin camps, 2,000 died during their two- to four-month stay there.[62]

Besides gathering people, Jin gathered loot of many sorts, so organizing carts and draft animals took some time, and the convoys of captives did not set off until the end of the third month of 1127. Nearly fifteen thousand captives were organized into seven separate convoys. The requisitioned urban residents made up the largest convoy with 3,412 commoners drafted for their special skills and 3,180 women, some perhaps wives or daughters of specialists, others women transported to serve as prostitutes, whether that had been their earlier profession or not.[63] When this convoy arrived in Yanjing on 5/27 their numbers were down to 2,900 women and 1,800 specialists, half of whom were promptly sent more than 600 kilometers further north to the Supreme Capital.[64]

The reason so many died on the trip was the harshness of the conditions. According to the *Record of the Bian Capital* (Biandu ji) by Tao Xuangan, those transported were grouped into troops of 500 and driven like sheep or pigs by several dozen mounted soldiers. Most were city dwellers not used to walking long distances, and if they fell behind they were beaten or killed, so that bodies littered the fields they passed.[65] The survival rate of children in particular was very poor. Women were often transported in carts, which sometimes overturned. Worse, they often could not avoid being raped.[66]

Each night tents would be set up and rice distributed. According to Cao Xun, the Jurchen generally erected a wooden barrier around the camp, with gaps between the planks that allowed people on the inside to see out and outside to see in.[67] The deportees had to find their own firewood and water.

Since they were not allowed out of the camp, they soon learned to pick up what water and wood they could while they were traveling and save it for the evening.[68]

The townspeople's convoy reached Yanjing on 5/27, after two months on the road (a slow pace for 650 kilometers). Half were immediately sent on to the Supreme Capital. Zhao Zizhi described what happened to those who stayed in Yanjing: "On the order of the Jin ruler the physicians, musicians, palace servants, craftsmen, and astrological service officials who were forced from Kaifeng to Yanjing were not made to move again, and were adequately accommodated in several temples. The palace servants became the property of the ruler, the physicians opened shops, the musicians performed, the astrologers offered services, the craftsmen plied their trade, each in their own ways making enough to clothe and feed themselves."[69]

Part of what made it difficult to support themselves was that the city was filled with others forced there: "Residents of nearby counties and prefectures that fell [to the Jurchen] were all forced to move north, in the millions, to Yanjing. Both the noble and the base, the strong and the weak, faced the misery of starvation. Bodies were piled up, bones exposed in the fields. The strong who did make it to Yanjing had to find a way to support themselves. Those with resources opened shops or businesses; those without borrowed or stole; the old and the weak begged for food in the market."[70] The craftsmen and other urban residents who were moved to Yanjing and the Supreme Capital largely disappear from the written record at that point. Their individual fates undoubtedly varied, depending not only on where they ended up, but also their own ability to make the best of their situations. As a group they seem to have done better than the Song imperial clansmen, who died at such a high rate that it is difficult not to think that the Jin state was trying to kill them off.[71]

THE MONGOLS AND THE STATE OF YUAN

The scale of Mongol-forced relocations dwarfs that of the three earlier dynasties. Not only were Chinese moved north, but Europeans and Central Asians were moved east. In this chapter my attention is not on the non-Chinese that the Mongols brought to Mongolia or China, a subject that has been widely studied.[72] Instead, my focus is on the transfer of Chinese, subjects of Jin or Song, to places so distant from their homes that they had little hope of ever returning. Evidence is largely of two sorts—reports of substantial groups of Chinese in Mongolia or further west and records of people being taken captive and moved away, often with nothing known of their final destination.

The Europeans who reached Mongolia or China regularly made note of Europeans they encountered so far from home.[73] Chinese who traveled west, for similar reasons, sometimes noted when they came across Chinese in unexpected places. In 1221 and 1222, Li Zhichang traveled from Shandong to Mongolia, then west to Central Asia, stopping in Tashkent, Samarkand, and Balkh. He saw Chinese craftsmen settled in western Mongolia, Samarkand, and in the Upper Yenisei region of Siberia.[74] Peng Daya and Xu Ting sent as envoys to the Mongols saw Chinese working as herders, concluding that seven out of ten of the herders were Chinese.[75] Zhang Dehui (1195–1274) traveled to Karakorum in 1247 and reported seeing Chinese farmers living along the Kerulun River in mud huts growing hemp and wheat.[76] Liu Yu, traveling along with a mission in 1259, saw Chinese in four places. They were workmen "living everywhere" in Samarkand; in Beshbalik they were growing wheat, barley, and millet; further west they worked as guards; and in the city of Almalik they lived among the local Muslims.[77] Evidence of Chinese in Central Asia and further west is also found in Rashid al Din's *History*, written in 1310. He reported that Chinese had been moved to Marv (one of the cities in Central Asia whose population had been slaughtered), where they introduced a new type of millet, and he mentioned that some of them were later moved to Azerbaijan.[78]

How had Chinese ended up so far from home? The Mongol campaigns against Jin between 1211 and 1232 resulted in the capture of hundreds of thousands of Chinese. As they did in Central Asia, in North China the Mongols sometimes slaughtered everyone except for artisans or those they wanted as slaves or cannon fodder.[79] Recorded cases of sparing artisans before general slaughter include Guangning, Yizhou, Xuzhou, and Baozhou.[80] Many captives were taken to the Mongols' new capital of Karakorum. Archaeological investigations of Karakorum have uncovered the quarters of "metalsmiths, ceramicists, bead-makers, bone-carvers, and weavers drawn from such diverse regions as China, Tibet, Khwarazm, Volga Bulgaria, Uighuristan, and southern Siberia."[81] After Jin abandoned Yanjing in 1214, the Mongols "moved artisans from the Luo River area to fill it up" and put one man in charge of them.[82] Another group of artisans were brought to Hongzhou (western Hebei) in the early 1230s, where 300 weavers from Bianjing (the Jurchen's southern capital) were brought to work with another 300 from Central Asia.[83] When Bianjing fell in 1233, the Mongol general Subetei considered general slaughter. Yelü Chucai (1189–1243) argued that land without people is useless and pointed out to him that the city was full of such useful people as bow and arrow makers and armorers, as well as officials and the rich.[84] As a result, military men were given huge numbers of captives, often several hundred or even several thousand. In 1236 Ögödei took 72,000 artisan families and assigned his generals appropriate shares.[85]

Given the highly unstable situation in North China during the years when the Jurchens and Mongols struggled for domination, it can sometimes be difficult to tell whether people were being deported against their will or were refugees given an opportunity to escape danger. Consider those relocated by Shi Bingzhi, a Chinese strongman who had surrendered to the Mongols along with several thousand followers. The *Yuan shi* records: "[Mukhali] ordered [Shi] Bingzhi to supervise the surrendered men and their families and make a camp at Bazhou [Hebei]. Because Bingzhi was successful at comforting them, from far and near people came to join him, the number reaching 100,000 families. He then transported them to north of the desert [Mongolia]. On the journey, the surrendered people were starving, so Bingzhi fed them using the cattle and sheep that had been given to him, saving many lives."[86]

This passage makes Shi Bingzhi sound like a paternalistic patron who hadn't forced anyone to accompany him, but considering the fact that the people being transported lacked adequate food, one can see other ways to read it. C. C. Hsiao comments that "Bingzhi seems to have done much to assist the Mongols with their supply and manpower problems. It is said that, soon after submitting, he assembled more than 100,000 families in Bazhou alone and deported them to Mongolia—perhaps to serve as artisans, domestics and military colonists."[87] Igor de Rachewiltz more explicitly stresses the coercive side of transferring the surrendered, citing this case as evidence that the Mongols treated the population in North China as slaves.[88]

The Mongols executed the Xi Xia ruler when he surrendered in 1227.[89] With the fall of Jin, the Mongols marched out more than 500 members of the Wanyan imperial clan, then killed them all.[90] After the fall of Jin, the Mongols attacked Song territory in Sichuan, but did not wage all-out war to subjugate Song until the 1250s because they were busy elsewhere. In 1259, after capturing a city in Sichuan, more than 80,000 captives were taken, and an attack in Hunan resulted in 20,000 captives taken north.[91]

In contrast to how the Mongols treated the royal families of the Xia and Jin upon subjugation, a half century later they treated the surrendered Song empresses and the boy emperor relatively decently. In 1276 the Song surrender had been nearly unconditional: the empress dowager asked that the people of Hangzhou and the Song house be spared. The Mongol occupation of the city was done in an orderly manner, and orders were issued that everyone continue in their usual work, and many officials were offered the opportunity to serve the Mongols. The convoy carrying the imperial party and the treasures the Mongols had decided to bring north was much smaller than the one that left Kaifeng a century and a half earlier: about 300 officials and clerks, perhaps a hundred palace ladies, a few dozen eunuchs, and a hundred or more students from the imperial academy, along with about three thousand men as escorts. The trip was also much easier, at least for the first several weeks, as it was done by boat up the Grand Canal. It took two months to reach Yanjing, but almost half of that time was aboard boats. After spending a month in Yanjing, the imperial party was forced once more to move, this time to the Yuan Supreme Capital (Shangdu), where they met Kubilai. There the palace ladies learned that they would be married to local artisans (perhaps descendants of earlier deportees). Imperial clansmen do not seem to have been rounded up in Hangzhou, perhaps because few were there at the time. The main reason that few of them ended up in captivity, however, was that Pu Shougeng, the superintendent of foreign trade at Quanzhou, Fujian, defected to the Mongols, and whether on his own initiative or by command, had the three thousand imperial clansmen living there slaughtered. Many other clansmen went into hiding and took assumed names.[92]

In Chinese sources, one does not come across many cases of Chinese farmers or craftsmen who had been transported to Mongolia or further away, undoubtedly because they rarely rose to hold important political or military roles. Those transported at a young age, however, might prove useful to the Mongols because they could acculturate better. One example is Yang Weizhong (1206–60), who after being captured as a boy in Hebei was transported to Karakorum and assigned as an attendant attached to Ögödei's guard. He was young enough to acquire fluent Mongolian and with Ögödei's rise came to hold influential military and administrative posts.[93] Zhang Hui (1223–1285) offers a similar case. Captured at twelve or thirteen when the Mongols invaded Sichuan, he was taken to Hanghai in central Mongolia. After living there for several years, he could speak several of the local languages. On the recommendation of a Mongol official, he was assigned to work in Kubilai's princely establishment and from there rose to high office. He later went to considerable effort and expense to redeem people who had been captured, even establishing a monastery for those who were unable to return to their homes.[94]

Records of educated men who were taken captive by the Mongols are quite common in Chinese sources. Dou Mo (1196–1280) managed to escape captivity on his own (the only one to survive of thirty taken captive).[95] Usually they are mentioned because Chinese who gained influence with the new rulers took it upon themselves to try to gain their release. Yang Weizhong, for instance, recognized the Confucian teacher Zhao Fu (fl. 1235–1257) among a group of captives in Hubei and brought him north to Yanjing.[96] A Uighur Confucian scholar in Mongol service, Lian Xixian (1231–1280), "in addition to emancipating enslaved scholars," also "recruited many learned men for official appointment."[97] When Bianjing fell to the Mongols, many leading Chinese scholar-officials were captured, including Yuan Haowen (1190–1257), who wrote to Yelü Chucai pleading for his assistance in rescuing fifty-four Jin scholar-officials.[98] Xu Heng (1209–1281) was captured by the Mongols after they took Zhengzhou and spent two years in captivity, from 1232 to1234.[99] The Chinese general Yan Shi (1182–1240) was credited with paying ransoms to free Chinese scholars that other Mongol commanders had captured.[100] In these cases, there is no definite statement that the scholars were transported far from home. But the need to return freed captives is mentioned from time to time in surviving sources. For instance, in 1328 the government issued an order that people in both the capital region and throughout the country who had been captured by soldiers and made slaves should be sent back by the authorities, and in 1339 the government ordered that 100 people who had been captured by soldiers in Yunnan be released and given the wherewithal to return home.[101]

Artisans moved by the Mongols to where they were needed became hereditary artisan households, expected to train their sons to perform the same work they did.[102] Some artisans worked in government workshops, but others provided products as their tax and corvée obligation. After Kubilai took the throne, he had many artisan households moved to Zhongdu, probably already contemplating the building of a new city there, later called Dadu.[103] After the capital was moved to Dadu, more artisans were sent there, such as jade workers sent in 1261 and catapult builders in 1279.[104] In some cases, Kubilai had Chinese artisans communities moved back to China from Mongolia.[105]

The Mongols' transfers of artisans and others can be assessed several ways. A late Yuan author took pride in the quality of the work produced by transported artisans: "When our dynasty first gained control of China and set up institutions, all the artisans in the realm were taken to the capital, classified, and assigned to bureaus which kept records of their work, provided food, excused their families of other corvée, letting them concentrate on their art.

Therefore, the refinement of the craftwork of our dynasty is superior to that of earlier times."[106]

Much like the Kitans and Jurchen before them, the Mongols implemented harsher policies in their early decades. It is probably fair to assume that the generation who were forced to move far from home suffered the most, and that their children and especially grandchildren would be relatively adjusted to their place in the Mongol empire. Over time, especially once Kubilai succeeded as khan, the Mongols became more familiar with Chinese traditions of statecraft and came to appreciate their logic. By 1272, the Chinese official Wei Chu (1232–1292) argued that trying to confine a work force and send out search parties when someone fled was not worth the effort—it was better to simply recruit those willing to work for pay.[107] This way of thinking probably helps explain the gradual reduction in forced moves.

DISCUSSION

The four states treated in this chapter all pursued state interests. They sought to avoid domination by their neighbors and were alert to possible changes in circumstances that would allow them to redraw boundaries in their favor. Victoria Tin-bor Hui's description of the competition of the Warring States period would fit this period just as well: "Compelled by the pressure of war, rulers who wished to maintain survival, recover losses, or establish hegemony would have to strive to increase their military and economic capabilities."[108] But even if their goals were essentially the same, the strategies that the four states adopted were not identical.

The Song was the odd man out. From the evidence presented here, the three northern states all made greater use of forced relocation than the Song did; they took more people and moved them longer distances. Granted, there were differences among the Liao, Jin, and Yuan. Both the Kitans and the Mongols moved large numbers of people to put them to work. The Kitans saw these captives as assets. In place of acquiring grain from China proper (by raiding or trade), the Kitans moved farmers to places controlled by Liao and had them put fields to the plow to grow grain. They may have thought of them as slaves, but slaves who are useful to their owners. The Mongols were different. Sources for the early Mongols portray them as seeing little to lose by killing those they captured, the utility of terrifying nearby cities outweighing any useful work that the captives could have done. They made exceptions for craftsmen in short supply in their new cities, whom they relocated to where they could construct buildings, weave textiles, and do all sorts of other skilled work. As Thomas Allsen points out, nomadic societies find it difficult to produce from their own ranks all the specialists that they desire. In his assessment, "the Chinggisid practice of capturing, collecting, and redistributing human capital was firmly embedded in the demographic and ecological arrangements of pastoral nomadism and woven into the basic structures of Mongol imperial rule."[109] The Kitans and Jurchens had similar demographic and ecological challenges, and also appropriated Chinese labor when it was convenient for them, though not on the same scale as the Mongols. When numbers are supplied for households or individuals relocated by the Kitans, they are commonly in multiples of a thousand and occasionally in multiples of a hundred; for the Mongols, multiples of ten thousand are quite common.

Does the contrast between the Song and the northern states tell us anything interesting about the Song? Are there differences in military tactics, cultural attitudes, or state structure that help explain why Song did not copy the practices of their militarily more successful neighbors?

When thinking about forced relocations as a weapon of war, that is, a way to weaken an enemy, it helps to step back and think more broadly about what armies do with surrendered soldiers and civilians. Like most other premodern states, none of the four countries treated here had a concept of prisoners of war, to be routinely returned after the cessation of hostilities. Killing captives occurred with some frequency, and is recorded in sources over the centuries. Enslaving captives also occurred, especially, perhaps, in fighting between different nomadic polities. But there were also men who spoke out against both killing and enslaving people captured in war, whether soldiers or civilians. Chinese military treatises advised letting those who surrendered live.[110] In 642, the second Tang emperor Taizong (r. 626–649) took a stand against killing or enslaving the thousands of captives he took on the Korean campaign, offering to compensate his soldiers from his own funds rather than distribute captives to them as they had expected. In the end most of the captives were allowed to return home.[111] The Song founder expressed his opposition to slaughtering surrendered soldiers and civilians when he objected to a temple to martial heroes listing the Qin general Bai Qi, known for ordering the killing of people who had surrendered.[112] Chinese sources do not record similar sentiments among the commanders of the northern states, who are occasionally quoted as saying such things as "captives have always been enslaved."[113] Surviving sources, unfortunately, say little about the disposition of captives taken by the Song. A report on a victory might say so-many people were killed and so-many taken captive without any indication of what was done with the captives. Sometimes soldiers in surrendered armies may have been absorbed into the victor's armies. Occasionally the parties might negotiate an exchange; this was done in 1085 when returning one hundred captives was a major element in the agreement between Song and Xia.[114]

Song stands out more when the issue is civilian populations. In the wars that led to the founding of the Song, populations were not transferred. As the Song founders took the south piece by piece, they put in Song administrators and redrew the boundaries of the Song state to include the new prefectures, but the population was simply left in place, as were many lower-level officials. Song did have the royal houses and senior officials moved to Kaifeng. As Song Chen notes in the opening of his chapter in this volume, these officials were given government appointments and sent to parts of the country other than their former states. Their descendants often did quite well in the examinations, enabling the family to retain its elite status.[115] In battles between Song and the Kitans, Tanguts, Jurchens, and Mongols, Song did not routinely remove the people from places they secured. In fact, in 1122 Song was quite taken aback when they reached Yanjing to discover that their then allies, the Jurchen, had taken the residents of the city as booty, leaving it effectively empty.

Cultural differences between Song and the northern states may have played a part in differing treatment of civilian captives. In nomadic societies relocating was a routine part of life and not nearly as distressing as it was to sedentary people. Over the centuries, tribes had moved from one region to another for a host of reasons, sometimes coerced into moving, sometimes voluntarily seeking other pastures. Their tents could be moved, allowing them to bring their homes with them. In Chinese culture, by contrast, relocation carried many negative associations. One of the harshest punishments that could be meted out to criminals short of death was exile to another part of the country: the longer the distance, the harsher the penalty. Exile forced one to leave behind the graves of one's ancestors and homes or land that had been in the family often for generations.

Differences in attitudes toward ethnic mixing could also be a factor. Naomi Standen argues that ethnicity is not a helpful concept for explaining the choices men made to join Liao in the tenth century.[116] From the evidence on relocations, it does seem the case that Liao had no objection to Chinese living in their midst. The number of Kitans was never very large, so to build a powerful state they needed to absorb neighbors, and found nothing objectionable about settlements of Bohai or Han Chinese dotting the landscape. Not only were Song's challenges different, but Song statesmen also saw ethnic mixing differently. When clashes along the western border resulted in non-Han surrendering to the Song, the Song hoped to incorporate their land, leaving them in place, under their own headmen, and perhaps encouraging Han Chinese to move into the region as colonists. Song statesmen did not advocate moving the non-Han captives deep within Song territory.[117]

Did differences in the strength of Confucian ideas of governance matter? Yuan-kang Wang argues that Confucian emphasis on harmony and benevolent rule does not explain strategic choices made by the Song court, which are better explained by differences in military strength—the court chose to negotiate when it recognized that it could not prevail.[118] Even granting that, lower-level decisions such as whether to relocate people for state purposes could still reflect Chinese traditions. A good example here is the handling of defeated rulers and their courts. Song moved Li Yu, Qian Chu, and other former rulers to Kaifeng, where it provided for them generously and regularly invited them to court. They did this to show that the moral power of their ruler and his dynasty attracted notables from afar. Reducing their social rank or exiling them would have weakened this message. The three northern states, in their early conquests of Chinese states, did not follow this logic. Both Liao and Jin moved conquered rulers and their courts far beyond their capitals and out of sight. The Mongols killed all the members of the Jin imperial clan that they could find, but two generations later, by which time many Confucian scholars had entered Mongol employ, the young Song emperor and his regent were spared. More familiarity with Chinese traditions would seem to be the central difference here. By the 1270s the Mongols found it expedient to consider how their Chinese subjects and especially the educated elite would look on an action.

These contrasts between Song and its three northern rivals lend weight to the idea of Song exceptionalism. The difference is not merely that the Song economy was more commercialized than the Liao, Jin, or Yuan, but also that the Song state made more use of market principles. If we think of people as economic goods, then forced relocation represents not only a coercive exercise of state power but also an extreme manifestation of the command mobilization of economic resources. From this perspective it makes sense that forced relocation loomed larger as a tool of labor recruitment among the three nonmarketized states of Liao, Jin, and Yuan—at least in their early phases—than it did in either the Northern or Southern Song. Generations of scholars have stressed the growing importance of market over the command mobilization of resources through the course of the eleventh through the thirteenth centuries.[119] As Elad Alyagon reminds us in his chapter, the

Song state even relied on hiring men rather than conscription to recruit most of its troops, however poorly those troops were treated once they were tattooed and enrolled on the rosters. By the same token, Song Chen shows that by the Southern Song economic prosperity had trumped proximity to the national capital as the main determinant in the regional distribution of political success. The New Policies extended market principles through the hired service system and conversion of assessments of tribute, but even after the New Policies were repudiated, the trend toward use of market mechanisms continued. In the Southern Song, statecraft theorists, as Jaeyoon Song argues here, insisted on the greater effectiveness of market over command approaches to land taxation and economic inequality. Cultural preferences may have tempered the Song state's recourse to mass, coercive population relocations. However, we should not overlook the impact of a Song commercial revolution that rendered the command movement of population less effective than economic incentives in getting people where they were needed. At no point did the Song state forgo the perquisites of command, as its corvée policies, militia conscription, and commodity monopolies demonstrate. Its limited recourse to mass population relocation mirrors the larger incorporation of the market into the repertoire of Song approaches to the exercise of state power.

NOTES

1   Colson, "Forced Migration," 15.
2   On Qin's transfers, see Ge Jianxiong, *Zhongguo yimin shi*, 2:59–64.
3   *Shi ji* 6.236; 239, 244, 256, 8.386. See also Ch'ü, *Han Social Structure*, 164; Lewis, *Space*, 172; Chang, *Rise*, 43, 45, 52.
4   *Shi ji* 253–54, 259, 3086; *Han shu* 2830; Chang, *Rise*, 52–58; Ma Feibai, *Qinji shi*, 916–29.
5   *Shi ji* 99. 2719–20; Ch'ü, *Han Social Structure*, 164–65, 410–11. On other Han moves, see *Song shu* 36.1092; *Wenxian tongkao* 318. 2502c; Chang, *Rise*, 72, 207–13; Ge Jianxiong, *Zhongguo yimin shi*, 2:120–22.
6   *Jin shu* 105.2745; *Wei shu* 2.32, 4A.75, 4B.100, 102, 105, 33.787, 35.815–16, 103.2293, 110.2849–50; *Bei shi* 98.3253; *Zizhi tongjian* 132.4148–49; Graff, *Medieval Chinese Warfare*, 60–61; Kang, "An Empire for a City," 167.
7   *Bei Qi shu* 2.18; *Wei shu* 12.298; *Bei shi* 5.184; Jenner, *Memories of Loyang*, 100–101.
8   Graff, *Medieval Chinese Warfare*, 82–83.
9   *Zizhi tongjian* 177.5516; Wright, *Sui Dynasty*, 153–54.
10 *Zizhi tongjian* 202.6379. The exact number of commoners is given as 12,807 in the Korean history *Samguk sagi* 三國史記; cited in Bai Genxing, "Ruxiang suisu," 73.
11 See Elad Alyagon's chapter in this volume.
12 For Liao, see Wittfogel and Feng, *Chinese Society, Liao*, 508–23. For Jin, see Franke, "The Chin Dynasty," 274–75. On the Mongols' military system, see Allsen, *Mongol Imperial-*

ism, 195–202. On Chinese soldiers sent as colonists to Mongolia, see Wu Songdi, *Zhong-guo yimin shi*, 4:649–50. On the militarization of the New Policies *baojia* militia system see Smith, "*Shuihu zhuan* and the Military Subculture of the Northern Song," 380–98.

13 For an example of onerous labor service, see Chan, "Labor Service," 638–39, 651, on the labor service imposed in 1158–59 on two million workers from all over the country to build palaces in Kaifeng.

14 *LS, juan* 37–41.

15 Wittfogel and Feng, *Chinese Society: Liao* is still of value on the tribal structure of the Kitans.

16 Bohai (or Balhae in Korean), the state to the east of the Kitans, stretched eastward to the Sea of Japan and northward into what is now Russia. Bohai was of mixed ethnic identity when it was founded in the seventh century, and its ruling family was from the former Korean state of Goguryeo, but by the tenth century, to the Kitans at least, the people were simply Bohai people.

17 Based on *LS, juan* 37–40.

18 *LS* 37.443. Estimates of distances are based on distances given in Google Maps for modern towns in approximately the same place.

19 *LS* 37.447.

20 *LS* 34.396.

21 The population numbers are included in *LS, juan* 37–41, but disproportionally for the Supreme Capital circuit. The two smallest counties listed had 300 and 500 households (*LS* 37.449). Unfortunately, there is no evidence on which to judge whether the population of these units had grown or shrunk since their founding.

22 *LS* 38.468, 39.487, 40.497, 40.500, 501.

23 *Qidan guoshi* 8.76.

24 For one exception, see *LS* 39.487.

25 See Twitchett and Tietze, "Liao," 70–72.

26 *LS* 37.446–47, 38.468.

27 *Zizhi tongjian* 286.9351; *Xin Wudai shi* 72.899; *Qidan guoshi* 3.39. When the new administrator inspected the city, he found only about 700 people still there. Reportedly over 100,000 bodies were collected for burial in a large mound. The slaughter of the city seems to have been particularly grisly. Reportedly, the troops tossed babies in the air and speared them for fun.

28 On this rebellion, see Wittfogel and Feng, *Chinese Society: Liao*, 314, 419–20, 519–22.

29 *LS* 37.440.

30 *LS* 38.461–62.

31 *LS* 74.1233–34. For a detailed study of his descendants, see Crossley, "Outsider In." As she shows, some of Han Zhigu's descendants became aristocrats, intermarrying with leading Kitan families.

32 *LS* 109.1480–81. On officials who were captured by Liao forces during the Five Dynasties, see Standen, *Unbounded Loyalty*. One of her main themes is the ease with which men who had served another state took up employment with Liao.

33 *Jiu Wudai shi* 85.1126–27; *Xin Wudai shi* 17.178. The Kitans also took material booty, including books and pictures, the stone classics, the water clock of the Bright Hall, musical instruments and scores, ritual paraphernalia, and so on. *LS* 4.60.

34 *Zizhi tongjian* 286.9350.

35 *Xin Wudai shi* 17.178; trans. Davis, *Historical Records of the Five Dynasties*, 166. Cf. *Jiu Wudai shi* 85.112627; *LS* 4.59.

36 *Jiu Wudai shi* 85.1127–28; *Xin Wudai shi* 17.178–79; Davis, *Historical Records*, 166–68.

37 *Jiu Wudai shi* 85.1128–29.

38 *LS* 75.1238; trans. Wittfogel and Feng, *Chinese Society: Liao*, 112.

39 *LS* 98.1416–17. How Liu Shen phrased his objections is not recorded.

40 *LS* 104.1455.

41 To give a sense of the difference in the quantity of sources, whereas the modern punctuated edition of the standard history for the Liao has five volumes, that for the Song comes to forty volumes. The difference in the survival of collected works and other sorts of texts is even more dramatic. There are 360 volumes of the *Complete Song Prose* (Quan Song wen), but only three volumes for the *Complete Liao and Jin Prose* (Quan Liao Jin wen). The explanation for this difference is probably not only that the Song lasted a century longer, but also that its Chinese writing population was much larger.

42 Kurz, *China's Southern Tang Dynasty*, 111–13.

43 Lau and Huang, "Founding and Consolidation," 227–28; *SS* 478.13860–64, 479.13878–81, 480.13899–916, 481.13927–29, 482.13940–41.

44 *CB* 10.225, 20.442–43. Lorge, "Resistance," 125.

45 *SHY* Fanyi 1.11a. See also *SS* 5.78, 272.9304; *CB* 27.621–22, which do not mention the number of households or that they were returning to former lands.

46 *CB* 35.777–78. Cf. *SHY* Fangyu 8.32.

47 *CB* 168.4048.

48 *Jin shi* 46.1033. For other examples, see *Jin shi* 75.1719, 133.2844.

49 *Jingding Jiankang zhi* 43.44b.

50 The survival of multiple sources probably reflects the fact that many literate people were among those transported, and more crucially because the Song government survived after the loss of a big chunk of its territory, many of those who escaped or were released made their way back to the Song and reported their experiences, including Qin Kui and Gaozong's mother. Many of these accounts survived because they were quoted extensively in *Sanchao beimeng huibian*. Other important sources are the accounts preserved in the *Jingkang baishi*.

51 Ebrey, *Emperor Huizong*, 475–98.

52 *Wengzhong renyu* 73–84.

53 *SCBMHB* 72.153.

54 *SCBMHB* 78.211.

55 *SCBMHB* 78.212–13.

56 *Jingkang jiwen* 37.

57 *SCBMHB* 78.212.

58 *Nanzheng luhui* 174.

59 *Nanzheng luhui* 139.

60 *SCBMHB* 77.209–10; *Jingkang yaolu* 15.303.

61 *Nanzheng luhui* 139.

62 *Song fu ji* 243–44.

63 *Song fu ji* 244–50

64 *Shenyin yu* 199; *Song fu ji* 249. *Shenyin yu* says that they arrived in Yanjing on 5/17. Poor survival of deportees was not unprecedented and has been recorded for earlier deportations as well. For instance, a third of the 10,000 families that the Northern Wei forced to move to Pingcheng in 426 died on the road, and two or three out of ten of those taken captive with the fall of Jiangling in 554 were said to have died on the way to Chang'an. See *Zizhi tongjian* 120.3789–91, 165.5123.

65 *SCBMHB* 99.401.

66 *SCBMHB* 89.313; *Shenyin yu* 195.

67 *Beishou jianwen lu* 6; *Shenyin yu* 192.

68 *Beishou jianwen lu* 6–7.

69 *SCBMHB* 98.396. See also *Shenyin yu* 199.

70 *SCBMHB* 98.396.

71 The original 5,600 clansmen was reduced to 900 in less than two years and down to 500 four years later. See *Song fu ji* 244–45.

72 See, Dawson, *Mongol Mission*; Franke, "Sino-Western Contacts under the Mongol Empire"; Rossabi, "The Muslims in the Early Yüan Dynasty"; Allsen, "Ever Closer Encounters"; and de Rachewiltz, "Turks in China under the Mongols."

73 See, for instance, Dawson, *Mongol Mission*, 15, 66, 70, 129, 157, 179.

74 Waley, *Travels of an Alchemist*, 72–73, 93, 124.

75 *Heida shilüe* 86–87.

76 *Yutang jiahua* 85.

77 *Changchun zhenren xi you ji*; trans. Bretschneider, *Medieval Researches* 1: 78, 124, 126, 127.

78 Allsen, "Ever Closer Encounters," 9.

79 On Mongol slaughter of city-dwellers in Central Asia, see Boyle, *Genghis Khan*, 85–86, 91–92, 99–107, 115–22, 127–28.

80 *YS* 119. 2932 163. 3819; *Jingxiu ji* 4/2b.

81 Allsen, *Commodity and Exchange*, 35.

82 *Jingxiu ji* 9, *Jingxiu ji*, Yiwen 3.8a–9a.

83 *YS* 120.2964; Allsen, *Commodity and Exchange*, 43–44.

84 *Yuan wen lei* 57.16b-17a.

85 *YS* 123.3023.

86 *YS* 147.3478.

87 de Rachewiltz, *Service*, 28.

88 de Rachewiltz, "Personnel and Personalities," 132. See also Wu Songdi, *Zhongguo yimin shi*, 4:641, where he writes, "After Shi Bingzhi surrendered to the Mongols, he was ordered to lead 100,000 families who had been captured by the Mongols and move them to north of the dessert, which is an example of people from the Central Plain who were captives and taken north."

89 *YS* 120.2956; Dunnell, "The Hsi Hsia," 213.

90 Franke, "The Chin Dynasty," 264.

91 *YS* 3.53, 4.63.

92 Jay, *A Change of Dynasties*, 36–44; Chaffee, *Branches of Heaven*, 242–59; Davis, *Wind against the Mountain*, 115–26. The itinerary of the royal party from Hangzhou to Yanjing and Shangdu is translated by A. C. Moule, "Hang-chou to Shang-tu A. D. 1276."

93 de Rachewiltz, *Service*, 185–94.

94 *YS* 167.3923–24.

95 *YS* 158.3730.

96 de Rachewiltz, *Service*, 187, 418.

97 de Rachewiltz, *Service*, 498.

98 de Rachewiltz, *Service*, 156, 199, 301–2, 307. For the case of Wang E, spared execution after the fall of Caizhou, where the Jin had its last stand, see de Rachewiltz, *Service*, 303.

99 de Rachewiltz, *Service*, 418.

100 de Rachewiltz, *Service*, 66.

101 *YS* 32.719, 41.872. For other examples of slaves being freed, see Meng Siming, *Yuandai shehui jieji zhidu*, 198–201.

102 On artisan as a census category in the Yuan period, see Oshima, "The *Chiang-hu* of the Yuan"; Ju Qingyuan, "Yuandai xiguan jianghu yanjiu"; and for a précis of Ju's article, see Chü, "Government Artisans."

103 *YS* 6.105.

104 *Yuan wen lei* 42.19a; *YS* 10.210.

105 Allsen, *Commodity and Exchange*, 35.

106 *Yuan wen lei* 42.22a. For a very positive assessment of the hereditary status of artisans under the Mongols, see Rossabi, "The Reign of Khubilai Khan," 448–49, based largely on Ju Qingyuan, "Yuandai xiguan jianghu yanjiu."

107 *Qingyai ji* 4.23a-b.

108 Hui, *War and State Formation*, 38.

109 Allsen, "Ever Closer Encounters," 6.

110 Lo, "Chinese Just War Ethics," 418–22.

111 *Jiu Tang shu* 199A.5325. On Taizong's policies toward non-Han peoples, see Abramson, *Ethnic Identity*, 145–49.

112 *SHY* Li 16.5a.

113 *Nanzheng luhui* 141–42.

114 Forage, "The Sino-Tangut War of 1081–1085," 18.

115 See also Chen, "Managing Territories from Afar," 102–12.

116 Standen, *Unbounded Loyalty*, esp. 26–32.

117 For an example, see Smith, "Irredentism," 289–90. Song's southern and western borders are also relevant here. On them, see von Glahn, *Country of Streams and Grottos*.

118 Wang, *Harmony and War*.

119 For William McNeill it is this transition from a command to a market economy that characterized the place of the Song in global military history: McNeill, *The Pursuit of Power*, chapter two. William Liu, "The Making of a Fiscal State in Song China," further develops the idea that the Song was precocious.

REFERENCES

PRIMARY SOURCES

Bei Qi shu 北齊書, by Li Baiyao 李百藥 (565–648). Beijing: Zhonghua shuju, 1972.

Bei shi 北史, by Li Yanshou 李延壽 (active 7th century). Beijing: Zhonghua shuju, 1974.

Beishou jianwen lu 北狩見聞錄, by Cao Xun 曹勳 (1098–1174). CSJC ed.

Beishou xinglu 北狩行錄, by Cai Tiao 蔡絛 (fl. 1100–1130). CSJC ed.

Changchun zhenren xi you ji 長春真人西遊記. In *Wang Guowei yishu* 王國維遺書 Shanghai: Shanghai guji shuju, 1983.

Han shu 漢書, by Ban Gu 班固 (32–92 CE). Beijing: Zhonghua shuju, 1962.

Heida shilue 黑韃事略, by Peng Daya 彭大雅 (active 13th century) and Xu Ting 徐霆 (active 13th century), annotation 箋證 by Wang Guowei 王國維. Beijing: Wendian ge shuzhuang, 1936.

Jin shi 金史, edited by Tuo Tuo 脫脫 (1313–1355) et al. Beijing: Zhonghua shuju, 1975.

Jin shu 晉書, by Fang Xuanling 房玄齡 (578–648). Beijing: Zhonghua shuju, 1974.

Jingding Jiankang zhi 景定建康志, edited by Zhou Yinghe 周應合 (1213–1280). Song-Yuan difang zhi congshu ed. Taibei: Guotai wenhua shiye, 1980 reprint.

Jingkang jiwen 靖康紀聞, by Ding Teqi 丁特起 (d. ca. 1135). CSJC ed.

Jingkang yaolu 靖康要錄, by Wang Zao 汪藻 (1079–1154), CSJC ed. 3882–86.

Jingxiu ji 靜修集, by Liu Yin 劉因 (1249–1293). Siku quanshu ed.

Jiu Tang shu 舊唐書, by Liu Xu 劉昫 (887–946). Beijing: Zhonghua shuju, 1975.

Jiu Wudai shi 舊五代史, by Xue Juzheng 薛居正 (912–981) et al. Beijing: Zhonghua shuju, 1976.

Liao shi 遼史, edited by Tuo Tuo 脫脫 (1313–1355) et al. Beijing: Zhonghua shuju, 1974.

Nanzheng luhui 南征錄彙, by Li Tianmin 李天民 (Jin). In *Jingkang baishi jianzheng* 靖康稗史箋証, compiled by Cui'an 確庵 and Naian 耐庵, edited by Cui Wenyin 崔文印. Beijing: Zhonghua shuju, 1988.

Qidan guoshi 契丹國史, by Ye Longli 葉隆禮 (*jin shi* 1247). Guoxue jiben ed. 1938.

Qingyai ji 青崖集, by Wei Chu 魏初 (1232–1292). Siku quanshu ed.

Sanchao beimeng huibian 三朝北盟會編, by Xu Mengxin 徐夢莘 (1126–1207). Taibei: Dahua shuju reprint of Shixue yanjiushe, 1939 punctuated ed.

Shenyin yu 呻吟語, anon. In *Jingkang baishi jianzheng* 靖康稗史箋証, compiled by Cui'an 確庵 and Nai'an 耐庵, edited by Cui Wenyin 崔文印. Beijing: Zhonghua shuju, 1988.

Shi ji 史記, by Sima Qian 司馬遷 (145?–86? BCE). Beijing: Zhonghua shuju, 1962.

Song fu ji 宋俘記 by Kegong 可恭 (Jin). In *Jingkang baishi jianzheng* 靖康稗史箋証, compiled by Cui'an 確庵 and Nai'an 耐庵, edited by Cui Wenyin 崔文印. Beijing: Zhonghua shuju, 1988.

Song huiyao jigao 宋會要輯稿, edited by Xu Song 徐松 (1781–1848) et al. Beijing: Zhonghua shuju, 1957.

Song shi 宋史, edited by Tuo Tuo 脫脫 (1313–1355) et al. Beijing: Zhonghua shuju, 1977.

Song shu 宋書, by Shen Yue 沈約 (441–513). Beijing: Zhonghua shuju, 1974.

Wei shu 魏書, by Wei Shou 魏收 (506–572). Beijing: Zhonghua shuju, 1974.

Wengzhong renyu 甕中人語, anon. (Song). In *Jingkang baishi jianzheng* 靖康稗史箋証, compiled by Cui'an 確庵 and Nai'an 耐庵, edited by Cui Wenyin 崔文印. Beijing: Zhonghua shuju, 1988.

Wenxian tongkao 文獻通考, by Ma Duanlin 馬端臨 (ca. 1250–1325). Taibei: Xinxing shuju reprint of Shitong ed.

Xin Wudai shi 新五代史, by Ouyang Xiu 歐陽修 (1007–1072). Beijing: Zhonghua shuju, 1974.

Xu zizhi tongjian changbian 續資治通鑒長編, by Li Tao 李燾 (1115–1184). Beijing: Zhonghua shuju, 1985.

Yutang jiahua 玉堂嘉話, by Wang Yun 王惲 (1227–1304). Congshu jicheng ed.

Yuan shi 元史, edited by Song Lian 宋濂 (1310–1381) et al. Beijing: Zhonghua shuju, 1976.

Yuan wen lei 元文類, by Su Tianjue 蘇天爵 (1294–1352). Siku quanshu ed.

Zizhi tongjian 資治通鑑, by Sima Guang 司馬光 (1019–1086). Beijing: Zhonghua shuju, 1956.

SECONDARY SOURCES

Abramson, Marc S. *Ethnic Identity in Tang China*. Philadelphia: University of Pennsylvania Press, 2008.

Allsen, Thomas G. *Commodity and Exchange in the Mongol Empire*. Cambridge, UK: Cambridge University Press, 1997.

———. "Ever Closer Encounters: The Appropriation of Culture and the Apportionment of Peoples in the Mongol Empire." *Journal of Early Modern History* 1, no. 1 (1997): 2–23.

———. *Mongol Imperialism: The Policies of the Grand Qan Möngke in China, Russia, and the Islamic Lands, 1251–1259*. Berkeley: University of California Press, 1987.

Bai Genxing 拜根興. "Ruxiang suisu: Muzhiming suozai re Tang Baiji yimin de shenghuo guiji" 入鄉隨俗:墓誌所載入唐百濟遺民的生活軌迹. *Shanxi shifan daxue xuebao (Zhexue shehui kexue ban)* 38, no. 4 (2009): 72–80.

Boyle, J. A., trans. *Genghis Khan: The History of the World-Conqueror by Ata-Malik Juvaini*. Manchester: Manchester University Press, 1958.

Bretschneider, E. *Medieval Researches from Eastern Asiatic Sources*. 2 vols. London: Trübner, 1910.

Chaffee, John W. *Branches of Heaven: A History of the Imperial Clan of Sung China*. Cambridge, Mass.: Harvard University Asia Center, 1999.

Chan, Hok-lam. "The Organization and Utilization of Labor Service under the Jurchen Chin Dynasty." *Harvard Journal of Asiatic Studies* 52, no. 2 (1992): 613–64.

Chang, Chun-shu. *The Rise of the Chinese Empire*. Vol. 1: *Nation, State, and Imperialism in Early China, ca. 1600 B.C. – A.D. 8*. Ann Arbor: University of Michigan Press, 2007.

Chen, Song. "Managing the Territories from Afar: The Imperial State and Elites in Sichuan, 755–1279." PhD diss., Harvard University, 2011.

Chü, Ch'ing-yüan. "Government Artisans of the Yüan Dynasty." In *Chinese Social History: Translations of Selected Studies*, edited by E-Tu Zen Sun and John De Francis, 234–46. Washington, D.C.: American Council of Learned Societies, 1956.

Ch'ü, T'ung-tsu. *Han Social Structure*, edited by Jack L. Dull. Seattle: University of Washington Press, 1972.

Colson, Elizabeth. "Forced Migration and the Anthropological Response." *Journal of Refugee Studies* 16, no. 1 (2003): 1–18.

Crossley, Pamela. "Outsider In: Power, Identity, and the Han Lineage of Jizhou." *Journal of Song-Yuan Studies* 43 (2013): 51–89.

Davis, Richard L., trans. *Historical Records of the Five Dynasties*, by Ouyang Xiu. New York: Columbia University Press, 2004.

———. *Wind Against the Mountain: The Crisis of Politics and Culture in Thirteenth-Century China*. Cambridge, Mass.: Council on East Asian Studies, 1996.

Dawson, Christopher. *The Mongol Mission: Narratives and Letters of the Franciscan Missionaries in Mongolia and China in the Thirteenth and Fourteenth Centuries.* New York: Sheed and Ward, 1955.

de Rachewiltz, Igor. "Personnel and Personalities in North China in the Early Mongol Period." *Journal of the Economic and Social History of the Orient* 9, nos. 1–2 (1966): 88–144.

———. "Turks in China under the Mongols: A Preliminary Investigation of Turco-Mongol Relations in the Thirteenth and Fourteenth Centuries." In *China Among Equals,* edited by Morris Rossabi, 281–310. Berkeley: University of California Press, 1983.

de Rachewiltz, Igor, et al. *In the Service of the Khan: Eminent Personalities of the Early Mongol-Yüan Period (1200–1300).* Wiesbaden: Harrassowitz, 1993.

Dunnell, Ruth W. "The Hsi Hsia." In *The Cambridge History of China.* Vol. 6: *Alien Regimes and Border States, 907–1368,* edited by Herbert Franke, and Denis Twitchett, 154–214. Cambridge, UK: Cambridge University Press, 1994.

Ebrey, Patricia Buckley. *Emperor Huizong.* Cambridge, Mass.: Harvard University Press, 2014.

Forage, Paul C. "The Sino-Tangut War of 1081–1085. *Journal of Asian History* 25 (1991): 1–27.

Franke, Herbert. "The Chin Dynasty." *The Cambridge History of China.* Vol. 6: *Alien Regimes and Border States, 907–1368.* edited by Herbert Franke, and Denis Twitchett, 215–320. Cambridge, UK: Cambridge University Press, 1994.

———. "Sino-Western Contacts under the Mongol Empire." *Journal of the Hong Kong Branch of the Royal Asiatic Society* 6 (1966): 49–71.

Ge Jianxiong 葛劍雄. *Zhongguo yimin shi* 中國移民史, vol. 2. Fuzhou: Fujian renmin chubanshe, 1997.

Graff, David A. *Medieval Chinese Warfare, 300–900.* London: Routledge, 2002.

Hui, Victoria Tin-bor. *War and State Formation in Ancient China and Early Modern Europe.* Cambridge, UK: Cambridge University Press, 2005.

Jay, Jennifer. *A Change in Dynasties: Loyalty in Thirteenth-Century China.* Bellingham: Western Washington University, 1991.

Jenner, W. F. J., *Memories of Loyang: Yang Hsüan-chih and the Lost Capital (493–534).* Oxford: Clarendon Press, 1981.

Ju Qingyuan 鞠清遠. "Yuandai xiguan jianghu yanjiu" 元代係官匠戶研究. *Shihuo* 1, no. 9 (1935): 367–401.

Kang, Le. "An Empire for a City: Cultural Reforms of the Hsiao-wen Emperor (A.D. 471–499)." PhD diss., Yale University, 1983.

Kurz, Johannes L. *China's Southern Tang Dynasty 937–976.* New York: Routledge, 2011.

Lau, Nap-yin, and Huang K'uan-chung. 2009. "Founding and Consolidation of the Sung Dynasty under T'ai-tsu (960–976), T'ai-tsung (976–997), and Chen-tsung (997–1022)." In *The Cambridge History of China.* Vol. 5, Part 1: *The Sung Dynasty and Its Precursors, 907–1279,* edited by Denis Twitchett and Paul Jakov Smith, 206–78. Cambridge, UK: Cambridge University Press.

Lewis, Mark Edward. *The Construction of Space in Early China.* Albany: State University of New York Press, 2006.

Liu, William Guanglin. "The Making of a Fiscal State in Song China, 960–1279." *The Economic History Review* (2014): 1–31.

Lo, Ping-cheung. "The *Art of War* Corpus and Chinese Just War Ethics Past and Present," *Journal of Religious Ethics* 40, no. 3 (2012): 404–46.

Lorge, Peter. "Fighting against Empire: Resistance to the Later Zhou and Song Conquest of China." In *Debating War in Chinese History*, edited by Peter Lorge, 107–39. Leiden: Brill, 2013.

Ma Feibai 馬非百. *Qinji shi* 秦集史. 2 vols. Beijing: Zhonghua shuju, 1982.

McNeill, William H., *The Pursuit of Power: Technology, Armed Force, and Society since A.D. 1000*. Chicago: University of Chicago Press, 1982

Meng Siming 蒙思明. *Yuandai shehui jieji zhidu* 元代社會階級制度. Beijing: Zhonghua shuju, 1980.

Moule, A. C. "Hang-chou to Shang-tu A.D. 1276." *T'oung Pao*, second series 16, no. 3 (1915): 393–419.

Oshima, Ritsuko. "The *Chiang-hu* of the Yuan." *Acta Asiatica* 45 (1983): 69–95.

Rossabi, Morris. "The Muslims in the Early Yüan Dynasty." In *China under Mongol Rule*, edited by John D. Langlois Jr., 257–95. Princeton: Princeton University Press, 1981.

———. "The Reign of Khubilai Khan." In *The Cambridge History of China*. Vol. 6: *Alien Regimes and Border States 907–1368*, edited by Herbert Franke and Denis Twitchett, 414–89. Cambridge, UK: Cambridge University Press, 1994.

Smith, Paul Jakov. "Irredentism as Political Capital: The New Policies and the Annexation of Tibetan Domains in Hehuang (the Qinghai-Gansu Highlands) under Shenzong and His Sons, 1068–1126." In *Emperor Huizong and Late Northern Song China: The Politics of Culture and the Culture of Politics*, edited by Patricia Buckley Ebrey and Maggie Bickford, 78–130. Cambridge, Mass.: Harvard Asia Center, 2006.

———. "*Shuihu zhuan* and the Military Subculture of the Northern Song, 960–1127." *Harvard Journal of Asiatic Studies* 66, no. 2 (2006): 363–422.

Standen, Naomi. *Unbounded Loyalty: Frontier Crossings in Liao China*. Honolulu: University of Hawai'i Press, 2007.

Twitchett, Denis, and Klaus-Peter Tietze. "The Liao." In *The Cambridge History of China*. Vol. 6: *Alien Regimes and Border States, 907–1368*, edited by Herbert Franke and Denis Twitchett, 43–153. Cambridge, UK: Cambridge University Press, 1994.

von Glahn, Richard. *The Country of Streams and Grottoes: Expansion, Settlement, and the Civilizing of the Sichuan Frontier in Song times*. Cambridge, Mass.: Council on East Asian Studies, Harvard University, 1987.

Waley, Arthur. *The Travels of an Alchemist: The Journey of the Taoist Ch'ang-ch'un from China to the Hindukush at the Summons of Chingiz Khan*. London: Routledge, 1931.

Wang, Yuan-kang. *Harmony and War: Confucian Culture and Chinese Power Politics*. New York: Columbia University Press, 2011.

Wittfogel, Karl A., and Feng Chia-sheng. *History of Chinese Society, Liao (907–1125)*. Philadelphia: American Philosophical Society, 1949.

Wright, Arthur F. *The Sui Dynasty*. New York: Knopf, 1978.

Wu Songdi 吳松弟. *Zhongguo yimin shi* 中國移民史. Vol. 4: *Liao Song Jin Yuan shiqi* 遼宋元時期. Fuzhou: Fujian renmin chubanshe, 1997.

Glossary of Chinese Characters

anchashi 按察使
Anji 安吉 (prefecture)
Ansu 安肅 (prefecture)
Ayuwangsi 阿育王寺

Bai Qi 白起
baiguan 稗官
Bao Zheng 包拯
Baoguosi Daxiong Baodian 保國寺大雄寶殿
baoyi 保毅
baoyi gongjianshou 保毅弓箭手
Baozhou 保州
Bazhou 霸州
beiming 碑銘
Bi Zhongyou 畢仲游
Bian 汴
Bianjing 汴京
Bianxiu Zhongshu Tiaoli Si 編修中書條例司
biji 筆記
Bingzhou 并州
Bishi 秘史
Bola 撥剌
budao 不道

Cai Bian 蔡卞
Cai Jiao 蔡交
Cai Que 蔡確
Cai Tao 蔡絛
Cai Tiao 蔡絛
Cai You 蔡攸
Cai Xiang 蔡襄
caizhi yi fa 裁之以法
Cao Bin 曹彬
Cao Jing 曹涇
Cao Si 曹耜
Cao tai huanghou, Empress Dowager 曹太皇后
Cao Wei 曹瑋
Cao Xun 曹勳
Cao Zu 曹組
Caozhou 曹州
chafangshi 察訪使
Chang 常 (prefecture)
Chang Zhi 常秩
Changba 長霸 (county)
Chen Dong 陳東
Chen Fuliang 陳傅良
Chen Jian 陳薦
Chen Jizhi 陳及之
Chen Jun 陳均
Chen Shidao 陳師道
Chen Xinghua 陳省華
Chen Yaozuo 陳堯佐
Chen Zhizhong 陳執中
Cheng Hao 程顥
Cheng Yi 程頤

Chengdu 成都 (prefecture)

chengmai 承買

Chengtian 承天 Liao Empress Dowager

chengxiang 丞相

chi 尺

Chi 池 (prefecture)

Chongwenyuan 崇文院

Chu 處 (prefecture)

Chuan Xia 川峽

Chuanfa yuan 傳法院

Chuanxia 川峽

Chuguo 楚國, Princess

Chun 春 (prefecture)

Ci ke qibainian wu qingdong 此可七百年無傾動

Consort Wei 韋賢妃

Da Yanlin 大彥琳

Dabei Baoge 大悲寶閣

Dabeisi 大悲寺

dang 黨

daoxue 道學

Datong 大同

Dayunyuan Dafo Dian 大雲院大佛殿

di 詆 (vilify)

di 帝 (emperor)

dili zhi 地理志

Ding 定 (prefecture)

Ding Du 丁度

Ding Teqi 丁特起

Ding Wei 丁謂

Dong Zhongshu 董仲舒

Dou Mo 竇默

Dou Yuan 竇元

doujian 都監

Du Chang 杜常

Du Yan 杜衍

Du You 杜佑

duda tiju chamasi 都大提舉茶馬司

Dujusi 獨居寺

duliaojiang 都料匠

dutiju shiyisi 都提舉市易司

Fan Chunren 范純仁

Fan Chunyou 范純祐

Fan Xiwen 范希文

Fan Yu 范育

Fan Zhongyan 范仲淹

fangtian junshui fa 方田均稅法

Feng Jing 馮京

Fengqiumen 封丘門

Feng-Shan Monastery 封禪寺

Fengxiang 鳳翔

Fo dashi zhi ruixiang ye 佛大士之瑞相也

focha 佛剎

Fogongsi Shijiata 佛宮寺 釋迦塔

fotu 佛圖

Foxiangge 佛香閣

fu 府 (administrative unit)

fu 俘 (captive)

Fu 福 (prefecture in Fujian)

Fu 撫 (prefecture in Jiangxi)

Fu Bi 富弼

fuguo 富國

Fusheng tayuan 福勝塔院

Fushengta 福勝塔

fushu 府署

futu 浮圖

Gao tai huanghou, Empress Dowager 高太皇后

Gao Yi 高益

Gaoliang River 高梁河

Genyue 艮嶽

Geng Nanzhong 耿南仲

Geng Yanxi 耿延禧

gou 溝

Guang 廣 (prefecture)

Guang'an 廣安 (prefecture)

Guanghua 光化 (prefecture)

Guanghua Monastery 廣化寺

Guangnan 廣南

Guangning 廣寧

guangyong 廣勇

Guo Chengyou 郭承祐

Guo Jun 國均

Guo Kui 郭逵

Guo Ruoxu 郭若虛

Guo Shenxi 郭申錫

Guo Zi 郭諮

guwen 古文

Han Gang 韓綱

Han Jiang 韓絳

Han Qi 韓琦

Han Tuozhou 韓侂胄

Han Wei 韓維

Han Yi 韓億

Han Yu 韓愈

han 函

Hang 杭 (prefecture)

Hanghai 杭海

Hanzhou 漢州

Hedong 河東

Heisha 黑殺

Henan 河南 (prefecture)

heqing 河清

Heyang 河陽

Hong 洪 (prefecture)

Hu 湖 (prefecture)

Hu Yin 胡寅

Huai 淮

Huan 寰 (prefecture)

Huang Qianshan 黃潛善

Huang Zongxi 黃宗羲

Huanglong 黃龍 (prefecture)

Hui 徽 (prefecture)

huiyao 會要

Hunyuan 渾源

Ji 吉 (prefecture)

Jia Changchao 賈昌朝

Jia Changling 賈昌齡

Jia Wei 賈緯

Jia Yan 賈琰

jian 監 (prefectural level unit)

Jian 建 (prefecture)

jian zhong baoning 揀中保寧

jianbing 兼併

Jiang 江

Jiang Teli 姜特立

jiangbingfa 將兵法

Jiangling 江陵 (prefecture)

Jiangnan 江南

Jianning 建寧 (prefecture)

jianya 監押

Jianyuan 諫院

jianzheng zhongshu wufang gong-shi 撿正中書五房公事

jiaozhi zhi dao 教之之道

Jiaxing 嘉興 (prefecture)

Jidu Temple 濟瀆廟

Jidumiao Qingong 濟瀆廟寢宮

Jie 階 (prefecture)

Jin 金 (prefecture)

jinbi yinghuang 金碧熒煌

Jinci 晉祠

Jing 涇

Jingdong 京東

jingjie 經界

jingjie fa 經界法

Jingkang 靖康

Jingnan 荊南

Jinguangming jing 金光明經

jingtian 井田

Jingyuan 涇原

jinjun 禁軍

jinxi 近習

jinzhong 禁中

jiuren 久任

jueqiao 絕巧

jun 軍 (army)

Jun 均 (prefecture)

juntian 均田

kai qianmo bian 開阡陌辯

Kaibao Monastery Śarīra Tower
     開寶寺舍利浮圖舍利塔

Kaibao zang 開寶藏

Kaogongji 考工記

Kong Yingda 孔穎達

Kou Zhun 寇準

kuai 澮

Lady Xing 邢夫人

leishu 類書

Li Chunnian 李椿年

Li Daochuan 李道傳

Li Fu 李孚

Li Gou 李覯

Li Hong 李紘

Li Ji 李及 (prefect)

Li Ji 李稷 (cruel official)

Li Qingchen 李清臣

Li Tang 李唐

Li Tao 李燾

Li Xiu 李秀

Li Yu 李煜

Li Zhaoliang 李昭亮

Li Zhichang 李志常

Li Zhuo 李擢

Li Zongyi 李宗易

Lian Xixian 廉希憲

Liang Shicheng 梁師成

Liangzhe 兩浙

Liaoyang 遼陽

licai 理財

Liji 禮記

Lin Zhiqi 林之奇

Lin'an 臨安 (Hangzhou, capital of
     the Southern Song)

Lingbiao 嶺表

Lingganta 靈感塔

Lingyinsi Shita 靈隱寺石塔

Linhai 臨海

Linhuang 臨潢 (prefecture)

Linjiang 臨江 (prefecture)

Liu Hang 劉沆

Liu Hui 劉輝

Liu Jizong 劉繼宗

Liu Shen 劉伸

Liu Yin 劉 因

Liu Yonggui 劉永規

Liu Yu 劉郁

Liu Zongyuan 柳宗元

Long Dayuan 龍大淵

Long 隆 (prefecture in Sichuan)

Long 龍 (prefecture in Bohai)

Longde Gong 龍德宮

Longmen Shiku 龍門石窟

longmeng 龍猛

Longsheng 隆聖 (prefecture)

Longxing 隆興 (prefecture)

Longxingsi 隆興寺

Lord Cui 崔府君

Lou Yue 樓鑰

Lu 瀘 (prefecture)

Lu Chengjun 盧成均

Lu Duoxun 盧多遜

Lu Dian 陸佃

Lü Chengxiang 呂丞相

Lü Dafang　呂大防

Lü Gongbi　呂公弼

Lü Huiqing　呂惠卿

Lü Wenqing　呂溫卿

Lü Yijian　呂夷簡

Lu You　陸游

Lü Yuqing　呂餘慶

Lü Zhong　呂中

Lü Zuqian　呂祖謙

luan　亂

lüe　掠

Lügong　呂公

Luo River　洛水

luohan　羅漢

Luoyang　洛陽

Ma Duanlin　馬端臨

maiming　埋銘

Man Zhongxing　滿中行

Mei　眉　(prefecture)

men　門

Meng Xuanzhe　孟玄喆

Ming　明　(prefecture)

Mo Di　墨翟

mu　畝

muzhiming　墓誌銘

Nanhai　南海

Nankang　南康　(prefecture)

Nantasi　南塔寺

Ni Si　倪思

Nie Chongyi　聶崇義

ningchen　佞臣

Niu Sui　牛遂

nu　怒

Ouliseng　漚里僧

Ouyang Che　歐陽澈

Ouyang Xiu　歐陽修

Pan Mei　潘美

Pan Xiaochao　潘孝綽

Peng Daya　彭大雅

Pengdang lun　朋黨論

Ping　平　(prefecture)

Pingcheng　平城

Pingjiang　平江　(prefecture)

Pingshun　平順

Pota　繁塔

Pu Shougeng　蒲壽庚

Putuoshan　普陀山

qian babai guo　千八百國

qian　遷

Qian Chu　錢俶

Qian Hongchu　錢弘俶

Qian Kun　錢昆

Qian Liu　錢鏐

Qian Mingyi　錢明逸

Qian Yanyuan　錢彥遠

Qian Yi　錢易

qian　遷

qiangzhuang　強壯

Qianliao　遷遼　(county)

qianmo　阡陌

Qiantang　錢塘

Qin Gui　秦檜

Qin Xi　秦熺

Qinfeng　秦鳳

qing　頃　(unit of area)

Qing　慶　(prefecture)

Qingli shengde　慶曆聖德

qing zhongyuan　清中原

Qingyuan　慶元　(prefecture)

Qingzhou　慶州

Qinzhou　秦州

Qionglinyuan　瓊林苑

qu　區　(unit of space)

Qu　衢　(prefecture)

qu 驅 (to drive)

Quan 泉 (prefecture)

quanfu 泉府

qumin zhi zhi 取民之制

Quyang 曲陽

quzhi zhi dao 取之之道

Rao 饒 (prefecture)

raozhi yi cai 饒之以財

Renwang huguo bore buoluomi jing
 仁王護國般若波羅蜜經

renzhi zhi dao 任之之道

rili 日曆

ronglan 冗濫

Ru 儒

Rui'an 瑞安 (prefecture)

Ruisi Dian 睿思殿

Run 潤 (prefecture)

ruxue 儒學

ruzhe 儒者

Sanjing xinyi 三經新義

Shanwuwei 善無畏

Shaolinsi Chuzu'an Zhengdian 少林
 寺初租庵正殿

Shaowu 邵武 (prefecture)

Shaoxing 紹興 (prefecture)

She 歙 (prefecture)

Sheli Dian 舍利殿

Shen Gua 沈括

shendaobei 神道碑

sheng 升

shenke 神刻

shi 士

Shi Bingzhi 史秉直

Shi Daiju 石待舉

Shi Dingzhi 史定之

Shi Jie 石介

Shi Mijian 史彌堅

Shi Miyuan 史彌遠

shidafu 士大夫

shili qian 施利錢

Shiwei 室韋

Shouchangsi 壽昌寺

shoutian zhi zhi 授田之制

Shu 蜀

Shu Dan 舒亶

Shuang 雙 (prefecture)

shuli 俗吏

Shuo 朔 (prefecture)

Siling shuhua ji 思陵書畫記

Sima Guang 司馬光

Sinongsi 司農寺

Sizhou 泗州

Song Kuang 宋睍

Song Qi 宋祁

Su 蘇 (prefecture)

Su Che 蘇轍

Su Shi 蘇軾

Su Xun 蘇洵

sui 歲 (year)

Sui 綏 (prefecture)

sui 遂 (unit of length)

Sun Mian 孫沔

Sun Mou 孫侔

Tai 台 (prefecture on Southeast
 coast)

Tai 泰 (prefecture in Liao's Supreme
 circuit)

Taiping guangji 太平廣記

Taiping Xingguo Monastery 太平
 興國寺

Taiping yulan 太平御覽

taishang 太上

Taiyuan 太原 (prefecture)

Taizong shilu 太宗實錄

Tan 潭 (prefecture in Hunan)

Tan 檀 (prefecture in Liaoning)

Tang Shuyu 唐叔虞

Tao Xuangan 陶宣干

Temple to the Northern
    Peak 北嶽廟

Tian Kuang 田況

tiangong 天宮

Tianqingsita 天清寺塔

Tiantai 天台

tianwang 天王

Tianwang Dian 天王殿

tiju changping guanghui cang 提舉
    常平廣惠倉

tiju yiyong baojia 提舉義勇保甲

Tong Guan 童貫

Tongdian 通典

tongru 通儒

Tongzhi 通志

Tongzhou 通州

touzi qian 頭子錢

tufeng 土風

Wanfo Dian 萬佛殿

Wang Anshi 王安石

Wang Boyan 汪伯彥

Wang Deyong 王德用

Wang Fu 王黼

Wang Guo 王果

Wang Huaji 王化基

Wang Ling 王令

Wang Mang 王莽

Wang Pang 王雱

Wang Shouyi 王守一

Wang Xiu 王秀

Wang Yansou 王巖叟

Wang Zhengji 王正己

Wang Zhongzheng 王中正

Wang Zi 王鎡

Wangcheng 王城

wangji 王畿

wangtian 王田

wansheng 萬勝

Wei Chu 魏初

Wei Gui 韋貴

Wei Shaoqin 衛紹欽

Weizhou 渭州

Wen 溫 (prefecture)

Wen Yanbo 文彥博

wenxian 文獻

Wenyuan yinghua 文苑英華

Wenzheng 文正

Wu 婺 (prefecture)

Wu Anxian 吳安憲

Wu Daozi 吳道子

Wu Qi 吳起

Wutai 五臺

Wuyue Five Marchmounts 五嶽

Wuzhang he 五丈河

xi 徙 (to move)

Xi 奚 (ethnic group)

Xia 夏 (prefecture)

Xia Song 夏竦

xia'ang 卞昂

xian 縣

Xiang 相 (prefecture)

Xianggong Monastery 湘宮寺

Xiangguo Monastery 相國寺

xiangjun 廂軍 (provincial armies)

xiangjun 鄉軍 (local militia)

Xiangyang 襄陽 (prefecture)

Xiao Zhao 蕭照

Xiaozong shilu 孝宗實錄

Xihe 西和 (prefecture)

Xinding Sanlitu 新定三禮圖

Xinfa 新法

Xing furen 邢夫人 (Lady Xing)

Xingcita 興慈塔

Xinghua 興化 (prefecture)

Xingzhou 興州

xingzhuang 行狀

xiongwu 雄武

Xiu 秀 (prefecture)

xu 洫 (ditch)

Xu 許 (prefecture)

Xu Heng 許衡

Xu Ting 徐霆

Xu Wudang 徐無黨

xuanfushi 宣撫使

Xue Changru 薛長孺

Xue Kui 薛奎

Xun Yue 荀悅

Xuzhou 許州 (Henan)

Xuzhou 徐州 (Jiangsu)

Yan Shi 嚴實

Yang 揚 (prefecture)

Yang Huaimin 楊懷敏

Yang Weizhong 楊惟中

Yang Yi 楊億

yangzhi zhi dao 養之之道

yanlu 言路

Yanluo Fort 鹽濼

Yanshan 燕山

Ye Mengde 葉夢得

Ye Shi 葉適

Yelü Chucai 耶律楚才

yi 移 (to move)

Yi 宜 (prefecture)

Yijing Yuan 譯經院

Yin 銀 (prefecture)

Yin Zhu 尹洙

Ying 應 (prefecture in Shanxi)

Ying 瀛 (prefecture in Hebei)

Ying 郢 (prefecture in Jingxi South)

Yingchang 潁昌 (prefecture)

yinghao 英豪

Yingluan tu 迎鑾圖

Yingtian 應天 (prefecture)

Yingxian muta 應縣木塔

Yingzao chi 營造尺

Yingzhou 潁州

Yisu 易俗 (county)

yiwan 億萬

yiyong 義勇

Yizhou 懿州 (Liaoning)

Yizhou 益州 (Sichuan)

Yong'an 永安 (county)

Yongning Monastery 永寧寺

You 幽 (prefecture)

Youyang zazu 酉陽雜俎

Yu Delin 俞德鄰

Yu Fangjian 虞方簡

Yu Hao 預浩

Yu Jing 余靖

Yu Yunwen 虞允文

Yuan Haowen 元好問

yuanliao shengyuanzhi 員寮剩員直

Yue 越 (prefecture)

Yue Fei 岳飛

Yueyang lou ji 岳陽樓記

yuezhi yi li 約之以禮

Yun 雲 (prefecture)

yushitai 御史臺

Yuwen 宇文

zai de bu zai xian 在德不在險

Zanning 贊寧

Ze 澤 (prefecture)

Zeng Bu 曾布

Zeng Di 曾覿

Zeng Gongliang 曾公亮

zhang 丈

Zhang Bangchang 張邦昌

Zhang Bangji 張邦基

Zhang Dehui 張德輝

Zhang Dexiang　章得象

Zhang Dun　章惇

Zhang Fangping　張方平

Zhang Hui　張惠

Zhang Jie　章粢

Zhang Jun　張浚

Zhang Mian　張沔

Zhang Shizheng　張師正

Zhang Tangying　張唐英

Zhang Wenzhi　張盈之

Zhang Yinlin　張蔭麟

Zhang Yong　張詠

Zhang Zhongshu　張忠恕

Zhao Ding　趙鼎

Zhao Fu　趙復

Zhao Kuangyi　趙匡乂

Zhao Kuangyin　趙匡胤

Zhao Liangsi　趙良嗣

Zhao Shanxiang　趙善湘

Zhao Zizhi　趙子砥

Zhendan　震旦

Zheng　鄭　(prefecture)

Zheng An　鄭安

Zheng Xia　鄭俠

Zhengmen　鄭門

Zhenguo Monastery　鎮國寺

Zhenwu　真武

Zhenzhou　鎮州

Zhi Pan　志磐

zhizhi sansi tiaolisi　制置三司條例司

zhizhigao　知制誥

Zhongxing ruiying tu　中興瑞應圖

Zhongyong　中庸

Zhou Bida　周必大

Zhu Dunru　朱敦儒

Zhu Mian　朱勔

Zhu Xi　朱熹

zhuan　專

zhuanlunwang　轉輪王
　　(ćakravartin)

Zhuojun　涿郡

Zhuozhou　涿州

Zhuquemen　朱雀門

zhuru　諸儒

Zhuzi yulei　朱子類語

zixu　資序

Zong Ze　宗澤

Zu　祖　(prefecture)

zuzong zhi jiafa　祖宗之家法

Contributors

ELAD ALYAGON is completing a dissertation on the Song military at the University of California, Davis.

SONG CHEN is assistant professor of Chinese history at Bucknell University. He received his PhD from Harvard University in 2011 with a dissertation on the relations between the state and elites in Sichuan from the late Tang through the Song.

PATRICIA BUCKLEY EBREY is professor of history at the University of Washington. Her most recent books are *Accumulating Culture: The Collections of Emperor Huizong* (2008) and *Emperor Huizong* (2014). She is currently working on a book on China's history of repeated reunifications.

CHARLES HARTMAN is professor of Chinese studies at the University of Albany. He has published on topics ranging from Tang poetry to Song-Yuan painting. His recent research centers on the historiography of the Song dynasty in relation to Song political and economic history.

LI HUARUI 李華瑞 is professor of history at Capital Normal University in Beijing. He has written extensively on Song and Xi Xia history. Recent books (in Chinese) include *Production and Monopolization of Wine in the Song Dynasty* (2000), *The Relationship Between the Song and the Xi Xia* (2010), and *Disaster Relief in Song Dynasty* (2013).

TRACY MILLER is associate professor of art history at Vanderbilt University. Her research focuses on the culture of ritual sites, specifically the ways in which identity was expressed visually through the media of temples and their artistic programs. She is author of *The Divine Nature of Power: Chinese Ritual Architecture at the Sacred Site of Jinci* (2007).

PAUL JAKOV SMITH is professor of history and East Asian studies at Haverford College. Broadly interested in social, economic, political, and military history, he is the coeditor of the *Cambridge History of China* volume on the Song (2009). His current research is on war and politics in the Song.

JAEYOON SONG is associate professor of history at McMaster University. A specialist in intellectual history, he is the author of *Traces of Grand Peace: Classics and State Activism in Imperial China* (2015). His current research is on Southern Song critiques of Northern Song statecraft, especially the New Policies.

CONG ELLEN ZHANG is associate professor of history at the University of Virginia. Broadly interested in elite culture and social history, she is author of *Transformative Journeys, Travel and Culture in Song China* (2011). Her current project is a book on filial piety.

Index

Abaoji (Taizu of Liao, d. 926), 310–14, 317*table*

affines, imperial, 6*fig.*, 8; Cao Xun, 8, 65, 67; and Gaozong, 67; and Huizong, 66

Allsen, Thomas, 329

An Lushan Rebellion (755–763): and equal field system, 267; and Tang soldiers, 299

anchashi. See surveillance investigators

"Ancient Style" *guwen* movement: Fan Zhongyan and the reformers, 156

armies, imperial: area generals system, 289; *baojie*, 281, 282; rotation system, 288–89. *See also* military; soldiers; war

artisans, forced to move: in Chinese sources, 326; Han captives, 311; by Jurchen, 320, 321, 323; by Mongols, 324, 327, 328

Aśoka (ca. 304–232 BCE; r. ca. 268–232): and Qian Chu, 46; and Taizong, 7, 32, 45, 47, 48

Aśoka Monastery (Ayuwangsi), 45; and relic, 55n71

Avelokiteśvara (Guanyin): at Dabei Monastery, 38; at Longxing Monastery, 38

Bao Zheng (999–1062): condemnation of surveillance inspectors, 172

baojia (mutual surveillance units), 166*table*, 282–83

Baozhou mutiny: aftermath, 298–99; negotiations, 296–98; trigger, 293–94; violence, 295–96

Bei shou jianwen lu: account of Taizu's oath, 68–72

"benevolence" (*ren*), 62, 85

Bi Zhongyou (1045–1119), 178

Bishi, 85

Bishu manchao, 62

Blessed Success Pagoda Cloister (Fusheng Tayuan), 30

Bohai: and Kitans, 310, 311*table*, 312*table*, 317, 318; ethnic origin of, 333n16

Bol, Peter: on the *shi*, 10

Bola, 314

Bossler, Beverly: on Song elite continuity, 10

boundary measure (*jingjie fa*), 252; clarification, 258–59. *See also* land policies

Buddhism: building projects, 33–35

Buddhists, forced to move, 321

Bureau of Military Affairs, 66

Bureau of Policy Criticism, 161, 162, 170, 172*table*; and Wang Anshi, 174

bureaucracy: as focus of elite mobility strategies, 11; bureaucratic factionalism, 11–12; bureaucratic reforms under Fan Zhongyan and Wang Anshi, 13; changes in prefectural incumbency 11th to 13th centuries, 12; circuit intendants, 166*table*, 175; contests for bureaucratic positions, 11; controlling bureaucracy as key to reform, 158–61, 171; eleventh-century "bureaucratic boom," 11, 13; elite loss of confidence in, 12; Fan Zhongyan's analysis of, 157, 159; grand councilors and, 170; prefectural offices, 12–13; remonstrance agencies, 170, 171, 176; size of, 163; Wang Anshi's analysis of, 157, 159–60. *See also* Bureau of Policy Criticism; Censorate; factionalism; land, policies on; reforms; state

bureaucracy, appointment system of: appointments near homes, 115, 117*table*, 118; conflicting policy goals in, 118–19; cosmopolitanism of, 13, 113, 143;

www.ingramcontent.com/pod-product-compliance
Lightning Source LLC
Chambersburg PA
CBHW030911270326
41929CB00008B/658